T0326949

HEATHEN

HEATHEN

RELIGION *and* RACE *in* AMERICAN HISTORY

Kathryn Gin Lum

HARVARD UNIVERSITY PRESS
Cambridge, Massachusetts
London, England
2022

Publication of this book has been supported through the generous provisions of the
Maurice and Lula Bradley Smith Memorial Fund.
First printing

Library of Congress Cataloging-in-Publication Data

Names: Gin Lum, Kathryn, author.
Title: Heathen : religion and race in American history / Kathryn Gin Lum.
Description: Cambridge, Massachusetts : Harvard University Press, 2022. |
Includes bibliographical references and index.
Identifiers: LCCN 2021053223 | ISBN 9780674976771 (cloth)
Subjects: LCSH: Race—Religious aspects—Protestant churches. |
Race discrimination—Religious aspects—Christianity. | Race discrimination—
United States—Religious aspects—Christianity. | Protestants—United States—
Attitudes. | Paganism—United States—Public opinion.
Classification: LCC BT734.2 .G56 2022 | DDC 241/.675—dc23/eng/20220106
LC record available at https://lccn.loc.gov/2021053223

For my grandparents

CONTENTS

CONTENTS

A NOTE ON TERMS

I have chosen not to put "heathen," "heathen world," or "pagan" in quotes unless contextually necessary. This is for the sake of textual flow and clarity and should not be taken to indicate uncritical employment of the terms. I have chosen to capitalize "Black," "Brown," "Indigenous," and "White." The decision to capitalize "White" deliberately draws attention to Whiteness as a racial category rather than as the unmarked norm against which all other people are raced; see for instance Nell Irvin Painter, "Opinion: Why 'White' Should Be Capitalized, Too," *Washington Post,* July 22, 2020. I have preserved original spellings and punctuation in direct quotes and have chosen not to mark idiosyncratic or archaic spellings with "*sic,*" unless the meaning is obscured.

HEATHEN

PROLOGUE

Returning the Gaze

I started writing this book long before the COVID-19 pandemic engulfed the globe, before the murder of George Floyd gave rise to a national racial reckoning, before a new wave of anti-Asian hate swept the United States, before the discovery of hundreds of unmarked Native children's graves in Canada unleashed righteous fury at residential school systems. There is always a risk of dating a book by pegging it to a particular moment in time, but the world feels so much changed that to ignore this context is impossible. And yet the world is also still so much the same, in ways that tie directly to the story this book tells.

The story is, in some ways, very familiar. It is a story about how Americans have set themselves apart from a world of sufferers, as a superior people and a humanitarian people—a people who deserve the good fortune they have received and have a responsibility to spread it to others. What gives this book's version of the story specificity, and what makes it necessary, is the through-line that underlies it: the heathen, a figure and a concept that has been used repeatedly, whether named or not, as reason and justification for a range of actions that have stemmed from Americans' conviction that other people need to be transformed. The heathen is often imagined to be an antiquated figure and a primarily religious one whose significance has fallen as other categories of difference—particularly racial ones—have risen in importance. This book argues for the continued consequence of the concept of the heathen. My hope is that, by bringing together historical case studies and showing how they build on and resonate with one another over time, we can see the overlooked power of the heathen underpinning a White American Christian superiority complex, as well as participation in and opposition to the same by people historically considered to be part of the so-called heathen world.

To open with one contemporary example that shows the continued resonance of the heathen concept: on July 8, 2021, an article came out in the *American Conservative* by associate editor Declan Leary, expounding on the "meaning of the Native graves" discovered at residential schools in Canada. According to Leary, "the entire story" is "made up" because "we have *always* known that many children died in the residential schools," and the graves "are, in fact, the ordered and intentional burial sites of people we always knew were dead, and who died of more or less natural causes." (The "more or less" masks the physical brutality of the residential school system, not to mention the psychological trauma the schools wreaked on children and the families that waited for them to return.) Leary argues that "whatever sacrifices were exacted in pursuit of that grace"—salvation in Christ—"the suffocation of a noble pagan culture; an increase in disease and bodily death due to government negligence; even the sundering of natural families—is *worth it*."[1] To put it bluntly, Leary plays a heathen card to excuse death. Paganism or heathenism works here as a "get out of jail free" ticket that renders any harm excusable if done in the name of eradicating wrong religion.[2]

That Leary makes this kind of argument in 2021 might seem surprising. Few explicitly invoke the concept of the heathen or pagan nowadays, unless referring to Wiccans, Heathenry, or other movements that have taken the names to refer to revivals of pre-Christian folk traditions, a topic outside the scope of this book.[3] But Leary only exposes, in a particularly egregious way, an abiding sense of White Christian superiority that relies on a notion of the Other as deluded and in need of guidance and transformation.

Christians are hardly monolithic, of course, and others have been appalled and outraged by Leary's callous claims. The day after his article came out, Tyler Huckabee, the senior editor of *RELEVANT* magazine, wrote in response to Leary that "this sort of calculation is so inhumane it calls into question the author's understanding of Christianity. The sacrifice of Jesus Christ should motivate us to recognize the infinite dignity of each person as specially and uniquely loved by God."[4] And yet many Christians do not believe that the "dignity of each person" should eternally save them if they haven't accepted Jesus. And so they continue to grapple with how to respect the cultures and religions of people they believe need to be saved.[5] *RELEVANT* is a Christian multimedia platform that reaches an audience of roughly five million young adults in their twenties and thirties, many of whom are wrestling with the troubling legacies of the Christian faith that are baldly exposed in apologia like Leary's. "We're tired of the us-versus-them approach of previous generations," its mission statement proclaims. "We don't think believers should be known primarily for legalism and bigotry."[6]

RELEVANT's editors seek to reclaim Christian concepts that they feel have been hijacked by bigotry. Along these lines, in March 2020 *RELEVANT* featured an exclusive with Latino Christian hip-hop artist GAWVI on his album *Heathen*. "The word 'heathen' is a bold word that I feel the Christian culture requires an explanation for," GAWVI told *RELEVANT*. "To those who feel like they don't have it all figured out and are in hiding, I want the word *heathen* to bring them comfort, to let them know it is okay to embrace who you are and where you are in life. I want to give the word a new meaning of love and acceptance."[7] The concept of the heathen, in other words, is malleable and has never been the exclusive purview of people like Leary.

I am of the demographic *RELEVANT* seeks to reach. I grew up in a conservative church, fully of the belief that much of the world was heathen and needed to be saved. This belief was ingrained in me through ordinary sermons, occasional visits from missionaries, and a momentous musical experience that I participated in as a child in the early 1990s. I sang in the church children's choir, and every year we put on a show. Most of the time, we presented biblical stories—Noah, Jonah, Josiah, and so on. But one year we staged a musical, *The Mission Connection*, that is all about saving the world for Christ. *The Mission Connection* focuses on a train, the Jesus Express, that runs on "prayer power and can take its passengers to any mission field in the world."[8] One of the main characters, Hugo, is a "new Christian" who wants to understand the Great Commission. He hops on the Jesus Express and encounters a missionary named—what else?—Miss Shunary, who shows him around the world. I desperately wanted to be Miss Shunary, and I practiced her songs over and over to audition for the part:

Well, here I am,
Where is the glitter?
All I see all day is cactus plants and these big red ants, what a thrill.
You see my daddy's name is Dick Shunary,
and my momma goes by Stace Shunary.
And I'm their little baby Miss Shunary, Miss Shunary, just little ole me . . .[9]

But instead of the missionary, I was cast as a "Wanna Wiggle Indian," one of a group of six named "Who, What, When, Where, Why, and Wow." The "Wanna Wiggles" wear "Indian clothes" and converse in "Ugh's" and a broken English "that sounds like some disease." Their names cause confusion (to prompt audience laughter) when they speak with Miss Shunary. But at least they have speaking lines. The other people the Jesus Express encounters are "Jungle Jim," a "South-American Jungle Native" in "Jungle-style clothes," and "Muslim Mom," an "African Muslim" in "African clothes," neither of whom speaks. The stereotyped clothing of the Native characters is set against the "Basic All-American clothes" of the Jesus Express riders and serves to differentiate the choir kids who play the missionized from those who play the missionaries.[10]

The script indicates that Jungle Jim is "one of the hidden people": "tribes of people all over the world that are hidden from us." Serving him and his tribe is "Jack Taylor, a missionary pilot" who "has been here for years, translating the Bible into the languages of hidden tribes, while day by day helping to meet their material needs—like this well!" Meanwhile, the African mother is merely a prop to demonstrate the neediness of "the people in Senegal," who "are Muslims, and don't know about Jesus." She does not even get to carry her own baby, who is instead held by Bernice Miller, a missionary nurse. Miller expounds on the scarcity of food and the bodily diseases that she is trying to ameliorate. "If we care for their bodies," she says, "maybe they'll let the 'Great Physician' heal their souls!"[11]

Jungle Jim and the African mother are descendants of the heathen of yore. Heathens are supposed to be unable to care for themselves. They require not only the river of life but also clean water, and not only restoration of the soul but also bodily healing. The heathen category is expansive; Muslims slip in and out as people who are part of the Abrahamic traditions but supposedly "don't know about Jesus." *The Mission Connection* offers a world-encompassing orientation, evidenced not only by songs that take the Jesus Express from Brazil to the American West to Senegal but also by the musical's cover image, which features Hugo, the new Christian, derrière atop the globe in a posture of casual dominance. While the term "heathen" itself is never used, the "hidden people" with no clean water and the forlorn, sickly, and hungry Senegalese clearly derive from the needy heathens of yesteryear. The musical's cast of mostly mute Native people—playacted by Christian kids—also harks back to a long history of putting heathens (real or not) on display for Christian audiences to learn from, be entertained by, pray for, and pay for.[12]

Given the particular church context in which I grew up, my participation in this musical is not altogether surprising. The first church I attended, Holy Spirit Lutheran, was a Chinese mission branch of the Missouri Synod located near San Francisco's Chinatown and pastored by Wilbert Victor Holt, a returned missionary. Holt and his wife, Geraldine, had left on their mission to China on the heels of the Sino-Japanese War and on the brink of the Communist Revolution. They took up posts at the Evangelical Lutheran Church of China's missionary station at Enshiah, which featured a hospital, school, and orphanage in addition to a church. The Holts escaped

China for Hong Kong just before Mao Zedong's army took over Chongqing; there, they assisted refugees fleeing the mainland for the British colony and eventually helped to establish the Hong Kong Lutheran Synod and the first Lutheran seminary. By the time they came back to the States in 1962, Hong Kong boasted more than two dozen Lutheran churches and educational institutions. Holt founded Holy Spirit out of a storefront in Chinatown, eventually growing it into a large congregation aimed at evangelizing Cantonese-speaking Chinese immigrants in the San Francisco area.[13] My family was among them, my parents having come to the States in their early teens, after passage of the Hart-Celler Act of 1965 loosened long-standing restrictions on Asian immigration.

We attended Holy Spirit until I was seven, when my parents deemed it to be too far from our home and decided to try out the local Missouri Synod church, a predominantly German Lutheran congregation in a working-class suburb across the Bay. This is where I joined the church choir and sang in *The Mission Connection;* this is where I encountered missionaries who pled for our coins to send to the poor and starving children overseas. Pastor Holt and Pastor Wolkenhauer, the minister of the German Lutheran church, were among the kindest human beings I have ever known; compassion radiated from their countenances and gentleness from their calm baritones. I never felt anything less than a wholly beloved child of God in their eyes. And yet the church they served cast me in the role of a "Wanna Wiggle," destined for ignorance and eternal damnation but for the saving grace of the intrepid missionary.

The imperative to save the doomed heathen continues to animate the church; as of 2021, the Missouri Synod still features on its website's "Frequently Asked Questions—Doctrine" page a question reading, "What stand does our church take regarding the heathen who have never had the opportunity to hear the Gospel of Jesus Christ?" The answer is that the heathen are "without excuse" and that "we should seek to reach as many as possible with our own fearless witness and ardently support the missionary endeavors of our church on behalf of those whom we cannot reach with our own voice."[14] Growing up with this mentality I wondered, as a child, at the chance of my own birth in a Christian family in America, when I might have easily been born somewhere in the middle of heathen China, waiting to be rescued from my superstitious ways. I wondered about heathen ancestors I had never met, and I worried about what had happened to them. Mostly I felt lucky, but I also felt guilty about feeling lucky, because there were so many more perishing every day in the damning darkness of heathenism.

Fast-forward many years, and I realize that childhood me could be a primary source for adult me. Actually, adult me could still be a primary source for historian me. I continue to grapple with a faith that holds much meaning for me, but whose historical dealings with my people and other missionized groups have been fraught, to say the least. The lines between "us" and "them" blur in the case of converts who adopted and adapted some of the core values, practices, and beliefs of the religion that dubbed them heathen in the first place. Indeed, some converts even used the language of heathenism to refer to their former selves and their unconverted family and friends. As the daughter of a Christianized Chinese American family, I have come to realize that I am both the "us" and the "them," and that "my" history has been shaped by White Protestant Americans as much as the history of "my" people—the "heathen Chinese"—has helped to shape constructions of Whiteness, Protestantism, and Americanness. This book is the attempt of a historian and scholar of religion, then, to wrestle with the tradition that shaped me. I probe how it tried to change historically non-Christian people and people of color; how it has shed some of this past over time; but also what inheritances powerfully remain.

Even as it unveils the development and legacies of the figure of the heathen, this book also seeks to highlight the voices of those considered as such, who have taken on the concept and in some cases reclaimed and adapted it as an alternative to the ills that plague Western societies. For if White Protestant Americans have claimed the ability to speak for and about us, then why can we not also claim the ability to speak for and back to them? As Dipesh Chakrabarty puts it, "What allowed the modern European sages to develop such clairvoyance with regard to societies of which they were empirically ignorant? Why cannot we, once again, return the gaze?"[15]

INTRODUCTION

A Heathen Inheritance

B asil Miller, founder of World-Wide Missions and a minister in the Church of the Nazarene, had a heart for the heathen. He lamented the poverty, disease, and starvation that he saw in the regions his organization supported. In brochures, newsletters, and booklets, he called on Americans to feel a sense of gratitude and responsibility for their blessings vis-à-vis the rest of the world. While we savor our "filet mignon," he said, they crunch "fried grasshoppers." For Miller, this was no delicacy. "My two worlds"—the American world he lived in and the overseas world he was trying to save—"are literally worlds apart. In but few places do they touch. The demarkation between paganism and Christianity, civilization and hea-thenism, is sky-high and star-far." Miller wrote this in a 1971 autobio-graphical account, long after the label of "heathen" was supposed to have given way before color-based race talk as the primary mode for marking human difference.[1]

Even as he used the term "heathen," Miller also referred to his "two worlds" as "a white world and a colored world." "On my first trip around the world," he explained, "when I left Italy I began to search for a pair of blue eyes. Everywhere I found myself unconsciously looking for blue eyes. But through Africa, the Middle East, Turkey, Iraq, Iran, Afghanistan, Pak-istan, India and on up through Southeast Asia into Japan and Korea, there were no nationals with blue eyes. Every eye was dark." Miller asked, "What difference does this make?" and answered, "None except that I discovered much of the WORLD NO. II . . . is a colored world, mostly black." Race works here as a binary us versus them: the White and the Black, the helpers and the helpless, the "civilized" and the "heathen." Miller characterized everyone from Africans to Koreans as "mostly black," rendering "WORLD NO. II" as the religious and racial opposite of the "First World."[2]

Cover of Basil Miller, *Arms around the World: Missions World Wide* (Pasadena, CA: World-Wide Missions, 1971). Photo made available by Fuller Theological Seminary.

Miller used "WORLD NO. II—the world of abject poverty, dire need, bare existence, ignorance, and heathendom"—as a spur to gratitude and humanitarian feeling on the part of self-centered, spoiled Americans. "I had become quite dissatisfied with our home" in the first world, he admitted. "We had built it in 1945 during the war, and had lived there constantly. Much of it had become too familiar, and I was discontented—until I began to travel in my WORLD NO. II." Miller listed a litany of woes that the far-flung world of heathen poverty had in common: mud houses, no shoes, no cars, tattered or no clothes, insufficient food, no "fantastic electronic cookery." When Miller henceforth felt like purchasing some fancy new gadget, he would always feel "bombarded by WORLD NO. II" and refrain, guilted by the plaintive cries of beggar children, "pagan" villagers, and "nude girls": "Give us some of the simple things you have in WORLD NO. I. To us they would be luxuries." After returning to America from the world of heathenism and despair, said Miller, a sigh of relief practically exhaling off the page, "I sat down on the divan, somewhat frayed, and before me flashed my OTHER WORLD. I thanked God for the FIRST WORLD—my own, my native world."[3]

Miller's account, which he titled *Arms around the World*, raises the central and interrelated themes at stake in this book: the notion of the heathen as an elastic category that could stretch to incorporate people from all over the world; the significance of the heathen world to Americans' self-identification as lucky inhabitants of the "First World"; the responsibility this self-identification was supposed to entail toward the suffering heathen; and the attendant racialization of the heathen as non-White inferior and the Christian as White superior.

The Replacement Narrative

Miller's account might seem as though it should have come from an earlier century, when stories about the poor heathen were ubiquitous. But *Arms around the World* was published in the latter half of the twentieth century, when the figure of the heathen had largely come to seem an embarrassing relic of less tolerant times. Was Miller's take the last gasp of an outmoded view of the world? Or is there something more to it than that?

To answer this question requires reappraising a popular narrative about the relationship between religious and racial differentiation. I call this the "replacement narrative," and it holds that the figure of the heathen represents an older, binary form of religious difference that was eventually replaced by newer racial hierarchies. The replacement narrative does not help us to understand the simultaneity of religious and racial othering in Miller's account because it sees religion and race as categorically different: the religious subject is thought to be changeable through conversion, while the raced subject is said to be perpetually inferior by the color of their skin. Historian George Fredrickson articulates this position clearly when he writes in *Racism: A Short History* (2002), "If a heathen can be redeemed through baptism . . . we are in the presence of an attitude that often creates conflict and misery, but not one that should be labeled racist. It might be useful to have another term, such as 'culturalism,' to describe an inability or unwillingness to tolerate cultural differences, but if assimilation were genuinely on offer, I would withhold the 'R' word." For Fredrickson, racism requires a "mindset that regards 'them' as different from 'us' in ways that are permanent and unbridgeable."[4]

This story of racism's emergence is commonly linked to a tale of growing world religions awareness amid global exploration, such that as Europeans and Euro-Americans better understood religious variety and took note of apparent bodily differences between the world's people, racial knowledge replaced Christian knowledge as the primary way to explain human difference. Christian knowledge held that all humans are created of one blood, and that all people, after the fall of Adam and Eve, are born with the stain of original sin. All people also have the capacity to convert and be saved. Racial knowledge, by contrast, questioned whether all humans are made of one blood, and instead posited that there are physical differences that separate humans from birth. Racial knowledge tended to parse, split, and hierarchize, while Christian knowledge lumped the world's people into the saved versus the damned, the Christian versus the heathen. Christian knowledge, according to this story, tended to hold full-blown racism in check because of its insistence on monogenesis and the convertibility of Adam's descendants. Racial knowledge, by contrast, launched the West into a modernity characterized by the rapacious, scientifically supported exploitation of people of color regardless of their religious status.[5]

There is much to recommend in the replacement narrative. The chronological story it tells is dynamic and aligns well with the prevailing understanding of race in and out of the academy. Michael Omi and Howard Winant succinctly summarize this view in their classic *Racial Formation in the United States,* first published in 1986 and substantially revised since then. Understanding race as a socially constructed "concept which signifies and symbolizes social conflicts and interests by referring to different types of human bodies," they hold that religious "hostility and suspicion . . . cannot be understood as more than a rehearsal for racial formation, since these antagonisms, for all their bloodletting and chauvinism, were always and everywhere religiously interpreted." Scholars following the lead of Omi and Winant have sought to date when othering based on belief gave way to othering based on bodies, marking the uneven transition from the Middle Ages to modernity.[6]

Reappraising the Replacement Narrative

As clear as the replacement narrative might be in telling a story of change over time, it bears reappraisal on the basis of both the history it tells and the assumptions that underlie it. First, the history. Use of the word "heathen" in American English publications actually rose from the mid-eighteenth to the mid-nineteenth century, the period when Fredrickson explains that "full-blown biological racism" held sway.[7] The sustained rise in the term's use reflects the deliberate fashioning of the heathen world as a cohesive category in the eighteenth and nineteenth centuries. The idea of the heathen world was not unknown before then, but it flowered with the emergence of significant foreign missionary societies in England and the United States, including the Baptist Missionary Society in 1793, the London Missionary Society in 1795, and the American Board of Commissioners for Foreign Missions in 1810. The spread of racial science challenged the continued applicability of the older model of blanket heathenness and forced those who used it to explain how and why the model should continue to have explanatory power for a world where apparent physical differences could seem more salient than supposed spiritual similarities. In this context, White Protestants doubled down on the notion of heathenness as a term that could elide particularities, sweeping all who bore the label under the same heading of misguided and unfortunate souls who shared similar origin stories, landscapes, and bodies beneath any visible differences.[8]

This is not to say that the development of race as hierarchical differentiation did not also matter to Americans, not least to missionaries themselves. Beginning in the early republic, they developed "hierarchies of heathenism" to determine where to most efficiently and effectively marshal their resources. Those people who seemed least and most "civilized" were deemed most difficult to evangelize, whether because it would take too much effort to teach them, or because it would take too much effort to undo entrenched superstitions. Those in the middle of civilizational ladders were deemed most promising because they had some conceptions of religion but not so deeply ingrained as to prove near impossible to eradicate.[9]

Nevertheless, the idea of a vast heathen world that shared certain fundamental characteristics also continued to have purchase, helping to create the binaries that underlay colonial governance.[10] That those nearer the top of civilizational ladders were seen as especially difficult to convert demonstrates how, for White Protestants viewing the world, the overriding quality of heathenness outweighed any claims to civilization. Civilizational hierarchies hit a "heathen ceiling," so to speak, a ceiling that could only be (theoretically) broken through conversion. White Protestants held heathenism to be responsible for the stagnation of societies stuck below them on the civilizational ladder. Individual converts from those societies could be impressed into missionizing work or paraded as evidence of the possibility that the heathen could be saved, but ultimately, the heathen ceiling served to reinforce White Protestant exceptionalism over the rest of the world.

The idea of a heathen world in need was especially helpful for a young nation that was figuring out its global status, where European-descended settlers could not claim the land as the original birthright of their ancestors. Casting the pall of heathenness over that land and other far-flung regions of the world justified Anglo colonialism and alleviated anxieties stemming from increased awareness of other societies with different religious traditions and ways of life, and impressive inventions and architectural feats. For Anglo-American Protestants who sought to shape the nation in their own image, this adamantly included Catholic societies. Even as their worldviews shared some similarities with Catholics'—both rationalized colonization if lands were inhabited by heathens—Anglo-American Protestants viewed Catholics as insufficiently separate from the pagan Roman past and saw the people Catholics evangelized as essentially heathen still.

By the late nineteenth century and into the twentieth, use of the word "heathen" did in fact decline as it became an embarrassing term indicative of former intolerance and illiberality and the replacement narrative came to characterize the United States' very conception of itself. The myth of disenchantment, set forth most famously by Max Weber, allowed the West to imagine itself as "modern, rational, and secular," while believing that the "Rest" "languish[ed] in a fantastical world of tradition, superstition, and religion." The West came to see racism based on bodies as its "original sin," while religious fanaticism and extremism were thought to stain the soul of the "Rest."[11] But the replacement narrative's popularity reveals less a story of secularization, where religion wanes in importance, than of secularism, or the management of what counts as acceptable and unacceptable expressions of religion. In *Divine Variations: How Christian Thought Became Racial Science*, Terence Keel shows how "the secular acts as a mask for the religious." Instead of holding that "modernity naturally entails the erosion of religious influence over the structures of knowledge that govern social life," Keel argues that "a new story can be told . . . if we think of secularization not in terms of a rupture from the past but instead as a transference of religious forms into nonreligious spaces of thought and practice."[12] Along these lines, just because the word "heathen" fell into disrepute does not mean that the mental maps through which Americans envisioned the heathen world similarly disappeared. Indeed, it would be surprising if a concept that had captured the European, and then the Euro-American, imagination for so long had simply vanished because the word used to describe it came to be seen as intolerant. While a conservative missionary like Miller might continue to use the term "heathen" explicitly, mainstream missionary discourse now more commonly refers to the "unreached people" in the "10/40 window," the regions between 10 and 40 degrees latitude that are supposed to have the least access to the gospel. In secular discourse, the poor and needy heathen has been reborn as the starving child living in the "third world" or "developing world." To answer the opening question about Miller, then, his explicit use of the term "heathen" was, to some extent, anachronistic, but the ideas it invoked are hardly so. The figure of the heathen continues to stalk the secular categories that lump huge swaths of the world into a mass of suffering people whom Miller described not only as "heathen" but also as "black" and "colored."

Racism: A Heathen Inheritance

In addition to tracing this history, *Heathen: Religion and Race in American History* also operates under a set of assumptions about "religion" and "race" that are different from those animating the replacement narrative. *Heathen* joins a rich and growing body of literature that shows the continued importance of religion to racialization, and the earlier workings of race in religious othering.[13] One example of the latter is Geraldine Heng's work on the "invention of race in the European Middle Ages." She explains that the focus on bodies as the key signifier of race overlooks how "religion . . . can function both socioculturally *and* biopolitically."[14] For Heng, using euphemisms in place of racism—like "ethnocentrism, xenophobia, 'premodern discriminations', 'prejudice', 'chauvinism', even 'fear of otherness and difference'"—has the effect of "de-stigmatiz[ing] the impacts and consequences of certain laws, acts, practices, and institutions in the medieval period." In medieval England, for instance, not understanding the expulsion of Jews as an act of racial state formation ignores how "the lives of English Jews were *constitutive*, not incidental, to the formation of England's history and collective identity."[15] Englishness was formed in communal gossip about Jews as bloodthirsty ritual murderers, in the badges Jews were made to wear, and in the ultimate expulsion of Jews in the thirteenth century. The English were those who could tell the gossip, avoid the badges, and claim England as their birthright. By understanding religion capaciously, Heng pushes race before the replacement narrative's earliest origin stories.[16]

Similarly, by defining race capaciously, Sylvester Johnson, in *African American Religions, 1500–2000: Colonialism, Democracy, and Freedom,* pushes religion's significance beyond where the replacement narrative leaves it. If religion can function biopolitically, so also can race function outside biology, says Johnson, as "a colonial process that has constituted 'Europeanness and non-Europeanness' through material, discursive, and noncorporeal domains." Race, understood as a "*governing* formation . . . that has structured the *political rule* of Europeans over non-Europeans," turns non-Europeans into people who are perpetually in need of oversight and control.[17] Religion is a key domain that separates the European from the non-European but that also promises to bring them closer together through colonial converting and civilizing missions.

Such expansive understandings of religion and race underlie this book's story of how, in the American context, racial othering has been a "heathen inheritance." This is a play on Psalm 2:8, a favorite of missionaries: "Ask of me, and I shall give thee the heathen for thine inheritance, and the uttermost parts of the earth for thy possession."[18] The verse speaks to how the souls and soils of the heathen were linked as the rightful, God-given belongings of the Christian to renovate and take over. This linkage reverberates in American racism. Pushback against these processes has also been an inheritance of the people once considered to be part of the heathen world.

Where the replacement narrative sometimes implies that religious othering was gentler than racism because of its commitment to monogenesis and conversion, *Heathen* makes no such claim. It understands racism to include the binary perspective that supposedly inferior people cannot take care of themselves without the tutelage of superiors, a perspective that is expressed not just in the "beliefs and actions of individuals" but in a system of "cultural messages and institutional policies and practices," to use Beverly Daniel Tatum's classic formulation.[19] Classifying people as heathen has long served as a ticket of impunity to justify taking over their lands, and enslaving and reconstructing their bodies, in the name of saving their souls. Such classification has also justified violence against, and state exclusion of, people deemed heathen who have refused to accept or conform to such "assistance." Heathenness has never simply been about wrong and changeable belief. It also has to do with the manifold repercussions that wrong belief is supposed to wreak on lands and bodies, turning fertile soil into deserts and hale bodies into sickly ones, corrupted by idolatry, the oppression of women, and neglect of infants, the sick, and elderly. At times these repercussions could come to seem so entrenched as to render the heathen virtually unchangeable: not because an idea of inherent bodily difference necessarily replaced the "of one blood" theory, but because of the historical operations of wrong religion on bodies over time, such that the heathen—even if converted—is always playing catch-up to the White Christian.

Of course, racism does not take only this form, and this book does not claim to tell the only story of religion and race in America.[20] Still, the ways in which diverse people are lumped together as racial Others has received comparatively less attention than race understood as the hierarchical arrangement and treatment of people based on socially constructed meanings ascribed to skin color. Hierarchies of race emphasize difference, revealing how racial governance can work through a divide-and-conquer strategy that pits groups against each other. But racial governance can also work by overlooking difference—by grouping people from different countries and cultures together as simply "not White." Hierarchical and binary racialization coexist, with distinctions among groups deployed to lower the chances of multiracial alliances forming, while binary othering reinforces the position of Whiteness above a mass of others.[21]

This book shows the heathen's importance to racial clumping. The scholarship on racism and religion in the United States has tended to largely focus on Blackness as the primary locus of race, and on White Christian anti-Blackness as the primary locus of racism.[22] This is essential and important work. *Heathen* does not contest it but seeks to build on and out from it. As central as they are in the United States, Blackness is not equivalent to race, and anti-Blackness is not equivalent to racism. As scholar Judith Weisenfeld puts it, "Attending to the complexities of racialization in US religious history also requires that scholars refuse the conflation of race with blackness and understand racialized structures to affect, inflect, and infect the American religious world more generally."[23] This book tells a story of religion and American racism, then, that considers Black people alongside others who have borne the heathen label around the world.[24]

The heathen category has not only racialized those bearing the label as unable to care for themselves; it has also shored up the self-understanding of White Protestant Americans as people who hold themselves to be the heathen's savior. Benjamin Wisner, pastor of the Old South Church in Boston, summed up the power of the heathen world to shape this sense of identity in a sermon on "the moral condition and prospects of the heathen," given to the Foreign Mission Society of Boston in 1824 and reprinted for wider audiences in the *Monitor* and *Missionary Herald*. After detailing the moral and physical despair in which the heathen world languished, Wisner told his audience, "This remedy, my hearers, it is in your power to furnish to the perishing nations. . . . You behold them sunk in degradation and wretchedness; you see them hastening, as fast as the stream of time can carry them, to an eternity of woe! In the name of benevolence, in the name of philanthropy, I call upon you to contribute to their relief. . . . Have you the feelings of humanity? I wait for your reply."[25] Wisner crafts his audience as people with power over the life or death of heathens the world over. The activation of their own humanity and sense of superiority relies on the existence of "degraded" and "wretched" heathens for them to feel pity over and save. To borrow from Heng's formulation, the heathen world has been constitutive, not incidental, to White Protestant Americans' sense of history and collective identity.[26]

Yet even as the figure of the heathen underlies Whiteness as a quality of dwelling in and spreading the "light" to those languishing in "darkness," the notion of the American as spreader of salvation has not stayed exclusive to White Americans. Some Christian converts from missionized groups have also viewed their ancestors and unconverted relatives as heathens and sought to save them. Other converts have turned the label of heathen back on White Americans instead. They have diagnosed White American self-professed Christians as heathens and hypocrites for their racist behavior, separating Christianity from its White practitioners. The heathen label could also be co-opted as a term of resistance and empowerment by the people on whom it has been foisted. Yes, we *are* heathens, some have said, and proud of it. They have assessed Christianity against heathenism and found Christians lacking, discovering solidarity with others similarly clumped into the heathen world.

Continuity and Change

In his 1920 essay "The Souls of White Folk," W. E. B. Du Bois drew a withering portrait of Whiteness as an invented category characterized not so much by skin color as by an overweening superiority complex that veers quickly from humanitarianism into outright hostility once humanitarian overtures are rejected. As long as the recipient of White noblesse oblige fawns over the "gift" of White aid, "there is much mental peace and moral satisfaction." But as soon as the "black man begins to dispute the white man's title . . . ; and when his attitude toward charity is sullen anger rather than humble jollity; when he insists on his human right to swagger and swear and waste,—then the spell is suddenly broken."[27]

To apply Du Bois's insights to the heathen as object of White pity, it is when the spell is broken that the savable heathen becomes, for the White man, the irascible, eradicable Other. The potential for this is always and ever present in the changeable heathen, not replacing the heathen on a linear historical timeline but surfacing time and again to challenge and refuse to be the White man's burden. For the "Dark World," in Du Bois's words, knows the soul of the White man deeply: "We looked at him clearly, with world-old eyes, and saw simply a human being, weak and pitiable and cruel, even as we are and were." The "utter failure of white religion" struck the "Darker Peoples" with particular force, showing the hypocrisy and "self-deception" of "white Christianity" as a religion supporting White supremacy and plunder under the veneer of charity. Where White Protestants bemoaned how much of the world they believed was lost in heathen darkness, Du Bois proclaimed with a sense of power that "most men belong to this world. With Negro and Negroid, East Indian, Chinese, and Japanese they form two-thirds of the population of the world." It was in the "darker world" that Du Bois found hope: "A belief in humanity is a belief in colored men. If the uplift of mankind must be done by men, then the destinies of this world will rest ultimately in the hands of darker nations."[28]

Like Du Bois, this book gazes at the "souls of white folk," looking at how their gaze on so-called heathens reveals the constructed nature of their own sense of superiority. It also listens to those who countered, adopted, or recast the claims that White Protestant Americans have made about the heathen world and its descendants. I read these scripts and counterscripts as both a historian and a scholar of religion.[29] Kathryn Lofton explains the key distinction between the disciplines as follows: "If history in the academic sense marks difference—marks change over time—then religion is in part distinguished from history for its invocation of social forms iterated through repetition." Along these lines, I trace the story of the heathen world's origins, shape, and repercussions both chronologically and as a story of continuity, attendant to how history is itself, in the words of Linda Tuhiwai Smith, "a modernist project which has developed alongside imperial beliefs about the Other."[30]

The White Protestant Americans who professionalized the discipline in the late nineteenth century prided themselves on being progressive history makers, seeing the blessings of Providence in their technological inventions and world-conquering ambitions. They imagined the heathen world, by contrast, as a lethargic realm of unchanging pitiables, made such by their deluded and time-wasting devotion to false idols—whether of wood or stone, or of deified flesh and blood. As University of California professor William Swinton put it in a popular 1870s textbook, history "is the narrative of the rise and progress of those famous peoples whose doings constitute the history of *civilization*." For Swinton, "history proper concerns itself with but one highly developed type of mankind; for . . . the Caucasians form the only truly *historical* race." The very notion that history concerns movement over time was constructed against the idea of stagnant heathens subject to anthropological investigation while Caucasians were the authors and agents of historical writing.[31]

But ironically, White Protestant views of the heathen themselves reveal significant repetition over time. To emphasize this is not simply a disciplinary and methodological move but also an argument about Whiteness as a fragile religio-racial claim continually articulated with and against the figure of the heathen.[32] For if the heathen could convert, so also could the Christian backslide. Heathenness has functioned as a barometer of the abnormal, used to diagnose and condemn deviant behavior and belief not only in the heathen world but also at the heart of White Protestant America. The various idols Americans seemed to place before God—money, above all—blurred the lines between White Americans and the heathen and laid bare anxieties about whether America might, after all, be closer to the heathen world than not. The blurriness of categories called for the reinforcing of the same. The conviction that God favored Europeans with Christianization before much of the rest of the world, blessed them with the riches of America, and then sent them to the heathen world to save it required work to maintain. Constant invocation and reinvocation of the claim fortified White Protestant Americanness against its own precariousness. White Americans, then, did not only construct themselves in opposition to the heathen world. They constructed the heathen world to give themselves a venue for the evangelizing work that marked them as the givers rather than recipients of aid. Just as with Miller on his frayed divan, the heathen world has provided White Americans with a sense of gratitude for their privilege, a sense of guilt over their enjoyment of that privilege, and an outlet for the exercise of that guilt.[33]

To tell this story of the heathen's importance to American race-making, racism, and resistance against the same, *Heathen* begins by tracing how the parameters of the heathen world took shape. Part I considers the origins of the concept of the heathen and then shows how, despite the growing influence of scientific racism, Europeans and Euro-Americans imagined the heathen world as a sweeping realm that shared the essential commonality of requiring renovation. Part II looks at how Americans, having conceived of the heathen world as a realm that needed their help, grappled with what to do about supposed heathens in their midst and in regions they had economic and political interests in. The concept of heathenism both challenged and helped to define the American racial state, justifying inclusion and exclusion from the body politic. Finally, Part III considers how ideas about heathens have persisted to this day. Even as the term eventually fell out of favor, the concepts underlying it have continued to shape American approaches to a world in need, as well as ongoing critiques of the same by those historically clumped in the heathen category.

The story this book tells is as much about continuity as it is about change. Through one lens, we can see dynamic shifts in the idea of the heathen over time. But through another lens, we can see how long-lasting its implications have been. This book attempts to look through both lenses to offer a three-dimensional narrative that is attentive to the continued colonial thinking that tries to divide the world into a humanitarian "us" and a needy "them," as well as to the contingencies and counterscripts that rupture the colonizing frame.

PART I

Imagining the Heathen World

John Gast's 1872 painting *American Progress* is one of the best-known images from the nineteenth-century United States, reprinted in just about every contemporary American history textbook to illustrate the idea of manifest destiny. Columbia, a pale woman in a sheer white gown, wearing the Star of Empire on her complacent forehead, leads bearded White men from east to west. She carries a schoolbook and strings a telegraph line along the way. Steam engines follow her; partially clothed Native Americans and buffalo flee before her presence. Light bathes the image from the east, suffusing the darker clouds with sunbeams and forcing the Native Americans who look backward to shade their eyes as they gallop into the darkness.

Gast's was not the first image to employ such motifs of westward "progress." A much less familiar set of lithographs anticipates Gast's iconic artwork by four decades.[1] Printed on life membership certificates for the Missionary Society of the Methodist Episcopal Church beginning in the 1830s, the lithographs similarly feature a pale woman in a diaphanous white gown, moving from east to west. Light emanates from behind her, dispelling the darkness around her, as a figure cowers from its blinding rays.

These membership certificate lithographs also differ from Gast's painting in important ways. The central woman here is not America but an angel, bearing the Holy Bible instead of a schoolbook, and blowing a trumpet of the Lord instead of stringing a telegraph line. The light from the east emanates from a pointing hand instead of the sun, and in place of the Star of Empire, a dove of peace flies beside the angel. The scene below her is not primarily the American West, as in *American Progress,* but a montage of places depicting the heathen world, a realm Protestant Americans imagined to extend both geographically across the globe and temporally into the past. On the bottom right, a "converted Black family kneel[s] and reach[es] toward the heavens; broken shackles and swords beside them" suggest the Gospel's power to both set free and to pacify. In the middle, a missionary clad in a long black cape preaches to a group of Native Americans sitting in a semicircle by a cluster of tepees. These are the receptive heathens, the good

George A. Crofutt, *American Progress,* ca. 1873. Chromolithograph after 1872 painting of the same title by John Gast. Library of Congress, Prints and Photographs Division, LC-DIG-ppmsca-09855.

listeners for whom the river of life spills forth from a raised cross. To the left of the cross, a pale woman recoils from the angel, a snake around her neck. Her flowing white dress perhaps signifies the draped togas of ancient Greco-Roman pagans, while the objects in front of her may indicate the trappings of Roman Catholicism. A skeleton sporting a crown lies next to her, showing the deadly consequences of heathen unbelief on the fallen monarchs of yore. Behind her, a Mughal structure crumbles in the distance, a toppled Chinese-style Buddha at its base, representing the various heathens of the "Orient."[2]

As with Gast's *American Progress,* these images were likely meant to be displayed. Each certificate measures over sixteen by twenty inches. They are dated, inscribed with the names of the donor to the missionary cause and the amount expended, and signed by members of the missionary society. Their large size and official appearance communicated their importance. The individual details of each vignette invited close examination, rendering variations in skin color through lighter and darker shading, and differences in landscape with symbols like huts, tepees, palm trees, and temples.

But difference is not the only, or even necessarily the primary, significance the images convey. A viewer stepping back to take in the whole would

Missionary Society of the Methodist Episcopal Church, life membership certificate, Philadelphia, ca. 1835. Mezzotint (51×41 cm). Issued to Eliza J. Hamilton on April 7, 1846, signed by John Whitman, president, and Saml. Sappington, secretary. John Sartain, engraver, Edward Williams Clay, artist. Library Company of Philadelphia.

understand sameness, too: the sameness of the heathen world as a realm where differently appearing people, landscapes, and time periods belong on the same visual plane and require the same angelic intervention. Taken as a whole, skin color does not predict capitulation to the gospel, nor does the magnificence of a built environment. The heathen woman wrapped in snakes is the palest of all the bodies in the image, but also the most endangered. The fallen minarets and Buddha behind her may once have been impressive, but they are no match for the power of God. The juxtaposition of symbols conveys not ignorant confusion but purposeful conflation: the fundamental error and neediness of the heathen world no matter what its material manifestations might be.[3]

Viewers contemplating the certificate would have read an allegory of progress onto it, no less than in Gast's painting. The angel is sent by the hand of the Lord; everywhere the heathen must capitulate to the light or die in the darkness, as the proud buildings and despots of the heathen world crumble to the ground. The dynamism of this change could be seen on the static two-dimensional page, and the Americans whose names were proudly emblazoned on these certificates could witness the fruits of their contributions in the outstretched arms and patient postures of the saved, while hoping that their dollars might bring down other idolatrous temples and crush more obstinate heathen kings.[4]

Such dynamism and purposeful conflation of very different peoples and places are also apparent in nineteenth-century missionary maps that swathed the heathen world in undifferentiated colors like gray and brown. These maps were not merely matter-of-fact depictions of the world as it is, but showed what needed to be done to turn the drabness of the heathen world into the saving light (often rendered blue or yellow) of Protestantism. A typical such map was widely disseminated in the Congregationalist women's missionary magazine *Life and Light for Heathen Women,* which boasted a circulation of nearly four thousand women and one thousand life members a year after its inauguration. The map was first displayed at the Second Annual Meeting of the Woman's Board of Missions in Boston's Park Street Church on January 4, 1870. Explicitly dubbed a "Moral Map," it was painstakingly "drawn and painted for the use of the Board of Missions by Mrs. Miron Winslow" and "hung in full view of the audience," in order to show "the moral condition and religious aspect of the world, by the use of appropriately distinguishing colors."[5] Brown, for "Heathen," is the dominant color of the map; Protestants are a yellow that is few and far between. Yellow stars denote missionary fields that dot the edges of the heathen world in various places; the stars—representative of light—presumably augur Protestantism's eventual takeover of the world.

Winslow described the map for the audience, and her description, along with her map, was reprinted in the magazine. "Let us look at the eastern hemisphere," said she: "Asia is buried in the night of heathenism and Mohammedanism. Africa about equally divided between the same. . . . A sadly small portion of Northern Europe is Protestant. Turning to the western hemisphere, how large a portion of it we find still under the darkness of superstition! while the United States seems like a sun to scatter the moral darkness of the world. For this, God has opened the gates of mighty empires that had been shut during long ages."[6] Winslow knows the hand of God is in her map of the world no less than in the missionary certificates. Where the certificates show light emanating from behind the angel, light comes from the sun of US righteousness in Winslow's map. Through visual aids like these certificates and maps; in lectures, sermons, and displays; and in widely disseminated tracts, books, and magazines, Americans formulated their ideas about the heathen world as an elastic and shifting realm that could stretch to incorporate people and lands from past to present and from east to west, even as it could also recede before the saving light.

The heathen was not, of course, a nineteenth-century American invention. The figure of the heathen was born on the other side of the Atlantic. She was the younger, Anglo-Germanic, and sometimes indistinguishable sibling of the Latin pagan. Both the heathen and the pagan were defined by who they were not: not a Christian, not a Jew, not a Muslim. (In practice, ordinary Europeans tended to lump Muslims in with other heathens, while theologians and church leaders generally did not.)[7] The term "heathen," like "pagan," originally referred to the rustic country folk who resisted the spread of Christianity. It was not until the warring tribes of Europe were Christianized, and then set out in search of the treasures of other lands, that the elasticity and capaciousness of the heathen category grew to require broader explanation. The heathen were no longer just the uncouth people who lived on the outskirts of society. Europeans' realization that another world lay across the Atlantic generated new explanatory problems about the origins of, and similarities and differences between, heathen peoples the world over, particularly those whom the Bible did not explicitly reference. The idea of a heathen world grew out of attempts to explain what features the heathen shared in common, as Europeans and then Euro-Americans learned more about the diversity of the world's people and their practices, and attempted to differentiate themselves as superior. Euro-Americans continued to imagine heathenness as a cohesive category, even when the evidence gleaned from colonizing and missionizing ventures might seem to have pointed in a direction other than cohesion.

PRECEDENTS

E arly English travel literature did not enjoy a stellar reputation. Writers were known to exaggerate; some authors pieced together elaborate travel narratives solely on the basis of other publications. Fantastical stories of monstrous creatures, part human and part beast, tickled the fancy of readers but could hardly rescue travel literature from being "ranked among the lowest and least respectable kinds of writing." To preserve his reputation, clergyman and traveler William Biddulph published his 1609 *Travels of Foure English Men and a Preacher* under cover of an "editorial persona named 'Theophilus Lavender.'"[1] Lavender purported to have compiled the letters of William and his brother Peter from their journeys to "sundry" places, including "Africa, Asia, Troy, . . . and to the Blacke Sea," and "Palestina, Ierusalem, Iericho and to the Red Sea." The purpose of the text was to be didactic and moral, in contrast to the perceived frivolity of other travel literature. The title promised that the book would be "very profitable for the helpe of Trauellers, and no lesse delightfull to all persons who take pleasure to heare of the Manners, Gouernment, Religion, and Customes of Forraine and Heathen Countries."[2]

The primary lesson readers were to take from reading about these "Forraine and Heathen Countries" was gratitude for their own blessings and confidence in the superiority of Protestant Christianity. In the preface, Lavender set up a series of contrasts between "Heathen Countries" and England. The former were groaning under "tyrannous gouernment" while loyal subjects of the "good and gratious King" enjoyed the benefits of his "mercifull gouernment." The heathen lay in "blindness and palpable ignorance, not knowing the right hand from the left in matters that concerne the kingdome of Heauen," while the English luxuriated in the "inestimable benefit of the preaching of the word amongst them." Heathen women languished in "slauerie" and "subjection to their Husbands," while English women enjoyed such "libertie and freedome" as to teach them to "loue their Husbands." Heathen servants were "beate . . . like dogs," and their "poore men" "liue like brute beasts," which should encourage English servants to be "faithfull and dutifull to their Masters" and the English "poore" to "bee thankefulle to God for their benefactors." Even rich heathens were to be pitied, since "in other Countries no man is master of his owne," while rich men in England could rest in the confidence that they had "libertie and freedom" not only of their "Conscience and persons; but of their goods also."[3]

In a nutshell, then, "Forraine and Heathen Countries" served as a foil against which the English could reassure themselves of their political, economic, social, and religious superiority. In the English Protestant imagination, failing to recognize and worship the one true God had implications that reverberated throughout the lives of heathen individuals and their societies. "And who knoweth what good may redound vnto others, by reading of this discourse of other Countries?" asked Lavender. "For hereby all men may see how God hath blessed our Country aboue others, & be stirred vp to thankfulnes."[4]

But gratitude was not the only response that awareness of non-Christian, non-monotheistic cultures provoked. For gratitude raised other questions, too. Why were the English so peculiarly blessed (as they saw it)? Would they always remain so, even if they moved far away from England, perhaps even among the heathen themselves? And what could—and should—the English do about the supposedly lamentable condition of the heathen? Should gratitude be coupled with a sense of guilt for enjoying God's blessings without spreading them to others? Fundamentally, the imagined pitiful state of the heathen stoked uncomfortable questions about the reasons for human difference.

The Anglo-American save-the-heathen impulse drew from a much longer history of ideas inherited from centuries of philosophical and theological discussion, travel writing, and comparative colonial enterprises. As the English ventured into overseas empire, they drew from Greco-Roman precedent, scriptural authority and church teachings, and the Spanish example. A feeling of paternalistic guilt, combined with gratitude for the superiority of Englishness, formed one component of a larger set of attitudes toward the heathen: as innocent or demonic, virtuous or vicious, human or animal, natural-born slaves or changeable agents. This chapter sketches these precedents as essential to understanding the heathen's later development in the American imagination.

Barbaroi, Paganus, Haiþnô, and Savage

Ironically, the early colonists' thinking about the heathen owed much to a people they considered to be heathens or pagans: the Greeks. In Greek culture, the figure of the barbarian, which would later inform the Latin *paganus*, referred to foreigners who could not speak Greek. The *barbaroi*'s inability to use language in ways the Greeks understood was supposed to signify their inability to reason, to communicate clearly with each other, and hence to form themselves into civil societies or city-states (polis).[5]

While the Greek barbaroi were acknowledged to be humans, they were not humans of the same type as the *politēs*, or citizens. Adult male citizens occupied the highest position on an ontological ladder of development. They were closest to the gods, and they alone could aspire to the "life of happiness (*eudaimonia*) which is the highest end (*telos*) of all men." Women and children were below men, and barbarians were closest to the beasts. Their dwelling places outside cities, in the uncultivated forests and hills, was supposed to indicate their wild nature and communion with animals. They were also thought to exist in a constant state of mindless struggle with and against each other, since they lacked law and order.[6]

The associations that would become attached to the pagan drew from this notion of the barbarian; indeed, by the sixth century, the term "barbarous" had essentially "become synonymous with the term *paganus*."[7] The classical Latin *pāgānus* had originally referred to country-dwellers (from *pāgus,* or country district), villagers, and rural people, and also connoted "civilians" or "non-militants." After the Christianization of the Roman Empire, and around the fourth century AD, the term began to take on the additional meaning of those rustic people who continued to worship the old gods and did not adopt the new religion. The connection of the term to non-Christians was furthered by the self-identification of early Christians as soldiers for Christ, or *mīlitēs,* and thus non-Christians as pagans, or civilians.[8]

The Germanic term "heathen" (Gothic *haiþnô*) arose later; its origins are thought to be from the Latin *gentilis* (gentile) or *Hellenes* (worshipers of Greek divinities) and the Gothic *haiþi,* or heath. The idea that the heathen were gentile (that is, unbaptized) wanderers in the "heath," or wilderness, served as a rough translation of the Latin *paganus* and expressed a similar idea—that the uncouth tribes of the overgrown country resisted Christianization, in contrast to the people of the cities and towns. Another possible source for the term is the Armenian *het'anos,* for ethnic tribes or nations, and now translated as "heathen."[9] In the later American context, the terms "pagan" and "heathen" were used for the most part interchangeably, though as the encyclopedic late nineteenth-century New York *Century Dictionary* put it, "*Pagan* is sometimes distinctively applied to those nations that, although worshiping false gods, are more cultivated, as the Greeks and Romans, and *heathen* to uncivilized idolaters, as the tribes of Africa."[10]

Another important related term, the *sauvage,* or "savage," similarly connoted one who lived in the woods, from the Latin *sylvaticus,* meaning of the woods, or wild. As with the barbarian, pagan, and heathen, "to be savage meant to be living according to nature, in a manner 'closer to that of wild animals than to that of man.'" The figure of the savage drew from the popular European folk character of the "Wild Man of the Woods." The wild man was characterized by his hairiness and large size, and reputed for ferocity, sensuality, strength, and wilderness survival skills (not something to which genteel Europeans were supposed to aspire). In European folklore, the wild man could be a frightening, ogre-like figure but could also be seen as a noble savage, free from the constraints of civilization.[11]

In many ways, the terms Europeans used to describe outsiders were practically synonymous, and were often used as such. Still, there was a key difference between the figure of the pagan/heathen and the barbarian and savage: the emphasis on wrong (or no) religion that underlay the former category made religion, as opposed to region, climate, language, or descent, the primary explanation for human difference. And it carried with it the imperative to unheathenize. Pagans/heathens were also not just "wild" men to stay away from and keep out of civil society, but human beings who represented a wide array of social forms and customs, not all of which Europeans characterized as "savage." That is to say, while savages and barbarians were understood to be heathens (since Christianity was supposed to exert a civilizing influence on people), not all heathens were taken to be savages or barbarians. And as much as the knowledge of "Forraine and Heathen Countries" was supposed to inspire gratitude, a worry also lurked that exposure to other cultures might instead inspire envy and emulation. To what extent was this appropriate? Could Christians borrow and learn from pagans? And how could and should they go about convincing people who seemed already self-satisfied in their pagan resplendence of their need for the gospel?

The Pagan in Early Christian Theology

Case in point: the Greeks themselves. Though the figure of the pagan and heathen borrowed from the Greek barbaroi, the transmutation of the wild barbarian into the non-Christian pagan put the Greeks and Romans—the antithesis of barbarians (in their own eyes)—squarely in the pagan camp. Classical paganism presented a problem for the early church, as church leaders debated the merits of pagan virtue, the extent to which pagans could possess knowledge of God, and the possibility of pagan salvation.[12] On the one hand, Christian theologians were deeply influenced by Plato, Aristotle,

Plotinus, and others. But on the other hand, some argued that paganism was not a valid pathway to the truth, and that pagans were hell-bound sinners, not virtuous teachers. The Bible lent itself to multiple interpretations. Paul's famous sermon at Mars Hill, recorded in the book of Acts, suggested that the "men of Athens" were "too superstitious" yet also allowed that "THE UNKNOWN GOD" they "ignorantly worship[ed]" was the same God of the Christians: the "God that made the world and all things therein," who "dwelleth not in temples made with hands," and who "made of one blood all nations of men."[13] In other words, pagans and Christians alike owed their existence to and worshiped the same God, whether they knew it or not.

The first chapter of Paul's letter to the Romans presents another view of paganism that is "both more complex and less friendly to pagans than what Luke had attributed to him" in the sermon on Mars Hill.[14] Romans 1 articulates an idea of revealed religion that could hold pagans culpable for their unbelief but also offers the possibility that pagans could and should know about the one true God through nature: "For the invisible things of him from the creation of the world are clearly seen, being understood by the things that are made, even his eternal power and Godhead; so that they are without excuse." The text continues by criticizing idol worship as the "foolish" ideas of men who "knew God" but "glorified him not as God," instead turning his "truth . . . into a lie" by "worship[ing] and ser[ving] the creature more than the Creator." Thus God "gave them up to uncleanness through the lusts of their own hearts, to dishonour their own bodies between themselves."[15] The passage suggests that heathens could justifiably be held guilty for failing to clearly see God's hand in His creation. But it could also be read to suggest that heathens born out of reach of the gospel could still have a chance at salvation if they pulled the wool from their eyes.

The uneven process of Christianization required stark boundaries to be drawn between pagans and Christians. Each depicted the other in exaggerated terms. For the early Christians, the key characteristics that differentiated pagans from themselves were polytheism, idol worship, and sacrifice, whether of animals or of humans. Christians told stories of pagans' bloody rituals to Zeus, Jupiter, Pluto, Saturn, and Diana. They turned the gods into demons, as in the Council of Orléans's decree against eating "food immolated to demons" in 541. They constructed themselves, in opposition to pagans, as monotheists who did not bow down to images and who accepted Christ's atonement as the only possible and effectual sacrifice for their sins. Meanwhile, the Romans scorned the secret practices of Christians and spread rumors about what went on behind their closed doors, from orgies to ritual violence and cannibalism.[16]

But for all the differences set up by these dueling rumors, Christians and pagans in the Roman Empire shared common cultural heritage, and scholars have uncovered "pagan continuity" in Christian practices, such as the adoration of saints and prayers for the dead, shrines for healing, "dancing, feasting and the use of spells and divination."[17] Some early church leaders also found value in classical philosophy, developing those aspects of the scriptures that suggested that pagans could potentially be saved through a correct understanding of nature. Though ordinary Greeks and Romans might "dishonour" themselves in "lustful" and "unclean" behaviors, some early Christians saw the philosophers as wiser men in a foolish society who had partial access to the truth and even to the one true God, and whose texts could be profitably plumbed.[18] "Pagan apologists" also began to play up the similarities between their and the Christians' understandings of deity. As Plutarch (ca. AD 46–120) put it, "There are not different gods for different peoples; not barbarous gods and Greek gods, northern gods and southern gods. But even as the moon and the sun shed their light on all men, . . . however numerous may be the names by which they are known, so there is but one Intelligence reigning over the world, one Providence which rules it, and the same powers are at work everywhere. Only the names change, as do the forms of worship."[19]

By the second century, when Christian converts began to have greater access to education, including in classical philosophy, "they developed a much more unambiguously positive view of the wisdom of pagan philosophers, though one which—understandably in the polemical context—was none the less designed to show its inferiority to the Christianity which they preached."[20] Justin Martyr (d. 160) proposed that the "pagan thinkers had read Moses," and Clement of Alexandria (ca. 150–215) suggested that Christ's harrowing of hell (1 Peter 3:19–20) meant that all who had died before His coming now had a chance to receive salvation.

Clement's view would become popular in the Eastern church. But in the Western Christian tradition, attitudes toward pagan philosophy would take a different turn with the teachings of Saint Augustine of Hippo (354–430). Augustine wrote in a different context: the fall of Rome led by the Gothic leader Alaric. Like Justin and Clement, Augustine was also steeped in Platonic and Neoplatonic philosophy, but Rome's fall led him to see its people as prideful and their virtues as vices. According to Augustine, the pagan gods had failed to protect Rome—and indeed never had, given Rome's bloody history of violence and disaster. Augustine did not dismiss Rome's gods as "simply figments of the imagination" but instead viewed them as lesser supernatural beings: possibly angels but more likely demons, the false worship of which distracted people from the one true God.[21]

Augustine admitted that the pagan philosophers did not necessarily worship the gods of the people, and that some of them even seemed to believe in, and provide Christians with valuable ways of thinking about, God. But Augustine nevertheless found the philosophers to be "without excuse" because they failed to see their need for a mediator—Christ—instead putting faith in themselves. For Augustine, salvation was only possible through Christ, and hence "what does it profit someone proud and who, for this reason, blushes at the wood of Christ's cross, to see from far off his country beyond the sea?"[22] This line of reasoning also shaded Augustine's thought on the inability of pagans to act virtuously. True virtue must be done for the sake of the true God; virtuous acts done on behalf of humans might lead to earthly happiness and tranquility but were ultimately false virtues that did nothing for eternal happiness.

Augustine's views spread as Europe was haltingly Christianized. While local temples were sometimes preserved for community events, Christians "theatrically" destroyed the objects they housed—statues, images, trinkets— thus "demonstrating the power of Christianity over the old gods."[23] By the medieval era, various theologians were grappling with Augustine's teachings on the false wisdom and virtue of pagans and the surety of their damnation. Some felt that Augustine had gone too far. The French scholastic Peter Abelard (1079–1142), in his letters to Heloïse on theological matters, modified Augustine's uncompromising position and instead suggested that "it accords with piety and reason that whoever, recognizing by natural law God as the creator and rewarder of all, adhere to him with such zeal that they strive in no way to offend him . . . : such people, we judge, should by no means be damned." Abelard even proposed that "what is necessary for them also to learn in order to be saved will be revealed to them by God before the end of their lives, either through inspiration, or through someone sent by whom instruction may be given about these things."[24] In other words, God could send direct and salvific revelation to those out of reach of the gospel. To believe any less of Him would be neither "pious" nor "reasonable." As Abelard's framing of the issue demonstrates, the question of the pagan's potential to be saved was also a question about the nature of God. Where Augustine emphasized pagan pride and the inadequacies of pagan wisdom and virtue—hence damning pagans by their own sins alone—Abelard focused on how a reasonable God could not permit pagans who acted morally and piously to perish eternally.

By the following century, as medieval academies enshrined the study of Aristotle as a necessary part of higher education, Thomas Aquinas (1225–1274) argued that Christians' use of a pagan corpus was defensible and desirable. According to Aquinas, even without the benefit of revelation, "reason, rightly used, will show the falsity of heretical doctrines and arrive at many of the truths of Christian theology, which, on the basis of revelation, it can extend harmoniously." Aquinas was such a fan of Aristotle that he devoted "his later years to a precise, sentence-by-sentence exposition of his major texts."[25]

Contemporaneous Pagans

The medieval respect for past pagan philosophers would cast a long shadow on Europeans' growing awareness of contemporaneous pagans in other regions of the world. The popular mid-fourteenth-century *Book* [or *Travels*] *of John Mandeville,* written not from firsthand observations but from the anonymous author's perusal of other travelers' books, introduced readers to distant lands and their peoples and practices. Printed in French, English, Latin, German, Italian, Irish, Danish, and Czech, the *Book of John Mandeville* "presented new and formerly restricted material and ideas to a wide, general, and not necessarily highly educated audience."[26] The author drew from Odoric of Pordenone's (1286–1331) highly negative accounts of pagan cannibalism, idol worship, and self-mutilation. But where Odoric had dismissed these practices as demonic and impious, the author of the *Book* speculated about why pagans might actually want to engage in them. For instance, the author explained that "they think that the more pain and tribulation they suffer for love of this idol, the closer they will be to God and the more joy they will have in the world to come. . . . Hardly any Christian would dare to do a tenth part of it for love of his Christ."[27] At the level of popular reading, the account functioned to make pagans seem exotic but relatable, misguided but understandable. Toward the end of the book, the author even asserted that virtuous pagans might be blessed: "Although this people does not have the articles of faith which we have, none the less for their good natural faith and their good intention I believe that it is certain that God loves them and that God looks on their service favourably, as he did for Job, who was a pagan."[28] The author emphasized that pious present-day pagans could be as blessed as preincarnation pagans like Job, for whom "implicit faith" was widely accepted as enough.

Of course, holding out the prospect of theoretical salvation for pagans who followed the natural law still left the vast majority of (if not all) pagans without hope, for it was supposed to be well-nigh impossible for anyone but Christ to act thus virtuously after Adam's fall. The author of the *Book* admitted that most pagans were probably "hearing the voices of devils" through their idols rather than loving and serving the true God.[29]

For medieval Europeans, this seemed especially true of present-day pagans and heathens, to whom they accorded much less respect than to the ancient Greeks, and about whom they turned to the Greeks, and particularly Aristotle, to justify enslavement.

Aristotle had held that some humans are born naturally inferior and need the guidance and oversight of superior humans to lead them from their barbarous ways. These "natural slaves" were humans whose "intellect ha[d], for some reason, failed to achieve proper mastery over [their] passions." Natural slaves needed "stronger" men to make decisions for them and bring them out of their barbarism. Their enslavement was thought to be not only justified but also just, since "once the natural slave has been caught his condition must improve, just as the condition of the wild animal is said to improve once it has been domesticated."[30] In other words, to call people "natural slaves" was not simply a typological move but an argument about how they should be treated: like animals needing to be tamed.

Europeans added a Christian spin to Aristotle's arguments. Natural slaves were those who needed to be Christianized: heathens and Muslims. Muslims had their own views on who could be enslaved; Islamic law forbade "the forcible enslavement of fellow Muslims" but "gave religious sanction to the enslavement of infidels." Both Muslims and European Christians agreed that Africans were barbarous heathens whose worship of "fetishes" was base idolatry. Muslim traders enslaved "literally millions of blacks from sub-Saharan Africa," while the papacy "sanctioned their captivity on the basis that it could result in their conversion and salvation."[31]

Europeans' realization that the Americas existed led to debates about whether Native Americans were likewise "natural slaves" who could and should be held in captivity for the purposes of conversion. There was little question that they were heathens. The May 4, 1493 papal bull *Inter Caetera*, which divided the "undiscovered world between Spain and Portugal," made clear that a crucial justification for colonization was "to lead the peoples dwelling in those islands and countries to embrace the Christian religion."[32] Theologians like Aquinas had categorized those who never had a chance to receive the gospel as ignorant "through no obvious fault of their own." As applied to Native Americans, "most commentators were agreed . . . that [they] could have known nothing of Christ before the arrival of the Spaniards. They could not, therefore, convincingly be described as *inimicos Christi*."[33]

Native Americans were generally understood to be less culpable than Jews, Muslims, and Africans. During the Reconquista and its aftermath, Jews and Muslims were forced to convert or be expelled from Spain. Conversos came under intense suspicion and scrutiny. The Inquisition sought to sniff and stamp out secret Judaizing practices and evidences of Morisco obduracy. The notion of *limpieza de sangre* sorted people based on the closeness of their connections to conversos. Heathenness never neatly overlapped with the stain of blood impurity. In Spanish America, Native converts, who were understood to be formerly heathen, tried to claim limpieza by virtue of never having been exposed to Judaism or Islam before colonization. Since Africans came from an "Old World" context in which Christianity had made some inroads, and since they had been exposed and sometimes converted to Islam, they were unable to similarly claim complete heathen ignorance and came under limpieza suspicions more frequently. For Native converts and their descendants, by contrast, prior heathenness operated as a kind of shield against the even worse offenses of Christ-killing and Christ-denying. Ignorance was preferable to deliberate rejection.[34]

Still, the Spanish recognized differences among Native people, too, which made some seem more innocent and pliable, and others more guilty and subject to enslavement. The Native people of the circum-Caribbean, such as those Columbus first encountered, struck Europeans as naïve children who lacked recognizable religion just as they seemed to lack clothing, by European standards. (The assumption that one could be "pagan" but lack "religion" was not uncommon; "religion" was understood not as a generic concept but as a concept that applied to Christianity and to those beliefs and practices that resembled it.)[35] In the powerful empires of Mexico and Peru, by contrast, Spanish conquistadors were more likely to recognize the practices, beliefs, sacred spaces, and ritual experts of the Aztecs and Incas as dangerous and demonic inversions of "true" religion. As Spanish Jesuit missionary José de Acosta (1539–1600) put it, "It is a vulgar error to assume that the Indians are a single field or city, and because they are all called by the same name to ascribe to them a single nature and mind."[36]

Spanish debates over the justness of the conquest and the justness of enslaving Native people revealed varying assumptions about the causes of human difference. Some, like Juan Ginés de Sepúlveda (1490–1573), held that paganism was demonic, and sufficient argument for violent subjugation. As he put it, in what scholar Anthony Pagden calls "the most virulent and uncompromising argument for the inferiority of the American Indian ever written,"[37] their "paganism," their "abominable licentiousness," and their "prodigious sacrifice of human victims" justified "war against these barbarians." Indeed, "what is more appropriate and beneficial for these barbarians than to become subject to the rule of those whose wisdom, virtue, and religion have converted them . . . from being impious servants of the Devil to becoming believers in the true God?"[38]

But the theory of natural slavery, as defended by Sepúlveda and as applied to Native people, came under fire as theologians trained at the School of Salamanca, founded by Francisco de Vitoria (1492–1546), including Bartolomé de las Casas (1484–1566) and Acosta, dug deeper into the idea of natural law and the ability of humans to understand and follow it. Las Casas and Acosta both had direct experience in New Spain: Las Casas in Hispaniola and Cuba, and Acosta in Mexico and Peru. The Salamancans "held that the only possible legitimation for the conquest lay in the natural right of all men to communicate with each other, and in the Christian's right, under divine law, to be allowed to preach the Gospel to the heathen."[39] For the Salamancans, being allowed to preach to the heathen did not necessitate violently enslaving them for their own good.

Las Casas famously defended Native people as "gentle lambs," made by God to be "as open and as innocent as can be imagined. The simplest people in the world—unassuming, long-suffering, unassertive, and submissive."[40] But even as he paternalistically sought to protect Native people, Las Casas also advocated for African slavery to meet the labor needs of the colonists, reflecting the Spanish colonial tendency to see Native people as capable of purification (since they came from untouched regions of the world and "did not descend from deicides"), while "seldom allow[ing] black blood the possibility of full redemption." By the time the Spanish came to the Americas, they were already used to "linking blackness to both servitude and Islam" and to "seeing black skin color in negative terms."[41]

The forcible importation and conversion of enslaved Africans also put them on a different social level from that of Native people, whose connection to the Crown was supposed to be voluntary and contractual, and whose conversions were also seen as such in Castilian law. The enslaved Africans' Christianization and their loyalty to the Crown was always suspect, whereas Native people were supposed to have "natural love for the territories that now belonged to the crown of Castile."[42] The Salamancans affirmed that Native people could be reasoned with; that they had access to the "light of natural wisdom," were fully capable of observing it, and could, through that observation, act virtuously and attain right knowledge of the world and its Creator. They often "fail[ed] to interpret the law of nature correctly." But this was not because they were "men without true minds," but rather because "the natural law, though generally considered to be immutable, is none the less frequently obscured." Unlike Christians, who had the light of revelation to snap their understanding of nature into clear focus, and who "rarely [went] astray except when they allow[ed] themselves to be drawn aside into sin by the machinations of Satan," pagans' lives were veiled by such error.[43] The Salamancans' understanding of *why* Native people were led astray by Satan differed in a key way from Sepúlveda's. For Sepúlveda and other defenders of the theory of natural slavery, it was due to their inherent inferiority. But for Acosta, "the incapacity of their minds, the ferocity of their customs, does not derive from natural inclination or from the effect of climate, so much as from a prolonged education and customs like those of beast."[44] Difference, to Acosta, was predicated on centuries of misguided nurture, as opposed to flawed nature.

Pagan Catholics

Where the Spanish drew from the legacy of the Reconquista to justify violence against people for their religious identity, the English colonizers, who began arriving in the Americas later, fell back on the precedent of bloody colonial projects in Ireland to "conquer the barbarian, to recall the savage and the pagan to civility."[45] To the English, the Irish were the quintessential wanderers in the heath, the wild men who needed to be taught how to live in civil society. A wrong attitude toward the land reflected a wrong (heathenish) attitude toward its Creator, while "cultivated fields and enclosed grounds" represented a correct (Christian) understanding of nature and of humans' appropriate relationship to it. For uncultivated land of "woddes, rockes, greete bogges, and barren grounde, being unmanured or tilled," encouraged "theym to lyve like wild and salvaige persones, onlie lyving by stelthe," without the responsibility that came with property ownership on settled parcels of land.[46] Just as the land needed to be "broken" before it could "be made capable of good seed," so "a barbarous country must first be broken by a war before it will be acceptable of good government," as one husbandry manual put it.[47]

But wildness and barbarism were not the only characteristics that English Protestants used to distinguish themselves from the Irish. The Irish were not merely civilizationally backwards; as unrepentant Catholics, they were religiously so. For English Protestants keen to separate themselves from Catholicism, the Roman Church was uncomfortably close to paganism still. Catholic veneration of images and relics, the cult of the saints and of the Virgin Mary, and allegiance to the pope all smacked of idolatrous avoidance of the one true God. The Irish had access to the truth, but the failure of the Protestant Reformation to take firm root in Ireland was proof of their essential heathenism, obstinacy, and guilt.[48]

Some observers of the Irish resorted to a hereditary explanation for their supposed heathenism. In *A View of the State of Ireland*, Edmund Spenser, who spent nearly two decades as a planter there, explained that the Irish descended from "first the Scythian, then the Gaules, and lastly the English." The Scythians were Eurasian nomadic peoples derided as barbarians by the Greeks, while the Gauls had been Celtic animists. According to Spenser, this commingling explained "by what meanes the customes, that now are in Ireland, being some of them indeede very strange and almost heathenish, were first brought in." As evidence of the continuity of these customs, he contended that the Irish showed lack of restraint at "their buryals, with dispairfull outcryes, and immoderate waylings"; this was "the manner of all Pagans and Infidels to be intemperate in their waylings of their dead, for that they had no faith nor hope of salvation."[49]

Even as Spenser made a hereditary argument for Irish customs, he also contended that environment and surroundings could contribute to the formation (or, as the case might be, degeneration) of character. The Anglo-Normans who had invaded Ireland four hundred years earlier had since become worse than the Irish themselves, "for the cheifest abuses which are now in that realme, are growne from the English, and some of them are now much more lawlesse and licentious then the very wilde Irish: so that as much care as was then by them had to reforme the Irish, so and much more must now bee used to reforme them; so much time doth alter the manners of men."[50] Colonizers always had to stay on guard lest they turn "heathenish" themselves.

Spenser had "puritan leanings."[51] The inclination of some Catholic thinkers, like Abelard and Aquinas, to allow for the possibility of pagan virtue and redemption did not sit well with Protestants who sought to purify the church of supposedly superstitious and idolatrous tendencies. They returned to the starker formulation of Augustine in seeing heathen virtue as unmitigatedly false and damnable. The Protestants' almost universal "refusal to allow that even pre-Christians were saved or that there was any reason why they should have been . . . unproblematize[d] the Problem of Paganism."[52] That is, instead of wrestling with whether pagans could be saved through adherence to natural law, early Protestant reformers tended to simply emphasize that salvation could only come through faith in Christ, the gift of which God granted to His elect alone. To Protestants worried about their own election and salvation, the pitiful conclusion that the heathen were hell-bound sinners who could have no second chances was hardly in question.[53]

English colonizers crossed the Atlantic to vanquish the conjoined twins of Catholicism and heathenism, much as they had tried to do in Ireland. North American English colonial identity was forged in triangulation between themselves, Native people, and Catholic colonizers. Their own brutal history with the Irish notwithstanding, the English were voracious consumers of the Black Legend, circulating Las Casas's "booke of the Spanish crueltyes with fayr pictures" (in the words of Sir Walter Raleigh, referring to an English edition of *The Destruction of the Indies* graphically illustrated by Theodor de Bry). For those poor Native people who had already encountered Catholic invaders, the kindness of the English—the way in which they treated Native people with "all humanitie, curtesie, and freedome"—was supposed to encourage them to "yelde themselves to her government and revolte cleane from the Spaniarde." The French colonizers, who began arriving in North America around the same time as the English, were not as famous for cruelty (more so for their reports of missionary martyrdom), but to the English, their willy-nilly baptizing of Native people, and their allowance of intermarriage and syncretistic practices, was just as bad from an eternal standpoint. They were damning the heathen still by sharing a paganized version of the gospel and making them think they were thereby saved.[54]

From "Poore Prodigalls" to "Bloody Heathen"

The earliest English colonists did not categorically imagine the heathen in the "New World" as inferior and needy. They lacked the Bible and knowledge of the one true God, but that just gave the English all the more reason to "come over and help" them, as the first Massachusetts Bay Colony seal famously proclaimed. The English also realized that they could learn from Native technologies and that, if anything, the English often needed Native people to come over and help them in basic survival skills.[55] They remarked on climate and natural resources with eager appreciation and looked forward to mutually beneficial relationships, as the English taught the deluded heathen the truths of the Bible and learned from Native people how best to exploit the lands on which they were intruding.

One of the earliest reports back, Thomas Hariot and John White's description of Sir Walter Raleigh's settlement at Virginia, was written with an eye toward boosterism and thus emphasized the ways in which Native people and Native lands seemed not entirely dissimilar from the English. White, an artist who had served as recorder on an earlier expedition, had been appointed governor by Raleigh. *A Briefe and True Report* was first published in 1588 with text by Hariot and then reissued with detailed engravings by Theodor De Bry based on White's artwork. The book aimed to "attract settlers and investors in a venture which seemed to promise rich rewards."[56] The men stressed the "comodities" available in the "new found land of Virginia," from "silke of grasse" and "worme silke" to furs, dyes, and sugar cane. They noted the availability of building material and explained that the Native people lived in enclosed towns with "howses" and "fields vherin they sowe their corne." White and Hariot distinguished separate sacred spaces in Native towns and also noted a hierarchical system of governance, indicating the "kings lodginge" in a map of the "Towne of Pomeiooc." The image made clear that the Carolina Algonquian people of Virginia were not nomads lacking in law, order, or something that could be identified as "religion," however wrong the English believed it to be.[57]

Of the character of these people, Hariot assured readers that they "are not to be feared; but that they shall haue cause both to feare and loue vs, that shall inhabite with them." They had "some religion . . . already, which although it be farre from the truth, yet beyng as it is, there is hope that it may bee the easier and sooner reformed." Though worshiping multiple gods—a key marker of heathenness—Hariot said that the Native people primarily reverenced "one onely chiefe and great God, which hath bene from all eternitie," and seemed to recognize that this God "so specially loued" the English as to provide them with "Mathematicall instruments, sea compasses, . . . a perspectiue glasse . . . , gunnes, books, writing and reading, . . . and manie other thinges."[58] The Carolina Algonquian people seemed suitably awed by these innovations, showed an interest in the Bible as the means through which the English had come to invent them, and hence seemed eminently convertible. The measured illustrations that accompanied A Briefe and True Report similarly depicted Native people as deluded and deprived but not demonic or unchangeable—certainly not people among whom to fear settling.

In a preface to the "gentle Reader," the text acknowledged that "man by his disobedience, weare depriued of those good Gifts wher with he was indued in his creation," but that the Native inhabitants of Virginia proved that God had not entirely abandoned those who were not favored with the revelation. "For although they haue noe true knoledge of God nor of his holye worde and are destituded of all lerninge, Yet they passe vs in many things." As an example of this, White and De Bry illustrated in painstaking detail "the manner of making their boates," which is "verye wonderfull." The conclusion of the volume also included some images of "the Inhabitans of the great Bretannie" to show how they "have bin in times past as sauuage as those of Virginia." The illustrations showed how the Picts once went about practically naked but for body paint and "did never felle to carye" the heads of their enemies after conquering them. Where Spenser had written of English degeneration in Ireland, the producers of A Briefe

"The trvve picture of one: Picte I," in *A briefe and true report of the new found land of Virginia, of the commodities and of the nature and manners of the natural inhabitants,* by Thomas Harriot and Theodor de Bry (illustrator) (Frankfurt, 1590). British Library, C.38.i.18.

and True Report included these images of the English to suggest how people could change for the better over time.[59]

Unfortunately for White and Hariot, the colony for which they had such high hopes disappeared soon after the appearance of De Bry's 1590 edition of their text. By the time White returned to Roanoke from a trip to England for supplies, the colonists were gone, raising anxieties that the Indigenous people were perhaps more "to be feared" than the *Briefe and True Report* had led on. Other English colonial ventures similarly began with high hopes for the convertibility of the heathen, but where Roanoke ended with the disappearance of the English colonists, English settlements in Jamestown and New England ended instead with the near genocide, enslavement, and forced removal of the Native populations. The susceptibility of Indigenous bodies to European diseases led colonizers to believe that they were physically inferior, and when devastated Native communities fought back against English encroachments and diseases, the colonists justified their even more brutal retaliations with demonization of Native people as incorrigible heathens. No longer were they innocents out of reach of the gospel: they had had a chance to follow it but, like the Irish, had deliberately chosen to continue in their wrongheaded ways.[60]

Such was the case in Jamestown, after the Powhatans, led by Opechancanough, killed more than 350 English settlers, burned their fields, and destroyed their houses. They must have done this at "the instigation of the Devill (enemy to their salvation)," wrote Edward Waterhouse, and hence "the Indians, who before were used as friends, may now most justly be compelled to servitude and drudgery."[61] This echoed Spanish justifications of Native slavery on the basis of their supposed demonic paganism. Turning to violence, the Virginia Company "repudiated its previous strategy of conversion and commonwealth and abandoned the notion that Indians were potential Christians."[62]

Puritan New England followed a similar trajectory. The conversion of some Native people to Christianity sparked hope that the colonists were fulfilling their responsibility to "come over and help." Unheathenizing them meant more than simply telling them the gospel: it meant moving them into praying towns where they were supposed to live like the English colonists, in settled dwellings tending cultivated fields, and with patriarchal families headed by Native Christian men who "used stern resolve when necessary but applied Christian love whenever possible."[63] A 1649 "Act For the promoting and propagating the Gospel of Jesus Christ in New England" established a corporation in England to manage and collect lands and money for the work of heathen evangelization. The act exulted in the changes reported by "divers faithful and godly Ministers" who had been preaching the "Gospel to them in their own Indian Language." These ministers explained how "divers the Heathen Natives of that countrey" were "not onely of Barbarous are become Civil, but many of them forsaking their accustomed Charms and Sorceries, and other Satanical Delusions, do now call upon the Name of the Lord." The act was to be read by ministers throughout England and Wales in order to "exhort the people to a chearful and liberal contribution."[64]

The 1652 *Strength out of Weaknesse; Or a Glorious Manifestation of the further Progresse of the Gospel among the Indians in New-England* continued the boosterish tone of the 1649 act. Though the Native people had "wasted the remainder of Natures Riches to the utmost degeneracy that an Immortall rationall being is obnoxious unto," the volume explained, the Lord had now "powred his Spirit on the seeds of the Heathen, & his blessing on their Off-spring." The result could be marked both on the lives of the heathen, and on the land itself: "In the Wildernesse are waters broken out, and streames in the Desert, the parched ground is become a Poole, and the thirsty Land—springs of water: in the Habitation of Dragons where each lay, there is grasse with Reeds and Rushes."[65] A letter reproduced later in the same volume, by John Endecott, provided specifics as to how Native Christians were transforming the landscapes on which they lived, not only with productions of the soil but also the built environment. "To tell you of their industry and ingenuitie in building of an house after the *English* manner . . . , their being but one *English*-man a Carpentere to shew them, being but two dayes with them, is remarkeable."[66] Trees had become raw material to fell and hew, creating more empty space for planting crops, mowing grass, and constructing further buildings. Endecott explained that the Native Christians had also built a fort and bridge, and intended to build a water mill, further bringing the landscape under human control. Of course, Endecott and other English colonists failed to recognize that Native people had already wrought changes to the land, albeit with a less invasive environmental impact.[67]

But, as in Jamestown, things would take an ugly turn. The colonists' land hunger, the decline of the fur trade, and the spread of liquor led to increasingly tense relations between colonists and the local Wampanoag people and their Narragansett and Nashaway/Nipmuc allies. As the situation soured, leading to what became known as King Philip's War after the sachem Metacom, known as King Philip to the English, the colonists' self-identification as God's New Israel encouraged a shift in thinking about Native people. From savable, electable, prodigal brethren whose heathen ignorance could be reversed through the creation of praying towns and other evangelization efforts, Native people became unholy, willfully sinful, demonic Canaanites who deserved, even demanded, to be destroyed.

In his 1676 *A Brief History of the Warr,* published soon after hostilities had ended, Increase Mather depicted the "Heathen in this Wilderness" as "Thorns" in the colonists' sides, used by God as punishment for English backsliding, but ultimately struck down by God for their iniquities. "For it hath not been brought to pass by our numbers, or skill, or valour, *we have not got the Land in possession by our own Sword, neither did our own arm save us,*" said Mather. "But God hath wasted the Heathen, by sending the destroying Angell amongst them, since this War began."[68] Mather admitted that Native Christians had come to the assistance of the colonists, but when all was said and done, the New Englanders, as had the Virginians, not only violently suppressed Metacom's resistance but also enslaved survivors, sending them from New England to "Barbados, Bermuda, Jamaica, the Azores, Spain and Tangier."[69]

Mather likely helped publish another popular text that emerged in the aftermath of King Philip's War: the 1682 captivity narrative of Mary Rowlandson. It quickly raced through multiple editions (four in its first year of publication) and historians estimate that "the second and third editions alone sold more than one thousand copies," meaning that "many people read, or heard read aloud, each copy," including "large numbers of ordinary colonists."[70] In an era in which most families only owned and read a bible and an almanac, Rowlandson's graphic account provided some didactic entertainment that could be consumed without guilt. She described the Wampanoag, Narragansett, and Nashaway / Nipmuc party that held her captive as "wretches," "bloody Heathen," "merciless Heathen," "Infidels," "Wolves," "roaring Lyons," "Salvage Bears," "hell-hounds," "Barbarous Creatures," and "wild beasts of the forrest." They took her deeper and deeper into the wilderness, where their own bodies became one with the woods: "The *Indians* were as thick as the trees."[71] To Rowlandson, the difference between Christian colonists and Native heathens manifested physically. At one point, she thought she had come across some "*English men,* . . . for they were dressed in *English* Apparel, with Hats, white Neckcloths, and Sashes about their waists, and Ribbonds upon their shoulders: but when they came near, there was a vast difference between the lovely faces of Christians, and the foul looks of these Heathens."[72]

Rowlandson claimed that her Native captors brought hell to earth: "Oh the roaring, and singing and danceing, and yelling of those black creatures in the night, which made the place a lively resemblance of hell," she described. "So like were these barbarous creatures to him who was a lyar from the beginning." In contrast to the corporation's earlier account, Rowlandson described Native people not as pitiable creatures needing to be freed from the snares of the devil but rather as devils themselves. She wondered at the "strange providence of God in preserving the heathen," even in providing food for them where "there was nothing to be seen" in the "wilderness." But like Mather, she concluded that God had only allowed them to prevail in order to test the colonists' faithfulness, much as He had allowed the devil to test Job. When His anger at English backsliding was at last spent, "the Lord had not so many wayes before to preserve [the heathen], but now he hath as many to destroy them," and "hurll'd themselves into" a "pit . . . as deep as hell." The colonists saw themselves as partners with the Lord to "destroy them."[73]

In order to justify the brutal retaliation colonists enacted to wrench compliance from Native souls and soils, later generations emphasized just how difficult was the situation their forebears had encountered. In his 1721 *India Christiana*, Increase's son Cotton Mather described, disapprovingly, the Native peoples' supposed refusal to be awed by Euro-American ways, in direct contradistinction to earlier boosterish accounts. "Tho' they saw a People Arrive among them . . . who had *Houses full of Good Things*, vastly out-shining their squalid and dark *Wigwams;* And they saw this People Replenishing their *Fields*, with *Trees* and with *Grains*, and useful *Animals*, which until now they had been wholly Strangers to; yet they did not seem touch'd in the least, with any *Ambition* to come at such Desireable Circumstances, or with any *Curiosity* to enquire after the *Religion* that was attended with them," Mather marveled. For Mather, it was their "*Religion*" that explained the colonists' houses, fields, and beasts of burden. Lacking these things, the Native people became, in his view, even less "useful *Animals*" than the domesticated beasts of the colonists: "To *Humanize* these Miserable *Animals*, and in any measure to *Cicurate* [tame] them & *Civilize* them, were a work of no little Difficulty."[74]

The Birth of Race?

Some scholars have seen this trajectory, from helpless (and helpable) to hereditary heathen, even heathen animal, as marking the origins of race in British North America.[75] They have suggested that contemporaneous theological developments contributed to this birth of race, as some theologians began to suggest that religious identity could be inherited. As Thomas Blake wrote in 1644, "So the child of a *Turke* is a *Turke;* The child of a *Pagan* is a *Pagan;* The child of a *Jew* is a *Jew;* The child of a *Christian* is a *Christian*." After King Philip's War, Increase Mather similarly described "the line of Election" as running "(though not wholly, and only, yet) for the most part, . . . through the loins of godly parents." The notion that some people were simply unconvertible, which emerged from "the ruins of the Anglo-Indian Christian commonwealth," also characterized English dealings with enslaved people of African descent, who likewise came to be seen as hereditarily heathen.[76]

And yet the idea of heathenness as a changeable status requiring assistance did not disappear.[77] Nor did the idea of Christian identity as changeable: that one could turn from the salvific truth to damnable falsehood. The English acknowledged that their own ancestors had been non-Christian "savages," as De Bry's engraving of the Picts in White and Hariot's volume suggested. In later centuries other Euro-Americans would draw on the same idea of Europeans' savage and pagan ancestry as evidence of the teleological development of "Western" culture and the salutary influences of Christianity in bringing it about. But the flip side of the teleological argument was the possibility of backsliding. For the English in North America, the lurking fear was that their heathen roots were showing—that they were becoming more brutal colonizers than the Catholic Spanish, and possibly more violent still than their heathen antagonists, whether in the Anglo-Powhatan wars of the 1620s or King Philip's War in the 1670s. This fear did not abate over the course of the seventeenth century. Just because they increasingly declared that being English meant being Christian and White, and that being African or Indian meant being heathen and non-White, does not mean they necessarily believed that the equations were firm. Declaring them so could be a way to mask anxieties about their own saved status. For all Rowlandson's and Mather's commentary about Native people acting like devils, after all, the English also worried that they themselves might be in the sway of the devil, as the witch trials of the 1690s made abundantly clear.

Moreover, the idea that one could inherit religious proclivities from one's forebears did not necessitate an understanding of religion as innate. It could also suggest an understanding of culturally transmitted religion shaping human difference over time. The notion of heathenism as a familial identity passed down through generations of wrong teaching and wrong traditions could make it seem very hard for heathens to convert—but that did not necessarily imply that they could not ever convert, or that subsequent generations, exposed to Christian "civilization" for a longer duration, could not eventually become unheathenized.

The imperative to obliterate the culture of changeable heathens operated as a different kind of violence from the enslavement and extermination of people understood to be innately inferior, but it was violence nonetheless and could go hand in hand with the other. To see heathenness as changeable was not "better than" or "less racial" than to see the Other as unchangeable. The resilient idea of heathenness as a status out of which one could and should convert need not be relegated to a pre-racial religious past but rather can be seen as an essential part of the ongoing racialization of colonized peoples: as suspended in a godforsaken status, always in need of becoming something else, and always requiring European instruction to achieve and maintain transformation.[78] Instead of asking when (changeable) religious difference became (intrinsic) racial difference, then, we might ask how heathenness could be used to explain seemingly entrenched human difference. The next three chapters take up this question, as we move ahead to eighteenth- and nineteenth-century European and Euro-American speculations about heathen origins, landscapes, and bodies in light of growing efforts to taxonomize and classify the diversity of the world's customs, regions, and people.

2

ORIGIN STORIES

Nicholas Noyes, a Salem minister who had presided over the witch trials, was miffed. In the wake of King Philip's War and the witch craze, allegations that America was full of unsavable heathens showed no signs of abating. Some seemed ready to give up on the continent altogether. In a 1698 election sermon, Noyes admitted that New England had fallen from its pious precedents, and that its colonists had not done enough to "come over and help." But the minister, who had been born in Massachusetts Bay Colony and graduated from Harvard University, also sought to defend his natal home and its soul-saving mission from European naysayers. New Englanders just needed more time. "Methinks men should not be hasty to Reprobat a Fourth Part of the World, without Express Order from Heaven," he clucked.[1]

America's detractors held all sorts of theories about the origins of the land and its inhabitants that led them to conclude that Native Americans were reprobated pariahs. "I know not how it came to pass, that Conjectures about *America* have been so various, strange and uncomfortable; as to its Rise, State, and final Destiny," Noyes complained. One "*Burnet* M.D." claimed that the original Americans "came not out of the Ark" and "descended not from *Noah*. And indeed they are beholden to him, that he let them descend from *Adam;* and did not bring them out of the Slime." Another "annotator on the Bible (who is otherwise a very worthy man) . . . alloweth the *Americans* to be descended of *Noah;* but by *Cham;* and thence gathers that they shall not be gathered into the Church." Meanwhile, "others have *conjectured* that *America* will be the head Quarters of *Gog* and *Magog;* and that it will be *Hell* it self. This is worse and worse still!" Noyes exclaimed.[2]

The theories that his contemporaries offered for the origins of Native people were familiar ones used to explain the origins of so-called heathens around the world. Noyes's defense of Native Americans did not disclaim their heathenness but affirmed that the heathen were made "of one blood" with "all Nations of Men." According to Noyes, the derogatory origin theories about the heathen that classified them as barely human and cursed "tend[ed] to discourage all Endeavours for the Conversion of the *Indians.*" He was unwilling to give up the converting mission. In Noyes's framing, the heathen were children of Adam and Eve who had originally had access to the truth but had become like the prodigal son in the Bible, having "gone into a far Country, in esteem *dead* and *lost.*" But like the prodigal son's father, God would eventually bring the American heathens back: "What ever any think of *America;* If the great Shepherd have a *lost Sheep* in the *American* Wilderness; He will go after it till he find it."[3]

Noyes's sermon pointed to the many questions raised by the issue of heathen origins, especially once Europeans realized that people lived on the other side of the Atlantic. Were the heathen across the globe the siblings of European Christians who had originated in the same milieu, but wandered away and needed to be called back to the fold? Or did they come from such separate, antediluvian origins that they shared virtually no similarities with European Christians? And how had heathen beliefs and practices arisen and been sustained? Had the heathen the world over all wandered from the truth in the same way or differently? Had they ever known the truth?

This chapter assesses European and Euro-American ideas about the origins of heathenism. Despite the proliferation of new information about the various people grouped under the broad category of heathen, and despite growing recognition of different traditions that might be labeled with terms other than "heathen" (like "Boodhist" or "Hindoo"), Euro-Americans did not jettison the all-encompassing nature of the term. Instead, they posited shared histories of religious degeneration for the world's heathens that drew from older conjectures and dovetailed with increasingly popular theories about bodily degeneration as the explanation for physical differences among the world's people.[4]

These bodily theories posited decline from an ideal Caucasian form due to the influences of climate and environment on the blood. Drawing on the ancient Greek "father of medicine" Hippocrates, who had proposed a climatic theory of human difference, sixteenth-century French law professor Jean Bodin joined geographical with biological determinism, suggesting that the interplay between environment and "the inborn nature of each race" determined their "bodies and behaviors." In the eighteenth century, Carl Linnaeus and his student Johann Friedrich Blumenbach built on Hippocrates and Bodin to classify humans into types: European, Asian, African, and American. Blumenbach explained that these types varied in "bodily constitution, stature, and colour" and that this variance could be attributed "almost entirely to climate alone," which caused humans to degenerate from what he saw as the "ideal type": the "most beautiful race of men, I mean the Georgian" from the Caucasus Mountains. By the mid-nineteenth century, French aristocrat Arthur de Gobineau ossified Bodin's and Blumenbach's climato-biological determinism to declare the fixed "inequality of the human races," positing that there were only three ("white, yellow, and black") and that the latter two were "degenerations" from the "white race," which is "superior to all others in beauty." Gobineau's project was to prevent the "pollution of white blood by inferior elements": seeing the races as biologically distinct, he warned of the dangers of admixture that could lead to degeneration of the "white race."[5] In the midst of these developments, the idea of heathenness as a quality underlying apparent physical differences did not disappear. Far from it. Europeans and Euro-Americans also constructed the heathen world as a coherent and meaningful category whose intertwined origins and common features they alone could see and explain.

Degeneration Theory

One of the most influential theories of pagan/heathen origins held that they were, essentially, degenerated Christians. This theory was advanced long before the idea of bodily degeneration, by the Christian historian Eusebius (263–339). He held that the original and "most ancient race of humans," the pre-Mosaic Hebrews, had been "one and the same" with Christians. The Christians of today carried that pure past forward, but all other groups represented "deviations" from it. Even the later Jews and Muslims, not to mention pagans, could be classified as heretical Christians according to this schema.[6] Characterizing non-Christians as degenerated Christians enabled Europeans and Euro-Americans to cram people with varying conceptions of their own origins, and different ways of understanding time and history, into a single chronology that aligned with biblical genealogies of deviation from original purity. For Europeans and Euro-Americans, scripture was not just theology: it was history. By the nineteenth century, "many scholars still operated within the Biblical scheme of universal chronology, a matter of approximately six thousand years." This meant that all other claims to history were seen as pretensions that could not be trusted.[7]

Noah and his offspring loomed large in attempts to figure out when the heathen had degenerated. The Bible proclaimed that not only were all humans descendants of Adam, but all living beings were also descendants of Noah and the inhabitants of his ark. This biblical account reined in polygenetic and pre-Noahic theories of heathen origins, especially once it became apparent, from the reports and images sent back by colonizers, that various heathens were actually humans and not strange creatures, part person and part beast. Noah and his family had been beneficiaries of direct patriarchal revelation, and thus his descendants could not be said to have simply "strayed into error and superstition inadvertently through lack of exposure to the Christian message."[8] Instead, those who had turned to paganism were guilty of directly violating and corrupting a pure revelation that they had once possessed.

Moreover, some had supposedly strayed to paganism more quickly and completely than others. The myth of Ham, or curse of Canaan, held that because Noah's son Ham mocked his father's drunken nakedness as he lay sleeping, Ham's son Canaan was forever cursed to be a "servant of servants . . . unto his brethren," Shem and Japheth (Genesis 9:18–27). Over time, Ham came to be identified with Africans, Shem with Jews, and Japheth with Europeans. Ham and his offspring became the "ultimate representative of the heathen" since, according to the story, they had been first to disobey, were guiltier than the others, and were subject to deserved enslavement.[9]

Theologians devoted much energy to determining from which Noahic line other peoples of the world had originated. They also traced other peoples' deities back to Noah himself. For instance, some saw the Chinese Fohi, the god of creation, as Noah, believing that the ark had come to rest in China. Theologians yoked Eusebius's theory of Christian heresy to euhemeristic interpretations of heathen myths in order to "unma[sk] . . . the traces of Biblical history which lay beneath the legends and cults of pagan cultures." The court mythographer Euhemerus of Messina (fourth century BC), himself a pagan, had held that the gods and goddesses were actually historical human beings who had been deified, and that mythological accounts of their exploits were real historical events that had been embellished.[10]

American Amnesiacs

Adapting a Eusebian approach, Spanish Jesuit José de Acosta promoted a hypothesis about the Noahic roots of Native Americans that became "the most widely accepted version of the peopling of America" in northern Europe.[11] In his 1590 Historia Natural y Moral de las Indias (Natural and Moral History of the Indies), he surmised that the inhabitants of the "New World" must have "crossed to these parts from Europe or Asia or Africa; but how and by what route they came we must still ask and seek to know."

Acosta rejected the possibility of a "second Noah's Ark" that brought men to the "Indies," since in his estimation, Native people lacked the technology to undertake serious and deliberate ocean travel.[12] Acosta also dismissed other theories of Native people's origins, such as that they came by way of Atlantis, or that they descended from the Lost Ten Tribes of Israel.

Acosta instead hypothesized that there must have been a land bridge in the vast, unexplored regions to the north that connected Eurasia with the Americas, allowing humans and animals to cross over. He believed that the migrants had originally come from "civilized and well-governed countries" not more than a few thousand years ago (after the days of the Lost Ten Tribes) but that they had since degenerated. According to Acosta, they had already been wanderers from civilization even before they crossed the land bridge, having "strayed from their land"—the familiar motif of the heathen wanderer—in search of more space. By the time they came to settle in the "New World," they had "no more laws than a bit of natural instinct . . . and at most a few customs left over from their original country." Hence "it is not difficult to believe that they forgot everything in the course of a long time and little use."[13]

Acosta surmised that these amnesiac Eurasian migrants quickly became susceptible to the wiles of the devil, who had "retired to the most remote places" of the world after "idolatry was rooted out in the best and noblest part of the world": Christian Europe. Acosta admitted that many Native Americans still had some notion of a single, superior creator god whom they worshiped, "gazing heavenward," which suggested that they retained some glimmers of original truth. But the devil had encouraged the American migrants to corrupt their worship of this superior deity, so that it now stunk to heaven and offended the "most high God."[14]

Acosta extended his theory of the demonic encouragement of idolatry to other "heathen peoples" around the world, too, comparing and conflating Native American with Japanese, Chinese, and Greco-Roman beliefs and practices. He delineated a hierarchical and historical understanding of the different types of people and paganisms in the world. At the bottom were nomadic people, "savages who are close to beasts and in whom there is hardly any human feeling." Their paganism consisted of the worship of natural objects—like the sun and moon, stars, mountains, and trees. They had no literacy and hence no way to preserve their own history short of myth. Next were those who had some political, religious, and economic forms, and who had hieroglyphic or image-based means of record-keeping. Their paganism added the worship of animals to the worship of natural objects. And finally, there were stable societies of literate pagans, like the Aztecs and Inca, and also the Chinese and Japanese, who lived in cities under hereditary rulers, and who were governed by complex laws. According to Acosta, their paganism was the most extravagantly idolatrous, as they developed anthropomorphic figures to worship, and elaborate rituals overseen by ritual experts, often entailing bloody sacrifices.[15]

Though he sought to differentiate between more and less "advanced" pagans, Acosta also crafted a shared heathen heritage among these disparate groups when he explained that the "same belief" in a single supreme god "exists, after their fashion, in the Mexicans and the Chinese today and in other heathen peoples," but that "the devil has encouraged idolatry so much in all heathen lands, to the point that scarcely any people can be found who are not idolaters." There were two reasons for this. First, the devil, in his pride, sought to "steal and appropriate to himself in every way he can what is owed only to the Most High God" by making himself the object of humankind's worship (all idols are thus versions of the devil). Second, the devil sought to make himself, who lacked the capacity for eternal life, superior to humans by taking away their chance at eternal life, for "idolatry . . . is the cause and beginning and end of all evils."[16] Yet Acosta believed that God could turn this evil into good. Satan's primary trick was to divert pagans from worship of the Creator to worship of the created / creature. But the devil imitated the rites and ceremonies of true religion out of his "envy and desire to compete with God." Thus, despite all his nefarious machinations, through the "Lord's providence," "that trickster the devil is tricked in return," as his mimicry of true religion made it easier for the heathen to see the parallels between their ways and Christianity, and ultimately, to convert.[17]

Acosta's books were widely read and translated into multiple languages (Spanish, Latin, English, German, French, Italian, and Dutch). His hierarchical theory of human difference would find parallels in later teleological explanations of human development, such as the four-stages theory of Scottish Enlightenment thinkers, which classified humans into "primitive" hunter-gatherer societies, shepherding societies, agricultural societies, and commercial civilizations. The four-stages theory also looked to factors like environment and climate in explaining human difference.[18] But the thing about heathenism was that, even as it stretched to cover different societies, it still remained a blanket term that was useful precisely because it was so all-encompassing. For when Europeans like Acosta looked at the world, even if they noticed and tried to explain distinctions between people, they fundamentally still saw themselves as different on another order of magnitude, and all pagans as sharing some essential characteristics, due to their idolatry, that kept them firmly beneath the heathen ceiling.

Indigenous Origins:
Lafitau's Unifying "System"

In the early eighteenth century, Joseph-François Lafitau (1681–1746), a Jesuit missionary from Bordeaux who worked among the Mohawk people (Kanien'kehá:ka) at Kahnawake, elaborated on Acosta's theory of Indigenous origins to build his own "system" of comparative ethnology and theology. Lafitau offered a Eusebian and euhemeristic explanation for the customs of the "Sauvages Amériquains." In the years between his work and Acosta's *Natural and Moral History,* other explanations had been offered for the origins of Native Americans. These included Hugo Grotius's (1583–1645) contention that the original settlers were seafaring Vikings (supporting the colonial claims of the Swedish crown) and, more controversially, Isaac La Peyrère's (1596–1676) polygenist thesis in *Prae-Adamitae* (1655) that there might have been humans before Adam and that the flood had been limited. La Peyrère's book was translated into multiple languages and reprinted numerous times, but it also "immediately provoked a tremendous anti-pre-Adamite backlash." Copies of the book were burned, La Peyrère dubbed a heretic, and plentiful refutations produced. Nevertheless, La Peyrère's "devastating ensemble of amateur theology" opened the door to later challenges against scripture.[19]

Lafitau was firmly in the camp of those who sought to defend scripture. In his 1724 *Moeurs des Sauvages Ameriquains, Comparée aux Moeurs des Premiers Temps* (*Customs of the American Indians Compared with the Customs of Primitive Times*), lauded now as "one of the first works of ethnography in the West,"[20] Lafitau took stock of existing scholarship, which he critiqued as "faulty" since "they have been made from imperfect and superficial records only." By contrast, he promised "that a new study," based on the firsthand experiences of himself and other Jesuit missionaries, "will set forth more detailed and unusual data which will have, at the same time, the charm of novelty."[21]

Lafitau "operated within the intellectual paradigms of earlier Jesuit missionary-scholars," including Acosta, whose actual experience in the Americas gave him more authority than others who offered armchair speculations.[22] Lafitau supported Acosta's theory of a land bridge that connected Europe and Asia with the Americas, and argued that the physical features and spiritual nature of Native people conformed to the inhabitants of the Old World. Where Acosta ultimately concluded that "there is no sure way to establish the Indians' origin," Lafitau thought that the ancestors of the Native Americans were the "barbarians" of Greece. They were doubly outsiders, since even the pagan Greeks had considered the barbaroi to be uncouth, barely human babblers who lacked social organization.[23]

Though Lafitau agreed with Acosta that the peoples of the Americas had long been "held in slavery by the demon, buried in the darkness of error," he did not focus on demonic imitation and temptation as the primary explanation for heathen idolatry. Like Eusebius, Lafitau explained that all forms of pagan religion were heretical deviations from what was, "in truth, only one religion," which was "pure and holy in itself and in its origin, a religion emanating from God who gave it to our first fathers." Adam and Eve were not only the "first lawgivers, the first propagators of religion": they also, by virtue of being the first humans, became the first and foremost wrongfully deified creatures, the "principal objects of pagan mythology historically." Ceres, Isis, and the Phrygians' Mother of the Gods were none but Eve; the male gods of the pagans were corruptions of Adam.[24]

Lafitau dubbed this euhemeristic theory his "system," the key to understanding the origins of religion both true and singular, and false and plural. He brought Acosta's amnesiac theory into it: "It is easy also to conceive, in this system, how this religion, pure and simple in its origin, could have been altered in the course of time, ignorance and the passions being sources which poison the best things and from which, infallibly, confusion and disorder rise." And he claimed that his system of the unitary origins not only of humanity but also of religion helped to explain "how, in spite of the alteration of religion, in spite of the changes made in it among the different peoples of the world, there is everywhere, nevertheless, a certain uniformity in the myths which have some connection with the truth."[25] Just as all pagans had degenerated, so they also could be regenerated, which was the noble work of missionaries like himself. As Lafitau wrote in his "Dedication to His Most Serene Highness Monseigneur the Duke of Orleans First Prince of the Blood," "I flatter myself that I am presenting you with a spectacle . . . of a religion which you respect and love. You will see it, My Lord, come out pure from the hands of God, disfigured afterwards by the obscurity of centuries and the corruption of mankind, but triumphing, nevertheless, over both of them, and finding in their errors even, enough to prove its existence, its truth, its unity."[26]

In claiming the unity of humankind through descent from Adam and the unity of human religion through descent from divine revelation, Lafitau aimed to debunk those who said that Native people lacked "any sentiment of religion, . . . law, social control, or any form of government"[27] (commonly expressed in the phrase *ni roi, ni loi, ni foi:* no king, no law, no faith). Lafitau was writing not only post–La Peyrère but also in an Enlightenment context in which some radical thinkers threatened to expose the origins of all religions as human-made. "Atheism was the great bugbear of the time,"[28] and if it turned out that a majority of the world's newly "discovered" peoples had "no idea of any God," then the "atheist would seem to reason correctly," Lafitau admitted, that the religion "found among others is the work of human prudence and an artifice of legislators who invented it to lead the people by fear, the mother of superstition."[29]

Of course, as a good Jesuit, Lafitau could hardly hold that to be the case. He viewed Iroquoian accounts of their own origins as "myths so absurd that one can only very reluctantly report them," while crediting scriptural and Western accounts as "history." To be fair, Lafitau *did* report Iroquois myths, which is why his *Moeurs* has been recognized as a valuable early ethnography of Iroquois ways; nevertheless, he was not only interested in the particularity of American customs and traditions for their own sake, but for the sake of showing how similar they were to those of other pagans across time and space, and how vestiges of original truth remained in them. In outlining the "story that the Iroquois tell of their origin and that of the earth," for instance, he took care to show how, "investigating a little, we distinguish in it the woman in the earthly paradise, the tree of the knowledge of good and evil," et cetera. Lafitau also noted similarities between the Iroquois "fable" and "Homer's story of Até's fall," which also traced back to "Eve's fall and the banishment of our first ancestors."[30] He included Native Americans in a shared heathen history that traced back to what he saw as the very beginnings of humanity and religion.

The frontispiece to the 1724 edition illustrates Lafitau's goal not only of "learning the characteristics of the Indian and informing [himself] about their customs and practices" but also of seeking "in these practices and customs, vestiges of the most remote antiquity," which would prove common origins. The frontispiece shows a Greek-style muse "in the attitude of writing, at that moment making a comparison between several monuments of antiquity: pyramids, obelisks, statues of gods," and so on, and the "travel Relations, maps, travel books and other curiosities in the field of Americana in the midst of which she is seated." Approaching her are "two genii" who are helping to "assembl[e] these specimens for comparison," and "[Father] Time, whose function is to make all things known and to reveal all things in the end." The bearded and winged Time shows the muse a vision that reminds her that all specimens trace back to the same "origin of man, the heart of our religion," illustrated by the figures of Adam and Eve below the tree of the knowledge of good and evil. Light skin and Romanesque noses characterize all the figures in the image, visually suggesting the collapse of non-European peoples' own histories and conceptions of time into Western embodiments of the same.[31]

Frontispiece, Joseph-François Lafitau, *Moeurs des sauvages amériquains, comparées aux moeurs des premiers temps* (Paris: Chez Saugrain l'aîné . . . Charles Estienne Hochereau . . . , MDCCXXIV [1724]). Library of Congress, Rare Book and Special Collections Division.

Even as he described Native Americans' skin color ("bronze" and "reddish") as different from that of Europeans, Lafitau further collapsed Native people into an Old World paradigm when he said that they "are born white like us." Skin color was not a marker of inherent difference to Lafitau, but subject to the whims of environment, culture, and even thought. (Similar speculations had been advanced about the skin color of Africans, which was sometimes attributed to the effects of the sun, but also to the curse of Canaan.)[32] According to Lafitau, just as heathenness was a later corruption of original purity, so also was Native Americans' skin color a subsequent add-on: "Their nakedness, the oils with which they grease themselves, the sun and open air bronze their skin afterward." In the case of the "Carib" of the West Indies, said Lafitau, a "reddish" skin color could even be attributed to the "imagination of their mothers who, finding beauty in this colour, transmit it to their offspring."[33] For Lafitau, the particular characteristics and customs of Native Americans, from their origin stories to their physical appearance, showed not how different they were but how similar to others past and present. The effect was to fold them even further into his unifying "system" of heathen error.

Comprehensive Claims: Picart and Bernard's Compendium

Around the same time that *Moeurs des sauvages amériquaines* came out, another, vaster compendium was published that sought to sweep not only "idolatrous peoples" but all the "ceremonies and religious customs of the various nations of the known world" together into a comprehensive series. The influential set was written, edited, and published between 1723 and 1737 by Huguenot Jean Frédéric Bernard and engraved by recent Protestant convert Bernard Picart. Having fled to the more tolerant Dutch Republic amid religious persecution in France, Bernard and Picart framed the massive compendium of seven folio volumes, the first of its kind, as a fair treatment and comparison of religions around the world. Seeking firsthand sources wherever possible, Bernard and Picart offered their compendium in support of "those voices arguing for religious toleration." Instead of "attribut[ing] New World customs and rituals to the power of the devil's seduction" like Acosta, for instance, "they sought out the different ideas and practices concerning devils around the world. Were not all the religions of the world in some fundamental ways alike?"[34]

Theirs was not dissimilar to Lafitau's systematizing project, but with a Protestant twist. While some recent scholars have held up Bernard and Picart as essentially "an ideal version of us: open-minded, curious, and patient with difference," others have highlighted how their compendium was ultimately crafted in the service of Protestantism.[35] Both were true. For their time, Bernard and Picart were insatiably curious, committed to broad information gathering, and willing to draw comparisons between Christian and non-Christian customs and beliefs. Steeped in an Enlightenment context of skepticism, perhaps best encapsulated in the publication, within their Amsterdam circles, of the satirical *Treatise of the Three Impostors* (the three referring to Jesus, Muhammad, and Moses), Bernard and Picart "invited readers to distance themselves from their own beliefs and customs and to think about religious practices around the globe."[36]

But they also included an "explosive preface and introductory essay" that told readers how they should rightly interpret the rich data and engravings in the series. Like Lafitau, Bernard sought to show how all religions shared a common origin, whose truth they had warped over time: "Man by Degrees began to lose the true Idea of the divine Being, and took upon him to attribute corporeal Qualities, or human Frailties to him. . . . He added Superstition to his Worship, served God under corporeal Notions, and being no longer capable of contemplating him in Spirit, whether through Pride, Fear, or Weakness, he was pleased to represent him by Images, Statues, &c."[37] Here Bernard evinced a Protestant understanding of "true" religion: one that was originally spiritual as opposed to corporeal, mental and interior as opposed to physical and embodied. Like Lafitau, Bernard too pointed to Adam and Eve's fall as the origin of religious error, but he was less interested in tracking how Adam and Eve were euhemeristic prototypes of all pagan myths than in crafting a hypothetical history of the corruption and degeneration of "pure" religion over time and across societies. And unlike Acosta's account of amnesia, Bernard's account was less about forgetting original truth and more about erroneously and licentiously embellishing on it.

In the "Dissertation upon Religious Worship" that opened the folio set, Bernard explained that communication with the divine had once been simple and direct. But people soon ignored that "*Jesus Christ* forbids his Disciples to lengthen them by vain and impertinent Repetitions," and hence "'tis very probable, that the Prayers of Idolaters might be very tedious," while some "Christians . . . have fallen into the same error." Sacrifice represented another attempt to connect to and appease the Divine. According to Bernard, the "first Race of Men" (apart from Cain and Abel) most likely "did not offer up unto God any Blood-Offerings" or confine their supplications to the halls of temples; rather, they simply "used at first to invoke him in the open Fields, or every Man in his own Habitation, without the least outward Shew, Mystery, or any of those human Inventions, which in process of Time produced the Irreligion of some, and the Bigotry of others." But over time, "some Men, who were warmer Zealots than the rest of Mankind, shook off the Cares of Life, gave over all bodily Labour, and grew indolent, idle, and even savage from their enthusiastic Veneration for their Gods." Thus arose priestcraft—a "numerous Crowd of worthless Creatures, who pretend a Right to serve at those Altars which maintain them"— instead of the priesthood of all believers. And "True Religion by Degrees became less Spiritual, though more over-run with Ceremonies, and the false, more mysterious and fantastical." This was a jab at Catholics (corruptors of "true religion") no less than heathens (practitioners of "false" religion) and also indicated that "Ceremonies" in the title was no neutral term, instead reflecting this corruption.[38]

Bernard went on to explain how "sensual Pleasures" and "Debauchery" crept into heathen worship. Just as repetitious prayer and sacrifice were fallen attempts to reach the divine, so the "antient Heathens" believed that music and dance might "appeas[e] the Anger of their Gods." This belief carried into the practices of "the modern Heathens, even the most barbarous amongst them," whose "antic Gestures" reflected an incorrect understanding of what pleased the divine. Even the "Christians themselves can scarcely suppress this indecent and licentious Custom in their religious Worship," Bernard accused, pointing to the festivals, "masquerades," and "grossest Buffooneries" of European folk. Such "outward Ostentation" was hardly indicative of "a solid Piety." Instead, it was like the affected behavior of a man whose mannerisms were so governed by ceremony and pomp that one could scarcely discern the real person beneath the surface. "With all their Ceremonies," such men "find it a hard Matter to pass in the World for Persons of an agreeable Conversation. . . . We beg leave to compare such People to those who adhere to all religious Customs, as if they were the very Essence of Religion itself."[39]

Like Lafitau's, the "astounding frontispiece" engraved by Picart provides a visual key to understanding his and Bernard's perspective.[40] The figures' garments and actions, and the distanced placement of temples and idols in the background, indicate where the authors' sympathies lie. The lengthy caption accompanying the image begins by drawing the viewer's attention to "CHRISTIAN RELIGION," embodied as a plain white-robed and pale-skinned woman sitting "at the foot of a great tree holding open the BIBLE." (The tree, as the caption later explains, also "represents the Christian religion.") To her right is "REFORMATION," a modest woman clad in head covering and simple garb, who embraces the tree with a "pruning knife," which she has used to "cut back the ceremonies and abuses depicted by the dead branches." Immediately to the left of "CHRISTIAN RELIGION" is a dour and bearded *"Franciscan Monk"* who "is trying to close [the Bible] with one hand while pointing with the other to the book on which is written COUNCILS and TRADITIONS on which leans the Roman Church," personified as a richly robed woman wearing a beehive of a crown. The Roman Church stands proudly atop both a *"Rabbi* who has been knocked down holding the PENTATEUCH" and the "ROMAN EMPIRE," staking a supersessionist claim as God's new chosen authority. That Bernard and Picart are hardly neutral

Frontispiece, Jean Frédéric Bernard and Bernard Picart, *The Ceremonies and Religious Customs of the Various Nations of the Known World . . .* (London: printed by William Jackson, for Claude Du Bosc, 1733). Reproduction © The Trustees of the British Museum.

with respect to the Roman Church can be further seen in the figure of "Superstition," a woman bedecked in dark robes and a crown of thorns, who hands a "globe that signals Imperial Authority" directly from pagan to Catholic Rome. Additionally, although the Roman Church holds an olive branch "that she seems to be offering to all the other religions that wish to return to her bosom," the caption calls the viewer's attention to a "little serpent . . . snaking in the branch, and the chain hanging from it," which "make known that her apparent mildness always hides some venom and that slavery is all that one should expect from her."[41]

The image and caption initially seem more neutral with respect to "the diverse peoples who have embraced the *Mahometan Religion*"; at the bottom front of the image, Picart simply depicts "ALI successor to MAHOMET" explaining the "KORAN" to a variety of turbaned listeners. Their placement at the front might reflect the more recent origins of Islam, but their proximity to damned souls writing in the flames of hell at the bottom right is surely no accident. Those labeled "*Idolatrous Peoples*" in the series receive the least description and are relegated to the far background of the image, which shows naked people paying obeisance to the "*Pagodas and Gods* of the East Indies" and "West Indies," and the "*Idols* of the Lapps, etc.*" Implied through this perspectival choice is that these far-off people and their religious infrastructure are furthest from the truth in comparison to the Abrahamic people who occupy the visual foreground, closest to the tree of Christianity.[42] The far-off people might be curious to read about and gawk at, but ultimately they are interesting and important not so much for their own sake and their own particularities but for showing the diversity of error in the ceremonies and customs with which humans worshiped the divine.

Though Bernard and Picart offered the most comprehensive treatment of the "ceremonies and religious customs of the various nations of the known world" to date, then, they ultimately framed all the data they presented as part of a sweeping and synthetic history of unnecessary embellishment in religious worship. That this theme was picked up by their readers can be seen in later compilations based on their work, such as the American textbook writer Charles Goodrich's *Religious Ceremonies and Customs, or, The Forms of Worship Practised by the Several Nations of the Known World, from the Earliest Records to the Present Time. On the Basis of the Celebrated and Splendid Work of Bernard Picart* (1834). Writing after the evangelical revivals of the eighteenth and early nineteenth centuries spurred the Protestantization of the American populace, Goodrich augmented the theme of increasing error over time.[43] The entire history of all non-Christian religions, said he, could be traced to "the darkened views and evil feelings inspired by the depraved heart," from which "proceed all those fatal mistakes about God . . . which distinguish every nation, and every portion of the world, except where the Bible is strictly received as the rule of life."[44]

Christianity's Heathen Origins?

The question of heathen origins took a turn in eighteenth-century British North America as a new wave of overt skepticism challenged the reigning paradigm in which the heathen were depicted as degenerates who had once possessed the truth. The simmering skepticism and free thought that formed an antagonistic backdrop to Lafitau's and Bernard and Picart's early eighteenth-century volumes flowered in the later works of David Hume and Thomas Paine. Hume and Paine turned the degeneration theory of heathen origins on its head. Instead of holding that Christianity was the first religion of humanity and that everything else departed from this original truth, Hume claimed, in his *Natural History of Religion* (1757), that "polytheism or idolatry was, and must have been, the first and most ancient religion of mankind."[45] He said that the "various and contrary events of human life" created a need for explanation. The unpredictable and the uncontrollable gave rise to fear and worry, especially in "primitive" ages. To assuage their anxieties and give meaning to a confusing world, the "ignorant multitude" of early humans filled it with a host of idols and deities on whom they could pin that which could not otherwise be explained, and to whom they could offer their worship in an attempt to change their situations.

Hume argued that monotheism emerged from polytheism (and not the reverse). Among some "vulgar" polytheists, one god might arise from among the pantheon of deities as particularly powerful and worthy of worship. "In their anxiety to please and praise this god, worshippers will continually try to outdo their predecessors by attributing greater and greater powers and perfections to him." Eventually "they will reach a point where they represent this god as infinite and entirely perfect, whereby they render his nature inexplicable and mysterious."[46] But this was no teleological or laudable process of forward-moving religious progress. Rather, Hume saw the emergence of one god out of pagan polytheism as rooted in irrational processes of competition, fear, and appeasement. Hence his conclusion that "the religious principles, which have, in fact, prevailed in the world," are more the "dreams" of "sick men" or "the playsome whimsies of monkeys in human shape, than the serious, positive, dogmatical assertions of a being who dignifies himself with the name of rational."[47]

For his part, Paine attempted to apply the same folksy reasoning that characterized his blockbuster revolutionary treatise, *Common Sense* (1776), to his attack on revealed religion in *The Age of Reason* (1794). In the former treatise, Paine had taken a stance on religion that was palatable to his audience, citing scripture and appealing to the authority of the Christian God as the only sovereign to whom obeisance was due. To make his antimonarchical case, Paine had pointed to heathens as the originators of king-worship: "It was the most prosperous invention the Devil ever set on foot for the promotion of idolatry. The Heathens paid divine honors to their deceased kings, and the Christian world hath improved on the plan by doing the same to their living ones." Here Paine echoed the euhemeristic theories of earlier writers, who claimed that the heathen gods originated as wrongfully deified human beings. According to Paine, the Jews had originally had "a kind of republic administered by a judge and the elders of the tribes." It was only under a "national delusion" that they began "hankering . . . for the idolatrous customs of the Heathens."[48]

But it was actually not such a far step from this line of reasoning in *Common Sense* to *The Age of Reason*. If the ancient Jews had been deluded by their heathen neighbors, Paine said, such was also the case with the early Christians. Where Christian theologians had tried to find explanations for heathen divinities in the Bible, Paine instead tried to find origins for Christian divinities in heathen myths. "It is . . . not difficult to account for the credit that was given to the story of Jesus Christ being the son of God," said Paine. "He was born when the heathen mythology had still some fashion and repute in the world, and that mythology had prepared the people for the belief of such a story. Almost all the extraordinary men that lived under the heathen mythology were reputed to be the sons of some of their gods." Thus "what is called the Christian church sprung out of the tail of the heathen mythology." Not only was Jesus just another human hero resulting from "the intercourse of gods with women," but "the trinity of gods that then followed was no other than a reduction of the former plurality . . . the statue of Mary succeeded the statue of Diana of Ephesus; the deification of heroes changed into the canonization of the saints . . . and Rome was the place of both. The Christian theory is little else than the idolatry of the ancient Mythologists, accommodated to the purposes of power and revenue; and it yet remains to reason and philosophy to abolish the amphibious fraud."[49] Paine's polemic could be seen as a Protestant critique of Catholicism taken to an extreme, but he went further than connecting Catholicism to paganism, critiquing the "myths" of Christianity more broadly for their absurdity and unreliability.

Splendida Piccata or Sanctified Raillery?

Paine went too far for most Americans. *The Age of Reason* made him a pariah; Protestants summarily quashed it as heretical and dangerous.[50] Paine and Hume may have been more extreme in their views than most. Still, the issues they raised, of whether Christianity was on a par with other mythologies, reverberated in debates over the revival of classical education.[51] The generation of curriculum for colonial institutions of higher education resurrected older questions about the propriety of teaching pagan philosophy and raised newer questions about whether ancient Greco-Roman heathenism was any different in its origins from the heathenism of present-day Native Americans, Africans, Chinese, and others.

The revival of the classics in the colonies paralleled their rebirth in Enlightenment Europe. From the Venuses and Apollos that decorated Versailles and the royal library in Vienna, to the "coy little nymph or a cavorting satyr" that flitted across the fine china of Josiah Wedgwood and Sons, the classical gods were everywhere. Europeans and Americans devoured the words and sought to emulate the worlds of the Greek and Roman philosophers, which informed everything from republican political theory to the appropriate education of women.[52]

But the revival of the classics did not strike everyone as a positive development. Transatlantic debates over classical education played out in newspapers and books that circulated between England and the colonies in the eighteenth century. A piece in the first volume of the *London Magazine,* for instance, which was widely read by American Whigs, took issue with those "who were for prohibiting the use of *Pagan* Authors." Titled "Of the Law of Nature, and State of the Heathen," the 1732 article lamented that opponents of the classics "not only imagine, that since the Fall of *Adam,* Mankind have no *Liberty* to do *Good,*" but they "also . . . seem to deprive the Heathen of all Manner of *Grace; as* if God had entirely forsaken them, and they had no Share in his inestimable *Bounty* for Man's Redemption." But "is he not the God of the *Heathen* as well as of the Christians?" There must be "some other *Rule* for human Actions besides the *written Word,*" the article determined, and "this Rule could be no other than the *Law of Nature* and of *Right Reason,* imprinted *in their Hearts;* which is as truly the *Law* and *Word* of God . . . as that written in our *Bibles.*" To say otherwise—to hold that the "*Virtues* of the Heathen" could only be "*Vices*"—was to commit a "much more pernicious Error" than to advocate for teaching the classics, the piece concluded.[53] In so claiming, the author took on such esteemed canon as the *Book of Common Prayer,* which maintained that "works done before the grace of Christ, and the inspiration of his Spirit, are not pleasant to God." A product of the English Reformation, the *Book of Common Prayer* held that only acceptance of Christ's sacrifice was salvific. Another supporter of the Greco-Roman classics called for this article of the *Book* to be struck out. To say that the good deeds of the heathen were nothing but "*splendida piccata*," or "gilded evils," the author wrote, was "sanctified raillery" that suggested a God who was merely a ruthless, arbitrary tyrant.[54]

Where Acosta, Lafitau, and Bernard and Picart had convicted the heathen for their abandonment of religious truth, supporters of the classics declared that the heathen had not lost, forgotten, or abandoned anything. Rather, the truth was always available to them, written on their hearts, revealed in nature, and capable of guiding all their actions. The possibility that the heathen might be saved by something extra-biblical went against the Protestant dicta of salvation by faith alone, in the Bible alone, through grace alone. To rest faith in the law of nature was to assume that nature was orderly, predictable, and didactic, showing the way things were supposed to be, revealing the logical hand of a reasonable Creator, and ultimately providing enough instruction to save. In this deistical theory of natural religion, God was transformed from a choosy deity who picked only some to receive His special revelation, into an impartial, fair Creator who gave all humans the opportunity to discern the truth. In this line of thinking, value could be gleaned from all religious traditions, and superstitious myths could be sifted out of Christianity no less than from the *Odyssey* or *Mahābhārata*.

But even as this theory opened the door to a new view of religion as plural and comparable, it also opened the door to a newly pernicious possibility, in which those people who failed to grasp the truth (as understood by Europeans and Euro-Americans) could be directly blamed for inherent defects of mind and inability to comprehend the law of nature. It was not coincidental that the move toward natural religion among some "enlightened" thinkers precipitated a move toward measuring skulls and attempting to determine, on purely naturalistic grounds, the supposed physiological and biological reasons for human difference. This move also helped to explain how the ancient pagan Greco-Roman philosophers could be raised up for renewed adulation while the contemporaneous heathens of the world could be dismissed as ignorant, stupid, and degenerated. Since the classical Greco-Roman philosophers—ancestors of Europeans—were upheld as supremely reasonable men born with fully capable intellects, it seemed to follow that they had understood this natural religion and the "God-given natural laws" by which it operated, and were thus at least as suitable for study as the supernaturalistic and miraculous revelations passed down in the Bible.[55]

Not so, said John Wilson of the Philadelphia Friends' Latin School, who complained in 1769 that classical education was "the grossest absurdity that ever was practiced" and that it "contributed more to promote Ignorance, Lewdness & Profanity in our Youth than anything I know besides."[56] The anticlassics side of the debate held the Greco-Roman heathens to be degenerates from original revelation as much as any other heathens currently living. None other than Jonathan Edwards sought to bring all heathens back into the same history of shared degeneration when he—in unpublished manuscript writings that he may have intended to compile into a magnum opus—struggled with the threat of deism and its accusations of partiality against the Christian God. Edwards read widely as he "confronted the gods" of other peoples, from Native Americans to the Greeks and Romans. In coming to grips with both the diversity of beliefs and similarities in customs across cultures, he echoed earlier origin accounts about all of humanity's shared descent from common forebears. A "trickle-down process of revelation" from Noah's sons to their heirs helped to explain similarities, he thought, though "a religious law of entropy" "inevitably caus[ed] the revelation to be distorted, resulting in superstition and idolatry."[57] Edwards was less disparaging of Greco-Roman and Chinese philosophies than of Native American traditions and Islam, but there is no definitive evidence in his unpublished works that he ever went against the traditional Protestant conclusion that any of the heathen, without the gospel, could be saved. Because the original revelation had "trickled down to them" but they had failed to improve on it, it was "their own damned fault," and not God's, that they were condemned.[58]

Hannah Adams's "Impartial" Account

Debates over the classics took on new meaning after the United States broke ties with Great Britain, as Protestants worried about the moral foundations of a nation founded on the republican model of Greece and Rome. They feared that the failure to acknowledge the sovereign God, and to take seriously His divine economy of rewards and punishments, was to emulate the dangerous example of heathens who worshiped idols. America could be a republic, but it had to be a Christian republic under the divine kingship of God.[59] Otherwise it would follow the unfortunate precedent of the Greeks and Romans—its people into eternal damnation and its republic into colossal ruin.

Into the fray came a woman from the small town of Medfield, Massachusetts, eighteen miles southwest of Boston.[60] She held Unitarian convictions and felt that there was real value in learning about heathen religious practices and beliefs, if only to refine one's understanding of the truth and superiority of Christianity. Hannah Adams's (1755–1831) sickly constitution as a child meant that she was not able to attend school with the other children of the town. What she lacked in formal education she made up for in voracious reading. As she later explained it, she thereby acquired a wider view of the world than she might otherwise have had, since "the books chiefly made use of" in the "country schools, at that time," were "the Bible, and Psalter." Adams devoured novels, poetry, histories, and biographies. "I remember that my first idea of the happiness of Heaven was, of a place where we should find our thirst for knowledge fully gratified," she wrote in her *Memoir* years later.[61]

Adams's father struggled financially, and when she was in her teens he began taking on boarders to help pay the bills. These boarders taught Adams "Latin, Greek, geography, and logic," and one of them "awakened [her] curiosity" by showing her a manuscript of "Broughton's Dictionary, giving an account of Arminians, Calvinists, and several other denominations which were most common." Before this she had not read any works of religious controversy, but now, as she wrote, "I assiduously engaged myself in perusing all the books which I could obtain. . . . I soon became disgusted with the want of candor in the authors I consulted, in giving the most unfavorable descriptions of the denominations they disliked." So Adams took it upon herself to do a better job, reading, compiling, and drafting a manuscript by her own "rules," even while supporting herself during the Revolutionary War by weaving bobbin lace. The publication of Adams's *Alphabetical Compendium of the Various Sects* in 1784, which went through four substantially revised editions, brought her financial stability and literary renown, in both the United States and Great Britain.[62]

Adams attempted to craft a compendium of the world's religions that avoided one-sided labels like "Heretics, Schismatics, Enthusiasts, Fanatics, &c." and that allowed adherents of "modern sects" to "speak for themselves."[63] Some scholars have accordingly characterized her work as "impartial." Like Bernard and Picart's *Ceremonies,* it was, for its time, a groundbreaking publication that introduced generations of American readers to the religious traditions practiced by each other and the rest of the world.[64] Adams herself noted, in her *Memoir,* that reading religious debates in order to prepare her text had led her to "suff[er] extremely from mental indecision, while perusing the various and contradictory arguments adduced by men of piety and learning in defence of their respective religious systems." She attributed this to her lack of preparation, prior reading history, and sex: "Reading much religious controversy must be extremely trying to a female, whose mind . . . is debilitated by reading romances and novels." Adams admitted, "I never arrived to that degree of decision that some have attained on that subject."[65]

Even so, despite the seeming openness and humility that her "researches" had engendered, Adams remained assured of the superiority of Christianity vis-à-vis heathenness. She ultimately claimed, "My conviction of the truth of divine revelation, instead of being weakened by all my researches, was strengthened and confirmed," especially so in the direction of Unitarianism.[66] Adams did not include "heathen" among the pejorative appellations she wanted to avoid (later compilers writing in the same vein would explicitly avoid the term).[67] In her fourth and most thorough edition, the *Dictionary of All Religions and Religious Denominations* (1817), Adams defined "HEATHEN" as "a term which, like Gentiles, was applied formerly to all nations by the Jews, and is still applicable to all pagan nations." Her definition of "PAGANS" circled back to "heathens, and particularly those who worship idols. The term came into use after the establishment of christianity; the cities and great towns affording the first converts, the heathens were called Pagans, (from *Pagus,* a Village,) because they were then found chiefly in remote country places; but we use the term commonly for all those who do not receive the Jewish, Christian, or Mahometan religions."[68] Adams divided "The Pagans" into four groups:

I. The Greeks and Romans, and others who admit their refined system of mythology.
II. The more ancient nations, as the Chaldeans, Phenicians, Sabians, &c.
III. The Chinese, Hindoos, Japanese, &c.
IV. The Barbarians, as the Indians of North and South America, and the Negroes of Africa.[69]

While Adams's exhaustive account of over thirty-five entries on various heathen or pagan traditions provided specific and detailed information culled from her wide-ranging reading, she nevertheless ultimately grouped all together as errant polytheists (defined as "those who worship many gods. See *Pagans*").[70]

Adams's introduction elaborated on this clumping. At "the time of Christ's appearance on earth," she said, "all the heathen nations"—including the Greeks and Romans—were a mass of ignoramuses who "worshipped a multiplicity of gods and demons, whose favour they courted by obscene and ridiculous ceremonies, and whose anger they endeavoured to appease by the most abominable cruelties. Every nation had its respective gods," most of whom "were either ancient heroes, . . . or kings and generals who had founded empires, or women who had become illustrious. . . . The natural world furnished another kind of deities," particularly the "sun, moon, and stars." According to Adams, all of these pagans suffered under a "sacerdotal order, which was supposed to be distinguished by an immediate intercourse and friendship with the gods" but "abused its authority in the basest manner, to deceive an ignorant and wretched people." Echoing Bernard and Picart, Adams accused paganism in general of being a "totally external" religion of forms and ceremonies that was "not calculated to promote moral virtue." And thus it was that "at this time Christianity broke forth from the east like a rising sun, and dispelled the universal religious darkness which obscured every part of the globe."[71]

In individual entries, Adams explained how particular heathen peoples had degenerated from Noahic origins. The "great and ancient nation" of China, she noted, had originally had a "patriarchal" religion that was "supposed to be derived from Joktan, the brother of Peleg," descendants of Noah's son Shem. But "this has degenerated to Paganism, which among their *literati* may be refined to a sort of philosophical atheism; but among the vulgar is as gross idolatry as that of other heathen nations." The "Hindoos, or Hindus, otherwise called *Gentoos,*" also derived from Shem's stock. Said Adams, the original "colony" migrated to India after the flood and "flourished for a long succession of ages in primitive happiness and innocence; practiced the purist rites of the patriarchal religion, without images and temples, till at length the descendants of Ham invaded and conquered India, and corrupted their ancient religion."[72]

Adams did not forward a Noahic origin theory for "NEGROES, (The) natives of Africa."[73] That she remained mute on a biblical origin point for people of African descent helps to explain why some African Americans actually argued for descent from Ham in order to claim biblical personhood and history, and to defend against contentions that they were of pre-Adamite and not fully human stock. African Methodist Episcopal minister Benjamin Tucker Tanner, for instance, strongly asserted that "Ham is the father of all Africa, and the Negro being of Africa, is necessarily of Ham. The Negro is a man. He is of Adam. He is of Noah. The Negro is a brother."[74] Some African Americans claimed a proud heritage for Ham's descendants, despite Noah's curse against Ham's son Canaan, citing Psalm 68:31 ("Princes shall come out of Egypt; Ethiopia shall soon stretch out her hands unto God").[75]

Adams also made no speculations about biblical origins in her five-page entry on Native Americans (whom she termed "INDIANS"), an intriguing choice considering that authors from the earlier Acosta to her contemporary

Elias Boudinot were much engaged in that topic.[76] A year before the fourth edition of her dictionary was published, the elderly Boudinot came out with *A Star in the West; or, a Humble Attempt to Discover the Long Lost Ten Tribes of Israel, Preparatory to Their Return to Their Beloved City, Jerusalem* (1816). Contra Acosta, he argued that "there is a possibility, that these unhappy children of misfortune, may yet be proved to be the descendants of Jacob and the long lost tribes of Israel." Boudinot laboriously endeavored to prove his point over the course of his three-hundred-page book, even contending that the Jewish ancestors of the Native Americans had wandered and gotten lost precisely because they had sought to avoid the surrounding heathen (Acosta had rejected the lost tribes theory on the opposite basis that, since the Native Americans were heathens, they had obviously not come to America to flee from other heathens).[77] Adams included no such theories in the fourth edition of her dictionary, instead grouping Native Americans with other heathens while recounting "some striking peculiarities of their ancient pagan notions and idolatries." She quoted from missionary David Brainerd's account of Native American origins: "It is a notion pretty generally prevailing among them, that it was not the same God that made them who made us; but that they were created after the white people; and it is probable, they suppose their God gained some special skill by seeing the white people made, and so made them *better.*"[78] Adams let this origin story stand on its own without comment. Still, the general discussion of paganism in the dictionary's introduction made the point for her: that the supposition that Native Americans were "*better*" was foolish since their traditions were of a piece with those of other pagans who needed the "light" of Christianity to "dispel" their "darkness."[79]

While Adams's dictionary did not resolve debates over the classics, then, it did provide a popular framework and typology for thinking about where the Greco-Romans fit into the world's religions—the pagan camp—by an author whose Unitarianism put her somewhere between the Jonathan Edwardses and Thomas Paines of her time. For Adams, pagans were still worth studying even if they were wrong.

Pre–World Religions?

In one sense, the quest for heathen origins can be read as a familiar story about how the singular "religion" (as in Lafitau's scheme) became the plural "religions" (in Adams's *Dictionary*). In this teleological account, the two-part division of the world into Christian versus all others ("true religion" versus wrong, false, or demonic religion) gave way to the four-part division of the world into Christian, Jewish, Muslim, and heathen/pagan, which would ultimately lead to the rise of "world religions" by the end of the nineteenth and early twentieth centuries.[80] Adams's work is a trailblazing step in the direction of an impartial and academic study of religion, according to this view.

But as much as it cracked open the heathen category and differentiated between the peoples and religions that composed it, Adams's compendium, like those of Lafitau and Bernard and Picart before her, also cemented the coherence of the category by continuing to narrate the shared history of pagan degeneration into idolatry, priestcraft, and empty ritual. The degeneration theory, as we have seen, could be rooted in the Christian idea that all descendants of Noah could be held culpable for once possessing the revealed truth and losing it. It could also be rooted in the Enlightenment notion that all humans had original access to natural light but that some humans' ability to see and understand it had declined over time and in different environments. Either way, it constructed the heathen as an umbrella category of people who shared a history, regardless of the unique manifestations their deviance had later taken.

This meant that the contemporary heathen and the ancient heathen who had rejected the Christian message could be thrown into the same basket, a useful tactic for Protestants who thought that the classics did not deserve to be put on a pedestal. As Benjamin Wisner put it, "The ignorance of the Heathen now on the earth, (from which, it is said, their wickedness proceeds,) springs from the same source as did that of the Heathen of whom Paul speaks; for the Heathen are as truly rational now as they were then, and the 'invisible things of God' may be as 'clearly seen from the things he hath made' now as they might have been then." And hence, since their original forgetting of God was "voluntary," the heathen, whether now or then, were uniformly under the sentence of damnation. Their shared origins led to their shared demise, inspiring generations of missionaries to save those still living.[81]

The long history of the emergence of "world religions," then, is also a story about the ratification of heathenness as a still coherent concept, even after it became clear that the category was much more capacious than originally imagined. It is a fact that eighteenth- and nineteenth-century Europeans and Euro-Americans were learning more about different practices and beliefs, and that many were swayed by the virtues of classical paganism contra the vices of contemporary heathenism. By the end of the eighteenth century, the broadness of the idea of heathenness, from past to present, and from Atlantic to Pacific, came under fire in debates over the classics. But Adams's popular *Dictionary* and later American reprints and abridgements of Bernard and Picart's *Ceremonies* reaffirmed the category of "heathen/ pagan" in shared origin stories that differentiated the heathen from those who had not only retained and received the light but also (supposedly) improved on it, and now claimed the right to spread it over "those regions of midnight darkness" in which the heathen dwelled.[82] The category's coherence was further solidified by American Protestants like Wisner who, in the nineteenth century, set out to convert—and in the process construct—the heathen world for a new generation. Cognizant of theories on climate and geography as the cause of human difference, they nevertheless cast religious error as the underlying factor explaining the inability of heathens to care for their lands and bodies.

3

LANDSCAPES

On a Monday evening in early spring 1834, Thomas Smith Grimké regaled a Charleston audience with an *Address on the Power and Value of the Sunday School System in Evangelizing Heathen and Re-constructing Christian Communitys*. Grimké opened with a lengthy hypothetical scene. Imagine a remote island, he said. Mountains undulate against the open sky, and waterfalls cascade gently from their highest peaks to the valleys and glens below. The island is lush and beautiful, its natural environs untouched by the hand of "civilized" man. But this is no proverbial deserted island, for it is inhabited by "a race, at once artless in manners, kind in their affections, and obedient to the dictates of natural justice." The people of the hypothetical island are "ignorant of all but what nature taught them," living a pastoral life and unaware of anything beyond their view but the "sea bird, or the floating weed, or the water spout traveling along the horizon." But "the days of ignorance and simplicity were now to pass away forever: and civilized man was soon to appear before them, in all the power and glory of his marvelous achievments."[1]

First, a merchant ship appears. Finding that the inhabitants have little of value, and the island no gold or silver for the taking, it quickly departs. Next comes a ship of scientists, and then a battleship, which likewise see "nothing to covet and power nothing to subdue." Finally, a small, unassuming boat appears. "What stranger was this?" Grimké asked. "Was it the merchant vessel or the discovery ship, or the man of war, returnd to visit again the island solitude? . . . Those had forgotten the savage in his beautiful wilderness." But no: instead of the boom of cannons or the gleam of a telescope surveying the island for raw goods, "music, never heard before, filled the soul of the savage with solemn awe, with mysterious delight. It was the morn of the Savior's nativity, and was usherd in as became the missionary ship."[2]

It is the missionaries in their humble bark who see the real value in the island's soil and souls. Before stepping off the boat, the missionaries continue with their prayers and songs, giving "thanks for the preservation amidst the storm" and "be[seeching] a blessing on the dedication of themselves to the conversion of the heathen. They entrea[t] with many tears of faith and hope, that the heathen island before them might 'rejoice and blossom as the rose,' and 'the wilderness and solitary place might be glad' through their labors."[3]

Where the previous vessels saw the island as destitute and uninteresting, the missionaries read wilderness as the quintessential mark identifying the island as heathen, recalling the term's origins "from *heath,* barren, uncultivated," and signaling a field ripe for their intervention.[4] Despite the island's natural beauty and lush foliage, the missionaries still believe that it requires a different kind of blossoming, a scriptural reference to Isaiah 35 that signals the coming of the Glory of Zion: "The wilderness and the solitary place shall be glad for them; and the desert shall rejoice, and blossom as the rose. . . . And the parched ground shall become a pool, and the thirsty land springs of water: in the habitation of dragons, where each lay, *shall be* grass with reeds and rushes."[5] The preceding chapter of Isaiah explained that the wildernesses were such in the first place because of the anger of the Lord against unbelieving inhabitants: "And the streams thereof shall be turned into pitch, and the dust thereof into brimstone, and the land thereof shall become burning pitch. . . . And thorns shall come up in her palaces, nettles and brambles in the fortresses thereof: and it shall be an habitation of dragons, *and* a court for owls."[6] Steeped in the Bible, Grimké's fictive missionaries would have seen the island through the interpretive lens of both Isaiah 34 and 35, understanding the beasts of the fictive island as "wild" and its foliage as prickly and overgrown, all due to the sin of its inhabitants, before even stepping foot on it. Only with such a view could they believe in their own presence as heralding the "blossom[ing]" of the "rose" and "rejoic[ing]" of the "desert."

This chapter explores how missionaries and other travelers understood and described the landscapes they labeled "heathen," focusing primarily on the years between the founding of the American Board of Commissioners for Foreign Missions (ABCFM) in 1810 and the late nineteenth century. Protestants affiliated with the ABCFM and other evangelical organizations are the primary characters in this chapter and Chapter 4 because their tracts, magazines, and memoirs dominated nineteenth-century American publications about the world.[7] The nineteenth-century missionizing impulse brought the insecurities of the new nation together with the millennial hopes of American Protestants, promising to raise the global profile of the United States as it sought to save the world. The homogenizing force of the heathen world as a realm made such by religious error operated to firmly separate the United States from the benighted world at large.

Americans looked at this world with keen and particular interest as to how they might profit both its inhabitants and themselves. Although they recognized and made much of the differences between taro patches and savannahs, "rude" huts and densely packed cities, they nevertheless also swept them under the imagined rubric of untamed wilderness rendered such by the intransigence of the heathens who dwelled there. No matter how verdant or arid, they held that all heathen landscapes shared the same problems and needed the same kinds of intervention. Just as Isaiah 34 explained the desolation of the land as a result of the Lord's anger against apostates, so American Protestants explained the fundamental unproductiveness and unprofitability of heathen landscapes as a result of the wrong religious orientation of their inhabitants. By picturing the heathen world as universally blighted despite differences on the ground, American Protestants gave themselves a reason to refashion heathen lands into productive sites for the extraction of agricultural and mineral goods, and as we shall see in Chapter 4, to reshape heathen bodies into healthy and efficient laborers who could help with the reformation of the land.[8] They also brought to the soil an intensely Protestant understanding of the changes that could be wrought by conversion. The change of heart, they believed, would redeem not only converts' eternal souls but also the soils on which they lived.

The Doctrine of Discovery

In his 2010 *The Christian Imagination: Theology and the Origins of Race*, theologian Willie James Jennings explains that "land and body are connected at the intersection of European imagination and expansion." Christian colonization provoked a violent rupture in which "the earth, the ground, spaces, and places [were] removed as living organizers of identity and as facilitators of identity."[9] Jennings explains how the Christian imagination divorced itself from the land. By claiming to replace Jews as God's chosen people, Christians uprooted themselves from a particular relationship to the land of Israel. While Israel continued to loom large in the Christian imagination, the literal, physical space of Israel was no longer the basis of Christian identity as it was for Jews. Unmoored from a particular place, Christians roamed the earth (flipping on its head the stereotype of the heathen as the quintessential wanderer), seeking to subdue, subdivide, stake ownership in, and sell it.

Christian European colonizers upheld the proper Christian as one who understood that the land was the creation of the one true God, given to men (gender-specific) as their burden to toil over and dominate. This right view of the land was supposed to produce a right attitude toward it: instead of idly plucking its fruits here and there and hunting its fish and game willy-nilly, people who knew the true God were to domesticate and regulate its productions and, in so doing, regulate their labor industriously. As Jennings puts it, "The new worlds were transformed into land—raw, untamed land. And the European vision saw these new lands as a system of potentialities, a mass of undeveloped, underdeveloped, unused, underutilized, misunderstood, not fully understood potentialities. Everything—from peoples and their bodies to plants and animals, from the ground and the sky—was subject to change, subjects for change, subjected to change. The significance of this transformation cannot be overstated. The earth itself was barred from being a constant signifier of identity."[10]

The papal bulls issued by Pope Alexander VI in 1493 and 1494 had divided the lands "discovered" and to be "discovered" between Portugal and Spain, by an imaginary line west of the Azores. The basis of the papal claim to these lands was that they were not inhabited by Christians, and that therefore "barbarous nations" needed to "be overthrown and brought to the faith itself."[11] This became known as the "doctrine of discovery," in which the heathenness of non-Christian people justified the takeover of their lands for the good of their bodies and souls, and for the good of the land itself. In the landmark 1823 Supreme Court case *Johnson & Graham's Lessee v. M'Intosh*, Chief Justice John Marshall, writing on behalf of a unanimous court, drew directly from the doctrine of discovery to maintain that Native people were merely tenants on, and not owners of, their lands. Marshall said that the doctrine of discovery was "confined to countries 'then unknown to all Christian people.'" On this basis had the first English explorers "assert[ed] a right to take possession, notwithstanding the occupancy of the natives, who were heathens, and at the same time admitting the prior title of any Christian people who may have made a previous discovery." Marshall claimed that "the charter granted to Sir Humphrey Gilbert, in 1578, authorizes him to discover and take possession of such remote, heathen, and barbarous lands, as were not actually possessed by any Christian prince or people. This charter was afterwards renewed to Sir Walter Raleigh, in nearly the same terms."[12] And now the federal government, as the lasting representative of these first Christian English "discoverers," alone could claim the right to possess the land, Marshall determined; the government allowed Native people to live on the land and transfer it to the government, but not to do with it as they pleased.

As Steven Newcomb (Shawnee-Lenape), director of the Indigenous Law Institute, has shown, the doctrine of discovery and Marshall's reference to the land as "heathen" did not simply constitute a throwaway statement about the past but rather a continued justification for the present and future. "Legal thinking," writes Newcomb, "is a product of the human imagination."[13] The imagination of Native people as incapable heathens, and of colonists not only as Christians but as God's New Israel, rendered Native lands subject to takeover, just as the heathenness and idolatry of the Canaanites was supposed to have justified the Israelites' violence against them and their lands. Winnifred Fallers Sullivan calls the court's use of the doctrine of discovery a "breathtaking stroke of originary violence" that Andrew Jackson and his followers used "to underwrite Indian removal." Even as Marshall later "repudiated" the doctrine, it was "too late." He died in 1835, and Jackson appointed justices to the court who were friendly to removal.[14]

The idea that Native peoples and the lands and landscapes on which they dwelled were uncultivated, barren, and in need of Christian intervention also informed Euro-American approaches to other regions of the world. The imaginative legacy of the doctrine of discovery emboldened them to see in inhabited and cultivated overseas landscapes evidence of how heathenism had rendered them wild and barren, as well as the potential of what they might become under the Christian teaching of European-origin peoples.

"The Heathen for Thine Inheritance"

This emboldened vision manifested in broad geographic surveys of the "known world," as well as in specific reports and descriptions of particular places.[15] Congregationalist minister Jedidiah Morse provided a best-selling instance of the former with his *American Universal Geography*. In addition to his work as a geographer, Morse had a hand in founding some of the most significant evangelical undertakings of the early nineteenth century, including the missionary magazine *Panoplist* in 1805, Andover Theological Seminary in 1808, the New England Tract Society in 1814, and the American Bible Society in 1816.[16] For Morse, geography was a religious pursuit that revealed God's hand in creation. First published in the late eighteenth century and updated and reprinted manifold times in the century following, his *Geography* surveyed the histories, natural productions, and customs of the globe and found that all came up short relative to Europe. America was still "in its infancy," but Europe, as the source of its pioneering people, was the "most important grand division of the earth." Despite its small size, "nature has enriched the European continent with every species of minerals," and on top of that, "as the European nations have the skill of making the best use of their natural productions, and have taken care to transplant into their own soil as many of the foreign productions as their nature will permit, Europe, upon the whole, must be allowed to be one of the richest parts of the globe." Morse explained Europe's success as a factor of "the christian religion," for "wherever the christian faith has penetrated, learning, industry and civilization have followed."[17]

Morse drew on climatic theories to explain how the natural landscape of Europe had produced a world-conquering people.[18] It was not that God had particularly blessed Europeans with fertile soil, balmy weather, and compliant beasts. To the contrary, said Morse, "the greatest part of Europe is under the influence of a climate, which being tempered with a moderate degree of cold, forms a race of men strong, bold, active and ingenious." The cold weather made the land less productive than in other regions and had "forced [Europeans] by necessity to make the best they can of the smaller share of vegetable and animal treasures, which their soil produces." These providentially ordained "natural disadvantages" had, "by dint of the ingenuity and perseverance of the inhabitants, given rise to numberless arts and sciences, which have been carried to a great degree of perfection." In other words, what set Europeans apart was their ability to make the land blossom through innovation born of God-given necessity and encouragement.[19]

For Morse, the same could not be said of other regions of the world. He explained that "Asia and Africa have immense deserts, such as are no where to be found in Europe"; these arid expanses were partly the result of "natural and insuperable disadvantages of situation," but also due to "want of industry, which is at once the cause and effect of desolation." And so it was—in Morse's view—that "Europe has reduced to its subjection a great part of the other quarters of the world," from the Americas to the oceanic islands, and from Asia to Africa, "so that nearly half of the inhabited world bows to Europe."[20]

In his September 1821 *Sermon, Delivered Before the American Board of Commissioners for Foreign Missions, at Their Annual Meeting in Springfield, Massachusetts,* Morse drew an explicit connection between the heathenism of these supposedly blighted parts of the world and the responsibility of Christians to take them over. "The heathen nations, and those now buried in the darkness and delusion of Mahometanism, are a very large proportion of the inhabitants on our globe," he said. (Morse lumped heathens and Muslims together here, much as ordinary Europeans had long done.) He continued, "The world, since the fall of man, has been, and is still, principally under the immediate dominion of Satan." But the verse Morse chose for his text, Psalm 2:8, a favorite of missionaries and their boosters, promised Satan's overthrow: "Ask of me, and I shall give thee the heathen for thine inheritance, and the uttermost parts of the earth for the possession." Morse read the Psalm as a doctrine of discovery. It was, he claimed, a "prophesy concerning the Kingdom of CHRIST," which promised its eventual "exten[sion] over the whole world." Understanding the heathen as the inheritance of Christ, and their lands as His rightful possession, rendered the entire heathen world ripe for the taking of Christ's representatives on earth. Even if the taking was hard, the fact that it was prophetically foretold meant that Christ's kingdom would brook no opposition. Any resistance was futile: for "why did the heathen rage and the people imagine vain things?"[21]

Morse explained that having the "heathen for his inheritance" and the "earth for his possession" was a "parallelism"—that is, claiming the heathen and owning their land went hand in hand, and entailed Christ's "enjoying and delighting in them, as his purchase, his property, as a sanctified, obedient people, bringing forth the fruits of righteousness to his praise, and rendering him the homage, service and gratitude due to him as their Lord." The agricultural terminology—fruits of righteousness—was deliberate and signaled the blossoming of the heathen world once it was made Christ's "property." Morse extended the agricultural metaphor to Gentile believers, too, who "are now, as Israel was formerly, 'GOD's husbandry,'" while "the Church is CHRIST's inheritance, his 'garden.'"[22]

Some objected, Morse acknowledged, that "savages can never be tamed" and that "the work of converting the world is impracticable, visionary, utopian. Educate them in the best manner you can, their original character will remain unaltered;—and much more of the same purport." In other words, Morse was aware of the notion of innate heathenness, but he rejected it: "Will any one venture to say, that GOD cannot fulfil this promise to his Son? Cannot he do what he pleaseth with creatures which his own hands have formed? Will any deny that he can give a *new heart* to whomsoever he pleaseth . . . ? Yes, GOD *can* give the blessing of a new heart to a wild Indian, to a Hindoo, a Turk, a negro, a Hottentot, as easily as to the most enlightened, polished, and best educated, in civilized nations." And once their hearts were renewed, said Morse, it would "invariably produc[e] a new character, and always the same character, whether possessed by Jew or Gentile, Indian, Turk, Hindoo, or Hottentot." For "GOD, we see is compassionately concerned for *all* men, without distinction of nations or character. None are sunk so low in ignorance and stupidity, as to be considered unworthy of his notice and compassionate care."[23]

Here Morse showed how the blanket thinking that underlay the category of "heathen" had its corollary in the broad category of "Christian." The conflation of Christianity with Whiteness was never absolute. A number of missionaries advocated on behalf of the humanity, shared siblinghood, and Christian potential of the non-White people they evangelized. But we should not necessarily see in this an older, kinder form of othering that virulent scientific racism would eventually overthrow. For in the idea that a *"new heart"* could undo all the trappings of "nations or character"—indeed, producing *"always the same character"* in converts—we can also see the cultural and agricultural conformity that conversion was supposed to produce, entailing the attempted destruction of entire ways of life and the transformation of bodies and lands in addition to souls.[24] Different kinds of racial thinking coexisted and interacted, and we fail to capture the full range of othering in which Americans engaged if we assume that one (hereditable, biological othering) overtook and eventually replaced another (religious changeability).

"Neglectful of Their Fine Soil"

If Morse's geographic work shows the comprehensive global imagination that crafted the landscapes of the heathen world as desolated and needy, specific reporting from Anglo-Protestant mission fields variously cemented and challenged this view. Of the early fields evangelized by the ABCFM, Hawai'i galvanized public attention as a paradigmatic example of a heathen land successfully overhauled by American intervention. (In describing fictive missionaries on a hypothetical island, Grimké may well have been influenced by the experiences and testimonies of real-life missionaries to the Hawaiian Islands.) Hawai'i was one of the first places to which the ABCFM sent stand-alone missionaries and became one of its most vaunted success myths.[25]

In spurring support for the Hawaiian mission, the ABCFM amplified (and amply embellished) the 1818 *Memoirs of Henry Obookiah*. 'Ōpūkaha'ia was an adult of twenty when he left Hawai'i in 1807 to work aboard fur-trading ships traveling from the islands to North America to Macao. He eventually found his way to New England, where, as scholar David Chang explains, he was curious to learn about Christianity as part of his long-standing interests in religion, spurred by his earlier training for the Hawaiian priesthood. Despite his age and education, the ABCFM missionaries framed 'Ōpūkaha'ia's life as that of "a lost man-child far from home with inarticulate urges toward Christian enlightenment." They read into him what they wanted to see, and then read his life onto that of his countrypeople, believing that the missionaries could evangelize the islands as readily as they had converted him. "Desacraliz[ing] the Hawaiian landscape" for Hawaiians, they resacralized it for themselves.[26]

Hiram Bingham, who led the first ABCFM company to the islands, described the missionaries' arrival to Oʻahu in terms no less than biblical. Bingham figured Oʻahu as a kind of Promised Land coupling intense natural beauty with the blight of heathenism. Ascending Punchbowl Hill to survey their new surroundings, he and his fellow missionaries felt like Moses standing at the "top of Pisgah." But unlike Moses, who was "forbidden" from "entering it, even to exterminate the insufferable idolatry," Bingham and his fellows saw the land as theirs. Where once the land had witnessed the battles of Kamehameha for the unification of the islands, now "it was to be the scene of a bloodless conquest for Christ. . . . With all its mental and moral darkness, and heathen pollution, . . . it was contemplated as a scene of peculiar and thrilling interest, as a field of toil and privation, . . . where heathenism was to be extirpated, and churches were to be planted, watered, and made to flourish." The agricultural metaphors here (a *field* of toil; churches to *plant*) pointed to the excursion's conclusion, which turned the metaphors quite literal: "We returned at evening, presenting to the rest of our company fresh productions of the soil, and our report of the land of which we were to take possession."[27] Not only had the missionaries been looking, they had also been plucking, perhaps tasting, and collecting samples of the soil and its produce. They saw, as part of their task, the overhaul not just of the spiritual but also of the physical landscape.

Given the long-standing association between heathens and the wild heath, the ABCFM missionaries were predisposed to believe that Hawaiians were, by inclination or aptitude, dwellers of unimproved lands. Samuel Whitney and Samuel Ruggles visited the island of Kauai soon after the first company landed on Oʻahu. Said Bingham of their journey, "Having explored portions of the island, finding the people scattered, poor, debased and neglectful of their fine soil, these brethren returned to Oahu . . . having brought with them, as proofs of the kindness of the friendly king and his heathen queen, Kapule, a present of cocoanuts, calabashes, oranges, pineapples, fans, fly-brushes, spears and shells, thirty mats, one hundred kapas, and three hogs." Someone who lacked preconceived notions about the heathen and the barren wildernesses in which they dwelled might have come to a very different impression about the land and its people based on the richness of the offered gifts.[28]

Though Hawaiians had supposedly failed to improve the land, they could not be accused of being removed from it. If anything, the missionaries thought they were too close to it. Their thatched habitations were, in Bingham's words, "adapted to the taste of a dark, rude tribe, subsisting on roots, fish, and fruits, but by no means sufficient to meet their necessities, even in their mild climate." To Bingham, their exposure to this climate also made them susceptible to stimulants: "Nothing . . . would be more natural than that a heathen people occupying such habitations, and going bare-headed in the sun, should feel a depression or heaviness,—a tendency to listlessness, and even lethargy, which demands the stimulus of tobacco, rum, or awa, to give temporary relief."[29] This choice of words was significant. In 1836, the missionaries to Hawaiʻi published a volume titled *The Heathen Nations: Or, Duty of the Present Generation to Evangelize the World*. They listed a series of characteristics that supposedly could be found in the heathen and stood in the way of their salvation, including "apathy, listlessness, imbecility of mind, torpitude of intellect, vacuity of thought, inability to reason, and the like."[30] Putting this list alongside Bingham's focus on climate raised a chicken-and-egg question: Did the climate cause heathen listlessness, or did heathen lethargy explain a failure to build more permanent dwellings, which in turn allowed the sun to lull them into still further lethargy? Since heathens covered the world and climate varied from place to place, the problem, for the Hawaiian missionaries, lay with heathenism: climate could exacerbate and help to explain superficial differences in heathen built environments, but it could not be the root cause. As Titus Coan, who arrived in the mid-1830s, put it, Hawaiians were "naturally indolent. This has been fostered into a national trait by circumstances. A warm climate does not require energy in labor. A perpetual summer gives no occasion to lay up stores for a fruitless winter. We teach them industry, economy, frugality, and generosity; but their progress in these virtues is slow. They are like children, needing wise parents or guardians."[31] For the missionaries, unheathenizing them meant taking them out of the heath: changing not only their relationship to the "one true God" but also their relationship to, and manner of living on, the land.

Thanks to a series of remarkable engravings, we have evidence of what extirpating heathenism was supposed to do to the islands. The engravings were made by Native Hawaiian students at Lahainaluna, a seminary on the island of Maui, and they were based on images sketched by missionaries, showing the progress they had supposedly made and the buildings they had erected, like schools, churches, and Western-style houses. The images were used in Hawaiian classrooms and sent back to friends, relatives, and supporters of the mission in America. Lahainaluna Seminary was itself a model of what missionaries hoped for the islands. Founded in 1831, it was the "first secondary school west of the Rockies," and within several

Lahainaluna, Na Bailey i kakan, Na Kepohoni i kaha (Lahaina, HI, n.d.). Library of Congress, Prints and Photographs Division, LC-DIG-pga-13413.

John Warner Barber, sketch of Cornwall, Connecticut, 1835. In *Connecticut Historical Collections: Containing a General Collection of Interesting Facts, Traditions, Biographical Sketches, Anecdotes, &c.,* by John Warner Barber (New Haven, CT: J. W. Barber, 1836). Reproduction courtesy of the Department of Special Collections, Stanford University Libraries.

years of its founding, a printing press that had been sent from Honolulu was turning out the "first newspaper published west of the Rocky Mountains."[32] An engraving by an apprentice named Kepohoni, from a drawing by missionary Edward Bailey, shows what Lahainaluna looked like roughly a decade after its founding. Faculty residences gather on the left. The two-story building in the center is the printing house. The large building to the right is the seminary building; the second story housed additional teachers' quarters overlooking the much smaller students' residences below. The neat parallel ridges in the foreground represent the school's farm.[33] The engraving might have depicted any idyllic preindustrial New England village and looks remarkably like an 1835 sketch of Cornwall, Connecticut, location of the Foreign Mission School founded by the ABCFM in 1817.[34] Also known as the "Heathen School," Cornwall was inspired by 'Ōpūkaha'ia, who became one of the school's first students.[35] To the Lahainaluna missionaries, a landscape melding Western-style buildings and small-scale farming sufficient to feed residents seemed ideally suited to their project of Christianizing and "civilizing" the "heathen" Hawaiians.

Hawaiians vigorously contested the assumption of post-missionary progress and pre-missionary stultification. Samuel Manaiākalani Kamakau was born on O'ahu five years before Bingham's band of missionaries arrived. In 1833 he came to Lahainaluna to study in its second class. In his adult life, Kamakau served on the Land Commission, in the House of Representatives, and in the Royal Agricultural Society. It was for his historical writing, though, which he pursued on the side, that Kamakau became renowned. One newspaper dubbed him "he who surpasses all living Hawaiians in his knowledge of the ancient traditions and history of his race."[36] Kamakau converted from the Congregationalism of the New England missionaries to Catholicism as an adult, seeing in it "an affirmation of the spiritual power of Kānaka [Native Hawaiians] and their land," even as he described Hawaiian religion as "pagan."[37] He compared Catholicism to Hawaiian religion and "interview[ed] kūpuna who were knowledgeable and willing to share their wisdom with him." In 1841 Kamakau helped to organize the first Hawaiian Historical Society, Ka 'Ahahui 'Imi i na Mea Kahiko o Hawai'i Nei. The society sought "to obtain and preserve all historical data possible which bore on the origin of the race, and to obliterate the common belief among some foreigners who claim this is a wandering race which was lost in a storm and driven by winds to these shores. . . . A great many things being circulated by these foreigners are not so."[38]

Among the things that were "not so" was the Protestant missionaries' claim that Hawaiians had been wandering heathens who were "neglectful of their fine soil." Kamakau countered, "My people have been cultivators from very ancient times; it was by agriculture that they made a living for themselves."[39] Traditional Hawaiian cosmology held that the people and the land, or 'āina, were siblings; the land, as elder sibling, sustained the people, while the people took care of the land. The Indigenous land tenure system, called the ahupua'a, subdivided the land in triangular wedges that began at the mountains and extended to the sea, so that each had a varied mix of soil and climate conditions. Joint and varied responsibilities between chiefs, administrators, and commoners served, in the words of scholar Hokulani Aikau, to "[maintain] the productivity of the 'āina, and in turn ensured the health of the Kanaka."[40] In other words, Hawaiians, too, saw the state of the soil and themselves as linked. The kapu, or taboo, system not only ritually regulated the relationships between commoners, chiefs, and natural and supernatural forces but also conserved the land and the abundance of the sea. By restricting the gathering of certain plants and sea creatures at various times, the kapu system ensured that the soil would not be overworked or the ocean overfished.[41]

Kamakau described how the kapu system also ensured that plants had the proper amount of time to mature before being harvested: "After the prayer to Kanepua'a had been uttered," he wrote, "the patch became tabu." After a month or two, "the soil that had been heaped into mounds was seen to have been pushed aside . . . , and the stem ends of the plants were exposed. . . . [The farmer] was filled with happiness, and his lungs palpitated with joy. . . . At night as he rested he thought of his crops with happiness and desire, as a lover thinks of his beloved one."[42] Another Hawaiian historian, Kepelino Keauokalani, who was Kamakau's junior by fifteen years, similarly rhapsodized about the farmer's life: "In old days the farmers wept when they became disabled from work, because they loved their plants. 'Plants are beloved children,' said the farmers. Blessed were the Hawaiian people when their hands were occupied with work!"[43]

"The Contrast Was Remarkable and Complete"

If Hawai'i's soil was thought to be full of fertile potential, which Native Hawaiians had supposedly failed to take advantage of (per the missionaries' blinkered view), Anglo-American travelers to Africa initially believed that the climate there was so hot and the region so landlocked and arid that the life it managed to sustain was not only heathen but also barely human. In forming their impressions of Africa, antebellum Americans were influenced by the story of Scottish Congregationalists Robert and Mary Moffat, who had been sent by the London Missionary Society to South Africa. An 1846 American Sunday-School Union abridgment of Robert's memoirs, *The Gospel among the Bechuanas,* described "the natives, throughout southern Africa," as "like plants on a sterile soil, stunted in growth, while under better circumstances the same race would be as trees instead of shrubs." Quoting Moffat, the narrative explained that "they have neither house nor shed, neither flocks nor herds. . . . Accustomed to a migratory life, and entirely dependent on the chase for a precarious subsistence, they have contracted habits which could scarcely be credited of human beings. . . . Hunger compels them to feed on every thing edible." Where Bingham had criticized Hawaiians' thatched huts for exposing them to the sun, Moffat asked whether the "domiciles" of the "Bechuanas" (Tswana people) were even "the abodes of human beings? In a bushy country, they will form a hollow in a central position, and bring the branches together over the head. Here the man, his wife, and probably a child or two, lie huddled in a heap, on a little grass, in a hollow spot, not larger than an ostrich's nest."[44]

According to Moffat, the Tswana people were not idolatrous heathens but rather "had no ideas of religion." Their landscapes had "no sacred streams," and the missionary "seeks in vain to find a temple, an altar, or a single emblem of heathen worship." Instead, "Satan has employed his agency, with fatal success, in erasing every vestige of religious impression from the minds of the Bechuanas, Hottentots, and Bushmen." In other words, where other people classified as heathens were criticized for worshiping the creation instead of the Creator, the natives of South Africa, according to Moffat, were so degenerated that they worshipped nothing at all. Said Moffat, quoting fellow Scottish missionary John Campbell, "They looked upon the sun . . . with the eyes of an ox." Moffat complained of difficulty in telling them "that there was a Creator, the governor of the heavens and earth," since they had not even an "altar to an unknown God" on which to erect a Christian scaffold.[45]

But as different as South Africa might have seemed from Hawai'i, or any other part of the heathen world, ultimately *The Gospel among the Bechuanas* affirmed that "whoever goes to preach the unsearchable riches of Christ among the heathen, goes on a warfare which requires all prayer and supplication, to keep his armour bright, and in active operation, to wrestle and struggle, and toil, in pulling down the strongholds of Satan, whether in Africa, India, the islands of the Pacific, or in the wilds of America."[46] José de Acosta's theory about the shared demonic roots of heathenism loomed still. The underlying sameness of Africans with others in the heathen world meant that, no matter the aridity of the climate, unrelenting heat of the sun, or dryness of the land, which supposedly made them "plants on a sterile soil," their hearts could be renovated just as much as any other heathen's. And what is more, this could be accomplished without removing them from the land that had supposedly stunted them—instead, the land itself could and would be turned from heath to garden once the hearts of its inhabitants were changed. Souls and soils existed in symbiotic relationship, and missionaries and officials were confident that both could be made to blossom.

In 1829 Mary Moffat wrote to a friend in England that she and her husband had made a number of converts who "are becoming generally more civilised. The station affording great facilities for agriculture, it is carried on to a considerable extent. The missionaries have now fine gardens, vineyards, orchards, and corn-fields, so that they have our example, which they follow very well." Christianization meant civilization meant cultivation. And along with cultivation came wage work, barter, and trade. Before the missionaries established their "fine gardens," they complained that the locals would come at night and abscond with their produce, or divert the missionaries' irrigation streams to their own patches of vegetation. But now, said Moffat, "the head of each family has a garden on the mission-ground" (all the easier to closely supervise), "and all who have that privilege are bound to work (*for wages*) whenever their services are required for building, agriculture, or any public work. Their industry enables them to barter very profitably." New desires arose with new wages, and the converts bought more and more European goods to outfit their gardens and homes. In making the land blossom as the rose, the Moffats also created an economy that lined European pockets. And "the contrast was remarkable and complete."[47]

In addition to the Moffats' work in South Africa, Sierra Leone and Liberia were other paradigmatic African landscapes often held up as examples of missionary success, where the "contrast was remarkable and complete." When Assistant Agent of the United States Ephraim Bacon published journal extracts from his tour of Sierra Leone in 1819–1820, he included in the volume and flagged in the title "Cuts, showing a contrast between two Native towns, One of which is Christianized and the other Heathen." The former was Regent's Town. The view is similar to Lahainaluna and Cornwall, in which small structures dot a natural landscape. Clearly visible in the woodcut is a church, the largest building in the town, and a number of roofed dwelling places.[48]

The accompanying description explains the before and after that viewers were supposed to read into the landscape. Before the missionaries' arrival, the text claimed that

"View of Regent's Town." In *Abstract of a Journal of E. Bacon, Assistant Agent of the United States, to Africa: with an Appendix, containing interesting accounts of the effects of the Gospel among the Native Africans. With Cuts, showing a contrast between two Native towns, One of which is Christianized and the other Heathen,* 2nd ed., by Ephraim Bacon (Philadelphia: Clark and Raser, 1822). Library Company of Philadelphia.

in some huts, ten of them were crowded together; and, in others, even fifteen and twenty: many of them were ghastly as skeletons: six or eight sometimes died in one day; and only six infants were born during the year. Superstition, in various forms, tyrannized over their minds: many devil's houses sprung up; and all placed their security in wearing gregres. Scarcely any desire of improvement was discernible: for a considerable time, there were hardly five or six acres of land brought under cultivation; and some who wished to cultivate the soil, were deterred from doing so by the fear of being plundered of the produce.[49]

But now, the text asserted, they are "steady, sober, and industrious . . . active and serviceable men." And the "town itself is" said to be "laid out with regularity—nineteen streets are formed, and are made plain and level, with good roads round the town—a large stone church rises in the midst of the habitations. . . . The state of cultivation further manifests the industry of the people—all are farmers—gardens, fenced in, are attached to every dwelling—all the land in the immediate neighbourhood is under cultivation."[50]

"From London Missionary Papers" (view of "Heathen" town). In Bacon, *Abstract of a Journal*. Library Company of Philadelphia.

The text luxuriated in listing the goods produced by the Christian Africans of Regent's Town: "There are many rice-fields; and among the other vegetables raised for food, are cassadas, plantains, coco, yams, coffee, and Indian corn—of fruits, they have bananas, oranges, limes, pineapples, groundnuts, guavas, and papaws,—of animals, there are horses, cows, bullocks, sheep, goats, pigs, ducks, and fowl." The list recalls the gifts Samuel Ruggles and Samuel Whitney received on their visit to Kauai, which convinced them of the richness of its soil. Included as this was in a US agent's report, it is not difficult to see the desire for a two-way exchange of goods: delicious and exotic African (substitute Hawaiian, Chinese, Indian, et cetera) produce in exchange for European and American commodities. And furthermore, the productivity of the Native people "relieve[d] from all expense, on their personal account, that government to which they pay the most grateful allegiance."[51] For the colonizers, it was the best of all worlds: unproductive heathens, who did nothing with their land but grovel on top of it in sickly huts, turned into industrious Christians, producers, and consumers.

To Anglo-American readers, by contrast, the "Heathen town" would hardly be recognizable as a town at all if it were not labeled as such in Bacon's title. Where Robert Moffat complained that the "Bechuanas" lacked any kind of religion, the "Heathen town" here is dominated by an idol, described as "one of those frightful figures which the Africans make of the devil."[52]

The only visible structure in the woodcut is a tent, signifying imperma-
nence. In the background, African people dressed only in loincloths or
skirts appear to dance, a sharp contrast to the top hat–wearing White missionary in the foreground, who is accompanied by two Christianized assistants, also clothed from head to toe. The woodcut depicts the African
people in the background as doing nothing productive; they have changed
no features of the land, and their energies have instead been misspent on
building the idol.

"They Are Pagans; Every Person"

If conversion was supposed to renovate the land in those parts of the heathen world where Americans ignored evidence of cultivation, what of heathen environs where they did not? Anglo-Americans looking at India and
China found them to be a problem for the paradigm of wild and overgrown
regions that needed intervention. Jedidiah Morse, though he dismissed the
desolate deserts of Asia, nevertheless noted the exotic lushness, built environment, and productivity of Asian landscapes. In his *American Universal
Geography,* Morse depicted Asian environs as so naturally fecund and fertile that they had come to sustain dense populations whose early histories
outranked the rest of the world's in development and innovation. This was
due to the divine's decision to "place his once favourite people, the Hebrews,"
in Asia; "It was here that the great and merciful work of our redemption
was accomplished by his divine Son; and it was from hence that the light of
his glorious gospel was carried with amazing rapidity into all the known
nations." But from these glorious beginnings, when in Asia "the first edifices
were reared, and the first empires founded, while the other parts of the globe
were inhabited only by wild animals," Asia had fallen into overpopulated
decrepitude as Christianity had departed her warm climes for the colder
north. Now they were all "generally heathens and idolaters." Asia's was the
musty luxuriousness of the old rich, for it remained "superior" to "Europe
and Africa in the extent of its territories," Morse said, as well as in "the se-
renity of its air, the fertility of its soil, the deliciousness of its fruits, the fra-
grancy and balsamick qualities of its plants, spices and gums; the salubrity
of its drugs; the quantity, variety, beauty, and value of its gems; the richness
of its metals, and the fineness of its silks and cottons."[53]

Such salivating description belies a colonizer's gaze at the seductive richness of surveyed lands. Writing at a time when the productions of the
"Orient"—such as fine china, silks, and teas—were highly desired, Morse
acknowledged that "all the inhabitants of the more southern regions" had

shown remarkable "ingenuity in various kinds of workmanship, which our most skilful mechanicks have in vain endeavoured to imitate." He admitted that "the Chinese agriculture is carried to a high state of improvement," and "the culture of the cotton and the rice fields, from which the bulk of the inhabitants are clothed and fed, is ingenious almost beyond description." Indeed, it was primarily in landscape cultivation—"in their gardening and planning their grounds"—that "they hit upon the true sublime and beautiful."[54]

And yet, for all that their landscapes appeared well designed, verdant, and abundant, in reality, Morse claimed, they were as disordered and in need of intervention as any other part of the heathen world. For—and here Morse drew from Aeneas Anderson's *Narrative of the British Embassy to China, in the Years 1792, 1793, and 1794*—"though the soil is rich and every spot tilled, it affords but a scanty supply for its numerous millions. Creatures which die with disease, and even the vermin, which swarm over their own bodies, afford them a repast. . . . They are Pagans; every person, from the meanest peasant to the monarch himself, has an altar and *deity* of his own."[55] The idea that "Asiatics" like the Chinese could not feed their swelling populations but with the diseased carcasses of similarly malnourished animals and the rats and mice that fed on them would be repeated when Chinese migrants began arriving in America in the second half of the century, as we will see in Chapter 6.

A similar move from impressed appraisal to dismissive discounting occurs in Charles Lloyd's two-volume *Travels at Home, and Voyages by the Fire-Side, for the Instruction and Entertainment of Young Persons*. Lloyd was a Welsh minister, farmer, and schoolmaster. *Travels at Home* was first published in London in 1814 and, as a result of its popularity, reprinted in Philadelphia two years later. "The judgment of the public, which is the best, may be inferred from the rapid sale of the former edition," Lloyd gloated in the 1816 reprint. As the title suggests, *Travels at Home* offered children a way to imaginatively voyage to exotic places from the comfort of home, under the guidance of parents, free from the dangers of "carriages overturned, from restive horses, from shipwreck, from rocks and precipices, from wild beasts, and from savage men."[56] Families were to spread open maps and geographies in front of them as they read the book out loud. To make the reading more entertaining, Lloyd narrated the book from the multiple perspectives of a family sitting around the fireplace: "Mother" and the children, "Eliza" and "Charles," describe and remark on what they see with awe, disgust, pity, and surprise, while "Father" provides background information and directs their emotional reactions toward moral judgments of the regions through which they travel.

Mother and the children marvel at China. Donning "robes of invisibility," they gawk at the scenery, which appears to be "rich in every accommodation," with "fine roads," endless rows of cultivated crops, and a "deep green appearance." Mother cannot help herself; she exclaims at "the vivid cast of the painting [of Chinese buildings], and its uncommon excellence and neatness." She even admits that her "admiration of this race has been powerful. It has not diminished by examining every thing in detail."[57] Here Mother gives voice to European awe at the longevity of Chinese civilization and desire for finely crafted Chinese objects.

But Father reminds her not to be swayed by these superficial sights. Not only do the Chinese eat carrion, he says, but they are also "not a very happy people," for they "are too numerous for the extent of the land" and too hidebound to leave it. They are subject to famine all the time because they are practically bursting their borders but will not leave to form colonies elsewhere because of their pagan attachment to the "tombs of their ancestors." Lloyd genders Mother and the children as reactive and emotional; Father is the masculine voice of reason and expertise. Mother capitulates and acknowledges that "with all their sagacity then, [the Chinese] want yet to be enlightened in things of great importance. Probably if they possessed the Christian religion, its benevolent and generous principles might help to direct their frugality and industry towards securing a larger portion of happiness and comfort."[58] Wrong religion is the reason for underlying unhappiness.

If ancestor worship spells the doom of the Chinese, idolatry looms large as the family gazes on Indian environs. In the antebellum Anglo-American imagination, India often figures as the quintessential representative of the heathen world, with lurid tales of gargantuan idols, violent festivals, and bodily mortifications titillating readers and illustrating the full-fledged effects of heathenism on a landscape and a people.[59] Passing by the "Island of Elephants," Father points out the "monstrous figures" that "represent the Indian false gods" at the "subterranean temples" the family passes. In reply to Eliza's shock at witnessing these "graven images," Father explains that

these people, though the eternal power and Godhead of the Almighty are clearly understood from the works of his hands, have either made very little use, or a bad use, of their reason. They have adopted fantastic fancies which induce them to imagine that there are various divinities belonging to the air, earth, sea, rivers, mountains—Such is the ignorance that prevails every where, when men have not the benefit of divine revelation! Even the Greeks and the Romans, who were in many respects very wise and cultivated, knew little about religion. They had their Jupiter and Apollo, and others; and goddesses too, of whom the Hindoos are particularly fond. Christians in Catholic countries worship the Virgin Mary, whom they call the mother of God.[60]

Here, Father describes a broad world of willful heathen ignorance, stretching from India in his present day to the ancient Greeks and Romans. The inclusion of Catholics under the umbrella of idolatrous ignorance recapitulates Reformation-era Protestant polemics about the Catholic worship of images and statues, still going strong in the nineteenth-century Anglo world.

In contrast to her initially positive impressions of China, in India Mother shudders: "My feelings are indescribable, when I find myself thus in the temple of idols! A sort of awe, approaching to horror, seizes me." Here Lloyd uses the character of Mother to instruct Anglo readers how they are to react to accounts of heathen lands. Instead of being seduced by descriptions of exotic statues and colorful temples, they are to be disgusted and horrified, made to feel that in these locales, in the presence of idols, "we really stand where we are cut off from intercourse with God!"[61]

For Lloyd, heathenism was to blame for the failure of Chinese to leave their ancestral stomping grounds and look elsewhere for sustenance, and it was to blame for the failure of Indians to use "their reason," causing them to unproductively litter the land with soul-destroying idols. As Anglo-American technologies increased Britons' and Americans' ability to exploit the land, later commentators increasingly blamed heathenism for Asians' lack of innovation. Because they failed to understand the true nature of creation—made by God, for the dominion of man—and saw the actions of spirits in the caprices of nature, they reacted with cowed submission to bad harvests, failed crops, and inclement weather. Hoping to propitiate their spirits and ancestors, they used the best parts of the land for temples and graves, and on the rest of the land they continued to employ the age-old agricultural implements that their forefathers had developed. The only reason their lands still bore fruit at all was because of the hospitable climate, the soil's fertility, and the swarming populations of abject subjects who toiled over its insufficient productions. An 1863 article and image from the American Sunday-School Union's periodical *Child's World* is emblematic of this perspective. The image suggests backwardness as half-clothed "Hindoo native[s]" hold on to the tails of oxen while standing on a harrow. Even though they are assiduously trying to make the land blossom as the rose, the most they can do to the soil is "RUDE FARMING," limited by the meager weight of their own, frail bodies. The article assures, "When Christianity takes root among heathen nations, all the arts of life will soon follow."[62]

"Rude Farming." In *Child's World* 2, no. 9 (May 9, 1863). Library Company of Philadelphia.

As the article implies, nineteenth-century Anglo-Americans connected right religion—Protestant Christianity—to the technological prowess necessary to exploit the land to its full potential, if not beyond. Inventions like the steel plow, mechanical reapers and threshers in the 1830s, the steam-powered grain elevator in 1842, and the expansion of the railroad in the latter part of the century made it easier for Americans to work the soil, make it blossom, and ship its products far and wide.[63] Anglo-Americans read these developments as gifts from a God who preferred them above all other people. At the root of such conviction was the belief that Anglo-American landscapes benefited from the providential introduction of machines that allowed them to take rapid possession of the land and increase its productions manifold times, creating surfeits of raw goods and foods that could be exported and sold after the (White) population was fully satiated. By contrast, the fecundity of Asian landscapes only seemed to be enabled by the sheer numbers of Asian pagans available to cultivate the soil, but constrained by the lack of technological advancements that were enabling White Americans to plow through the American West. Heathenism kept souls mired in superstition and soils insufficiently cultivated by "rude farming." It prevented people from understanding the true workings of nature and unlocking the God-given scientific principles that had allowed White Protestants to obtain dominion over the land.[64]

"We Regret the Loss of Our Former Ways"

But not everyone celebrated the rapidity with which Anglo-American agricultural innovations enabled the plunder of the land. By and large, missionaries with the ABCFM envisioned remaking heathen landscapes through the introduction of yeoman farming, encouraging converts to tend gardens that could supply fruits and vegetables, and raise livestock that could produce dairy and meat, for their own and neighboring communities. They had in mind the ideal New England village, with bucolic pastures and farmhouses arranged in an orderly grid around the lifeblood of the community: the village church. This was also the model that home missionaries sought to impose on settler communities in the nineteenth-century American West, even though New England itself was rapidly changing through the introduction of industrial technologies and factory towns.[65]

A closing glance at the Hawaiian case illustrates how these changes could affect the missions field. In Hawai'i, the changes to the land were so meteoric that the tensions between the Indigenous system of shared cultivation and the missionaries' yeoman farms soon paled before the rise of large plantations that threatened the link both Hawaiians and missionaries saw between the physical and spiritual welfare of the soil and its cultivators. The Organic Act of the 1830s gave "foreigners who swore allegiance to the Kingdom of Hawai'i the right to own land." The Māhele of 1848 privatized land more broadly, turning it into a commodity to be bought and sold. King Kamehameha III encouraged native Hawaiians to purchase land before foreigners could snap it up. But scholars' estimates of the amount of land that actually went to Native Hawaiians range from less than 1 percent to only 26 percent of the total number of acres sold by the time of annexation in 1893.[66] "So great was the change" wrought by the Māhele, Titus Coan observed, "that a large class of the natives could not believe it to be true. Many thought it a ruse to tempt them to build better houses, fence the lands, plant trees, and make such improvements in cultivation as should enrich the chiefs, while to the old tenants no profit would accrue."[67]

The Māhele priced lands according to desirability; gone were the diverse wedge-shaped divisions of the ahupua'a. Fertile lands and those close to the ocean went to wealthy foreign investors. In 1852 missionary David B. Lyman wrote to family back in the States that "large capitalists are coming in to settle in the Islands. . . . Most of them are not pious men. To have most of the lands in few hands & the most of the people employed as hired laborers, is not much calculated to make them an independent people."[68] Instead of small taro ponds or limited farms, the landscape was changing to one of large-scale commercial plantations that needed an additional labor force to work: the Chinese, whose own supposed heathenism in turn threatened to unmoor the missionaries' paternalistic efforts at cultivating their Hawaiian "children." As Lyman's wife, Sarah, put it, "Foreigners are increasing on some of these islands & are establishing themselves on farms. Chinese laborers are coming in. . . . They are industrious & enterprising. But they are as ignorant of true religion, as the veriest heathen in a heathen land & are like to remain so, for ought I know."[69]

Coan's autobiography vividly illustrates the conflicted response of missionaries to these changes. Here is his description of Maui in 1882: "This district is now full of agricultural energy. Vast fields of sugar-cane wave where weeds grew before; crushing-mills groan, boiling-trains steam, smoke-stacks puff, centrifugals buzz, and ship-loads of sugar are produced in and around Wailuku. Extended and expensive ditches bring water from the mountains of East Maui, converting vast fields of dry and hot sand into rich and productive soil. . . . All would be matters of rejoicing and congratulation could we but report equal progress in moral and spiritual power."[70] Missionaries were caught between celebrating these rapid changes and realizing that massive agricultural upheaval could be more of a hindrance than a help to their project of converting the Hawaiian people. The rapid reshaping of the Hawaiian landscape spelled demographic disaster for the missionaries' attempt to reshape Hawaiians' souls. "The plantations do not replenish our town with Hawaiians," Coan admitted; "on the contrary, while foreigners of many nationalities, especially the Chinese, are increasing, our native population is perishing."[71] By the late 1850s, the Native population had been "reduced by 75 percent or more from its pre-contact level."[72] Broader moneymaking ambitions were turning the land into a source of wealth instead of the source of spiritual and physical health that both missionaries and Hawaiians had believed it could and should be.

Where missionaries like Coan were ambivalent about these changes, Hawaiian historian Kepelino condemned them in no uncertain terms. Hawaiians had once been generous, he wrote, sharing the fruits of their labor. But "at the coming in of American education the humble time passed and a period of arrogance began which has persisted until now." "As for us," he concluded, "we regret the loss of our former ways."[73]

4

BODIES

O n the third of September 1817, forty-one-year-old Lyman Beecher ascended the pulpit of Boston's Park Street Church to deliver an ordination sermon for the church's new pastor and for five men who had recently been commissioned "as missionaries to the heathen." After expounding on the perfection of biblical law, Beecher, ever the willing pugilist, took on the objections of those who thought missions were a waste of time. "There are not a few, who seem to regard the Heathen as not accountable for their depravity of heart, or criminal for their idolatry, and scarcely for their immoralities," said he. These wrongheaded souls held that the heathen were merely the "guileless children of our common father," so "what need then of all this sympathy for the Heathen"?[1]

Well, said Beecher, let them taste the fruits of their own false theory. If they think the heathen are mere innocents, let them "make the exchange": "Give them your bibles, and pastors, and Sabbaths, and receive their idol gods, and Brahmins, and religious rites."[2] What then would American society look like? Beecher drew on popular stereotypes about the heathen, derived primarily from the Indian context, to paint what he surely thought was a ghastly scene:

> Roll through your streets the car of Juggernaut, "besmeared with blood of human sacrifice," and covered with emblems of pollution. . . . Kindle up the fires, that shall consume annually, . . . two hundred and seventy five widows on the dead bodies of their husbands, and leave behind thousands of children, doubly orphans. Welcome to your shores the religion, which shall teach your children, when you are sick, to lay you down by the cold river side to die; and when their mothers shall shrink from the glowing flame, with their own hands to thrust them in. Welcome to your hearts a religion, which shall teach you to entice your smiling children to the waves, and plunge them in.[3]

Beecher's dire word picture, which found renewed life when his sermon was published a decade later, shows how heathenness operated as an embodied category as much as a spiritual one. In a century that saw the spread of scientific racism and the parsing of human difference on the basis of skin color, skull shape and size, and other supposed physiognomic characteristics, the older, broader category of "heathen" nevertheless retained a powerful salience rooted in ideas about bodies ravaged by misguided beliefs—bodies that needed the oversight of Protestants in order to be saved from themselves and each other. American Protestants in the nineteenth century continued to hold that God had made all the nations of one blood, and that therefore all the nations were convertible.[4] But they ascribed to entrenched heathenism the cause of physical distress manifesting on bodies inhabiting the "dark" and "benighted" regions of the heathen world.

Heathens were those who wasted the perfectly fine flesh God had given them by offering it up to false idols. They ignored their own sick and hastened to death their closest kin. Just as diverse heathen landscapes could be recognized by the blight that supposedly lurked beneath the surface of even the most beautiful natural environments, so too did all heathen bodies supposedly harbor the blight of premature death, even if they looked different on the surface, even if some were admired for their external fortitude and nobility of form, and even if White people actually worried more about the susceptibility of their own bodies to inhospitable climates in the heathen world. This chapter considers the heathen body as imagined by nineteenth-century Americans, showing along the way how the normative figure of American religious history—the White American Protestant—was constituted in opposition to diseased, dying, and damned heathens. The nineteenth-century save-the-heathen impulse assured and reassured Americans that they were helpful and healthful humanitarians in contrast to the poor heathen, whose sorry end, without missionary intervention, was foretold from their moment of birth.

Race, Religion, and Romans 1

If Isaiah 34 and 35 filtered Americans' views of heathen landscapes through the lens of moral blight, the first chapter of Paul's Epistle to the Romans served the same purpose with regard to heathen bodies. In his Park Street sermon, Beecher used it to justify his claim that "the Heathen are not holy," whatever the missions' opponents might say. Rather, they are "filled with all unrighteousness, fornication, wickedness, covetousness, maliciousness," "without natural affection, implacable, unmerciful."[5] In their tortured but useless attempts to save themselves, the heathen were supposed to actively neglect each other—indeed, to lack even the "natural affection" to care for their own children and parents.

In his 1824 *Moral Condition and Prospects of the Heathen,* Benjamin Wisner also drew from the first chapter of Romans to craft a broad heathen world that stretched from past to present and that was linked by the unfortunate ramifications of idolatry on the human body. Said Wisner, "*Whatever the Bible declares concerning any description of character in one age, is true of the same description of character in all ages.*" The "Eastern idolaters" and the "savages of the west" were just as guilty as the Greco-Roman and other heathens of biblical times who, "when they knew God, they glorified him not as God; but became vain in their imaginations, and changed the glory of the incorruptible God, into an image made like to corruptible man, and to birds, and four-footed beasts, and creeping things." The heathen both past and present were "given up to vile affections" and to the most shameful "uncleanness." As present-day evidence of this, Wisner cited Dr. William Ward's *View of the History, Literature and Mythology of the Hindoos,* which held that the "characters of the gods, and the licentiousness which prevails at their festivals . . . , with the enervating nature of the climate, have made the Hindoos the most effeminate and corrupt people on earth. Fidelity to marriage vows is almost unknown among them: the intercourse of the sexes approaches very near to that of irrational animals." Here Ward joined the Enlightenment interest in climate as a key cause of human difference, with idolatry, which he blamed for licentiousness, corruption, and bestial behavior.[6]

Wisner professed some embarrassment at "enter[ing] into this disgusting detail" but claimed that it was "necessary," and that what Ward said about the "Hindoos" was equally applicable to others in the heathen world. Having corrupted the true God by turning His image into the likeness of creeping and crawling things, so too did the heathen corrupt their bodies by engaging in "filthy" acts that turned them into little more than animals. Wisner was also confident that even those heathens who seemed, superficially, to be less given to "abominable vices" would prove over further inquiry and examination to be equally "disgusting," just as had been the case with the "South Sea Islanders, the Hindoos, the Chinese, &c." Thus, in one fell sermonic stroke, did Wisner craft a heathen world that extended both into the past and across the continents, all of whose inhabitants were so contaminated by the "guilt and pollution of Heathenism" as to be unworthy of heaven.[7]

The inclusion of biblical-era Greco-Roman heathens in the same category as Asians, Africans, Pacific Islanders, and Native Americans harked back to debates about the classics and raised questions about racial theories that held the Greeks and Romans to be the progenitors of the "West." Wisner and others squared these issues with the confidence that the Greco-Roman heathen of biblical times had been brought out of their degradation by Christianity centuries before and spread Christianity northward, so that Euro-American Protestants came from a long lineage of already reformed peoples. Wisner and others did not deny their heathen heritage, but since their ancestors had given up heathenism long ago, they maintained that European and Euro-American life-spans were longer, their bodies less weak, their behaviors no longer animal-like, and their characters cemented as rescuers of their less fortunate "brethren." Race is constructed here as the historical operation of heathenism and Christianity on different peoples, as bodily deviance becomes religiously wrought over time.

"What Will Become of the Baby?"

Drawing on the same kinds of sources that nineteenth-century Protestant Americans used to picture the heathen in their own imaginations, we turn now to their views of the heathen through life's stages. One small volume for children began, "A Hindoo mother sits at the door of a little hut. Her infant son is asleep on a mat, spread on a sort of bench, and a strip of blue cotton is so placed as to shelter it from the wind and sun. *What will become of this baby?*" The volume's title echoed the question and was published by the New York Sunday School Union sometime between 1856 and 1868. Any idyllic illusions young readers might have had when picturing the opening scene of mother and child—helpfully provided as the frontispiece to the volume—were quickly pierced by the following paragraph: the reader learns that the mother is "a heathen" living in a "dark land," and "What will become of this baby?" becomes an ominous harbinger of woe.[8]

In the American imagination as filtered through Romans 1, heathen parents could not be relied on to care for their own and infanticide was common. As one children's story put it, as if it were a given matter of fact, "Heathen parents do not love their children as Christian fathers and mothers do. They often kill their little ones, especially the little girls."[9] Charles S. Stewart, a missionary to Hawai'i in the 1820s, believed that heathens lacked "*natural affection,*" and claimed in his travel journal that "in those parts of the Islands where the influence of the Mission has not yet extended—*two thirds of the infants born perish, by the hands of their own parents, before attaining the first or second year of their age!*" Stewart and his wife, Harriet, had themselves recently welcomed a son, an experience that undoubtedly colored how they interpreted the supposed domestic mores of the heathen.

Frontispiece to *What Will Become of the Baby? With Three Other Stories about Children in Heathen Lands.* New York: Carlton and Porter for the Sunday School Union, [1855?]. Library Company of Philadelphia.

Everything they felt, the heathen must not be feeling, or else the distinction between the missionizer and missionized would break down and Romans 1 be proven wrong.[10]

Stewart took it upon himself to inhabit the mind of a heathen mother, using his own assumptions about proper Christian motherhood to draw a sharp contrast: "The very periods, when the infant of a Christian mother, is to her the object of intense solicitude, and of the deepest anxiety—in times of sickness, suffering and distress—times at which, the affections of the parental bosom are brought into the most painful exercise—are those when the mother, here, feels that in her child she has a care and a trouble, which she will not endure." Indulging fantasies about careless and unfeeling heathen women oblivious to the cries of their own, Stewart alleged that, instead of "attempting to alleviate [her child's] pains, she stifles its cries for a moment, with her hand—hurries it into a grave already prepared for it—and tramples to a level the earth, under which, *the offspring of her bosom is struggling in the agonies of death!*"[11]

Nor were heathen women only unfeeling euthanizers of the sick and suffering, he claimed: "Not unfrequently, [infanticide] is provoked by the simple necessity of half an hour's additional labour a day, for the support of the child, till it can seek its own living; and sometimes, merely, because its helplessness would interfere, for a period, with the freedom and pleasure of the mother!" Stewart sketched the hedonistic heathen as a mother unworthy of the title, a lazy woman who cared more about herself and her own enjoyment than about her children. The "crime" of infanticide, said he, was "so relentless, as to sink the guilty perpetrators of it, below the nature of the brutes." This set up the necessary contrast with the Christian mother, whose sensitive feelings were ever alert to the needs of her child, and which rendered her unquestionably human and not brute. Stewart opined, "Happy indeed is the people whose God is the Lord!"[12]

The Stewarts' story was more complicated than Charles let on in his journal. Though he suggested that the wont of the Christian mother was to do nothing but tend to her child's every need with earnest solicitude, his wife, Harriet, was not able to do so for their own infant son. Pregnancy and childbirth had left her greatly weakened and hardly able to care for herself. Fortunately for her and her baby, the Stewarts were accompanied by Betsey Stockton, a skilled nurse and the first single woman to serve as a foreign missionary. Stockton had been enslaved in the family of the College of New Jersey's president, the Reverend Ashbel Green. Emancipated soon after her conversion in 1816, she had initially sought to serve as a missionary to Africa but had been importuned to accompany the Stewarts to Hawai'i, where she was tasked with taking care of their household in addition to teaching school on the islands. Stockton's contract specified her status as "neither . . . equal nor as a servant," stipulating that she was to be treated "as a humble christian friend, embarked in the great enterprise of endeavoring to ameliorate the condition of the heathen generally, & especially to bring them to the saving knowledge of the truth as it is in Jesus." It was Stockton who helped the Stewarts preserve the semblance of Christian humanity, raising them above the "nature of the brutes" who ignored their young, by taking care of ailing mother and child.[13]

Stockton brought to the Islands similar assumptions about heathen animality that the Stewarts did. In the journal she kept about the voyage, she described her first impression of Hawaiians:

> Two or three canoes, loaded with natives, came to the ship: their appearance was that of half man and half beast—naked—except a narrow strip of *tapa* round their loins. When they first came on board, the sight chilled our very hearts. The ladies retired to the cabin, and burst into tears; and some of the

gentlemen turned pale: my own soul sickened within me, and every nerve trembled. Are these, thought I, the beings with whom I must spend the remainder of my life! They are men and have souls—was the reply which conscience made.[14]

Heathenness operated here to explain the animalization of certain humans, rather than innate animality explaining heathenness. "They are men and have souls," Stockton reminds herself, even as she has been conditioned to be "chilled" by the sight of "half man and half beast." By all accounts, Stockton thrived on the islands. Even as she continued to serve the Stewart family, she also established herself as a teacher in the school they opened at Lahaina on the island of Maui. Though she thought she might spend the rest of her life there, the Stewarts brought her back to the States to continue caring for their household when they returned in 1826 due to Harriet's continued health problems.[15]

"The Hard, Bitter Lot of Women"

To return to the "Hindoo" baby: What will become of him? Luckily for him, he is a son. Though Stewart claimed that unfeeling and lazy heathen mothers killed their infants irrespective of gender, his represented only one end of a spectrum of views. On the other end was a view of the heathen mother as the poor victim of a despotic society, whose sad plight as a long-suffering member of the female sex provoked her to kill her girl babies as an act of mercy. Emma Pitman, in her circa 1880 *Heroines of the Mission Field. Biographical Sketches of Female Missionaries Who Have Laboured in Various Lands among the Heathen,* offered a contrast between the Christian and heathen, much as did Stewart. But her heathen mother was pitiable and pitiful rather than callous and cold, the woman's social context explaining her sorry situation in contrast to the loved and cherished "English mother." Using the "Hindoo" as the quintessential heathen, Pitman alleged that "the Hindoo wife is shut up in her apartments like a prisoner, or waits upon her lord and master like a slave." Just a child herself of "between five and twelve years," she counts it a "calamity" if she has a girl, "and sitting in the hopeless night of heathenism, contemplates the future of the child" and "regrets that it was ever born. And then, frequently, after hugging her baby to her bosom with convulsive sobs, she gives it to the Ganges, that it may at least secure heaven, and avoid the hard, bitter lot of women in India."[16] An illustration of the scene showed decidedly unchild-like women, clothed only from the waist down, sending a baby into the river

"Hindoo Mother Consigning Her Child to the Ganges." In *Heroines of the Mission Field. Biographical Sketches of Female Missionaries Who Have Laboured in Various Lands among the Heathen,* by Emma Pitman (New York: Anson D. F. Randolph, [1880?]). Library Company of Philadelphia.

on a bed of rushes as they sprinkle flower petals over its stiff form. The drawing's explicit rendering of the women's naked forms suggests how publications about exotic heathens could titillate American audiences and provide them with sensational but acceptable material about deviant but beautiful bodies. But for the nakedness, the scene would have also reminded nineteenth-century readers steeped in the Bible of Moses, sent by his mother, Jochebed, down the Nile when Pharaoh decreed death for infant boys. But here the baby is a girl and her fate is death and despair for her people, where Moses's was life and salvation for his.

In building her tale of heathen womanly woe, Pitman may have been aware of and drawn from an earlier tract that was published and republished numerous times in the 1830s, *Condition and Character of Females in Pagan and Mohammedan Countries.* The tract claimed to present "a simple statement of facts" attested to by "men of different characters and professions—by protestants, catholics, infidels, and pagans—by geographers, travellers, and missionaries." Through the male authority of these diverse figures, the tract presented the "heathen female" as "despised," "degraded and miserable in the extreme." This began at birth: "The heathen female is viewed with contempt from the morning of her existence. The birth of a daughter, in most unevangelized countries, is an occasion of sorrow. She is frowned upon by her parents and relatives, and her sex is often a sufficient reason for putting an immediate end to her existence." If she were spared, the "heathen female" would soon be "betrothed" or "sold," and if she were in the "higher ranks in almost every pagan and Mohammedan country," into a polygamous union. The treatment of women serves as the theme that unifies "Pagan and Mohammedan" countries, no matter how "civilized" or "barbarous," under the broad heading of "heathen." This was the case from past to present: "The females of Greece and Rome, 1800 years ago, were in many respects, regarded and treated as are those of Turkey and Hindostan at the present time. Impurity and infanticide were *common* among the former, as well as the latter. Heathenism in every age and every country is essentially the same."[17]

The inclusion of "Mohammedans" in the category of "heathen" reflects how missionaries to the Middle East were trained at the same institutions, read the same material, and brought with them the same assumptions that American Protestants held about the rest of the heathen world. At the same time, they viewed Islam as unique—a "far more difficult and dangerous problem than that presented by the idolatry of the Indians or Hawaiians" because of its power, its reach, and its literary basis.[18] The first American mission to Palestine and later Syria was launched from Andover, Massachusetts, in 1818, as missionaries Pliny Fisk and Levi Parsons were tasked with "acquir[ing] particular information respecting the state of religion . . . in Asiatic Turkey" and with "ascertain[ing] the most promising place for the establishment of christian missions, and the best means of conducting them."[19] Historian Ussama Makdisi points out, "By its own admission, the board was to dispatch missionaries to an empire about which it knew virtually nothing." The knowledge vacuum meant that existing ideas about the broader heathen world could readily fill the void. Even as Fisk and Parsons were encouraged by reports of the uniqueness of their field—Palestine serving as the backdrop to biblical history—they were also handed the same instructions "recently given to fellow missionaries destined for the Sandwich Islands," fortifying the "dichotomy between the singular American Christian missionaries and the generic 'perishing heathen' they were meant to save."[20] The combination of uniqueness and genericness was not distinct to the Middle East mission; each American Board of Commissioners for Foreign Missions field provided data on how heathenism wrecked soils and souls in specific contexts, but the explanation remained the same: ignorance of the one true God and adulation of the creation rather than of the Creator.

Rather than blame female infanticide on the brutality and callousness of heathen women, as Stewart might have done, the *Condition and Character* tract blamed it on the "disease" of heathenism, which "plunged" heathen societies into "ignorance," "pollution and wickedness." As much as heathen societies were said to worship created things, they did not adore their women, claimed the tract—much the opposite. The tract pointed to topsy-turvy heathen societies that forced women to do hard labor while men either performed the milder domestic tasks typically reserved for Christian women or whiled the time away. As proof, the tract cited evidence from places as far-flung as Ceylon, China, and South America. In Ceylon, "a recent traveller was surprised to see strong and healthy men engaged in washing, ironing, preparing muslin dresses, and other similar employments, while slender females were passing the streets, carrying heavy burdens, or laboring in the fields." Meanwhile, in China, women were forced to "perform the duties of boatmen" and of "agricultural labor, frequently with an infant on their backs," while "their husbands are gaming, or otherwise idling away their time." One observer was shocked to see a "wife dragging the light plough, or harrow, while the husband was performing the easier task of sowing the seed." Similarly, a "Jesuit missionary assures us, that he has seen a woman and an ass yoked together to the same plough, while the inhuman husband was guiding it and driving his team." All of this made life nearly unbearable for heathen women, claimed the tract, rendering their decision to kill their own infant girls understandable if deplorable.[21]

The tract used one South American "Indian mother" as a spokesperson for "the condition of millions of her sex." Upon being censured by a missionary "for the destruction of her female infants," the mother supposedly said, "I would to God, father, I would to God, that my mother had by death prevented the distresses I endure and have yet to endure, as long as I live." Complaining about the menial labor women faced while their husbands hunted for pleasure and got drunk, she continued, "And what have we to comfort us for slavery that has no end? A young wife is brought in upon us, who is permitted to abuse us and our children, because we are no longer

Condition and Character of Females in Pagan and Mohammedan Countries
(New York: American Tract Society, 183[?]). In *Tracts of the American Tract
Society: General Series* (New York: American Tract Society, various dates).
Princeton Theological Seminary.

regarded. Can human nature endure such tyranny? What kindness can we
show to our female children equal to that of relieving them from such oppression, more bitter a thousand times than death? I say again, would to
God my mother had put me under ground the moment I was born."[22] The
anonymous woman's words are filtered through the memory and mores of
the missionary, who hears what he wants to hear: that heathens have it all
wrong when it comes to the organization of society; that women are forced
into drudgery while heathen men enjoy themselves; and that as a result heathens are mired in a death spire whereby, eventually, women and girl
children will be no more, men will have no one to take care of things, and
society will be unable to reproduce itself.

The image accompanying the tract illustrates its assumptions about wom-
anhood and religion. It offers a cloistered scene: a woman with pale skin
and white clothing lounges on a mat against a tufted pillow, at first glance
suggesting the supposed heathen laziness to which Stewart had alluded. But
the woman is also looking out a minuscule window, through which beams
of light illuminate her face and reveal the darkness in which she lies. Instead of a scene of laziness, the image might alternatively be read as a scene

of subjection and imprisonment. A poor woman, whose innate virtue and innocence are signaled to an audience accustomed to the imagery of white-as-pure, is forced into a sordid situation. She has been caged and corrupted. It is heathenism, not skin color or civilizational status, that imposes this condition of sexual and menial slavery on women and that makes the heathen mother so woeful and so willing to kill her own daughters.

Heathens need Christians to save them, not just spiritually but also physically, then. For though women are "designed by their Creator to belong to the fairest and loveliest portion of the human race," they are in heathen lands "despised, oppressed, and sunk down in pollution and guilt," a situation whose deadly ramifications reverberated throughout heathen societies. But the damage was reversible, the tract assured readers. Offering proof from Tahiti, the tract said, "The mild influence of Christianity has effected the entire abolition of infanticide, and revived the parental affection and tenderness originally implanted in the human bosom. The mother, who had been guilty of destroying her helpless offspring, may now be seen coming into the place of public worship with her little babe in her arms, gazing with evident tenderness upon its smiling countenance."[23] The message was clear: Christianity could unheathenize and restore suffering societies, saving women and their babies from servitude and death.

"He Will Be Taught to Worship False Gods"

But to return to our "Hindoo" baby once more: he is a boy, so he lives. What happens to him then? Is it really so lucky for him that he is spared by his "heathen mother"? Not so, the Sunday School Union book maintained. For "if the infant lives, he will be taught to worship false gods." He will learn that "there are three hundred million of gods, some black and others white; some red and others blue . . . some like to men, and some to monkeys. . . . He will be told that they quarrel and fight with one another; that they lie, steal, and commit murder."[24] And he will be told, the story suggested, that this is all well and good and deserving of worship and praise.

In an 1845 ordination sermon boldly titled *The Theory of Missions to the Heathen*, Rufus Anderson, secretary of the American Board of Commissioners for Foreign Missions and influential theorist of missions, contended that there were two kinds of errant minds that characterized the heathen world. In "those heathen nations which make the greatest pretensions to learning, as in India, we find but little truth existing on any subject." The "Hindoo" baby might receive training in "history, chronology, geography, astronomy," but educated heathens' ideas of such were "exceedingly destitute of truth," as were "their notions of matter and mind, and their views of creation and providence, religion and morals." In such nations, it was "*plenitude of error*" with which the missionary had to deal— "the unrestrained accumulations and perversions of depraved intellect for three thousand years." As for "savage heathens," said Anderson, "it is *vacuity of mind,* and not a *plenitude,* we have to operate upon. For the savage has few ideas, sees only the objects just about him, perceives nothing of the relations of things, and occupies his thoughts only about his physical experiences and wants. He knows nothing of geography, astronomy, history, nothing of his own spiritual nature and destiny, and nothing of God."[25] According to Anderson, both classes of heathens presented problems for the missionary: brains from the former required expunging; brains from the latter required filling.

As with infanticide, the blame for heathen ignorance was laid squarely at the foot of the "heathen mother." Nineteenth-century American readers would have learned that the mind of the heathen mother was as shackled to false gods as her body was captive to despotic husbands and social structures. Her "education is neglected," claimed the 1830s *Condition and Character* tract. "This is true of every rank and in every country where the Bible has not rescued woman from her degradation. It is a natural consequence of the contempt in which she is held."[26] Enslavement of body explained stagnation of mind, and vice versa. Heathenism created a self-perpetuating cycle of error.

Because women were responsible for raising children, the supposed ignorance of heathen mothers infected entire societies. "Human society depends upon woman for its moral tone. . . . If woman goes downward, and becomes the creature of ignorance and superstition, the entire community or nation is dragged after her—there is no help for it," wrote the Reverend Ross C. Houghton in the 1877 *Women of the Orient: An Account of the Religious, Intellectual, and Social Condition of Women in Japan, China, India, Egypt, Syria, and Turkey.* "Heathenism insists upon her becoming, and forever remaining, man's helpless, trembling slave." Houghton declared that "woman, more than man, perpetuates [the] idolatry" of heathenism. For "religion is largely left to the women. The majority of strict worshipers in most heathen temples are women. . . . Crafty priests are much more successful in working upon the superstitious credulity of women than men."[27] The trope of the easily preyed-on and ignorant woman was not exclusive to the heathen world; it was also familiar to antebellum Americans wary of confidence men and snake oil salesmen who sold the promises of salvation for the adoration and money of female flocks.[28] While overly charismatic

Protestants could come under suspicion, it was more often Catholics and Mormons who earned such scorn and who were smeared with allegations of sexual impropriety. They were also painted with the broad brush of heathenism.

The *Condition and Character* tract upped the ante by spelling out what some "heathen" priests required of their female proselytes. Because women were "superstitious," a "natural consequence of their ignorance," they easily became "the dupes of the most detestable and wicked impositions from their impious priests, the Brahmins." Citing an anonymous American missionary, the tract accused the priests of assault in the name of helping women to overcome infertility. Priests would instruct barren women to "remain in the temple during the night, performing their devotions," and "if their worship is accepted they will be visited by the god. They return home without the least suspicion of the horrid deception practiced upon them by the Brahmins, supposing that they have had intercourse with the deity of the temple." And this was just on ordinary occasions: "during the festival months," the missionary accused, "there is one vast scene of impurity and wickedness." Not surprising, editorialized the pamphlet, for the heathen are *"generally guilty of the transgression of the seventh commandment"* (thou shalt not commit adultery). Polygamous heathen men had multiple wives either locked up or doing hard labor for them. But "in violating the laws of morality, they act in perfect obedience to the dictates of their religion," for their gods and priests did much the same.[29] Again, Romans 1, with its injunction about heathens reducing the incorruptible God to corruptible creeping things, loomed large.

"This Is Heathenism"

In some cases, the consequences of heathenism were imagined to be so severe that they could turn the heathen into the living dead and damned. In his 1870 *Letters from India, China, and Turkey,* Bishop Edward Thomson of the Methodist Episcopal Church connected hell in the life to come with a hellish existence now. He wrote, "Oriental idolatry has touched bottom. As I stood in the holy city of Benares, every sense disgusted, and every feeling merged in indignation, contemplating the stupidity, the odiousness, the obscenity, the discord, the beastliness of that center of pagan worship, I thought, Surely it can get no lower without opening the mouth of hell." Drawing on the degeneration theory of heathen origins, Thomson "exclaimed within myself, 'Almighty God! to what depths of darkness and depravity are thy rational creatures capable of descending, when they turn away from the revelation of love and mercy!'" Heathens did not originally have disgusting, obscene, and bestial bodies—they had sunken into that state. Continuing with his alignment of heathenness with hellishness, Thomson said, "As I looked upon a Fakir seated by the Ganges, naked, haggard, worn to a skeleton, and covered with ashes, I thought I knew what it is to be damned."[30] White observers like Thomson liberally salted their accounts of suffering heathen bodies with their own reactions of dismay, disgust, and pity. Asserting such sensations created distance between them and the people they described for readers back home, and taught readers how they should react, too.

The bodily effects of heathenism were understood to differ depending on whether one lived in Anderson's regions with "pretensions to education" or in his regions of "vacuous savagery." In the former zones, where idolatrous heathen mothers raised societies of benighted heathen people, purposeful self-mutilation was said to be the result of heathens fruitlessly trying to "obtai[n] the favor of their gods, and [be] happy after death."[31] In the latter regions, less-than-purposeful bodily harm was thought to result from the ignorance of heathens who lived like animals and suffered from exposure to the elements. In both zones, disease was also rampant because heathens failed to understand its root cause, ascribing it to angry gods and spirits instead of to maltreated God-given bodies. And in both regions, too, heathens were thought to evince a lack of charity toward the sick and dying, preferring to selfishly focus on their own vain hopes for salvation or bodily preservation rather than on ameliorating the pain of those around them.

The author of *What Will Become of the Baby?* used popular tropes about Hinduism in India to demonstrate the disastrous bodily effects of heathenism: "Some roll on the ground after a great car, or chariot, on which an ugly idol is placed. Others roll over and over for many miles, till they reach some spot where a temple stands. Some have large hooks passed through the tender parts of their backs, and are then drawn up to the top of a high pole, where they swing aloft in the air. Many stand between two fires and are sadly scorched; or wear large iron collars on their necks; or stretch themselves on beds of spikes."[32] Rather than read bodily mortifications as evidence of great piety, nineteenth-century Protestants largely interpreted them as evidence of religion gone awry. "Poor creatures!" wrote an "Aunt Margaret" in another children's story about "the heathen." "They think that this is the way to have their sins forgiven,—the way to get to heaven." The accompanying illustration showed a half-clothed heathen man grown so stiff in his unrelenting idol worship that his upraised arm "grows that way and [he] cannot put it down again."[33] Such an interpretation of bodily expiations was colored by anti-Catholic sentiment, which

The Heathen.   p. 59.

"The Heathen." In *Aunt Margaret's Twelve Stories, to Illustrate and Impress Important Truths* (1856; Philadelphia: American Sunday-School Union, 1893). Library Company of Philadelphia.

held Protestants to rightly focus on interior belief while Catholics—who had insufficiently separated from ancient heathen practices—wrongly fixated on exterior bodily penances in vain attempts to save themselves.

"Strange as all this may seem to us," the Sunday School Union story opined, "the cruel religion of the Hindoos teaches them to do such things; and who can tell but that some of them may be done by the tender little babe now gently sleeping at its mother's side?" This "tender little babe" might also grow up to neglect his own mother as he focused on "obtaining the favor of their gods, and of being happy after death." Said the text, "Should the little babe become a man he will worship the river Gunga. He will believe that the sight or the touch of its waters will take away sin. Or, it may be, that to the banks of this river he will bring his mother when sick, or old, or near to death, and will make her drink of the stream and will rub her body with its mud; and there on the edge of the river he will leave her to perish." At least the text implied that this babe, grown into a man, might try to help his mother, albeit misguidedly.[34]

The same was not assumed of or granted to other parts of the heathen world. Where India was thought to represent a more "civilized" heathen zone, White travelers in regions they described as "savage" (per Anderson's dichotomy) rendered their inhabitants barely better than animals. *The Gospel among the Bechuanas* connected blighted landscapes to suffering bodies, describing the "degraded heathen" of South Africa as almost entirely focused on bare subsistence. As a result, they supposedly gave little thought to anything else and "kn[ew] no God, kn[ew] nothing of eternity." Even animals were thought to have more pity on their sick and dying than the heathen. Because the "poorer classes" were "struggling for existence," Robert Moffat claimed that "when the aged become too weak to provide for themselves," they are "not unfrequently abandoned by their own children, with a meal of victuals and a cruse of water, to perish in the desert. . . . In one instance I observed a small broken earthenware vessel, in which the last draught of water had been left. 'What is this?' I said, pointing to the stakes, addressing Africaner. His reply was, 'This is heathenism;' and then described this patricidal custom." This was an "awful exhibition of human depravity," as Moffat put it, "when children compel their parents to perish for want, or to be devoured by beasts of prey in a desert, from no other motive than sheer laziness, or to get rid of those on whose breast they hung in helpless infancy."[35] The assumption that "sheer laziness" was the reason for leaving parents to die echoes similar claims made about infanticidal mothers and parents. And so the sorry lot of the heathen came full-circle in the imagination of the Anglo-Protestant missionary. Heathenism taught parents to abandon their children and children their parents. Whether in China or India, Hawai'i or South Africa, and whether primarily idolatrous or primarily ignorant, "this is heathenism," and the consequences redounded to heathen bodies in similar ways.

"To Save Some of These Races from Entire Annihilation"

But in the Protestant imagination, the heathen were not thought to be unsavable, whether in body or soul. Just as with the soil, so bodies and souls were linked, and changing one promised to change the other. Mission theorist Rufus Anderson maintained that the healing of souls *must* precede the healing of bodies, but missionaries on the ground were deeply troubled by the physical suffering they believed to be a manifestation of heathenism.[36]

They hoped that medical interventions might have a greater immediate impact, or perhaps even open the door to gospel preaching. As London missionary Richard Marley put it in his 1860 *Medical Missionaries; Or, Medical Agency Cooperative with Christian Missions to the Heathen,* "The Missionary message is the ultimatum, the essential of salvation; but the Medical office capacitates for its more effectual discharge, its readier reception, its swifter extension." Marley recounted the "pregnant testimony" of a missionary who wished he had had medical training "when visiting a sick Indian, sinking rapidly through want of proper treatment." Said the sick man's father, "You talk of your God being so powerful and good, . . . yet there lies my son, and yet you are unable to obtain any help from him for my son!" Marley editorialized that had "the Medical Missionary been present, capable of administering remedies permitted to arrest the premature stroke of death, could there be a question of the comparative influence of the two different agencies on the Missionary result?"[37]

One of the authorities Marley cited was medical missionary Daniel J. Macgowan, who served in China under the American Baptist Board of Foreign Missions. In October 1842, Macgowan gave a talk before the Temperance Society of the College of Physicians and Surgeons of the University of the State of New York, outlining the "claims of the missionary enterprise on the medical profession." Macgowan wanted to rally his audience to the missionary cause, so he reminded his listeners that "it is frequently the indispensable duty and the highest triumph of the accomplished practitioner to heal the maladies of the body, by attacking the mental influence which has produced or exasperated them." For "the reciprocal action and reaction of the informing spirit upon the material frame it occupies . . . are so intimate, that religious belief and all kindred subjects become thus for certain purposes, and within certain limits the legitimate object of medical inquiry." Macgowan staked space for doctors in matters of the soul, and for the missionary "as a fellow laborer in the fields of science."[38]

The mental influence at play in the missionary enterprise was heathenism. The physician, claimed Macgowan, "cannot but feel more sensibly than any other class, the cruelties of heathenism, and the butchery of those tender mercies which it affords to the sick and the dying." Citing evidence from China, Macgowan said that even "though she has attained the highest degree of civilization, of which a nation is capable without the gospel, [China] presents perhaps more physical suffering, from want of medical knowledge, than any other portion of the globe." Their physicians are "ignorant," he said, but worse than that was the "neglect and indifference on the part of those who surround the sick bed." Citing additional evidence from the kinds of textual sources featured in this chapter, Macgowan sketched an entire heathen world whose maltreatment of the body, and lack of care for their own sick and dying, necessitated Western intervention. He re-hashed familiar tropes about "the sick Hindoo" choked "with handfuls of the mud of the Ganges" and left to die by "his murderous relations," and about sick Hawaiians whose restorative food, prepared by missionaries for their recovery, was instead "devoured by their friends."[39]

What was it about heathenism that caused this supposed level of igno-rance about the body? According to Macgowan, heathens' bodily neglect traced all the way back to biblical times: "Ancient heathenism knew not the orphan-house, the infirmary, or the hospital. To *Christianity* we owe *these*, and the healing art must ever cherish a grateful sympathy in the labors that extend this beneficent religion." The idea that Christianity alone was charitable was a popular one in the nineteenth-century English-speaking world. If Christianity was the opposite of heathenism, as Anglo Protestants wanted to believe, then it stood to reason that everything heathenism was, Christianity was not. So while heathenism taught that sickness was caused by evil spirits and angry idols who needed to be placated in ways that harmed rather than healed the body, Christianity taught that God granted to humans the ability to find scientifically based medical treatments to ad-dress the body's ills. Indeed, God called on physicians, "in imitation of the Saviour, 'to heal all manner of diseases.'"[40] Prayer was fine but not exces-sive prayer or bodily penances: trust was key. And while heathenism taught selfishness and neglect of the sick and dying, Christianity taught charity and the love of neighbors writ large.

The problem was that this did not actually hold true. Macgowan himself admitted that heathens could not be entirely to blame for their precarious bodily straits: "Many regions of the pagan world are at this time enduring fearful miseries, which they trace directly and undeniably to their intercourse with our commerce and our civilization. The voyager has often discovered some far island of the deep, only to corrupt and enslave its inhabitants" and to introduce "novel and hideous diseases." Macgowan even acknowl-edged that although they had inherited a lack of charity from ancient hea-thenism, heathen bodies were not intrinsically different from Christian ones, or even necessarily inferior. It was "our people" who have "entailed upon pagans some of the most loathsome and frightful contagions to which the human frame is liable, in this way mutilating their manly forms, poisoning their offspring, and rapidly depopulating the beautiful islands they inhabit." British opium and American rum, Western diseases and weapons—not just misguided beliefs—had ruined the noble forms that God had originally given the heathen. So Western doctors had a threefold duty to care and intervene: first "from regard to the heathen as members of the great brotherhood of man," second because the West was not off the hook for the suffering heathens faced, and third because Western doctors had "in our power in a measure" the ability to "save some of these races from entire annihilation."[41]

But Western "help" was not always welcome, and when it was rejected, heathen intransigence was blamed, not Western civilization. Dr. Kate C. Bushnell, who also served as a medical missionary to China later in the century, was less than forgiving when she described a case of what, to her, was an avoidable death due to misguided belief. Writing for *Heathen Woman's Friend*, a monthly newsletter published by the Woman's Foreign Missionary Society of the Methodist Episcopal Church, Bushnell larded her narrative with frustration and exasperation sufficient to convey a deep sense of her own superiority and right(eous)ness. She recounted how a man had asked her to help his sick wife. She was at first pleasantly surprised to find that the husband and wife lived in "the best native house [she] had ever entered," an "unusually cleanly looking, well-built Chinese home." But she "had not been in the house long before discovering that heathen darkness and stupidity were not less familiar to this household of wealth and leisure than to the meanest hut [she] had ever entered." Bushnell swooped in and discovered that the woman's "case was one of unusual severity." She administered aid and then left for supper with the stern injunction that the woman needed "good nursing." "In accordance with Chinese stupidity," however, the family "were unmindful of everything else" Bushnell said once she informed them that the woman's "chances for life" were "slight."[42]

Given the long odds for survival, the family turned to the supernatural to save the woman—something Methodists might well have done under similar circumstances, though Bushnell did not acknowledge as much. Feeling concerned that "the woman would be neglected," she decided to return to the house after dinner. Bushnell's description of what followed is laden with sensory detail. It was a "very dark, cold, rainy night," and her "chair coolies" had to "pi[ck] their way through the mud and water" in order to get her to her destination. Once there, she heard the sound of "screaming and crying" and found "the first room illuminated and crowded with men, boys, and women, who were engaged in worshipping a huge brass idol." Bushnell believed that the loudest one, who was "throwing himself about in a most frantic and idiotic style," was "evidently hired for the purpose." Catching a few words here and there, she understood him to be saying "prayers for the evil spirit to leave the sick woman."[43]

Passing through the "confusion and excitement," Bushnell entered the sick room, where she was "dismay[ed] to find the patient sitting on the edge of a bed in this cold, damp, room, half naked, feet almost bare, shivering with cold, and groaning with agony." Bushnell determined that the family meant to bring the brass idol in, so that the sick woman could "prostrate herself before it." Bushnell prayed. Asking for "wisdom and prudence," she told the family that they must "choose quickly now between [her] advice or the worship of the idol." Adopting a sternly maternalistic tone, she continued, "If I doctor you, you must stop all this excitement *at once,* and get into a warm bed. See! I am ready to depart. Shall I go or stay?" The family was clearly skeptical about the doctor's ability to cure their loved one, given her pessimistic assessment of the woman's health. They allowed her to stay but did not unquestioningly accept her advice. Where Bushnell prescribed broth and Western medicine, the family proffered pork and rice. When the wife ultimately died "in heathen blackness and despair," Bushnell concluded that her demise was caused by heathen idolatry, hardheadedness, and neglect, while the family blamed the "foreign doctor," whom they deemed "a fool." Bushnell framed her entire encounter with this woman and her family as a spiritual battle over a heathen body, titling her article for the *Heathen Woman's Friend* "Competing with an Idol."[44]

"We Almost Forget That They Have Been Heathen"

But when Western medicine worked, it could be an effective way to create converts from heathens. Creating converts meant more than fixing souls, despite what Anderson might say: it meant producing healthful bodies, properly clothed bodies, and efficiently laboring bodies that conformed to Western gender roles. After detailing the sorry life of the "Hindoo" baby if left to rot in the imagined sinkhole of heathenism, *What Will Become of the Baby?* took a choose-your-own-adventure turn to "dwell on more pleasing and hopeful" prospects:

> *What may become of the baby?*
> A missionary from England or America may cross the stormy seas, and travel far up in the country, "in perils by land, in perils by water, in perils among the heathen"; and at last he may come to the village where lives the little babe when grown to be a little boy.
> The missionary stands under the shade of a tree, and preaches to the heathen.[45]

The missionary has caught the child just as his heathen mother is about to fill his brain to the brim with idolatrous errors. The missionary preaches that "the idols cannot save" and that "Jesus Christ is the only Saviour," who is "able and willing and waiting to save *them*." It takes "many visits" before "some destroy their idols" and desire to learn more. The missionary decides to stay; he builds a "school-house for the children of the heathen; and among the first scholars is that little boy of whom we now speak." The boy learns to read the Bible and throws away "the wicked shasters, or sacred books of the Hindoos." His brain packed with Christian teachings, he "grows into early manhood," when he makes a definitive declaration for Christ and "boldly stands forth in the midst of the heathen as a disciple of Christ." After which he himself becomes a missionary and "goes among his own people to tell them of the great change he feels. . . . What a contrast is there."[46]

The fictional and hypothetical *What Will Become of the Baby?* did not spell out the bodily transformations the converted boy was supposed to experience, though they were certainly implied in the contrasting way the story outlined the ill effects of heathenism. Other texts, ostensibly about real people and real situations, were more explicit about the salutary effects that conversion was supposed to have on heathen bodies. One story, recounted in an obituary for Yankton Sioux (Ihanktonwan Dakota Oyate) patriarch Francis (Saswe) Deloria, also involved a case of spiritual warfare over a sick woman, but this one ended in a strikingly different way from the situation so exasperatedly described by Bushnell. Deloria and his wife were members of the Episcopal Church when she was "taken very ill," and "no one expected her to recover." The obituary, written by missionary Joseph Witherspoon Cook, explained, "If there is anything more than all others which tries the principles of our Indian converts, it is times of sickness." Sensing weakness in the face of desperation and death, "conjurors" would "come with bold assertions that they know just what is the matter, just where the evil spirit lurks, and that unless they are allowed to practice their art the person will undoubtedly die. One can well see that with an ignorant and superstitious people such argument would be most powerful, because the appeal is to their fears and deals with the unknown." But Cook noted with satisfaction that Deloria "drove them away, saying, that he had chosen the white man's way, and that if his wife died in it it was all right; that the whites who know more than the Dakotas about medicine and disease were doing all they could for her; and that being Christians they would not go back to the worship of the devil."[47]

Deloria (as filtered through Cook) expressed particular distaste for the "women" who, "as is their custom, came to mourn and bewail [his wife], not out of love and respect for her, but hoping to seize upon all the goods of the family." According to Cook, Deloria "drove them all away," railing against their wails as "the devil's works." The sounds produced by heathen bodies could only be interpreted by the Christian as evil and insincere, much as Bushnell viewed the "screaming and crying" around the Chinese woman's sickbed as disorderly and disgusting rather than distraught. It is ultimately a spiritual remedy that cures Mrs. Deloria: "I [Cook] visited her and at her request administered to her the Holy Communion, and to the astonishment of all she began to recover." Deloria's faithfulness in casting out the medicine men and castigating the wailing women is rewarded with his wife's restored health; according to Cook, he "has several times since spoken of the matter and said that the whole history of the case had been such as greatly to strengthen the faith of them all in the Divine power of our holy religion and in the efficacy of prayer."[48]

Deloria himself had been a medicine man "in heathen darkness" (Cook's words) before his conversion.[49] Evidence from his descendants suggests that his turn to Christianity was motivated as much by practical concerns—of which healing was a key component—as by doctrinal affinity. Deloria had been baptized in 1871 and had sent his children to the Yankton mission school. His son, Philip Joseph Deloria, became an Episcopal priest; his grandson, Vine Deloria Sr., did likewise, while his granddaughter, Ella Deloria, became an anthropologist. Perhaps most famously, Francis's great-grandson, Vine Deloria Jr., after studying theology with plans to enter the ministry, became a prominent scholar and activist, author of *God Is Red: A Native View of Religion* (considered in Chapter 10), among many other books. According to Vine Jr., his great-grandfather accepted the missionaries' presence because he "saw that they represented the kind of life that the Yanktons would have to live in the future," and since "the Yanktons were now restricted to a small tract of land, they would have to support themselves in the white man's way."[50] Baptism held promise for Francis as a "ritual for healing." As a young man, Francis had killed four men with "legitimate" reason ("two of the cases involved in-laws who were wife beaters").[51] But every time he tried to drink a cup of water or coffee thereafter, Vine Jr. explained that Francis would see the faces of the men he had killed as "reflections, taunting him and uttering threats only he could hear." Francis "consulted the other Yankton medicine men about a cure for this condition," but to no avail. It was only after his baptism, at a celebratory feast to mark the occasion, that Francis "looked in his coffee cup and for the first time in years did not see any of the dead man's faces."[52] For Francis, it was baptism—just as it was Holy Communion in the case of his wife—that "provided the cure that eluded the Yankton medicine men."[53]

Converted heathen bodies were not only supposed to be internally transformed and (sometimes) healed, they were externally different, too. Often, this was signaled through a change in attire that—in the eyes of believers—allowed the erstwhile heathen's body to be restored to its original God-given propriety and dignity. Rufus Anderson recounted one such story in his *Memoir of Catharine Brown,* about a young Cherokee woman who became one of the nineteenth century's most famous converts at the Brainerd Mission School in Tennessee. Ironically, such memoirs—heavily edited and written over by missionaries—were often published after the untimely death of the convert, suggesting that not only heathen bodies but also Christian ones were subject to illness and premature passing. As much as medical missionaries lambasted heathens for their misunderstanding of disease and proper care, conversion did not actually promise good health, and exposure to European diseases could instead hasten demise. Memoirs of converts often took the form of heathen hagiographies, lamenting the premature loss of the saved but reassuring readers that their deaths were not in vain.

In the case of Catharine Brown, who died of tuberculosis at the age of twenty-three, Anderson used his own assumptions about heathen "vacuousness" to fill in what he thought Brown knew before her conversion: "her acquaintance with the *geographical features of the earth* . . . must have been exceedingly vague and limited"; "her apprehensions respecting the *human race* were so imperfect, that she supposed her own people a distinct order of beings"; and "her knowledge of *history*" was so "exceedingly confined" that past ages "must have been to her almost as much a blank, as ages that were to come." Not only did Christian education fill her brain with the Bible as "the wisest, most sure, most comprehensive history of man," Anderson claimed; it also gave her a new understanding of "worlds and suns and systems . . . wheeling, at the command of their Creator, through immensity," and of her own body as "of one blood" with the rest of humankind.[54]

All of these changes were internal. Anderson also cited evidence of the external changes wrought on Brown. He quoted at length a letter from Jeremiah Evarts, treasurer of the Board of Missions, who visited Brainerd to see the Cherokee children "lately rescued from heathenism." Brown, he noted, had once been "vain, and excessively fond of dress, wearing a profusion of ornaments in her ears." But after spending time at the mission school, "her trinkets have gradually disappeared, till only a single drop remains in each ear." Now, said Evarts, "if you were to see her at a boarding-school in New-England, . . . you would not distinguish her from well-educated females of the same age, either by her complexion, features, dress, pronunciation, or manners." The only thing that did make her stand apart was "her more than common simplicity and humility." Another man "favourably impressed" by Brown's "personal appearance" was Dr. Alexander

A. Campbell, with whose family she lived for several months. From a "wild, untutored girl," he wrote, she had become "graceful and polite, and benevolence beamed from her countenance. Some of my acquaintance were unwilling to believe she was an Indian."[55] The loss of Brown's ornamentation and her Christian education had essentially deracinated her in the eyes of Evarts and Campbell. They did not read race solely in terms of skin color but saw race as a constellation of religion, comportment, dress, speech, and complexion. The first four could be taught, while complexion could literally pale under the influence of Christian education.

Methodist Episcopal missionary bishop William Taylor explained why the loss of heathen ornamentation was so meaningful. Though he wrote in and about a different context (South Africa in the late nineteenth century), the idea that the heathen world was the same across time and space made his remarks more widely applicable. According to Taylor, taking off jewels and trinkets signified not only a changed fashion sense but also a wholly new sense of self. "There's a heathen doctor among the seekers," said he, "decorated with strings of beads, shells, and all sorts of trinkets and charms. He feels that these things are hindering his approach to Christ, and now he scatters them." Taylor claimed that none of the missionaries had asked the doctor and other seekers to do so, but that the seekers had themselves realized that "these are not simply the ornaments of their half-naked bodies" but "were the badges of their heathenism, their gods and charms, in which they trusted for health, good crops, good luck in hunting, deliverance from their enemies, and all those demands of human nature which God only can supply. Hence in accepting Christ they violently tear these idols off and cast them away." Yanking off the "badges of their heathenism" also changed their demeanors: "Many of those who an hour ago were roaring in the disquietude of their souls are now sitting quietly at the feet of Jesus with tearful eyes and smiling faces."[56]

Charles Stewart, the missionary to Hawai'i who had so lambasted the unfeelingness of heathen mothers, also celebrated the visible changes wrought in converts as evidence of their internal transformation. Visiting a man named Kaikioeva and his wife, Keaweamahi, Stewart commented favorably on the "neat and ornamental" furniture that they enjoyed, including a "handsome cabinet" and a "Chinese sofa," a "very large mahogany dining table," a "handsome card table and dressing case," and "a large and expensive mirror."[57] Such furnishings contrasted with the simple "huts" that Hawaiians had lived in before Western contact and that missionaries said exposed Hawaiian bodies to the warm climate and sun, rendering them "indolent."[58] But now, this husband and wife were fruitfully occupied among their bourgeois surroundings, one reading on the "Chinese sofa," and the other "writing a letter" at the "handsome cabinet." They "were both clothed in loose dresses, made in the European fashion; and in their persons, more in the furniture of their apartment, presented a strong contrast to the appearance they made but a year or two since, when seen only in unblushing nakedness: and when, they knew no higher subjects of thought or occupation, than to 'eat, drink, and be merry.'" Their demeanor had also changed: where they were once hedonistic and thoughtless, they were now "at all times modest, dignified and interesting." They were frequent attendees of the chapel and, "not unfrequently, are seen bathed in tears, under the preaching of the Gospel of Jesus Christ." Indeed, said Stewart, Kaikioeva's and Keaweamahi's characters were "so consistent with Christian propriety and purity, that, in our intercourse with them, we almost forget that they have been heathen."[59]

Of Markets and Men

And so visual transformation can be bought: living among nice things encourages the wearing of decent (in the eyes of Europeans) clothing; wearing decent clothing lends itself to dignified and useful behavior; dignified and useful behavior softens the sentiments so that tears can emerge where unfeelingness once reigned. And the heathen is forgotten (almost).

Creating a desire for European clothing also created a market for European cloth and a need for laborers to render it into garments. Missionary Mary Moffat "impress[ed] on [South African women] the necessity for abandoning their heathen dress," which consisted of "the skins of goats, sheep, and gazelles." "The *men* formed the skins into garments, no woman being ever known to attempt such a feat." Women had instead been accustomed to "building houses and raising fences." These reversed gender roles, as we have seen, were not acceptable to the missionaries, who saw them as inefficient and unfair to weaker women. Before the Moffats began their work, the local women mocked the European textiles brought by traders. But at the same time that her husband, Robert, was preaching the gospel and translating the Bible, Mary taught the women to believe that they were immodestly clothed. The "same Gospel which had taught them that they were spiritually miserable, and blind, and naked, discovered to them also that they needed to reform externally" and "to adopt those modes of comfort and cleanliness which they had been accustomed to view only as the peculiarities of a strange people." Soon the women began to clamor for European garments. Mary Moffat obliged by opening a sewing school. The women learned to wield a fine needle instead of "the handle of a pickaxe" or "trowel." After a while, "the demand for European produce [became] so great, that . . . something like three hundred thousand pounds' worth of goods annually pass[ed] through the missionary stations into the interior." Changing the women's clothing preferences not only revised gender roles and turned women into delicate textile rather than hard manual laborers, it also created a new, thriving market for European cloth where previously traders "could not obtain a single purchaser."[60] Heathen souls are cleansed; heathen bodies are cleaned and clothed; heathen women and men become efficient laborers at gender-appropriate tasks; European missionaries and traders, their pockets newly heavy, rejoice.

For White missionary boosters, then, conversion could make the heathen almost unrecognizable from the Christian. In the case of some exemplary converts, it could practically erase race in the eyes of the White beholder. We can best understand this effect if we see race-making as an ongoing process of differentiation between supposedly "superior" and "inferior" groups. Whiteness signified "superior" status based on "right" religion, which was supposed to have reverberating effects on governance, gender roles, education, medicinal practices, clothing choices, and labor on the land. For nineteenth-century Protestants, their religion was the master key that unlocked the other benefits that made White Americans the self-appointed teachers of the heathen. Once the heathen converted, they could theoretically claim access to these benefits of Whiteness, which has always meant more than skin color alone. But in reality, many converts continued to face suspicion over the genuineness of their conversions and were labeled with the oxymoronic terms "heathen converts" or "converted heathens" even after joining the church. Meanwhile, converts could turn the concept of the heathen back on White Christians to critique racism and hypocrisy. The blurriness of the categories of Christian and heathen underscores the instability of race, with particular consequences for the constitution of the American body politic.

PART II

The Body Politic

While White missionaries never tired of telling triumphant tales of heathen conversion, converts to Christianity also narrated their transformations in their own words, selectively adopting and rejecting the valences carried by the concept of heathenism. Uchimura Kanzō's *Diary of a Japanese Convert* is illustrative of the complicated relationship between the converting body and the American body politic. Born in Edo (now Tokyo), Japan, in 1861, and educated at Sapporo Agricultural College, Amherst College, and (briefly) Hartford Theological Seminary, Uchimura became known for founding the Mukyokai-shugi (Non-church Movement), an independent, "nonsacramental, largely nonliturgical mode of church life in implied criticism of historic Western Christianity."[1] His *Diary,* published in New York in 1895, was lauded as "the only book of the kind ever published in any language. . . . It touches upon many vital questions connected with Christian missions in 'heathen' lands."[2]

Uchimura knew that "the conversion of a heathen is always a matter of wonder." He maintained control over his own narrative and—to the extent that others read him as representative—that of other so-called heathens too. For Uchimura, conversion entailed a deliberate and considered undertaking of spiritual growth.[3] In contrast to missionary reports of heathen conversions, which often told of immediate night-to-day transformations as the heathen woke up to the obvious error of their ways, Uchimura depicted his conversion as a "slow and gradual process," which he painstakingly logged in his diary as a "biologist" might keep track of "all the morphological and physiological changes of a soul in its embryological development from a seed to a full-eared corn." Even at the point of writing, Uchimura professed uncertainty as to "whether I may yet find my present position to be still heathenish." He blurred the lines between the Christian and the heathen throughout his *Diary,* refusing, for instance, to denigrate his unconverted family members. His grandfather, he said, "was essentially an honest man." As for his grandmother, "a pathos there is in 'heathenism' so noble as hers. . . . Let the Spirit of God alone mould her, and no ill shall come to her well-tried soul."[4]

Uchimura was cognizant of sensationalist stories about heathen bodies that saturated Protestant print media, some of which he countenanced and others not. He thanked God that he had "never . . . tasted human flesh, or prostrated [him]self before the wheels of Juggernaut, or witnessed infants fed to gavials." Yet even as he nodded to these stereotypes, he maintained that heathenism was not all bad. "Our ideal mothers and wives and sisters are not very inferior to the conception of the highest Christian woman-hood," he wrote. Moreover, "I was spared much of mammonism, of the fearful curse of rum-traffic, so common in other *doms* than heathendoms. . . . That excitement and rush of the so-called Christendom which whirls men and women into premature graves was unknown to me. If heathenism is the reign of darkness, it is the reign of moon and stars, of obscure lights no doubt, but withal of repose and comparative innocence."[5] In Uchimura's rendering, heathen darkness was no damnable offense or terrifying abyss: rather, it was the quiet and peaceful gloaming of eventide.

Since he found much to admire in heathenism, Uchimura was slow to leave it behind. At Sapporo Agricultural College, he was the last of his class to convert. Everyone else found their way to Christian affiliation under the influence of the college's New England faculty. Uchimura "alone was left a 'heathen,' the much detested idolater, the incorrigible worshipper of wood and stones." Finally, he was "forced" to sign the "Covenant of Believers in Jesus" at Sapporo Agriculture. This went "against my will, and I must con-fess, somewhat against my conscience too." But even as he resented being forced into Christianity, the new faith changed him. Polytheism, as Uchimura described it, had been the worst part of heathenism. There were so many gods to propitiate that he had been lost in a "spiritual darkness . . . laboriously sustained with gross superstitions." His concern about satisfying the gods and the "contradictions" between what the various gods wanted had turned him into a "fretful timid child." Christian "monotheism made [him] a new man." No longer did he have to "appease [his] angry gods." The immediate sense of relief he felt in his newfound "spiritual freedom" created a "healthy influence upon [his] mind and body." Now, he strode confidently through the streets with his head "erect," reassured that the gods in temples could not "punish" him for failing to say prayers before each and every one. Now, instead of abstaining from certain foods, like beans and eggs, he could eat whatever he wanted. And now, instead of being distracted by heathen "superstitions," he could concentrate fully on his studies. "Re-joicing in the newly imparted activity of my body," Uchimura rhapsodized, "I roamed over fields and mountains, observed the lilies of the valley and birds of the air, and sought to commune through Nature with Nature's God."[6] For Uchimura, rejecting his former gods had significant bodily ramifications that changed his demeanor, his energy level, and his interactions with the built and natural environs in which he lived.

Even as he luxuriated in its fields and mountains, Uchimura soon became dissatisfied with Japan. "While yet a heathen, my country was to me the centre of the universe, the envy of the world." But "how opposite when I was 'converted'! . . . Soon an idea caught my mind that my country was really 'good-for nothing.' It was a heathen land which required missionaries from other countries to make it good. God of Heaven had never thought much about it." Uchimura determined to visit and study in America, convinced from what missionaries told him that it would be "a *Holy Land.*" His experience there was mixed. Arriving in 1884, he spent several years studying at Amherst College, where he grew firmer in the Christian faith and "found [him]self in a path which pointed heavenward." But he also found himself discomfited by the "great missionary meetings" held at the college and attended by thousands of interested women and men. While "these Mission-shows are inspiring," Uchimura said, "the worst lot" in them "falls to some specimens of converted heathens who happen to be there. They are sure to be made good use of, as circus-men make use of tamed rhinoceroses." These rhinoceroses, said Uchimura, are asked to "just tell us how you were converted" but only "in fifteen minutes and no more"! The rhinoceroses who "like to be seen and petted gladly obey the behest of these people" and "tell them how they ceased to be animals and began to live like men. But there are other rhinoceroses who do not like to be so used."[7]

Uchimura counted himself among the latter. How could he reduce his ongoing conversion process to a mere fifteen minutes? Why should he parade his conversion experience and his converting body before an audience? Why did missionaries always want obedient rhinoceroses to show the difference between heathenism and Christianity in the starkest of terms? "There are some people who seem to imagine that the cause of Mission can be upheld only by picturing the darkness of heathens in contrast with the light of Christians," he complained. "So they make a diagram showing heathens by jet-black squares, and Protestant Christians by white squares. Missionary Magazines, Reviews, Heralds, all are full of the accounts of the wickedness, the degrations, the gross superstitions of heathens, and scarcely any account of their nobleness, godliness, and highly Christlike characters make its way into their columns." If a convert spoke highly of their "heathenish" people, they received "no approbation." For Uchimura, this treatment of converts was not biblical. "I do not read in the Bible that Paul or Barnabus brought a Titus or a Timothy to Jerusalem for the purpose of making him sing Gentile songs, and tell the brethren there in his queer half-incomprehensible way 'how he cast his idols into fire and clung unto the

Gospel.'" Enough, said Uchimura: "I, a regenerate rhinoceros, advise the mission circus-men to be more considerate in this matter."[8] His entire *Diary* can be read as pushback against the reduction of converted bodies to grossly unnuanced entertainment meant to make Protestant Americans feel pity for the poor and deluded heathen and pride for their work in rescuing them.

Uchimura's experience in the United States—seeing how Americans treated him and other converts, witnessing how they worshiped Mammon, and most disturbingly, encountering their "strong race prejudice" against African Americans and Native Americans, and their exclusion of Chinese immigrants— shocked him out of his reverence for the land ("I was deceived!"). He moved from critiquing Americans' treatment of the converting body to critiquing the American body politic. The hypocrisy and racism he experienced in America made "Christendom appear to [him] more like heathendom" and rekindled his love for his homeland and his longing for the "Blessed Ignorance" that "satisfied [his] good grandma!": "Hers was Peace and mine is Doubt; and woe is me that I called her an idolater, and pitied her superstition. . . . I shall never defend Christianity upon its being the religion of Europe and America."[9] Uchimura's gradual conversion process, to an indigenized Christianity that did not depend on Euro-Americans, was made such not least by the "heathenish" behavior of Americans themselves.

Even as Euro-Americans were imagining the heathen world as a realm of blighted lands mired in darkness and inhabited by degenerated, diseased, and dying people, then, those very people were often more than clear-eyed on how they were being used to shore up the identity of *their* Other—the self-appointed White savior. To still affiliate with Christianity under such circumstances suggests not that converts were dupes pressured by colonial imbalances of power (though indeed such inequities should not be ignored) but that they managed to see through and to see something else in the religion on offer. Uchimura's critique raises the themes considered in Part II, of how the heathen concept could be deployed to demarcate certain groups as belonging to the body politic, others to be held at arm's length, some to be firmly excluded, and still others to be forcibly included. While White Americans imagined the heathen world as a realm beyond America's shores, they also grappled with what to do about those they considered to be heathens within the nation, others trying to come in, and those in parts of the world where the United States sought influence. But as Uchimura's application of the term suggests, the figure of the heathen or pagan could also be used to critique White Americans themselves. The stereotypes that White Americans built up around the heathen world turned the concept into a useful measure of deviance and deficiency that could be turned back on them when the United States "appear[ed] . . . more like heathendom" than the heathen world they were professing to save.

5

BAROMETER

In his *Diary,* Uchimura Kanzō recounted an anecdote that drove home for him the extent to which Americans' "race prejudice" overrode their claim to be Christian. "Down in the state of Delaware, whither I was once taken by a friend of mine as his guest," he wrote, "I was astonished to find a separate portion of a town given up wholly to negroes. Upon telling my friend that this making a sharp racial distinction appeared to me very Pagan-like, his emphatic answer was that he would rather be a Pagan and live separate from 'n——s,' than be a Christian and live in the same quarters with them!"[1] To choose to be pagan rather than live with African Americans struck Uchimura as the very antithesis of Christianity.

Uchimura was hardly the first to critique American Christendom as itself "Pagan-like" and to connect this critique to White Christian racism. In his incendiary *Appeal, in Four Articles: Together with a Preamble, to the Coloured Citizens of the World, but in Particular, and Very Expressly, to Those of the United States of America,* first published in 1829, David Walker charged that "the white Christians of America, who hold us in slavery, (or, more properly speaking, pretenders to Christianity,) treat us more cruel and barbarous than any Heathen nation did any people whom it had subjected, or reduced to the same condition." Walker had been born free in North Carolina to a free mother and enslaved father. He moved to Boston in the mid-1820s, where he operated a used-clothing store and wrote and published the *Appeal.* In it, he gave the lie to proponents of Southern slavery, who claimed that it was an extension of biblical slavery. "They tell us of the Israelites in Egypt, the Helots in Sparta, and of the Roman Slaves," he scoffed, but "those heathen nations of antiquity, had but little more among them than the name and form of slavery; while wretchedness and endless miseries were reserved, apparently in a phial, to be poured out upon our fathers, ourselves and our children, by *Christian* Americans!" Throughout the *Appeal,* Walker repeatedly found White American Christians worse than the so-called heathen they were trying to save.[2]

Walker's *Appeal* appeared in three editions before his untimely death in his early thirties in 1830. All editions were published in Boston and circulated in the South as Walker sent copies through the mail and through traveling contacts who read the *Appeal* aloud to enslaved people. Fearful of Walker's message, Southern authorities attempted to suppress it and other literature "*having a tendency* to create discontent . . . or insubordination" among free and enslaved African Americans.[3] Walker and his contacts found other ways to disseminate the *Appeal*. His Brattle Street store was usefully located close to the wharves, allowing him to sew copies into the linings of clothes that he bought and resold to sailors, and to smuggle pamphlets with other shipments.[4]

Building on Walker's critique, this chapter considers domestic uses of the "heathen" label among and as applied to Black and White populations in the United States and in the context of colonization and missionary efforts in Africa. Since missionary exploration and entertainment had long linked the heathen world to the foreign and to the inadequate, applying the term "heathen" to the domestic sphere became a rhetorically provocative way to malign the group labeled as such, whether it was White slaveholders depicting African Americans as virtual heathens in need of paternalistic oversight, or African Americans like Walker castigating White Americans as heathens for their racist hypocrisy.[5] The term "heathen" also served to mark off the boundaries of Whiteness in the United States, excluding those whose practices could be aligned with the heathen world abroad. For if heathen bodies could be regenerated through conversion, White bodies could also be contaminated through association with heathenness. It was the poor dwellers of the heathen world who were supposed to be swathed in darkness, in contrast to the lucky Protestants, of whom English-origin people believed they were the premier representatives.

In the domestic sphere, then, heathenness became a barometer of the deficient, against which to both deify and denigrate a genteel Anglo-Protestant norm, and to mark those who belonged and those whose actions made them seem to be a "foreign element" within the body politic. Diagnosing groups by the heathen barometer was a comparative move: it was not necessarily to say that they *were* heathens but to say that they *resembled* heathens in order to call into question their fitness as Americans.

"The Heathen of Our Land"

Heathenism had historically served to justify the enslavement of people of African descent. Ever-important biblical precedent held the heathenism of the Canaanites to be sufficient reason for their enslavement, and as the self-professed heirs of the Israelites, the English purported to copy their precedent. The conversion of African and African-descended enslaved persons to Christianity raised questions about whether a baptized slave should be manumitted; ultimately, planters instead decided to baptize slavery as a Christian institution. Protestant missionaries promised that Christianization would create better slaves who would be more trustworthy and hardworking as a result of conversion.[6]

By the nineteenth century, proslavery apologists picked up on this rationale with renewed vigor in response to a growing antislavery movement. They simultaneously recognized that the enslaved population was not as Christian as the ideology of Christian slavery had promised, while also continuing to laud the institution as the best means of unheathenizing and eternally saving African-descended people.[7] Charles Colcock Jones Sr. exemplified this position in his *Religious Instruction of the Negroes in the United States,* published in Savannah in 1842. Jones, a Presbyterian minister from Georgia, had been educated at Princeton Seminary. There, he had founded and helmed the Society of Inquiry Concerning Africans, which he "hoped . . . would encourage his classmates to reflect on their 'personal duties and responsibilities' to both slaves and free blacks." Jones supported missions with the enslaved population and became interested in the work of the American Colonization Society while a student at the seminary. Upon graduation and ordination, Jones returned to Liberty County, Georgia, where he eventually owned and managed three plantations while serving as a minister, professor, and missionary to enslaved people.[8]

In his *Religious Instruction of the Negroes,* Jones laid out the history of evangelization efforts with African Americans and concluded that although some had been converted, the vast majority had "been left . . . in moral darkness, and destitution of the means of grace." He contended that the "Moral and Religious Condition of the Negroes of the United States" revealed them to be "intellectually and morally a degraded people; the most so of any in the United States;—and while from their universal profession of the Christian system, and their attendance upon its ordinances of worship, and the absence of all fixed forms of idolatry, they cannot, strictly speaking be termed *heathen;* yet may they with propriety be termed the *heathen of our land.*"[9] Assessing African Americans by a heathen barometer, Jones found them to fit the bill, cataloging a host of characteristics that he believed made African Americans "the heathen of our land," including "ignorance of the doctrines and duties of Christianity," "confused" ideas about "the Supreme Being," "superstition," and "polygamy"—charges characteristically leveled against the heathen world. Jones admitted that although "the majority of them have access to some kind of means of grace, . . . they are not as efficient means as their necessities require; while multitudes of them are almost wholly destitute" and "left in next to absolute dependence upon the permission, the countenance and assistance of the whites."[10] Assuring his White readers that a focus on the spiritual condition of enslaved people would not affect their earthly status as property, Jones exhorted slaveholders to remedy the situation.

According to Jones, and in direct contrast to what Walker charged, Southern slavery was "identical" with the Old Testament slavery that the Jews had been "allowed" to practice, and "identical" with the New Testament slavery that "existed among the Greeks and Romans and Gentile nations." Therefore, the biblical precepts that governed ancient slavery applied equally well to the South and "by the providence and word of God are we under obligations to impart the Gospel to our servants." For Jones, the salvation of the slaveholder was tied to that of enslaved people: should the former neglect the souls of the latter, leading them to perish in eternal damnation, they would have to answer for it "in the day when God riseth up for judgment."[11]

Jones did not confine his arguments to the life to come; he also tapped into language about the character and consistency of White Americans in this life that would have been familiar to readers of missionary pleas in the nineteenth century. Just as the heathen world operated as a foil that allowed Americans to feel grateful and guilty for their own blessings, and as an outlet for Americans to activate their humanity through outreach to the heathen, so Jones connected his readers' treatment of the enslaved population to their own feelings of gratitude and professions of humanity. "We cannot disregard this obligation thus *divinely imposed*" to evangelize the enslaved, he wrote, "without forfeiting our humanity, our gratitude, our consistency, and our claim to the spirit of christianity itself."[12] There is a distinct echo here of Benjamin Wisner's "Have you the feelings of humanity? I wait for your reply."[13]

In the context of Southern slavery rather than the heathen world, though, "humanity" and "gratitude" carried different valences. Fully aware that his readers might not believe that "humanity" applied to the people they enslaved, Jones said otherwise, citing Christ's example of caring for even one wandering sheep. For Jones, recognizing the humanity of enslaved people was necessary in order to activate White Southerners' own claims to the same. Lest his readers be unsure of what "humanity" entailed, Jones defined it as "that kindness and good will towards our fellow creatures which prompts us to sympathize with them in their necessities and sufferings, and to exert ourselves for their relief." As for "gratitude," Jones defined it in a distinctly Southern context. Where American gratitude vis-à-vis the heathen world entailed feeling good about one's blessings as compared with the suffering world-out-there, slaveholders' gratitude, per Jones, entailed feeling indebted to the people they enslaved. For "they nurse us in infancy, . . . they constitute our wealth, and yield us all the comforts and conveniences of life." The "kindest and the most grateful return which we can make them," he maintained, "is to put them in possession of the richest gift of God to men, the Gospel of our Lord and Saviour Jesus Christ." Failure to do this, Jones warned, would "forfeit also our consistency," or the "correspondence of our conduct or practice with our professed princi- ples," and "an exceedingly rare virtue." White American inconsistency was already most glaring in the field of missions: "We have indeed assisted in sending missionaries to the heathen, thousands of miles from us; and to multitudes of destitute white settlements in our own country," Jones said. "This is all as it should be. But what have we done publicly, systematically and perseveringly for the Negroes, in order that they also might enjoy the gospel of Christ?"[14]

"To Disenthral Themselves"

Where Jones admitted inconsistency, African Americans saw outright hy- pocrisy. One of the abolitionists deeply influenced by David Walker's *Appeal* was Henry Highland Garnet, who had been born into slavery in Maryland in 1815 but escaped with his family as a child. Educated at the African Free School in New York City, at Noyes Academy in New Hamp- shire, and at the Oneida Institute in New York, Garnet became a Presbyte- rian minister and newspaper editor. Like Walker, Garnet charged his people with resisting the false narrative that slavery could save the souls of the enslaved if only slaveholders evangelized them, as Jones urged. In 1843, the year after the publication of Jones's *Religious Instruction of the Ne- groes,* at the National Convention of Colored Citizens in Buffalo, Garnet gave "An Address to the Slaves of the United States of America," exhorting them to fight back against their condition and seize their own freedom: for "if the ignorance of slavery is a passport to heaven, then it is a blessing, and no curse." Having been shut off from access to the true Word of God, the souls of the enslaved were imperiled, Garnet warned, and no false teach- ings by hypocritical enslavers would save them. They needed to free themselves.[15]

The twenty-seven-year-old minister presented a hypothetical example to illustrate his point: "If a band of heathen men should attempt to enslave a race of Christians, and to place their children under the influence of some false religion, surely, heaven would frown upon the men who would not resist such aggression, even to death." In the same way, said Garnet, if "a band of Christians should attempt to enslave a race of heathen men and to entail slavery upon them, and to keep them in heathenism in the midst of Christianity, the God of heaven would smile upon every effort which the injured might make to disenthral themselves." Like Walker, Garnet could not countenance the claims of slaveholders like Jones, who played the heathen card to argue that the bondage of bodies could be paid for by the salvation of souls. Souls could not be saved while bodies were enslaved, he warned. Garnet's intellectual debt to Walker was such that he included a copy of his own address, along with a "brief sketch" of Walker's life, in an 1848 reprint of the second edition of Walker's *Appeal*.[16]

Frederick Douglass, Garnet's junior by a little over a year, opposed his call to rebel at the 1843 convention. At the time, Douglass preferred William Lloyd Garrison's tactic of nonviolent moral suasion over violent resistance, and joined with other likeminded Black abolitionists to reject Garnet's address by a single vote.[17] Yet in his 1845 *Narrative,* Douglass also drew on the figure of the heathen to highlight White hypocrisy. Douglass had been born into slavery in Maryland in 1817, escaping to freedom as a young man in 1838. At this point in his career, he hoped to convince White Americans that slavery was morally hideous; the *Narrative* did that work powerfully. Where Walker had compared White Christians to ancient heathens unfavorably, and Garnet compared them to hypothetical enslaving heathens, Douglass, like Jones, brought up the heathen in the context of the foreign mission complex. In the appendix to his *Narrative,* he lamented, "We have men sold to build churches, women sold to support the gospel, and babes sold to purchase Bibles for the *poor heathen! all for the glory of God and the good of souls!*" Douglass's characterization of American slaveholding Christianity held it to be a humbug of misdirected humanitarianism: "They love the heathen on the other side of the globe. They can pray for him, pay money to have the Bible put into his hand, and missionaries to instruct him; while they despise and totally neglect the heathen at their own doors."[18] Douglass condemned the White Americans who bemoaned slavery overseas while engaging in the same at home. White American slaveholding Christians were no better than the heathens they were claiming to set "free" from idolatry and despotism. Measuring them against the heathen barometer, Douglass diagnosed them as indeed worse: serving the idol of King Cotton, they had become despots of the most abysmal variety.

Douglass and Garnet diverged further when the latter became an emigrationist toward the end of the 1840s, seeing a better future for African Americans outside rather than inside the United States. In 1852, Garnet headed to Jamaica, where he served as a missionary until his failing health required a return to the States. In 1881, he took up a post as US minister to Liberia, where he succumbed to malaria two months later. Though Douglass is now better known than Garnet, the latter's desire to evangelize Africa was hardly uncommon in the nineteenth century. Like Garnet, other African American Christians saw Africa as a site of hope but also as a heathen continent that required Christian renovation in order to realize its full potential.

"A Heathenish Way to Worship"

With emancipation, missionization efforts spurred by African American Christians for newly freedpeople and for Africans picked up steam. Black Christian leaders viewed both populations as in need of salvation and racial uplift defined by genteel Protestant Victorian mores—the freedpeople because they had been barred full access to the gospel, and Africans because they had been exploited for their labor rather than valued for their eternal souls.[19] To bring their brethren into the Christian fold required a rationale for why people of African descent should accept a religion that rendered their past heathen and evil and their history nonexistent. Ethiopianism, based on Psalm 68:31 ("Princes shall come out of Egypt; Ethiopia shall soon stretch out her hands unto God"), provided this rationale. It promised that God had a special plan for Black people, and as scholar Sylvester Johnson explains, it "reincarnated white defenses of slavery as the path of salvation for the 'Dark Continent.' It signified the black race as a divine instrument whose constituents would demonstrate to a hypocritical world an authentic Christianity."[20] Africans and African Americans might have endured the worst, but they would not suffer forever: the time was coming when God would lift them up to be a light unto the rest of the world. They, and not White Americans, were God's true New Israel, a long-suffering people whom God redeemed from slavery and chose for special oversight, just as He had rescued the Israelites from their bondage in the Old Testament.[21]

African Methodist Episcopal Church bishop Daniel Alexander Payne, born free in Charleston in 1811, subscribed to this conviction and dedicated his efforts after the Civil War to the evangelization of freedpeople in the South. He reassured them that the idea that God is "the God of the white man, and not of the black," is a "horrible blasphemy."[22] But even as he affirmed that God was on their side, Payne worried that the religious practices developed under slavery were "heathenish." In his *Recollections of Seventy Years*, published in 1888, Payne recalled how he had met with

Sunday-school teachers at Mother Bethel African Methodist Episcopal Church in Philadelphia and "showed them how England had become great by habitually making her people read the Scriptures . . . and how the colored race, who had been oppressed for centuries through ignorance and superstition, might become intelligent, Christian, and powerful through the enlightening and sanctifying influences of the word of God."[23] Payne's uplift theology promised that Christian instruction could jump-start a people from stagnation to development, from oppression to power.

Payne contrasted this vision of a churched people reading the scriptures together with what he viewed as a degraded and "heathenish" form of worship among the freedpeople. He wrote, "About this time I attended a 'bush meeting,' where I went to please the pastor whose circuit I was visiting. After the sermon they formed a ring, and with coats off sung, clapped their hands, and stamped their feet in a most ridiculous and heathenish way." Payne asked the pastor to put a halt to the dancing. He obliged, but the people continued "singing and rocking their bodies to and fro" for a quarter of an hour before Payne, unable to countenance this further, took "the leader by the arm" and "requested him to desist and to sit down and sing in a rational manner. [Payne] told him also that it was a heathenish way to worship and disgraceful to themselves, the race, and the Christian name." Payne's admonition did not meet with the reaction he had hoped; although the worshipers "broke up their ring," they "walked sullenly away."[24]

In the afternoon, Payne spoke with their leader again, who informed him that "sinners won't get converted unless there is a ring." Try as he might, Payne could not convince the leader to see the ring as "heathenish"; the leader instead let him know, in no uncertain terms, that "the Spirit of God works upon people in different ways." Payne left it at that, explaining in his *Recollections*, "I have been strongly censured because of my efforts to change the mode of worship or modify the extravagances indulged in by the people." He simply could not countenance the possibility that the "Spirit of God works upon people in different ways" and instead used all manner of terms to characterize the rings as "heathenish": "an incurable religious disease," "fanaticism," an "evil practice," a "disgrace," and, as "some one has even called it," a "Voudoo Dance" that left its participants "an easy prey to Satan."[25] For Payne, the wrong form of worship could doubly damn a people. At the supernatural level, it left them open to Satan's machinations, and at the earthly level, it left them vulnerable to the claim that their religious practices proved them to be essentially "primitive" and in need of continued oversight. As harsh as Payne's critiques were, he feared much worse from White people ruing the end of slavery and looking for every opportunity to keep African Americans in a condition of servitude.

Although Payne opposed emigration to Africa, focusing his energy on the uplift and education of his people in the United States, he encouraged African Americans to support missions to Africa. "At nearly all these places in the South," he wrote, "I organized Mite Missionary Societies, the first being at Mobile, and preached or lectured upon missionary work in Africa and in Hayti." As he drew near to death, Payne asked for God's blessing on his labors "for the benefit of all the generations and all the races," and for blessing on the work of "the living missionaries. . . . Let the victories of thy conquering cross be ever increasing! Let its living trophies in the heathen world be as innumerable as the stars in the skies, and as countless as countless sands upon the ocean shores! To all these glorious ends, O Lord Jesus, make thy aged and feeble servant helpful!" For Payne, the heathen barometer diagnosed African Americans in the US South as "heathen*ish*" because of their enthusiastic worship style, which jeopardized the reputation of the race. By contrast, Africans *were* heathens, "barbarous and savage men," "whom [missionaries] do not understand, and whom the heathen in turn do not comprehend."[26] Payne wanted his compatriots in the US South to distance themselves from their African past; hearing about and contributing to the salvation of the heathen world overseas was one way to do this.

"The Land of My Fathers"

Missionary Thomas Lewis Johnson took to heart what he heard about heathens in Africa. Born into slavery in Virginia in 1836, Johnson remained enslaved until the end of the Civil War. As he later described it in his 1892 *Africa for Christ. Twenty-Eight Years a Slave,* he had once been "superstitious, and believed in witchcraft and ghosts, as did all on the plantation. It was natural we should. Superstition is characteristic of the race in Africa. Having been brought to America, not permitted to be taught to read the Bible, and having every avenue to education closed against us, it was natural we should retain the superstitions of our fathers." Johnson became a Christian during the Great Revival of 1857 but was adamant that his Christianity was not just the unquestioning adoption of the master's religion, for, he said, "I had not much faith in what my master told me, and could not understand much of what he said." He converted not through the injunctions of a White preacher but with the assistance of a "coloured man on the street, named Stephney Brown," who "explained to [him] the simple Gospel, and how he had found peace." Pray that God will have mercy on you, Brown told Johnson, "for Jesus' sake," and have faith that He will answer, "just as you believe I would give you a glass of water if you asked me for it." The idea that God would respond as readily to a prayer for salvation as Brown would respond to a request for water filled Johnson with hope, gratitude, confidence, and the desire to spread the good news to Africa, "the land of my fathers." Even before he obtained his freedom, he longed to go to Africa as a missionary, "convinced that there were thousands in Africa who were heathen."[27]

After the Civil War, Johnson traveled to New York, where he soon realized that "there was almost as much prejudice against [his] race as in the South."[28] He and his wife then left for Chicago, where he worked as a waiter until receiving a call from a local Baptist congregation to take up a missionary position in Denver, Colorado. Johnson accepted the call, though he continued to pray for the opportunity to evangelize Africa. He finally received that opportunity, departing with his wife for England in 1876, where he spent two years studying at the Pastors' College before the two of them sailed for the west coast of Africa in 1878.

Johnson's experience in Africa reinforced his belief that "there were thousands" of "heathen" there, even as it assured him that they could be converted. Spending time in Sierra Leone, Liberia, and Cameroon, he brought to the continent many of the same assumptions about heathen lands that shaped White missionaries' views of the heathen world. Johnson was pleasantly surprised by areas that had been Christianized, seeing them as harbingers of Africa's future. He described Victoria, Cameroon, for instance, as "a beautiful little town of 500 inhabitants" that was "beautifully laid out with broad streets. Each house has a large yard and garden, in many of which are to be seen the palm, lime, cocoa-nut, bread-fruit, custard-fruit, orange, banana, and plantain trees. The cottages are neat and clean, built after the style of European cottages. These are occupied by the English-speaking people who are native Christians, and many of them have, for long years, been earnest workers for our blessed Jesus." But other parts of Africa Johnson described as mired in the "superstition and witchcraft" in which he himself had once believed. As he saw it, these regions were literally swathed in the shadows of the valley of death, as the remnants of human sacrifices littered the land. "The King's palace at Abomey is surrounded by a clay wall 20 feet high, the top of which is said to be covered with human skulls," Johnson wrote. Instead of caring for the land, Johnson believed that the unchristianized tribes of West Africa wasted their energies "continually at war. You hear of their DRINKING THE BLOOD AND EATING THE HEARTS of their enemies; of walls covered with human skulls; of a pavement made of human skulls, to walk on. Truly," he lamented, quoting Psalm 74:20, "'the dark places of the earth are full of the habita-

OUR DESTINATION AND SPHERE.

"Our Destination and Sphere." In *Twenty-Eight Years a Slave: or, the Story of My Life in Three Continents,* by Thomas Johnson (Bournemouth, UK: W. Mate and Sons, 1909). From the Schomburg Center for Research in Black Culture, Jean Blackwell Hutson Research and Reference Division, The New York Public Library.

tions of cruelty.'" An accompanying illustration zeroed in on a "human slaughter-house" watched by placid onlookers. The reader is placed in the position of an onlooker as well, made to feel the anxiety and dread Johnson experienced as he approached "our destination."[29]

Johnson went on to explain the attitudes toward the land purportedly held by these tribes. They "pay homage to lakes, rivers, and mountains, believing that their gods live there. In some places large houses are kept for serpents, and these miserable reptiles are worshipped. At Dix Cove, on the West Coast, it is said they have a crocodile which they worship." He

"Native work; Caps and Bags made of Grass, and an Idol Given Up by a Convert." In Johnson, *Twenty-Eight Years a Slave*. From the Schomburg Center for Research in Black Culture, Jean Blackwell Hutson Research and Reference Division, The New York Public Library.

described the Africans' attitudes toward the land, the weather, and the flora and fauna as "queer superstitions, and one must be among them to realize what slaves they are to them. When it rains they beat their drums to make it stop. There is a bird which makes a noise at night something like an owl. This is called a witch bird. When it is heard, the children are afraid to go out, and guns are fired to frighten it away."[30] To Johnson, Africans required emancipation from their fears of the environment, which would ultimately enable them to subdue the land and make the "habitations of cruelty" blossom as the rose.

The evidence of orderly Christian towns and gardens in other parts of Africa gave Johnson confidence that such a result could be achieved. Indeed, he never lost faith that asking God for transformation was as simple, and guaranteed as favorable a response, as asking a friend for a cup of water. Returning to the United States in 1880 due to his failing health, Johnson went on the lecture circuit as an expert on Africa, displaying large maps and exhibiting artifacts recovered from his travels, such as "an idol given up by a convert." He spread the word about what he had seen far and wide to White missionary associations and to freedpeople pining, like him, to evangelize the "dark" land of their forebears:

> "Come over and help us," is their cry,
> "Come now, oh, do not pass us by.
> We are seeking truth, we are seeking light,
> We seek deliverance from dark night."[31]

"And Yet Africa . . . Is Still Heathen!"

If Payne represents the concern for racial uplift at home, and Johnson for the evangelization of Africa, Alexander Crummell brought together both. He added, too, the fire of David Walker and Henry Highland Garnet at the hypocrisy of White Christian Americans. Born free in New York City in 1819 and extensively educated, Crummell, like Payne, had been initially opposed to colonization but became an emigrationist who focused his energies on Liberia upon moving there as a missionary in 1853. Crummell had been ordained as an Episcopal priest in 1844, eventually becoming the first Black graduate of Cambridge University in the same year that he left for Liberia. His experiences there—where he served not only as a missionary, founding churches and schools, but also as professor of English and philosophy at Liberia College from 1862 to 1866—turned him into one of the foremost advocates of emigration as a means to redeem Africa and fulfill the promise of Ethiopianism.[32]

In an 1865 address titled "The Regeneration of Africa," given before the Pennsylvania Colonization Society at the Church of the Epiphany in Philadelphia and reprinted in the 1891 *Africa and America: Addresses and Discourses,* Crummell articulated his vision of Ethiopianism and the connection he saw between Christianized African Americans and "still heathen" Africa. Crummell began by surveying the history of world missions and noted that the Great Commission ("Go, ye, therefore, and teach all nations, baptizing them in the name of the Father, and of the Son, and of the Holy

Ghost") had turned Christianity into the "foremost of all faiths," as its followers "lay themselves out at once, in most painful endeavors," to spread
the word. They had evangelized Asia Minor, "destroy[ed] all the paganisms of Europe," crossed the ocean to the "New World," and "bent [their]
energies for the conquest of Christ of the Pacific Isles." Crummell used
Hawaiʻi and other Pacific Island nations as examples of missionary success,
much as did the missionaries themselves: "Idolatry, in some islands, has been
entirely destroyed. Nations there have been born in a day; and such is the
influence of Christianity that the destruction of paganism is a certain event,
and at no distant day. Thus," he continued, "has the religion of Jesus, visited
with saving power, Europe, America, large sections of Asia, and the isles
of the sea." But "one great, melancholy contrast presents itself; two thousand years have passed away, and yet Africa, with her hundreds of millions
of souls is still heathen! The abominations of paganism still prevail through
all her vast domains!"[33]

Crummell was convinced that "Ethiopia is yet to 'stretch forth her hands
unto God'" and that the Great Commission "is as well a prophecy as a
mandate." And so he asked, "HOW SHALL THE REGENERATION OF AFRICA
BE EFFECTED?" Crummell believed that Africa needed external assistance
to be redeemed, for "you cannot find one single instance where a rude, heathen people, have raised themselves by their own spontaneous energy from
a state of paganism to one of spiritual superiority." Envoys of "superior
people," who would come in family groups "seeking a new home amid the
heathen population of Africa," were the best means to effect moral "elevation." Establishing "roots" in Africa, these emigrants would employ "Native heathens" to care for their families, cultivate their gardens, and labor
in their workshops. The "Native heathens" would in turn be "touched by
their civilized habits, and moved by their family prayers and Sunday teachings." Eventually the children of emigrants and the children of Natives
would marry and their "blood, at times, *both* Christianized," would "flow,
mingled together, through the veins of a new race, thoroughly indigenous
and native." For Crummell, this "new race" would be characterized not
by skin color but by shared ancestry and religion. He was adamant that
the "superior people" who could make the greatest impact on Africa's "regeneration" were African Americans, for "indigenous agency" was necessary to make the gospel stick, and African American emigrants could operate as Christian agents who were "somewhat native to the soil" and
"indigenous, in blood, constitution, and adaptability. Two centuries of
absence from the continent of Africa, has not destroyed his physical adaptation to the land of his ancestors." The White "foreign missionary," by

contrast, is "an exotic" who "withers and pines away" under the "burning sun of Africa."[34]

That African Americans were best suited to regenerate Africa also indicated, to Crummell, the need to raise their educational and civilizational levels. He returned to the States in 1873, founding and serving as rector of Saint Luke's Episcopal Church in Washington, DC, until 1894 and teaching at Howard University until 1897, when he founded the American Negro Academy, a society devoted to African American scholarship and the arts. In March 1897 Crummell gave the inaugural address for the academy, titled "Civilization, the Primal Need of the Race." Nearing eighty years old at this point, Crummell articulated a response to the view exemplified by Booker T. Washington in his 1895 Atlanta Exposition Address, that "those of my race" should focus on "industrial progress" and "cast down your bucket" in "agriculture, mechanics, in commerce, in domestic service, and in the professions."[35] Crummell raised themes that would be famously echoed by one of his protégés, W. E. B. Du Bois, in *The Souls of Black Folk* (1903). To Crummell, "the special race problem of the Negro in the United States is his civilization." He emphasized that he had a "higher conception of Negro capacity" than perhaps any member of the audience, but "as a race in this land, we have no art; we have no science; we have no philosophy; we have no scholarship." He lamented the materialism that others like Washington put forward as "the master-need of the race, and as the surest way to success." Instead, he advocated for the leadership of "trained and scholarly men of a race to employ their knowledge and culture and teaching and to guide both the opinions and habits of the crude masses" toward "that civilization which is the nearest ally of religion." For Crummell, as for Payne, racial uplift of the "crude" by the "scholarly" was essential to "break down the conspiracy which would fain limit and narrow the range of Negro talent in this caste-tainted country. It is only thus, we can secure that recognition of genius and scholarship in the republic of letters, which is the rightful prerogative of every race of men."[36]

In a subsequent address for the American Negro Academy at the end of the same year, "The Attitude of the American Mind toward the Negro Intellect," Crummell expanded on the reasons why he thought African Americans had been held back thus far. It was not for want of talent, since already "the race in the brief period of a generation, has been so fruitful in intellectual product." Rather, it was due to White Americans actively stamping out African American intellectual life. "Here was a people laden with the spoils of the centuries . . . and withal, claiming the exalted name and grand heritage of Christians," said Crummell. "By their voluntary act they placed right beside them a large population of another race of people, seized as captives, and brought to their plantations from a distant continent. This other race was an unlettered, unenlightened, and a pagan people." From the very start, the White "master race" "undertook the process of darkening their minds. 'Put out the light, and then, put out the light!' was their cry for centuries. Paganizing themselves, they sought a deeper paganizing of their serfs than the original paganism that these had brought from Africa." Crummell did not mince words as he, too, drew on the heathen barometer to accuse White Americans of turning their Christianity into a pagan sham by virtue of their active efforts "to stamp out the brains of the Negro!"[37]

"A Byword and a Reproach throughout the Civilized World"

Mary Church Terrell went further still in accusing White Southerners and their churches of an abiding ignorance, barbarism, and savagery that manifested in the horror of lynching. Born in 1863 to a later generation than Crummell, Payne, and Johnson and to parents who were formerly enslaved, Terrell was also an advocate of racial uplift and became one of the first African American women to receive a college degree, earning a bachelor's degree in classics and a master's in education at Oberlin in the 1880s. She went on to an illustrious career in education and was also active as a founder of the National Association for the Advancement of Colored People and as president of the National Association of Colored Women.[38]

In 1892 one of Terrell's longtime friends, Thomas Moss, a successful grocer in Memphis, was lynched alongside two of his coworkers. His death galvanized Terrell and Ida B. Wells into action.[39] In a 1904 article published in the *North American Review,* "Lynching from a Negro's Point of View," Terrell systematically dismantled assumptions regarding the reasons for lynching and argued, "At the last analysis, . . . there are just two causes of lynching. In the first place, it is due to race hatred, the hatred of a stronger people toward a weaker who were once held as slaves. In the second place, it is due to the lawlessness so prevalent in the section where nine-tenths of the lynchings occur." Where Protestant Americans—White and Black included—used the historical weight of heathenism to explain the supposed backwardness of much of the world's people, and the specific history of slavery to explain the supposed ignorance of the freedpeople, Terrell turned the tables and insisted that "the brutalizing effect of slavery" had turned White people into "bloodthirsty" "fiends." Slavery had made White women incapable of "mercy and compassion" and had turned White men into "debauch[ers]" of Black women. Their descendants—the "white men who shoot negroes to death and flay them alive, and the white women who apply flaming torches to their oil-soaked bodies to-day"—inherited their bigotry and cruelty.[40]

To show how warped White Southerners had become, Terrell cited excruciatingly graphic examples of torture. She charged Christians, specifically, with turning lynching into sick spectacle.[41] Describing the murder of Sam Hose, she wrote,

> The Sunday on which Sam Hose was burned was converted into a holiday. Special trains were made up to take the Christian people of Atlanta to the scene of the burning. . . . After the first train moved out with every inch of available space inside and out filled to overflowing, a second had to be made up, so as to accommodate those who had just come from church. After Sam Hose had been tortured and burned to death, the great concourse of Christians who had witnessed the tragedy scraped for hours among his ashes in the hope of finding a sufficient number of his bones to take to their friends as souvenirs.[42]

Just as José de Acosta had once accused Native Americans of perverting Christian rites through the influence of the devil, so Terrell implied the same with her description of American Christians' twisted search for "relics" among the bones of the lynched. She charged that "if the number of Americans who participate in this wild and diabolical carnival of blood does not diminish, nothing can prevent this country from becoming a byword and a reproach throughout the civilized world."[43] During a period when American imperialists trumpeted the advantages of Western Christian civilization to the heathen world, Terrell instead turned America into a horrifying and demonic embarrassment.

Lest readers think the behavior of Christians at the murder of Hose an anomaly, Terrell lit into the nation's churches more broadly, indicting them for their complicity with lynching. "The church puts forth so few and such feeble protests against lynching," she accused. "Thousands of dollars are raised by our churches every year to send missionaries to Christianize the heathen in foreign lands, and this is proper and right. But in addition to this foreign missionary work, would it not be well for our churches to inaugurate a crusade against the barbarism at home, which converts hundreds of white women and children into savages every year, while it crushes the spirit, blights the hearth and breaks the heart of hundreds of defenceless blacks?"[44] Terrell brought up the foreign mission comparison much as had

Douglass, in order to highlight American hypocrisy. Instead of focusing on White Americans' neglect of enslaved people and their descendants, though, she asked how Christians could send missionaries to the heathen in foreign lands while ignoring the heathenizing effects of "barbarism" on White Americans themselves. And where missionaries loved to linger on the supposedly sorrowful effects of heathenism on benighted women and children in the heathen world, Terrell expressly highlighted the baneful results of lynching on White women and children, who were "convert[ed] . . . into savages" as a result.

"The Heathenism of Our Religion"

Even as African Americans used the heathen barometer to shred apart the self-anointed supremacy of White American Christian civilization, others tried to double down on a conception of Whiteness based in the same, using heathenism as a smear against misbehaving and misbelieving White people whose practices made them seem unfit for the body politic. The heathen barometer worked here to demarcate the bounds of both respectable religiosity and racial identity for Euro-Americans of questionable racial and religious orientations. Since the heathen had become primarily associated with the nonwhite foreigner, to call a Euro-American a heathen in this context was not to highlight their hypocrisy, as Walker, Douglass, Terrell, and others had done. It was to render judgment on their supposed religious abnormalities in order to racialize their Whiteness as suspect.

Uses of the heathen barometer tracked with new waves of immigration to the United States, beginning with Irish Catholics in the 1840s and followed by increasing numbers of Catholics and Jews arriving from Germany, Poland, Italy, and eastern Europe from the mid- to late nineteenth and early twentieth centuries. These immigrants threatened the cultural clout of Anglo-American Protestants who were trying not only to shape the world in their image but also to keep their home country aligned with their vision of how a Christian nation should look. They used the heathen barometer to detect heathenness among Euro-Americans in regions of poverty and recent immigration, where children were kept from school and church in order to make money, and families seemed barely able to tell the Bible from a picture book. Catholic immigrants were particularly derided both for their supposed ignorance and for being too close to idolatry still, what with their veneration of the saints and the Virgin Mary. In his 1849 *Tales for Little Readers, about the Heathen,* for instance, Protestant medical missionary John Scudder told American children that there were "many millions of people" who "embrace the religion both of the Greek and Roman Catholic churches—a religion which is nothing more nor less than paganism, with a few Christian doctrines added to it."[45]

Meanwhile, in an 1859 volume titled *The Union Tabernacle; or, Movable Tent-Church*, Superintendent Edwin Long provided example after example of "home-heathenism as revealed by incidents," many of them involving poor German-speaking immigrants, whose pastors seemed no better than their parishioners. All throughout the States, Long claimed, "there are dark corners and remote settlements whose inhabitants live in almost total neglect of public worship and of all religion; and high up in the mountains are people who live in a state of almost abject and heathenish degradation." The idea that heathens could be found at "home" challenged the conception of the heathen world as a realm separated from Protestant America by its suffering bodies and benighted souls. But ironically, one of the signifiers of "home heathenism" also served to reinforce the boundaries between White America and the heathen world. According to Long, home heathens were clueless about the heathen world, and this very cluelessness helped to mark them as heathens. "I once heard a pastor plead warmly for the poor heathen 'out there near Jerusalem,'" said Long, "where mothers were throwing their babes to crocodiles, and men were being crushed by the car of Juggernaut." Long mocked the pastor's geographic confusion, relying on his audience's familiarity with tropes about heathen India to convey the pastor's own heathen ignorance. Long also derided a "grandmother" who "told [him] she had never been more than three miles from home in one direction. . . . She thought it strange that we preachers would come begging so often; for their church had certainly supplied all the heathen with the gospel." When asked "how many heathen she thought there were, she replied that there was a handful out on some island of the ocean." Ignorance of the extent of the heathen world made this woman a "home heathen," even as it normalized the idea that the *real* heathen world was foreign, extensive, and in need of sustained American intervention.[46]

The racialization of suspect religion also operated in the context of anti-Mormonism, particularly around polygamy.[47] Protestant missionaries described Utah as an exotic foreign mission field; in 1881 one asserted that "the same methods by which Christianity has been carried into the jungles of India and the wilds of Africa will be required to carry and hold it in Utah. The citadel of polygamous Mormonism must be invested by a Christian army, as other strongholds of heathenism have been besieged."[48] It probably did not help that Latter-day Saints pushed back against this racialization by using the heathen barometer against the "so-called Christian religion" too. In an 1887 editorial in the *Juvenile Instructor*, George

Quayle Cannon compared "modern Christianity" to heathenism, and not favorably: "Modern Christianity as a religion is a failure. True, it has its good points. It has a modicum of truth. But so have heathenism and the various religions believed in and practiced by those whom we call pagans. It is very unfashionable to say this. . . . Nevertheless, it is true; and many of the heathen nations are aware of it." Cannon criticized Christian missionaries for being "utterly inadequate to supply the spiritual wants or to reform the lives of the heathen who embrace it." In their attitudes toward Latter-day Saint teachings, he found modern Christians sorely lacking in comparison with heathens: "Christianity has gone down hill with wonderful rapidity since the year 1830, and its decline will undoubtedly continue. There is a good reason for this to be found in the fact that the fiercest persecutors of the truth have been the professors of so-called Christianity. In this respect heathenism has the advantage and contrasts well with it." Having rejected the "revelation of the gospel" sent by God in the person of Joseph Smith, modern Christians in the United States and Great Britain had lost "that portion of His Spirit which has previously rested upon them." Cannon admitted that "the elders of our Church, so far, have labored but little among the heathen." Still, he was convinced that when they did venture into the mission fields where Anglo-Christians had proved themselves failures, particularly among the "teeming millions" of Asia, "the power of God will be manifested as to convince the honest among them that this work is of God." Evangelizing the heathen *better* than Christians was a way for Latter-day Saints to prove that they were not themselves heathen but were, rather, the true favored children of God.[49]

Where Cannon critiqued "modern Christianity" from the vantage point of a Latter-day Saint, others used the heathen barometer from within. In 1891 George Augustus Lofton, a Baptist minister whose career spanned churches in Georgia, Tennessee, Missouri, and Alabama, delivered a two-sermon series on "modern Paganism." He excoriated the "heathenism of our religion," which he said was "in absolute conflict with its doctrinal, spiritual, and practical origin." "Our fashion and the craze of worship thereof are grossly paganistic," he griped. "The picture show, the theatre, the dance, the game table, the saloon—are all licentious and soul-damning specimens of paganism which keep sinners from Christ." And what was worse, "we bring this Paganism into our [^very] churches." Lofton used the heathen barometer to detect heathenism at the heart of Protestant practice. "You do not need a multiplicity of false gods, in idol shop and at brazen altars to have paganism. We have all this here in America, as in Asia, Africa and the isle of the Ocean." Lumping America in with foreign, heathen lands—the places late nineteenth-century imperialists were supposedly "rescuing" from the blight of ignorance—served as a purposeful blow to Americans' self-esteem.[50]

"We in Heathendom Have Never Seen the Like"

To apply the heathen barometer to the domestic sphere, then, was to call into question the Americanness and Christianity of the groups found to fit. When applied to and by African Americans, the heathen barometer both cast aspersions on White slaveholders who failed to Christianize them, and provided fodder for the internal project of racial uplift. When used on Euro-Americans, the heathen barometer cast doubt on their Whiteness as intertwined with their Americanness, Christianity, and claims to "civilization."

In the late nineteenth century, another group was also at the forefront of White Americans' minds when they worried about heathenism at home and their own susceptibility to it. Since the middle of the century, Chinese migrants had been coming to America's shores, first to seek their fortune in the gold mines and later to build the transcontinental railroad. The expansion of citizenship and suffrage after the Civil War did not benefit the Chinese, who faced increasing hostility leading ultimately to the passage of the Chinese Exclusion Act in 1882. Scholar Joshua Paddison explains that Republican and African American leaders "argued that it was not 'blackness' but 'heathenism' that rendered a man unfit for suffrage, opening the door for generally Christianized African American men to become full citizens while continuing to shut out Indian and Chinese men." As Paddison puts it, after the passage of the Fourteenth and Fifteenth Amendments, "a man's right to vote in the United States would no longer hinge on his whiteness but on whether he was or was not a heathen."[51]

In the next chapter, we turn to the question of how the Chinese came to be seen as quintessential heathens in the late nineteenth century, whose presence on American soil threatened to heathenize the entire nation and blast open the barriers that White Protestant Americans were trying so hard to construct between Christian America and the heathen world. In his *Diary*, after recounting the anecdote about the "friend" who "would rather be a Pagan" than live near African Americans, Uchimura Kanzō averred that while racism toward African Americans was an embarrassing reproach to White American Christians, "the prejudice, the aversion, the repugnance, which they entertain against the children of Sinim is something which we in heathendom have never seen the like." He highlighted the hypocrisy of missions to the Chinese overseas alongside their ill-treatment in the United

States, much as Douglass and others drew on the example of foreign missions to cry foul on American racism at home: "The land which sends over missionaries to China, to convert her sons and daughters to Christianity from the nonsense of Confucius and the superstitions of Buddha,—the very same land abhors even the shadow of a Chinaman cast upon its soil. There never was seen such an anomaly upon the face of this earth." Drilling into the very things that White American Christians believed made them special and superior, Uchimura stated in no uncertain terms, "The whole tenor of anti-Chinese laws appears to me to be anti-Biblical, anti-Christian, anti-evangelical, and anti-humanitarian. Even the nonsense of Confucius teaches us very much better things than these."[52]

6

EXCLUSION

For those concerned about the heathen world, nineteenth-century advances in transportation and communications machinery were truly revolutionary. Steam power made ocean travel quicker, and the railroad promised to vastly simplify overland journeys. Small wonder, then, that minister Calvin Colton implored Congress to move ahead with plans for a transpacific railroad in an 1850 speech: "God, from his throne in heaven, now seems to ask, '*who—who* will build me an highway to the heathen?'" Channeling the Almighty, Colton promised, "I will make of that nation the greatest of nations."[1] He and other champions of nineteenth-century American technologies hoped that these machines would facilitate not only the conversion of energy into useful forms but also the conversion of the world's heathen into useful Christians, even speeding the coming of the millennium, or thousand years of peace.

But Colton did not anticipate that the practical answer to his question might, in large part, be a people quickly smeared as quintessential heathens. Though some saw the immigration of Chinese laborers as a chance to eradicate their heathenness and revitalize their society through education in a Christian land, others quickly started to view the railroad not as a "highway to the heathen" but as a dangerous avenue to the importation of heathen labor for the enrichment of a few wealthy capitalists.

This chapter shows how and why heathenism became a justification for Chinese exclusion in the late nineteenth century. Scholars of anti-Chinese sentiment have tended to argue that it was fundamentally labor competition and racial antagonism, not religious hostility, that led to the passage of exclusion laws.[2] According to this point of view, the popularity of the label "heathen Chinese" can be explained quite simply by the surprising success of Bret Harte's 1870 poem about "Ah Sin," the "Heathen Chinee" with the "ways that are dark," who cheats at cards while pretending not to understand the game.[3] Harte intended the poem as satire, but it was not primarily read as such by those who were fearful of Chinese migration.

Cover of Bret Harte, *The Heathen Chinee,* with illustrations by S. Eytinge Jr. (Boston: James R. Osgood, 1871). This version contains a "Publisher's Note" stating that "MR. EYTINGE's illustrations to 'The Heathen Chinee' have been submitted to the author, and have received his approval. The present is the only illustrated edition of the poem published with the author's sanction." Rare Books 10597, Huntington Library, San Marino, California.

"Ah Sin was his name." In *The Heathen Chinee,* by Bret Harte, illustrated by Joseph Hull (Chicago: Western News, 1870). Rare Books 17012, Huntington Library, San Marino, California.

Drawings of Ah Sin as a childish or only vaguely human-looking creature with a long, tail-like queue reinforced the impression that the "Heathen Chinee" was a strange and unassimilable foreign element. After the publication of the poem, many politicians and demagogues used the same phrase as convenient shorthand for the negative qualities of Harte's Ah Sin: childishness, trickiness, thievery, and willingness to labor for cheap.

But Harte's poem was not the only reason that the label stuck, and "heathen Chinese" was not just an accidentally popular, casually applied epithet. Rather, "heathen Chinese" was a purposeful and political appellation that drew from the many associations that had become attached to the concept of the "heathen" over time. Though most anti-Chinese demagogues thought that the Chinese had a relatively advanced civilization, they reinforced the heathen ceiling, intentionally flattening racial and civilizational hierarchies under older and broader discourses about the sweeping similarities between the poor heathen of the world. They connected older assumptions about heathen landscapes and bodies to newer arguments about the relationship of heathenness to American money and machines. And they used the historical influence of heathenism to explain why the Chinese had developed to a point of unassimilability. The concept of heathenism shaped American racial governance: it became the reason why Chinese bodies were supposedly different, why Americans could never compete short of turning heathen themselves, and why, ultimately, the Chinese should be excluded from the body politic.

"The Greatest Heathen Empire of History"

China's heathenness had once been seen along the same lines as that of ancient Greece and Rome: as wise but misguided, rather than demonic and disgusting. Early Americans coveted fine Chinese porcelains, silks, and tea, and as we have seen, travelers to China commented on the orderliness and even beauty of its densely populated cities. Academics and missionaries were also fascinated by the Chinese classics and what these ancient texts might tell them about buried spiritual truths common to the human family. But the 1842 Treaty of Nanjing, which concluded the First Opium War, made China seem a little less formidable and impenetrable. It opened China's ports to British traders and merchants and ceded Hong Kong to the British. The United States and France made similar treaties for extraterritorial rights and "favored nation" status a couple of years later. In the 1844 Treaty of Wangxia, US citizens were, among other things, allowed to purchase land in treaty ports and build hospitals and churches there.[4]

Soon after, in 1845, a Chinese museum opened in the Marlboro Chapel in Boston, to serve American visitors newly curious about China. The accompanying *Descriptive Catalogue,* by John Peters Jr., represents a transitional moment in American attitudes toward China. On the one hand, it continued to depict China as a civilization worthy of respect for the stability of its government and its peaceful population, particularly in light of the country's geographical extent. "A happy, contented, and industrious population is a pretty sure indication that the government is, on the whole, well administered," the catalog stated. "The most powerful kingdoms of Europe are but of yesterday compared with China. While they count their existence by hundreds, she reckons hers by thousands of years, and is now in the enjoyment of a green old age under the administration of laws founded upon the precepts of her sages."[5]

On the other hand, China's "green old age" was quickly becoming a source for American contempt by the mid-nineteenth century. The promise of youth seemed to outweigh the dignity of longevity, and as Americans gained confidence in their national experiment, they increasingly saw "the ancient civilizations of China, India, and the Arab world" as "cultures that were past their glory."[6] The museum catalog drew a distinction between the Chinese who "live on the past" and "we on the future."[7] While the sages still delighted, the Chinese people increasingly struck American observers as deluded and in the sway of ignorant idolatry.[8] Americans were also put off by the fact that the Chinese seemed to consider them uncouth barbarians whose ways were not worth emulating. In other words, while missionaries often relied on wowing the heathen with the supposed superiority of American civilization, the Chinese seemed less than impressed.[9]

But gold was impressive. Chinese migrants started arriving on the Pacific Coast on the heels of the first gold-seekers. Almost as soon as they arrived, anti-Chinese violence and legislation followed, as miners jealously guarded their claims against the perceived intruders. The Foreign Miner's Tax, aimed at the Chinese, charged them a fee of four dollars per month (roughly half a month's typical salary). *The People v. Hall* case of 1854 made Chinese testimony impermissible in court. From 1864 to 1869, even more Chinese migrants came across the Pacific to work on the transcontinental railroad. The Burlingame Treaty of 1868 sought to establish most-favored-nation status between the United States and China and promised the Chinese that they could immigrate to and travel freely in the States. But this only raised tensions and hostilities further, as other laborers worried about competition and lowered wages.

In the meantime, missionaries also came to the West Coast, seeing the arrival of the Chinese as a providential occurrence that meant they might

not have to travel all the way to China to evangelize these particular heathen.[10] In America the Chinese were separated from family and friends, easier
to access, and hopefully more receptive to their lessons. As Daniel Cleveland, a lawyer for the Texas and Pacific Railroad, put it, "There is not one
among the many thousand Chinese in the state who would receive the missionary with disrespect, or refuse to listen to him."[11] Cleveland assessed the
character of the "Chinese in California" in a lengthy manuscript of the same
title that was never published. Others publicly countenanced his assessment
of the Chinese as "courteous" and "cordial," defending them in the face of
sometimes brutal maltreatment. In the February 1856 edition of the *Oriental,*
a bilingual newspaper started by Presbyterian William Speer, for instance,
an article entitled "Can the Chinese Be Converted?" laid the blame for the
low rate of conversions on their maltreatment: "Our impregnable belief is
that the Chinese can be converted, that the Chinese will be converted, and
that the chief obstacle is in us so-called 'Christians.'"[12]

Missionaries and other supporters of Chinese immigration characterized
them as superior to other heathens, and therefore worthy of better treatment. Cleveland reasoned that "[China] is the greatest heathen empire of
history, certainly the greatest of modern times."[13] In 1860 John Archbald
even dared to compare the Chinese with Americans: "What, after all, is the
difference between us and these despised dwellers in our land? Their institutions are different, you say." Though foreign, Archbald contended that
they had recognizable institutions that had lasted for generations, while
"neither Negro, Malay, nor American Indian has, or ever has had, institutions perfected to a similar degree."[14] Chinese migrants also tried to emphasize the differences between themselves and others whom they, like
Euro-Americans, claimed were "uncivilized." In a remonstrance to Congress after the *People v. Hall* case that Speer helped write and publish, they
expressed dismay that Americans had "come to the conclusion that we Chinese are the same as Indians and negroes, and will not allow us to bear
witness in your courts! And yet these Indians know nothing about the relations of society; they know no mutual respect; they wear neither clothes
nor shoes; they live in caves and wild places. When we reflect upon the
honorable position that China has maintained for many thousands of years,
upon the wisdom transmitted by her philosophers, upon her array of civil
and military powers, upon the fame of her possessions . . . and then behold
the people of other nations heap ridicule upon as if we were the same as
Indians,—we ask, is it possible that this is in accordance with the will of
heaven?"[15]

The Chinese appealed to racial hierarchy to try to contest racial clumping.
But as we have seen, the concept of heathenness that underlay the latter

was not a rung on a civilizational ladder or scale of development but a ceiling to the ladder that kept all below in a condition of damnable, across-the-board moral darkness. It did not matter how civilizationally "backwards" or "advanced" a people seemed, or how great a "heathen empire" they had built—if they were heathen, they were one and the same in their degeneration, degradation, and lack of saving knowledge and grace.[16]

"And Hear the Chinese Swarm like Rats"

Bringing the Chinese in line with other stereotypically heathen traits helped sweep them off civilizational ladders into the great level morass of heathen darkness.[17] As Part I of this book demonstrated, Americans believed heathen landscapes to be uncultivated and disordered, much like their hearts and minds, and heathen bodies to evince a lack of care and decorum. But as we have seen, in the case of landscape, the Chinese at first glance did not seem to fit. Speer, who had been a missionary in China before coming to California, described the "garden-like cultivation of the soil" there and the "hills with their irrigated terraces." Even anti-Chinese demagogues could not ignore evidence of Chinese agriculture. In a circa 1871 speech on the perils of "heathen Chinese" immigration before Congress, Democrat William Mungen begrudgingly acknowledged that "the minute attention they give to husbandry, the quantity of produce they extract from the soil, the care with which they restore to it the most insignificant element, and the manner in which they economize that produce, are no doubt eminently worthy of our attention and imitation in this country, where we so prodigally misuse the soil and so wastefully misuse its productions."[18] Yet Mungen explained that the only reason the Chinese were able to cultivate the soil so extensively was not that they possessed advanced technological skills, but that they had so many people. "Within a generation the Caucasian mind has devised cultivators, and steam-plows, and reaping-machines, and mowers, which enable one man to do the work of a hundred Chinese," he scoffed. Speer similarly admitted that it was only "by dint of the excessive toil of the vast numbers of people employed" that "the lands are as well cultivated and as highly productive as they are elsewhere by any improved system."[19] If Euro-Americans saw machines as a "measure of men,"[20] the Chinese failed to stack up, even if their agricultural environs looked as orderly as any Christian country's. It was the very thing that redeemed their agricultural landscape that doomed their built environment: China's plentiful people. And it was its plentiful people that brought Chinese environs in line with the perceived moral disorder of other heathen landscapes.

Americans transferred their assumptions about Chinese landscapes to the dwelling places of the Chinese in America. Commentators tended to focus on how crowded and squalid their living conditions were. James Haggerty, a former Union soldier and Andersonville survivor who traveled west with six ex-soldier companions in 1870, portrayed Chinatown in his travel diary:

> These block's are cut up into small alleyway's about ten foot wide with Tenement Houses on both sides the Tenements are cut up into small rooms like prison cells and hear the Chinese swarm like rats. . . . To have a good look at "China Town" start out In the after noon and go down Kearney Street until you come to Jackson Street turn down Jackson and there you are right in the middle of a crowd of jabbering tan colored galoots chattering like a crowd of monkey's all along the side walk are Chinamen selling fruit, vegitables, green's, etc. . . . they haller all the way down the street, untill you wish you had a good sized club so you could swing it around your head once and knock down a dozen or so.[21]

For Haggerty, the landscape was inseparable from the people. In fact, you could hardly *see* the landscape for all the people—if people they actually were.

Alfred Trumble, a self-styled "old Californian," described Chinese environs as resembling the nonsensical burrowing of animals. Though superficially the "main streets of Chinatown are innocuous enough to the view" and are "altogether bright enough and harmless enough to create rather a pleasing impression on the civilized eye," he warned that they "are but walls of the sepulcher. . . . Pass behind them, and the corruption they hide will speak for itself to every sense which is the attribute of decent men. The ramifications of Chinatown's byways are indescribable. Winding ways have been burrowed through the hearts of blocks as rats bore their way through solid walls. From serpentine alleys others branch out to end nowhere."[22] Just as did missionaries overseas, so observers of the Chinese in America connected the external appearance of their dwelling places to their spiritual condition. Trumble might just as easily have been writing about the "winding ways" of ignorance, darkness, and superstition burrowing through the hearts of heathens as he was about the alleys of Chinatown. It was surely no accident that he titled his anti-Chinese diatribe *The Heathen Chinee.*

Observers of Chinese livingscapes in the United States also never failed to comment on their temples, or "joss houses," often depicted as the nerve centers to which their winding streets led. Arthur Stout, a physician, noted in 1862 that "while but few are here, the occasional appearance of an idol temple may not be of consequence; but when, ere long, the immigration, if not prevented, will be immense, these people will claim permission to worship according to their Oriental doctrine." This would change the American landscape: "In every valley and over every plain Christian churches and heathen temples, side by side, will offer the grotesque contrast to the sight."[23] Soon more temples did crop up as "the Chinese . . . made up their minds to take a decided stand, and in the open air, before all men, declare their allegiance to the gods of their fathers," as a *San Francisco Chronicle* article put it. "Heathen" temples were easily recognizable, outwardly displaying the "grotesque symbols of their mysterious faith, wrought in the fantastic and peculiar style of Oriental art." They were also recognizable by sound—"unearthly noise connected with a heathenish rite"—and the smell of "suffocating perfume" from burning incense and paper money.[24] From time to time the Chinese took their rituals to city streets as well, as in a "heathen ceremony of driving the devil away," "performed by the Chinese" in Sacramento. An article about this ceremony that made it all the way to the London *Missionary News* in 1867 commented on "chants that were dolefully terrific," performed by "heathen priests" who had "arrived from San Francisco," as well as the sound of "gongs" and "hideous noises" as they "paraded the streets, bowing and chanting furiously." "Such is the heathenism in the so-called *Christian* country of America!" the article concluded with dismay.[25]

A foldout image of a "Gosh House" in Rev. Milton B. Starr's polemic, *The Coming Struggle; or What the People on the Pacific Coast Think of the Coolie Invasion,* illustrated the crowded interior of one such temple, showing a darkened space lit by a skylight, worshipers lying prostrate before dour bearded figures on daises, and other Chinese visitors chatting and going about their business in the same space. "There are such things as 'Gosh Houses' in San Francisco," the caption read. "There are a number of images in this temple, distinguished by no particular feature but unpronounceable names."[26] Translation: Why bother to learn anything specific about the beliefs and objects of Chinese ritual spaces and practices? If they were all just heathens anyway, as Starr repeatedly labeled them, they were all indistinguishable and nonsensical, just as were the alleys and byways of Chinatown.

"A Mere Animal Machine"

From the supposed crowding of the Chinese "in every hole and corner of these vast barracks," it was an easy slide to identifying the Chinese as heathen based on the condition of their bodies. Some observers claimed that, like a quick glance at Chinatown, first impressions of the Chinese might lead one to believe that they were clean and neat. "But cleanliness and neatness are very different matters," Trumble cautioned. "The one is a virtue, deep seated and far reaching, the other a simple acquirement, a mere veneer of decency, and that characteristic of Ah Sin [a nod to Bret Harte], which gains credit for a virtue, is simply a result of his imitative faculty." Even if one's Chinese domestic help seemed a "paragon of cleanliness," their manner of living when out of the eye of their employer was nothing short of pestilential, evidence that the Chinese did not know how to take care of themselves. Trumble shuddered at how "the scales of the leper fall upon the sound man in the bunk below him."[27] Starr, appointed "Grand Lecturer" of the People's Protective Alliance of California, an anti-Chinese and nativist organization, snuffed that "no European would occupy a dwelling once inhabited by the coolies, however thoroughly it might be renovated, *for fear of some contagious disease.*" "They menace us with a fearful pestilence hitherto unknown in America," he warned, and "we cannot escape retributive vengeance if we permit the heathen races to mingle with our population."[28]

Starr and others blamed Chinese women, who attracted not only Chinese men but also the "lower" classes of White people, for the spread of disease beyond the clustering crowds of Chinatown. "Their women sit in unblushing crowds by day and by night, in open view," he complained, "with manner and voice to entice our youth and adult men to their haunts of vice."[29] This was another common allegation about the heathen, as we have seen: that they did not elevate their women, who ended up in a condition of debased slavery and depraved licentiousness, and were, as a result, unable to be good mothers and uplifters of their people. Rev. S. V. Blakeslee, formerly a supporter of the Chinese, came out against them in an 1876 address published in a special report of the California State Senate. Blakeslee alleged that Chinese women made American converts to heathenism by spreading their immorality and disease to children as well as adults. They were a dangerous inversion of everything a nurturing Christian woman was supposed to be: "I saw, when walking a Chinese street in open day, at a distance from any American house, in Nevada City, seven boys under ten years of age in one of their women's houses. And here in Sacramento City, the police have told me that many times they have taken boys under eight years of age, and of respectable, wealthy families, from the occupied couches of Chinese creatures. . . . Can these evils be prevented in this Christian land? I know of no way in which they will be if this immense immigration continues."[30] Blakeslee could not even bring himself to refer to Chinese women as human beings.

Even as anti-Chinese demagogues applied blanket stereotypes about heathenness to them, the notion that the Chinese were different from other peoples, as evidenced by the country's longevity, remained influential. Instead of reading the difference as a sign of Chinese "advancement," though, some began to see it as a frightening indication that the Chinese were subhuman due to their ability to survive in the worst of conditions. Other so-called heathens were believed to be dying out due to their inability to care for their lives and their lands, and hence were worthy of pity and paternalistic assistance. But the Chinese seemed to need no help as far as base survival went, and hence needed no pity. Instead, the proper emotion they should call forth in the Euro-American was fear.

Most Chinese laborers were sojourning men who sent money back to families in China until they could themselves return, and so it made practical sense for them to share living spaces and live frugally. Opponents of Chinese immigration mostly recognized this, but that did not stop them from searching for something deeper than demographics to explain how the Chinese lived. In a speech before the 1877 Social Science Association of America, Hon. Edwin Meade claimed that the Chinese laborer "has evidently reached the minimum at which existence may be maintained, and he desires little more. His food is usually a little rice, sometimes, as in India, mixed with curry, in this country occasionally with a piece of pork or fish, the whole not costing over from twenty-five cents to fifty cents per week; besides, it is not exaggerated that he will feed upon the meanest kind of food, including vermin." Meade blamed the Chinese level of subsistence not on inherent biological differences but on "the operation of fifty centuries of paganism, poverty, and oppression," which "have made him—a mere animal machine, performing the duties in his accepted sphere, punctually and patiently, but utterly incapable of any improvement."[31] The Chinese needed so little to operate on that they were no longer men, and not even really flesh-and-blood animals, but animal *machines*.

While some capitalists trumpeted the machine-like quality of Chinese laborers as the most efficient way to build America's newest machines, Starr took issue with the idea that they might boost California's, and the nation's, economy. "Pro-coolie advocates assert that the importation of the pagans, as serfs, multiply industries and enrich the country by creating a demand for more skilled laborers, the same as the introduction of labor-saving machinery." But, said Starr, "there is a radical difference in the working and results produced by the two machines." Labor-saving machines were a sign that the people who made them understood that "Divine wisdom" gave them the "intellectual power to seize upon the forces of nature and make them instruments in his hands to overcome the obstacles of nature itself."

If a man could make natural forces his "servants," he could be "redeemed from the curse that he must earn his bread by the 'sweat of his brow.'" Such inventions also benefited the nation as a whole: "Every such invention implies growth and expansion, capability and power to develop the natural resources of wealth and intellect of the whole country." But "can we claim any such results from the incoming heathen?" Of course, Starr answered with a resounding "no." The heathen were stultifying influences on the nation who contributed nothing to its material, intellectual, or spiritual benefit. Unlike labor-saving machines that freed men for higher pursuits, heathen machines impoverished the nation, since, as subhuman beings, they were always able to work for less than Euro-Americans.[32]

"Proof That You Are Pagan"

But how and why did heathenism create this result? To understand the logic of the anti-immigrationists, we have to dig deeper into how most Americans conceived of the substance of Chinese religion at the time. They would have gleaned their information from articles like Augustus Ward Loomis's accounts in the *Overland Monthly,* which "examined the quirky, the material, and the picturesque, as well as the highly philosophical and intellectual . . . thereby open[ing] the door to a wider world of popular religious description."[33] In articles like the 1869 "Chinese 'Funeral Baked Meats,'" Loomis—who, along with his wife, Mary Ann, served as a Presbyterian missionary to China, to the Creek (Muscogee) Nation in Oklahoma, and among the Chinese in San Francisco—tried to explain the core of Chinese "religion" to curious readers. Though he glancingly acknowledged some differences between "the Buddhist doctrine, of purgatory," "the Tauists' notion respecting spirits," and "ancestral worship, which is older than the religions of Buddha and Tau," he alleged that "it is very seldom indeed we may meet with a Chinaman who has not his head full of the superstitions of all the three."[34]

American observers held that the Chinese, like other heathens, made the fatal mistake of deifying creatures rather than their Creator. In an article titled "Occult Science in the Chinese Quarter," Loomis explained that "Chinamen seem, indeed, to have a fondness for the marvelous; and, never having been taught to trace many of the ordinary phenomena of nature to their true causes, they are easily persuaded to attribute them to supernatural agency."[35] The primary false gods of the Chinese were thought to be their parents and ancestors. Some saw respect for ancestors as harmless, and even "praiseworthy, . . . indicative of noble feelings." Said Loomis, "People who see only these marks of respect for the dead, and know not how much idolatry is mixed with it, see nothing which is reprehensible but much that is commendable." But when "we become acquainted with some of their superstitions respecting the dead, . . . our admiration changes to pity." Loomis described the richness of Chinese provisions for the dead, which included "five kinds of animal food uncooked, and the five kinds which are cooked; also a variety of cakes and dishes of vegetables, with fruits, wine, and tea," and "whole fowls and fish fantastically ornamented; also a pig's head, or an entire hog; with pyramids of cakes and fruits, and vases of flowers." He also noted how expensive death was for the Chinese, and especially for Chinese immigrants, who had to pay a "special sum" to have their remains sent back to China: "As we see, it must cost a large amount for a Chinaman to die and to get finally laid down where 'the weary may be at rest.'"[36]

Loomis concluded his discussion of Chinese funerary practices with an expression of pity for the deluded Chinese. How pathetic their "heaven of tinsel money, tallow candles, paper garments, boiled rice, and samshu, with Chinese theatricals and Buddhistic mummeries intermingled." Much preferable was "a paradise in which hunger, thirst, and carnal desires may never more torment us." The "earnestness with which they endeavor to make provision for a future state" was admirable, he admitted, but "it makes us very sad to see how utterly mistaken they are." Still, as a missionary whose work was predicated on the possibility of heathen conversion, Loomis maintained that "there is room for them all in that place where 'the many mansions be,' and there is a power which is able to fit them for companionship with prophets and apostles."[37]

Speer believed that the "power" that could fit the Chinese for Christian companionship was not just the Christian God but the very machines they had been brought to America to build. From their labor on the railroads, he said, the Chinese would "learn to look for help and safety not to a dumb wooden idol, but to a mighty power which surpasses all they have ever imagined. It has limbs of iron, heart of fire, lungs of steam, ravenous appetite and thirst, with the strength of a thousand horses, and yet tractable to the touch of a man's finger. What a teacher is the steam-engine, in all its thousand applications in this country, to the strangers whose nation never till recently possessed one!" Speer claimed that "the events of the last thirty years have thoroughly waked the Chinese government to the necessity of fitting itself to cope with the powers of the West. . . . It has given license to telegraphic communication between its seaports. It will by degrees introduce railroads," which had hitherto not been built because of "*fung shwui*" superstitions and Chinese fears of disturbing the bones of their ancestors.[38]

Speer was a champion of the Chinese. Opponents of Chinese immigration took ideas such as those Loomis and Speer presented about Chinese ancestral worship and used them as reasons for Chinese incompatibility with American identity. The masses had turned ancestor worship, they said, into a stultifying superstition. Said Mungen, "It is . . . a most unequivocal form of idolatry. . . . It involves an untruth of the most serious and far-reaching character, namely, that the spirit of the dead are at liberty to visit their posterity; and it is also a proposition in mockery of common sense, namely, that the dead require articles of food, clothing, and furniture etherealized by fire." Mungen claimed that "this system has a most deleterious effect upon Chinese society. . . . Every man is taught to act and think and feel as his parents or progenitors do or have done before him, and so to venerate his ancestry, their remains and burial-places, that as they recede from him he comes to worship them, if he worships anything at all; and his only hope in the future is to lay his bones among them, to be in turn revered by his posterity. That is his future."[39] In other words, the Chinese future was stuck in the past.

The contrast between the stagnating East and the progressive West was a common Orientalist trope, and one that anti-Chinese lecturers perpetuated with relish in order to turn on its head the Chinese claim to superiority because of the antiquity of their civilization. "Although at a period as early as the date of Thebes, in Egypt, the Chinese had a settled form of government," Mungen crowed, "what are they now but a poor, miserable, dwarfish race of inferior beings, physically and mentally, and pagans at that?"[40] Since the Chinese were always looking to (and expending money on) the dead, they failed to improve their lives, their vast empire, or any place to which they migrated. The Reverend William Lobscheid, of the United German Evangelical Saint Mark's Church in San Francisco, alleged, "Is this lack of public spirit not a proof that you are Pagan, that you are determined to continue to be so . . . ?"[41] Here he echoed Benjamin Wisner, who accused "Paganism universally" of having "no charities. Throughout its widely extended domain, not a hospital, or an asylum, rears its head. Almost every where, the sigh of the orphan is unregarded, the tear of the destitute unpitied, the groan of the dying unheeded."[42] Since heathens / pagans were so worried about their false gods, they were said to pay little attention to the actual needs of the living. And the Chinese migrant failed to learn any productive lessons from his sojourn in America: "Returning to his native land, he is as ignorant of machinery as when he left, and the money he has earned is spent in feeding and clothing the spirits of the other world" rather than in nourishing or outfitting himself or his compatriots.[43]

As we have seen, Americans believed that paganism/heathenism could shape the bodily needs and social development of adherents over time, such that they became less than human. To claim that the Chinese were mere mindless machines, who needed little on which to subsist because they did little but mechanistically worship their dead, was not to say that heathenism was innate and could never be wiped out, but that missionaries should not deceive the public into believing that it could be wiped out quickly. Just as Chinatown always revealed disease beneath gilded surfaces, so the Chinese people, for now and for the foreseeable future, always revealed heathenism beneath supposedly civilized surfaces, because of its stultifying influences on their historical and human development (or lack thereof). Writers often used the term "heathen race" or "pagan race" to refer to the Chinese, highlighting the slide between religious and biological descent.

"Is Not Christianity Stronger than Heathenism?"

If the Chinese ability to subsist in subhuman conditions resulted from "the morass into which paganism has dragged them," in the words of Lobscheid, the Euro-American inability to do the same supposedly resulted from their Christian identity.[44] In contrast to the heathen Chinese, Christian Europeans proclaimed that they had "improve[d] the country" wherever they migrated. In America, they had "public spirit," which meant that they looked out for their living (not dead) families and friends, and felt an obligation to contribute to the maintenance of churches, missions, schools, and hospitals. They also had to spend money on clean clothing and food, and sufficiently spacious shelter for themselves and family, since, as John H. Boalt said before the Berkeley Club in 1877, "we have encouraged each other to think that overcrowding leads to immorality, that plenty of air and sunlight are necessaries of life, that our old and infirm must be properly cared for and kindly treated."[45] Blakeslee put it this way: without money, the "American laborer" (almost always imagined as a White man) would have to "live more nearly like a heathen" along with "his wife and children." The "Chinese, in his less expenses, can always underbid the American unless the American will descend to the same level with him, in a cheap, wretched, uncivilized, unchristian manner of living. But this inevitably involves similar degradation, immorality, and vice, or possibly worse."[46]

Euro-American laborers needed money to convince themselves that they were mindful men instead of mindless machines, and sympathetic and social Christians instead of selfish heathens. "The truth is, we have taught each other habits that are expensive," Boalt acknowledged. "The Chinaman is what he is because of China; the American is what he is because of America. Under the circumstances there cannot be a fair competition between them. You cannot give the American laborer a long line of Chinese ancestors."[47] But the emphasis on money as an American necessity raised an interesting tension. The American laborer had to walk a fine line between the pursuit of money for the sake of Christian manliness, which included providing for family, church, and state, and the pursuit of money for personal wealth and luxury alone. For money could be made an idol too, and as Starr admitted, "the idolatry of our own hearts is bad enough."[48] The capitalists who "imported" Chinese labor for the sake of enriching their pockets provided ample proof. Starr clumped the heathen Chinese together with these capitalists—both idolaters, and both threats to the nation—in contrast to the "honest laborer" who needed money to be a man. To the extent that "honest laborers" included Catholics, this represented an implicit shift from earlier Protestant rhetoric that clumped Catholics with heathens for their shared reverence of images and formalistic rituals.[49] Speaking for the laborer, the Congregationalist Starr claimed that "idolatry is not our God. It is not the God by whom we testify. It is not the God of intelligence and progression. It is not the God of civil and religious freedom. It is not the people's God. It is Nebuchadnezzar's golden image; will you bow down and worship that? No; rather pass through a storm of fire, heat seven times hotter than this nation ever endured before, and the God of your fathers, your God, will bring you out with heads unsinged and garments unscathed."[50]

Opponents of the Chinese also told Americans not to try to save money by buying Chinese-made items. The *Morning Call* of 1873 declared, "Let no one purchase a Chinese-made cigar, a pair of boots manufactured by a Chinaman, or a pair of duck pants manufactured by him, and storekeepers will cease purchasing these goods, and manufacturers to employ Chinese to make them." Better to spend a few more bucks to keep one's fellow Euro-American laborer employed and his family fed, so that he could spend a few more bucks to keep Christian society running, than to try to save a few cents here and there on goods made by the selfish heathen. With this context in mind, advertisements that proclaimed, "WHITE LABOR EMPLOYED EXCLUSIVELY," were not just about xenophobia and economic competition but also about the supposed social consequences of heathen labor, one of which was the abrogation of missions themselves, since White people could not support them if reduced to the salary of Chinese "machines."[51]

The argument that being a good Christian and good American required money allowed opponents of the Chinese to claim that their opposition was based not solely on crass materialism and class conflict but on piety and patriotism. For (and this is Mungen now, before Congress, no less) "our people are not rat-eating, snake-eating, cat-eating, pup-eating, rice-eating lazzaroni. . . . They look through nature up to nature's God"—instead of looking for gods in nature—"and feel themselves men. They draw their lessons from the divine precepts, and know that they have as large an interest in the great hereafter as the richest man in the country. Feeling and knowing this, they act like men, and are fully up to the standard of manhood among the most intelligent."[52] Mungen implied that the feeling of equality Americans derived from knowing that the laborer and the capitalist had the same chance at heaven made them live in the here-and-now as though they were deserving of the best, instead of being content with the worst.

Starr explained that the workingman's feeling of fundamental equality also animated America's republican government. The subservient Chinese might "tolerate" inequality, but liberty-loving Americans never would. And again, the difference could be explained by religious affiliation. Just as the Chinese were in perpetual subservient obedience to their ancestors, so they had been subservient to their emperor, the chief leader of their formalistic and baseless worship, for generations. The Chinese, said Starr, had been "locked up for centuries under tyrannical and superstitious service to the imperial majesty of Josh" and "are more easily deceived and enslaved than any other people."[53] If allowed to stay in America and if given the vote, they would too easily become "vassals to the wealthy," voting as the capitalists who had "imported" them here dictated. As Edwin Meade put it, "A republican or even liberal government of any form is to [the Chinese] quite incomprehensible. Government to their minds is a despotic power, in which they have no lot or part, except unqualified obedience. . . . Their superstitions, prejudices, and opinions have become as fixed as their habits of life."[54] Preserving the religious liberty and political equality of other Americans required preventing the heathen from exercising the same.

But "a taunting question is often proposed: Is not Christianity stronger than heathenism?" asked Blakeslee, with what we might surmise to be a hint of chagrin. "Is your religion afraid to meet the religion of the Chinese?" The question struck at the heart of what it meant to be "Christian" and "American" in the late nineteenth century. Confidence tangoed with anxiety, and this was extraordinarily so in the ways that anti-Chinese campaigners imagined themselves and their nation in opposition to the "heathen Chinese." Though everything in their worldviews dictated that Christianity should overpower heathenism, they worried that heathenism might overtake *them*. The number of converts missionaries had made was small, and as Blakeslee put it, "converts are not all on one side" either, "for an able deacon of a leading Congregational Church in San Francisco has written me, that where Americans have converted one Chinaman to Christianity, the Chinese, he believes, have converted ten Americans to real heathenism."[55]

Blakeslee defended Christianity as "*strong*" but admitted that "*Americans* are not always strong in Christian principle." This was especially apparent in boomtowns in the West, where the institutions of government and church struggled to keep up with the arrival of fortune-hunters and settlers. Moreover, though Christianity in itself was strong, that was no excuse to "open the gates of her fortresses to the enemy." Blakeslee described America as God's virgin stronghold for Christianity, which He had "kept . . . for thousands of years for the experiment of true Christian liberty," against the "petrified tyrannies, errors, vices, and irreligions of the old continents." But now, "to prostitute all American advantages and opportunities to a vast people, confirmed in old systems of debasement, idolatry, prejudice, immorality, and clannishness, . . . is exceedingly dangerous. It is exposing our whole country and its policy to volcanic eruptions of heathen hosts and abominations. 'Tis false Christianity, false benevolence, false patriotism." America, in Blakeslee's imagining, should be a fortress on a hill in order to preserve and develop its God-given identity, walled off from heathen intruders instead of welcoming them in.[56]

The Great Commission, or the Great Omission?

The idea that Americans should not allow heathens into their fortress called into question the theory that the heathens' arrival was providentially ordained by God to facilitate their conversion. Opponents of Chinese immigration argued that supporting their entry to the United States on missionizing grounds was a fallacy at best, and a "doctrine of devils" at worst, that provided pious cover for the rapacious greed of capitalists.[57] Father James Buchard, a Catholic priest of concealed Native heritage,[58] took the anti-missionary argument to one extreme when he said that the Chinese were constitutionally unable to become Christians, so that mission work was bound to fail: "Will you invite and bring in by thousands and hundreds of thousands this inferior race; these pagan, these vicious, these immoral creatures, that are incapable of rising to the virtue that is inculcated by the religion of Jesus Christ—the world's Redeemer"?[59] Missionary Otis Gibson angrily called this a "blasphemous utterance" that "should cause all believers in Christ to blush, to blush for very shame," as it went against the precept that God "hath made of one blood all nations of men." As he pointed out, the notion that "these Chinese are an inferior race, not capable of becoming Christians," plainly inferred "that to murder a Chinaman would not be a greater sin than to kill a monkey" (this also calls to mind Haggerty's nonchalant wish to "knock down a dozen or so" of "galoots chattering like a crowd of monkey's").[60] It also put to naught the Great Commission to "go ye therefore, and teach all nations, baptizing them in the name of the Father, and of the Son, and of the Holy Ghost." For if some men were mere monkeys (or machines), there was no point evangelizing them at all, whether in California or China. But since Buchard's own Catholic brethren had long-standing missions in China, Gibson concluded that he was going against his own church's teachings.

Nevertheless, Buchard's claim about the Chinese was a popular one, repeated in the press and taken up by rioters. Yet exclusion laws did not pass because of such extreme rhetoric alone. Many workingmen were already convinced by Buchard and the inflammatory remarks of anti-Chinese labor leader Denis Kearney well before exclusion made its way through the halls of government. It was not they who needed convincing. Anti-Chinese activists were aware that not only pro-Chinese ministers in California but also East Coast Protestants, who proudly claimed the heritage of antislavery and viewed the maltreatment of Native Americans with paternalistic pity, often looked askance at labor violence and unrest in California, seeing it as evidence of Californians' uncouth ways and pitying the Chinese for it. The American Board of Commissioners for Foreign Missions had, at the close of the Civil War, reaffirmed its commitment to the heathen, celebrated the Pacific Coast as a "broad and open gateway to the crowded millions of Asia," and affirmed that the nation's duty was not to "fenc[e] out the rest of the world, resolved to till with all painstaking our own fertile acres," but instead to "gir[d] ourselves, in a generous and manly spirit, for the work to which God calls us." Indeed, the ABCFM claimed that God had saved the nation in the late war so that it could take up mission work with a renewed sense of duty and gratitude and "successfully promote our national honor."[61]

It was promoters of this view of America who needed to be convinced that, in fact, fencing out the heathen was the right move. In order to gain wider national support in the churches and government, anti-Chinese lecturers and politicians had to take a more nuanced perspective that preserved the semblance of belief in monogenesis and missions (since they remained culturally regnant), while still arguing for exclusion. Starr did not deny that the Chinese could ever be converted—he just denied that the best way of effecting their conversions would be in the United States. "If ever Satan is transformed into an angel of light," said he, "it is when he brings a Bible doctrine and Christian ministers to justify his low, scavenger work of scraping up the scum and filth of heathenism and emptying it into the heart of Christianity." This, Starr maintained, striking at the holier-than-thou heart of the Eastern pooh-bahs, had been the excuse that proslavery ministers had offered to justify their peculiar institution. Eastern Protestants were claiming the wrong heritage if they thought that missionizing the Chinese in the United States was benevolent and providentially ordained. As "'the *love* of money is the root of all evil,' it is not strange that the worshipers of mammon should readily fall in with this scheme for enriching themselves," Starr accused, "but that Christians should be so 'blinded by the god of this world' as to believe the spurious doctrine, that God is sending the heathen here to be converted, is passing strange, for it is only a resurrection of the old pro-slavery argument, which being interpreted means, 'Let us do evil that good may come.'"[62]

Unlike Chinese heathenism, Starr claimed, African heathenism had never presented much of a threat. "The imported African was stripped of his idols and freedom. . . . He was not permitted to establish a Fetish temple, or perform a single act of his former stupid worship of material things that would corrupt the children of his master. Hence, as he gradually forgot the religion of his fathers, the transition from a material to a spiritual worship was a comparative necessity. . . . But, oh! at what a fearful price! . . . Do we wish to buy another experience like that?" Starr warned that another, worse war might be Americans' punishment if they continued to paint lipstick on the pig and justify the importation of heathens as a missionizing opportunity.[63]

Starr agreed that God had "made of one blood all nations of men," but argued that the Great Commission commanded Americans to "*go*" to the heathen, not to invite them in. California's pro-Chinese ministers were being lazy by sitting around and waiting for the Chinese to come here. As much as they trumpeted their Christian manliness, they were not being real men if they did not go abroad to the heathen world. He mocked their excuse, which instead made them handmaidens of greedy capitalists: "We can make money by their importation and cheap labor, while we save their souls. It will work like a 'labor-saving machine.'" But "nowhere are we told, directly, that the heathen are to come to civilization and establish idolatrous temples of worship." Starr argued that the Bible expressly prohibited such religiously promiscuous intermingling. "The Mosaic rule was, and the rule of the New Covenant is, 'to come out from among the heathen and be separate.'" Terrible things had happened to the Jews when they had mingled with the heathens, like the "death of Zimri and twenty-five thousand men, who brought heathen women into the camp of Israel." And terrible things were happening to America too, and would only continue to worsen if Americans failed to heed the "Divine injunction" to omit the heathen from their midst. By all means, go to China if you feel such compunction about the heathen, Starr urged. Otherwise, be prepared to "let the sons of Jeroboam marry the Zidonian princesses, who will bring with them the gods of their fathers, and entice our descendants to follow after their abominations."[64]

This line of reasoning—that the Great Commission required missionaries to go, and not stay—ultimately made its way into the halls of government and even the General Association of the Congregational Churches of California, which unanimously adopted a series of resolutions to modify the Burlingame Treaty to "restrict Chinese immigration" "and so relieve us from impending peril to our republican and Christian institutions."[65] In one of the interviews it conducted in order to formulate a recommendation, the Special Committee of the California State Senate heard from Rev. J. H. C. Bonte of Grace Church (Episcopal) in Sacramento. Bonte, like Starr, did not deny that "the conversion of the Chinese to Christianity is a consummation hoped for and believed in by every Christian," and expressed "no doubt whatever of the power of the gospel to regenerate the whole Chinese Empire." But Bonte claimed that "a heathen nation can be generally or permanently transformed only while in a settled condition, and while living in their natural surroundings." California was unsettled and its Euro-American population given to "hoodlumism and crime," Bonte acknowledged, making it hardly a favorable school for the Chinese. Moreover, "in [his] judgment, the Chinese exercise as much influence among the people of this coast in favor of paganism as the church among the Chinese in favor of Christianity." Hence "the grand contest, which is to end with the conversion of China, must be carried on in China," or it might end instead with the conversion of America to heathenism.[66]

"Unfortunately We Should Have Neither a Country Nor a People"

At the end of the day, then, the fear that America might turn heathen outweighed the hope that the Chinese in America might turn Christian. Of course, this was not the only reason why exclusion laws passed, but neither can we overlook the religious logic underlying exclusion. Scholars have tended to focus on the religious nature of support for the Chinese, and the economic and racial component of opposition to them. The typical story

"The Consequence of the Completion of the U.P.R.R.—a New Sect Is Added to Those Already in Existence." *Frank Leslie's Illustrated Newspaper,* July 3, 1869. Gale Primary Sources, Nineteenth Century U.S. Newspapers.

told is that the latter eventually overtook the former. But anti-Chinese racism was also shaped by religious rhetoric that painted heathenism as extraordinarily strong and dangerous. The Chinese provided a chilling lesson of how heathenism could stagnate an entire culture and change the bodies of an entire people. The antiquity of their empire showed how far the heathen could supposedly progress civilizationally, but also how meaningless the veneer of civilization was without the transforming power of Christ. According to some, the heavy burden of heathenism could even pull the Chinese lower than other peoples traditionally represented as less "developed," because it had permeated their culture for so long that they had become entrenched in their ways and more difficult to evangelize. The Chinese had perfected the art of temporal survival, but their existence was so rote and mindless as a result of centuries of obeisance to false gods that they had become machines more than men.

And so, encouraging Chinese immigration to build the glorious machines of which Americans were so proud led to a great and fearful irony in the minds of anti-Chinese demagogues. Instead of heralding the conversion of the heathen and coming of the Christian millennium, the railroad promised the very opposite if Chinese labor were not curtailed.[67] In the words of Mungen, "All white labor shall be thus superseded, and the great Chinese or pagan millennium of the party in power shall blaze forth illuminated with haloes of oriental splendor, intermingled with pigtails and chopsticks. . . . Then our people could out-manufacture and out-produce the world were it not for one thing—unfortunately we should have neither a country nor a people. If such a thing shall happen there will be a few prosperous and bloated masters, and hordes of Asiatic drudges." An 1869 image from *Frank Leslie's Illustrated Newspaper* dramatized the fear. According to the caption, the image showed "the consequence of the completion of the U.P.R.R. [Union Pacific Railroad]—a new sect is added to those already in existence."[68] Though not as overtly dehumanizing and demonizing as some other images from the period, the illustration nevertheless suggested that the railroad might have the opposite result of what boosters like Calvin Colton had hoped for, spreading the subservient worship of "bloated masters" by "hordes" of men in queues instead of serving as a "highway to the heathen."[69]

"This Is What Keeps Me the Heathen I Am"

Five years after the passage of exclusion, American readers heard from one of the "heathen Chinese" directly. Wong Chin Foo explained his perspective in an article titled "Why Am I a Heathen?" in the *North American Review*. Born in Shandong Province in 1847, Wong had been baptized at the age of twenty, but just a handful of years later—having studied in the United States in the interim and then returned to China—he was excommunicated from the Shanghai Baptist Church. In 1873 Wong embarked on a lecture tour of the United States, and the following year, he "declare[d] himself China's first Confucian missionary to the United States."[70]

In "Why Am I a Heathen?" Wong took up the same issues of money and machines that were so central to the debates over Chinese immigration. On one thing, Wong could agree with the anti-Chinese demagogues: that the Chinese were different from Americans, and that heathenism was responsible for the difference. But Wong turned the tables. Sure, heathens might not have innovated the world's latest machines. But they were happier as a result. Americans were committed to "the restless Christian doctrine of ceaseless action." They, and not the Chinese, were putting people out of work by creating machines, for "if my shoe factory employs 500 men, and gives me an annual profit of $10,000, why should I substitute therein machinery by the use of which I need only 100 men, thus not only throwing 400 contented, industrious men into misery, but making myself more miserable by heavier responsibilities, with possibly less profit?" Though the heathen might be accused of being machine-like men, Wong explained that they were satisfied to accomplish things through repetitive shared manual labor, for each person then had a role to play instead of becoming extraneous: "As the heathen does not encourage labor-saving machinery, I do not have to be idle if I don't want to, and, as a result, work is more equally distributed."[71]

Wong also defended heathenness against the charge that it made adherents not socially minded. Their care for older generations was perfect proof of their compassion for others, in contrast to the "Christian style," which is "for children to expect their parents to do all for them, and then for the children to abandon the parents as soon as possible." And he accused Christians of doing good only "for immediate honor and for future reward; he lends to the Lord and wants compound interest." Nor did Wong find the "future reward" of the Christians particularly appealing, if heaven included the likes of Kearney and dangerous criminals who had had deathbed repentances. "Suppose Dennis Kearney . . . should slip in and meet me there, would he not be likely to forget his heavenly songs, and howl once more: 'The Chinese must go!' and organize a heavenly crusade to have me and others immediately cast out into the other place? . . . while I, the good heathen (supposing the case), who had done naught but good to my fellow-heathen . . . , I was unmercifully consigned to hell's everlasting fire, simply because I had not heard of the glorious saving power of the Lord Jesus, or because the construction of my mind would not permit me to believe in the peculiar redeeming powers of Christ!" Christianity's exclusivism proved it unjust, said Wong, and the failure of Christians to abide by the Golden Rule proved them hypocrites. "This is what keeps me the heathen I am!" he concluded. "And I earnestly invite the Christians of America to come to Confucius."[72]

A month after the publication of Wong's article, a rejoinder, "Why I Am Not a Heathen," came out in the *North American Review*, written by a fellow Chinese immigrant, Yan Phou Lee. Lee was born in Guangdong fourteen years after Wong and came to the United States at the age of twelve under an educational mission established by Yung Wing, the first Chinese graduate of a North American university (Yale). Lee was embedded in a Christian household in Springfield and found his growing inclinations toward Christianity strengthened after hearing evangelist Dwight L. Moody at an 1876 revival. Lee matriculated at Yale, graduating in 1887, and authored the "first book published in English by an Asian American author," the autobiographical *When I Was a Boy in China*.[73] Where Wong renounced Christianity and gladly accepted the title of "heathen," Lee held firm to the faith and adopted some of the negative assumptions that Christians held about heathenism. "Having been a heathen myself, and an associate of the heathen," said he, "I am competent to say that they never do any good without expecting a return, or gaining some merit." Lee rebutted Wong's critiques of Christianity by "discriminat[ing] between true Christians and hypocrital ones. Confucius says: 'It is impossible to carve on rotten timber.' Christianity is not responsible for the acts of morally rotten men, and yet, where there is any soundness at all, it has demonstrated its power to heal and save." Many Christians were generous and kind, Lee affirmed, but he accused the Americans who persecuted the Chinese of having "perver[ted]" Christianity.[74]

Despite their differences, Wong and Lee both ultimately used the concept of heathenism against the White Americans who sought to exclude the Chinese from the United States. Lee applied the heathen barometer to bigoted White Americans by calling them heathens, too: "The ways of the American heathen and the Chinese heathen are wonderfully alike. Only the American may become a Christian whenever he chooses with greater facility than the Chinese. That is not saying, however, that the American heathen may not be worse than the Chinese." While Wong called on American Christians to become heathens, Lee called on "all heathen, whether American, or English, or Chinese, to come to the Saviour." For Lee, the power of conversion on the heathen was so transformative that even the likes of Kearney could repent and become a wholly new man: "Even if [he] should slip into the Heavenly Jerusalem, he would be lamb-like and would be heard to say: '*The Chinese must stay!* Heaven is incomplete without them.'"[75]

Whether they knew it or not, Wong and Lee wrote at precisely the same time that others were debating the very question of just whom heaven might be "incomplete without." We now turn from heathen exclusion from the body politic to the parallel question of heathen inclusion—on earth as it is in heaven.

7

INCLUSION

On May 5, 1893, a group of businessmen, missionaries' children, and professors held a luau in honor of Professor William DeWitt Alexander and Lorrin A. Thurston, son and grandson of Hawaiian missionaries. They might have enjoyed a roasted pig and some poi, but it is unlikely that they would have watched a hula. These men wanted the United States to annex Hawai'i, and part of their professed reason for this was to rid the islands of Hawaiian traditions like the "voluptuous obscenities of the Hawaiian hula—or cancan," as one attendee put it.[1] They viewed the hula as a heathen vestige that their parents were supposed to have eradicated, and justified annexation as a way to complete the task.

The luau's guests were instead entertained by a reading of an intercepted "SECRET MESSAGE" purportedly from President Grover Cleveland to Congress. The annexationists were unhappy with Cleveland for opposing their plans and attempting to reinstate the deposed Queen Lili'uokalani. They had conspired to overthrow her government in January of the same year, replacing it with a Provisional Government staffed by themselves and their supporters. Cleveland's memo—which was almost certainly satirical and written by someone else[2]—complained that the Provisional Government had attempted to assassinate him by soliciting a "kahooner" to undertake the "nefarious, heathenish, and diabolical practise" of "praying to death; a proceeding which is common in that benighted country, and which if successfully conducted, compasses the death of its object, or victim."[3]

The "kahooner" had illegally obtained "one of my old boots," this Cleveland protested, and with it had set up camp in "Lafayette Square, directly opposite to the White House," where "he proceeds, nightly, to germinate and project the unholy influences of the 'annanar' toward the Presidential Mansion, accompanying the same with incantations and a shuffling dance, which in itself indicates a heathen environment." Not only did he bring the songs and dance of Hawaiian heathenism to the nation's capital, Cleveland charged; he also brought a frighteningly otherworldly aura: "His eyes glow at night with a phosphoresent light and the unearthly glare can be distinctly seen from the White House. At times, the odor of sulphur eminates from the locality occupied by him, and dismal music proceeds from a crude instrument unknown to our civilization."[4]

Cleveland attributed to the "kahooner" a host of woes. The "first assault" left him prostrate "on the floor of the 'Blue Room,' as if [he] had taken an excessive quantity of cucumbers and watermellons." After that, a favorite dog was felled; next, a "valuable servant who prepares with rare skill the Presidential drinks" was "stricken with paralysis"; the "Presidential horses have been attacked with blind staggers"; and the "billy goat which draws the Presidential baby wagon" lost its hair. Cleveland submitted these strange occurrences to the "Super-natural department of the 'Smithsonian,'" whose experts determined their heathenish cause. He closed by importuning Congress to "invit[e] an International Convention which shall declare that such practices are contrary to the law of nations"—but not before sending his secretary of the navy to the "miserable pittance of a nation called Hawaii" to learn the practice of "annanar" ("praying to death") himself in order to make it work on Cleveland's behalf. The secretary's first mission was to send "the infamous Dole"—president of the Provisional Government and another missionary's son—"into an unholy grave."[5]

This satirical "SECRET MESSAGE" no doubt provoked laughs among the annexationists at the luau. The descriptions of the kahuna's "phosphoresent" eyes and "sulphur[ous]" odor; his supposed hexing of a billy goat and dog; and the purported training of the secretary of the navy in the kahuna's arts were exaggerated enough to communicate the memo's facetiousness. The idea that the Provisional Government would send a kahuna to kill Cleveland was also patently satirical, since the annexationists believed that Hawaiian spiritual leaders had an undue influence on the monarchy.

To laugh at heathenism instead of just trying to eradicate it might be seen as a step toward the category's decline. Yet the memo reached for comedy in still-regnant assumptions about the bodies, motions, sounds, smells, and afterlife of the heathen. The idea that a "heathen environment" could be created and recognized by dance and music recalled missionaries' and travelers' fearful but fascinated accounts of the people whose worlds they breached. The notice of glowing eyes evoked traditional depictions of the devil; the mention of sulphur called forth the lake of fire. The notion that a kahuna might be found to assassinate the president also emerged in the context of growing worry about the imperfect conversion of the islands to Christianity, despite the trumpeting of various boosters about the early missionaries' rapid success. Amplifying this worry helped proponents of Hawaiian annexation to justify their position. Presenting Hawaiians as still heathen worked to racialize them as still needy.

Where American politicians decided that the "heathen Chinese" should be excluded from their shores, they made very different decisions for others in the so-called heathen world whose lands and material goods they had an interest in. They played the heathen card to justify annexation of Hawai'i, control of the Philippines, and detribalization of Native Americans under the guise of incorporating them into the nation. By the late nineteenth century, declamations of the impending extinction of Native Americans, with the close of the frontier, became more frequent. Meanwhile, the populations of Hawai'i and the Philippines, unlike those of China, did not seem interested in coming to the mainland in large numbers, and thus their formal inclusion in the American empire did not threaten to heathenize it, unlike a supposedly massive influx of Chinese. Moreover, many Native Americans, Hawaiians, and Filipinos had already been exposed to Christianity, whether by Protestant or by Catholic missionaries. The problem with them (so the story went) was that they had insufficiently converted (if at all) and threatened to relapse into heathenism without American Protestant intervention.

But inclusion of the heathen was not the benevolent counterpart to exclusion. It was forcible and still exclusionary, in the sense that the practices identified as heathen were supposed to be policed out of the population as the rationale and condition for inclusion. This was the case not just on earth but also in heaven. For at the same time that annexationists were arguing for the inclusion of certain so-called heathens into the American empire, some theologians and writers were arguing for inclusion of the heathen in a kind of heaven after death. Anti-imperialists explicitly blamed American rapaciousness for the dire state of the heathen world and contended that the heathen should be able to enter heaven, or at least have a second chance after death, given the unfairness of their situation on earth. Mark Twain, in his satirical final publication, *Extract from Captain Stormfield's Visit to Heaven*, included a parade of heathens among the saved. "Have they really rung in Mahomet and all those other heathens?" asks the titular character, incredulously, of a heavenly denizen. "Yes," is the reply; "they all had their message, and they all get their reward. The man who don't get his reward on earth, needn't bother—he will get it here, sure."[6]

Yet just as significant strings came with the inclusion of heathens on earth, so also did strings attach to their inclusion in heaven. Their admittance was predicated on their pliancy and peaceableness in this life, which were read as harbingers of their ability and willingness to accept Christianity after death. This chapter considers the costs of inclusion on earth and in heaven,

then, taking as case studies Hawaiian annexation and a theological controversy at Andover Theological Seminary over the salvation of the heathen. For most Americans, the heathen were not to be allowed into heaven
to stay just as they were, but to accept Christ after death, just as heathens
brought into the American empire were not to stay as they were, but to
accept American oversight and adapt to American mores.

"Scratch the Skin and You Came
to the Heathen"

In 1870, at the fifty-year jubilee of the first American Protestant missionaries' arrival on the islands, Rufus Anderson published a "history of the
Sandwich Islands mission" titled *A Heathen Nation Evangelized*. He explained that Hawai'i had been "regarded as an experiment in missions"
and that its history offered "remarkable" results. Anderson lauded its "independent and constitutional government, with a native sovereign at its
head, and a government as confessedly cognizant of God's law and the
gospel, as any one of the governments of Christian Europe; and, what is
more, with a Christian community of self-governed, self-supporting
churches, embracing as large a proportion of the people, and as really entitled to the Christian name, as the churches of the most favored Christian
countries."[7]

Nathaniel Bright Emerson disagreed, even though he was the son of missionaries who had arrived on Hawai'i in 1832, a decade after the first
band led by Hiram Bingham. Emerson had served in the Union army before training to become a medical doctor and returning to practice on
Moloka'i and Honolulu. He took a keen interest in Hawaiian politics and
claimed that things had taken a turn for the worse beginning with the accession of King Kamehameha V, "a heathen of depotic will," to the throne
(r. 1863–1872). In a handwritten, heavily edited essay that he drafted in
the middle of the annexation crisis, titled "A Page from Hawaiian History,"
Emerson charged that "his whole reign was ~~the~~ a protest ~~of a powerful heathen will~~ against progress and an effort to reinstate the heathenism of his
ancestors, in which he was largely successful." Kamehameha V particularly
angered Euro-Americans who wanted more influence and sway in the government, because he had "cast away the constitution of good king Kamehameha III"—under whose reign Hawai'i's communal lands had been
partitioned in the Māhele—in order to reinstate more absolute power to the
Hawaiian monarchy. Kamehameha V's death brought the short-lived,
"loveable and lamented Lunalino" to the throne for thirteen months, fol-

lowed by the "election of that prince of corruption, David Kalakaua," who sought to reinstate the "obscene" hula, among other things.[8]

Emerson reserved his choicest condemnations for Queen Liliʻuokalani. Her accession, he explained, was originally "hailed[^seen] by the pious friends of good government as the occasion for [^indirect] appeals to her supposed kind womanly nature and to her educated Christian conscience [^in favor]on behalf of a return to the wise administrations of Kamehameha III & IV, and the lamented Lunalilo." Emerson (and other "pious friends") appealed to common assumptions about how Christianization was supposed to change gendered behavior. As we have seen, heathen women were commonly depicted as licentious, careless, and stubborn in their ways, or as abject and pitiable slaves in the thrall of their fathers and husbands. Either way, they were supposed to be uninstructable save for the converting power of the gospel. The Christian woman, by contrast, was supposed to have an educated mind of her own that was kind but firm in the moral convictions of its regenerated conscience. In this, Emerson claimed, Liliʻuokalani had proved deceptive and insincere. Though feigning Christian observance and church attendance, "she remained under the spell of the defunct gods of ancient Hawaii, walked on occasion walked unclad in their mystic processions in the dead of night, sacrificed at their shrines, and took ghostly counsel with the kaunas, the priests of Hawaii's ancient cult. It was but necessary [^but] to scratch the skin and you came to the heathen."[9] Religion constituted the body's true nature in this description of heathenness lurking just beneath the surface of the skin. To Emerson, Liliʻuokalani would not be someone whom American Protestants could easily sway or control, since she remained under the sway of "heathen" kahunas.

Emerson focused on the monarchs, who had been educated in Protestant schools and were supposed to be proof of the good work of the missionaries. Around the same time, Rev. James Bicknell, founder of the Association of Christian Workers for the Suppression of Idolatry, complained about the continued influence of heathenism among the Hawaiian people. He was as skeptical as Emerson about the triumph of the missionary project. The "majority of church members" are "not Christians," he alleged, "but semi-pagans worshiping Jehovah during health and the heathen gods in sickness." Native Hawaiians were understandably skeptical about the missionaries' God, whose arrival had coincided with the onslaught of deadly and widespread disease. Bicknell explained, "The natives reason that if Jehovah cares for nothing for the body, and will not hear prayer for its relief from sickness, of course the proper thing to do is to apply to the gods for the healing which Jehovah will not give. The tendency of present preaching is to confirm the people in idolatry."[10]

Bicknell and Emerson described a situation in which Christianity coexisted with the continuation of older practices that they identified as heathen: the one, officially sanctioned, provided common ground for Native Hawaiians to interact with Euro-Americans and gain their respect, and the other granted a sense of control in times of disease and death. Just as Emerson described the heathenism lurking just beneath the surface of Liliʻuokalani's skin, so Bicknell claimed that Christianity was only a "veneer" in Hawaiʻi, "spread over the surface of the religious life of most Hawaiian churchmembers. Satan in the form of fetich and ancestral worship, lies beneath. The preaching of the native Pastors does not exorcise the evil spirit." Indeed, many churches allowed people to continue traditional practices, so much so that Bicknell accused them of being more the "synagouges of Satan than temples of the Living God."[11] Decades of debate about heathenism's historical origins came crashing down as the old colonial pattern of equating Indigenous religion with devil worship reared its tired head again.

Policing Heathenism

Bicknell claimed that Hawaiian idolatry was now "subtile" and that the people "dislike greatly to be called pagans. They desire to present a civilized exterior though their minds be brimful of idolatrous notions. Tax a Hawaiian as being a hoomanamana case, and he will resent it. No matter how deeply he may be engaged in idolatrous practices, he will not admit it. He will deny stoutly that he is an idolater until he is found out, and his practices exposed." Though the Hawaiian Kingdom ostensibly recognized freedom of conscience, hoʻomanamana, which Bicknell understood as heathen "idolatry," was subject to governmental policing that went well beyond taxing.[12]

This had been the case since the abolition of the kapu system in 1819 and the adoption of Christianity by Queen Kaʻahumanu in 1825. The Hawaiian priesthood had been abolished, and kahunas forced to go underground with their practices. Lot Kapuāiwa, who became King Kamehameha V, and David Kalākaua (r. 1874–1891) encouraged traditional Hawaiian medicinal practices again (seen by Christians as idolatrous, superstitious, and dangerous). But even so, the constitutions and penal codes enacted under their reigns allowed for significant governmental oversight into matters of religion and medicine. The 1864 Constitution of Kamehameha V retained the language of earlier constitutions written with the assistance and support of missionaries; Article 1 provided that "God hath endowed all men with certain inalienable rights," and Article 2 stipulated that "all men are free to worship God according to the dictates of their own consciences; but this sacred privilege hereby secured, shall not be so construed as to justify acts of licentiousness, or practices inconsistent with the peace or safety of the Kingdom."[13] The 1887 Constitution, commonly known as the Bayonet Constitution because it was forced on King Kalākaua by antimonarchists at threat of deposition by armed militia, opened with the same articles.[14] It also took power from the monarchy and put it in the hands of the legislature and cabinet. The Constitution of the Republic of Hawaii, enacted by the Provisional Government that spuriously overthrew Queen Liliʻuokalani in 1893, opened with the same language of inalienable rights, freedom of conscience, and the privilege of what was now termed "Religious Freedom,"[15] but added that "the Legislature may provide by law, however, for the supervision, registration, control and identification of all persons."[16] The wording of all these versions left the door open for surveilling and punishing anything defined to be "licentious" or against "peace or safety."

The penal codes of the Hawaiian Kingdom expanded on what counted as dangerous, defining "any person who practices hoomanamana or pretends to tell fortunes," and "any person who practices anaana" ("the power of praying persons to death"), as "Vagrants.—Disorderly Persons."[17] The practice of medicine was also policed and licensure made mandatory. The codes outlawed traditional Hawaiian medicine, stating that any "practitioner who shall be convicted of the practice of anaana, hoopiopio, hoounauna or hoomanamana, shall forfeit his license."[18] (*Hoopiopio* and *hoounauna* were understood as divisions of the Hawaiian priesthood. Hoopiopio was roughly translated as "sorcery," while hoounauna was "the sending of evil spirits on errands of death."[19]) From the mid-nineteenth to the early-twentieth century, the punishments for such practices increased, from half a year of jail detention that could be avoided by paying a fine, to expulsion and hard labor not exceeding five years.[20] In a context in which Native Hawaiians were publicly rallying, petitioning, and protesting for the overthrow of the Provisional Government, and drawing inspiration from traditional practices and beliefs in doing so, these were significant threats.[21] The classification of Hawaiian traditions as "vagrancy" and as unauthorized medicinal practices moved them into the domain of that which could be penalized by secular authorities, despite the lip service paid to freedom of conscience.

For annexationists, such classification also worked to define King Kalākaua and Queen Liliʻuokalani as unfit to govern, since they engaged in the revival of Hawaiian traditions. In 1886 Kalākaua had created the

Hale Nauā Society, translated as the "House of Wisdom" or the "Temple of Science." It was modeled after other popular fraternal organizations but included women and excluded anyone without Native Hawaiian ancestry, thus putting it outside the control of White sons of missionaries, businessmen, and planters. Among the resolutions the Society adopted were several related specifically to the "survival and increase of the Hawaiian race and other races as well, . . . which are greatly reduced and dying." The Society resolved that a member should travel around the world to raise money for the purpose of fostering health and "to take one of the ancient artifacts of the Society and any other item to foster good will during the trip around the world." The Society kept a detailed record of its holdings, including "20 Stone Idols—Males and Females, Large and Small," and "5 Wooden Fish Gods." It used these artifacts not only to "foster goodwill" but also in rituals aimed at healing.[22]

The Hale Nauā's "Rules" indicated that the Society "does not conflict with the nature of religious worship."[23] The Society's constitution and by-laws declared that "the object of this Society is the revival of Ancient Sciences of Hawaii in combination with the promotion and advancement of Modern Sciences, Art, Literature and Philanthropy."[24] The Society incorporated rituals to the Christian God as well as nods to "the gods," especially the "all-powerful Kane." It also paid reverence to the ruling family. In a September 1888 session, the Society honored then-Princess Lili'uokalani: "Our great desire to number the good deeds that you have performed, Royal One, will never end—they are vast, deep and numerous extending to the very foundation of the native world, to Hawaii of the Keawe chiefs, Maui of Chief Kakaalaneo, Oahu of Chief Kuihewa, Kauai of Chief Manokalanipo, your family gods and ancestors of the night." The Society also honored King Kalākaua and his wife, Queen Kapiolani, with this prayer: "The one important thing that we have to place before you today are the prayers that our Great President in the Heavens continues to prolong your life, the life of the King, the royal family, the chiefs and your native race of people. . . . Long live the Sovereign in the almighty God."[25] The unique phrasing of this prayer implied the lower position of the "almighty God" (the "Great President") to the king ("the Sovereign"). Given that Kalākaua had recently been forced to sign the Bayonet Constitution, which reduced his power to that of a figurehead, the elevation of the king over the "Great President in the Heavens" suggested that the Christian God had been elected for now but might have to step down, and at any rate must share power with other supernatural forces. The implication was that this God could remain "President" only so long as he supported the Hawaiian sovereign and the health and welfare of the "native race of people."

In his ardor to suppress what he believed was idolatry, Bicknell worried about just this prospect. He predicted that the Hale Nauā "will, by giving Jehovah a place in the Hawaiian pantheon, be subversive of true Christianity. . . . The next move, no doubt, will be to adopt Jehovah into the family of gods, and out of the union of Christianity and paganism, evolve a hodge podge which will be called a 'national religion.'"[26] Bicknell and Emerson understood that the persistence of Hawaiian traditions, behind closed doors, gave the monarchy a basis of authority over which they had little power. Heathenism, they feared, was not just a threat to eternal souls— it was a political threat to American control. To them, the Hale Nauā's attempts to unite Hawaiian traditions with "modern sciences" and Christianity were a sign of the promiscuous mingling of the false with the true, of the heathenish with the progressive Christian. The monarchs and other members of the Hale Nauā must not be true converts, according to this line of reasoning, and hence they could not be trusted to govern their country, given the supposed inability of heathens to correctly understand and take care of their lands and their lives. The secular governance that White Protestants demanded relied on an understanding of the land as saleable rather than sacred, and of bodies as useful laborers rather than useless idol-worshipers.

And if the monarchs, who had received the best education at missionary schools, did not understand this, then, as the annexationists saw it, the Hawaiian people were even less to be trusted. In the words of Emerson in his handwritten "Notes regarding Hawaiian Annexation," "If it were [^desired]~~required~~ to find out what [^is] the real wish of a majority of the native Hawaiians is on the question of annexation to the U.S., it would require a commission of archangels to do it, and they would not be able to accomplish the task. The majority of the natives[^them] are not capable of forming an opinion on such a matter." Tapping into the familiar trope of the infantilized heathen who could not think for themselves, he continued, "They are a shortsighted set of children and will vote according to the [^instructions] of the last plausible demagogue who [^may sway their passions] addresses them. . . . Hawaiians are <u>unfit for self government</u>. They are not yet far enough advanced in <u>political intelligence</u> to be capable of that wise choice which is essential to government of the people by the people."[27] And hence, even though Kalākaua had been overwhelmingly elected by the Hawaiian people, and had appointed his sister, Liliʻuokalani, as his heir, annexationists like Emerson could delegitimize their right to govern their people.

And that is exactly what the annexationists did. Though Liliʻuokalani appealed to her God-given right to the monarchy in multiple letters to

American authorities (writing to President William McKinley in 1897 that she was "by the Will of God named heir-apparent" and "by the grace of God Queen of the Hawaiian Islands"), Hawai'i became a US territory in 1898. Lili'uokalani never stopped calling on the "people of this great and good nation, from whom my ancestors learned the Christian religion," to right the wrongs inflicted on her and her people. Fully aware of the exalted status of the Protestant God in American secular governance, Lili'uokalani—beneath whose skin supposedly lurked the heathen—rested her case in the hands of "the Almighty Ruler of the universe, to him who judgeth righteously."[28]

"Subject to Imposition of All Sorts"

Not surprisingly, White Americans' treatment of Native Hawaiians paralleled their oversight of other so-called heathens whom they sought to manage and include in the US empire at the turn of the century. Hawaiian annexation must be considered not only with the backdrop of Chinese exclusion in mind but also alongside fin-de-siècle US attempts to control the Philippines and Native American tribes. In the Philippines, US colonial officials adopted a similar strategy of governance as in Hawai'i, characterizing Filipino practices and sacred objects as superstitious and fanatical, and using such characterization to justify their own rule. The religious landscape of the Philippines, as understood by colonial administrators, included not only the "Christian population" (majority Catholics and a smaller number of Protestants) but also, in the classificatory scheme of American war correspondent Murat Halstead, Chinese, "Moors or Mohametans" (also commonly dubbed "Moros"), and "Heathen."[29] In practice, the distinctions between these other-than-Protestant groups collapsed in the surveillance of superstition and fanaticism, which "was applied frequently, though unevenly, to animists, Catholics, and practitioners of Islam," as scholar Jeffrey Wheatley explains.[30]

Just as traditional healing practices made Emerson and Bicknell allege a lurking heathenism in the Hawaiian population, rulers on down, so US colonial administrators in the Philippines believed that "the presence of superstitions and fanatical groups signaled the atavistic racial nature of Filipinos across the board."[31] In a speech before the Senate in June 1902, for instance, Albert J. Beveridge of Indiana, a strident jingoist who had earlier declared that the "Philippines are ours forever," provided supposed proof of entrenched Filipino heathenism. He quoted from "perhaps the very greatest oriental authority in the world," one Archibald Colquhoun. According to Colquhoun, "A great many old pagan beliefs and customs are said to survive, even after centuries of Christianity" in the Philippines. Colquhoun warned that if "suddenly released from all religious trammels save those he voluntarily assumes, [the Filipino] will relapse into a state of heathenism." Colquhoun attributed this relapse to a racial trait: "*The well-known tendency of the Malay is to revert—to return to his former state.*"[32] He might as well have said, like Emerson, that scratching the skin of the Filipino would reveal the heathen beneath.

Similarly, just as Emerson and Bicknell argued that heathenism made Hawaiians incapable of self-governance, so too did American imperialists in the Philippines make the same kind of claim. Said William Howard Taft, donning the characteristic blinders that helped him think the United States was not imposing while other competitors were, "90 percent or more are densely ignorant, superstitious, and subject to imposition of all sorts."[33] The idea that ignorance and superstition—long the hallmarks of heathenism—made people "subject to imposition" recalls José de Acosta's influential contention that the devil was the heathens' first master; the original imposter/imposer on weak-willed humanity. Unable to see that their only allegiance was to God, the heathen kept trying to appease representatives of the devil on earth, which left them subject to tyrannical rule. Rather than understanding their nation as another tyrant, Americans like Taft believed that it was the United States' responsibility to save the heathen from a cycle of oppression.

The treatment of Hawaiian and Filipino practices also drew from earlier and contemporaneous White impositions on Native people. The US government had long abused and limited Native sovereignty. In 1887 Congress passed the Dawes Severalty Act, the same year as the Bayonet Constitution in Hawai'i. Native tribes that had previously been removed to reservations had been subject to attempts by the Bureau of Indian Affairs and "Friends of the Indian" (Protestant reformers) to "civilize" them.[34] By the late 1880s, it was becoming brutally clear that the reservation system was leading to competition for scarce resources as White settlers continued to encroach, often violently, on Native lands. The Dawes Act disastrously responded to these issues by breaking up reservation land, seeking to push the assimilation process further by severing Native people from their tribal identities and communities. It promised a 160-acre allotment to each head of family (80 acres to the unmarried and orphans over eighteen, and 40 acres to those under eighteen) and provided a path to citizenship for those who accepted the allotment and "adopted the 'habits of civilized life.'" But the act ultimately resulted in a devastating 66 percent reduction of "Indian land holdings from 156 million acres in 1881" to "53 million acres in 1933."[35]

"St. Paul's Indian Boarding-School, Yankton Agency, Dakota." In Charlotte Everett [Cook] Webster Scrapbook, 1863–1961, Joseph Witherspoon Cook Papers, Collection of Samuel Derrick Webster, 1771–1966, mssHM 48551 (20). Huntington Library, San Marino, California.

The Dawes Act was followed by redoubled efforts to wipe out heathenism among Native people. The slogan "Kill the Indian, save the man" might as well have been "Kill the heathen, birth the Christian." As did their fore-bears, so late nineteenth-century missionaries and teachers touted visual evidence of what "unheathenization" had done to the lands and bodies of Native people. Artifacts pasted into the scrapbooks of Charlotte Everett (Cook) Webster, daughter of Joseph Witherspoon Cook, missionary to the Yankton Sioux (Ihanktonwan Dakota Oyate), are paradigmatic of the kinds of images White Protestants relished. Much like the depictions of trans-formed heathen landscapes seen in Chapter 3, a drawing of Saint Paul's Indian Boarding-School at the Yankton Agency features a caption that sig-nals the "before" that viewers were to read onto the image: "There was not a tree to be seen in the neighborhood when the school was begun."[36] In place of a barren, uncultivated landscape, viewers could now look upon a tidy grove of well-kept trees fronting the large buildings that made up the school.

Similarly, images of schoolchildren were supposed to be seen with all the stereotypical assumptions of a heathen "before" in mind. An article pasted into the scrapbook explained the "before," detailing "Mr. Cook's first

"St. Paul's School." In Charlotte Everett [Cook] Webster Scrapbook, mssHM
48551 (27). Huntington Library, San Marino, California.

sight" of the "wild Indians" he was to evangelize: "Scarcely a dozen were
in civilized dress. All were 'blanket' Indians, with the usual accompaniments
of paint, feathers, gewgaws, bows and arrows and pistols, as if they were
expecting some sudden appearance of their enemies."[37] This "before" contrasted with the many "after" images Webster tucked into her scrapbook,
such as a class portrait of unsmiling, short-haired, Western-clothed students
at Saint Paul's. Where missionaries touted such images as evidence of their
success, scholars now emphasize the severe costs of such "education for
extinction."[38]

Missionaries and other "Friends of the Indian" justified such harsh
measures—taking children from their parents, changing their names, cutting their hair, discarding their clothes, and forbidding their native tongues—
as necessary for the eradication of heathenism. In 1892 Daniel Dorchester,
school superintendent for the Bureau of Indian Affairs, wrote in his annual
report that the Native peoples' "principal religion is the darkest of superstitions, a pagan fetishism which controls the whole life." The abiding notion that paganism "controls the whole life" was what made it seem to be
the reason for, rather than just a synonym of, "savagery," "barbarism,"
and backwardness. Heathenism was supposed to keep people in the dark

about the true nature of the creation and who was in charge of it—God, who delegated power to men—and encourage people to grovel in ignorant fear before spirits and demons inhabiting the landscape and their bodies. Dorchester attacked the Indians' "darkest of superstitions" as "assum[ing] man's utter helplessness within the natural realm and excus[ing] crime," resulting in "lack of truthfulness, consistency, and moral consciousness." In keeping with the view of heathenism as at base the same despite differences in context, Dorchester also drew broad comparisons between Native American "heathenish" ways and the practices of other heathens both currently living and long dead. In the same report, he explained that the Pueblos "still preserve some of the most ancient heathen rites, linking them with the old idolatrous Canaanites of earliest recorded history."[39] Other reformers sounded similar notes; in 1892 Presbyterian John Menaul, who was a missionary at Laguna Pueblo, wrote in the *Home Mission Monthly* that "the heathen customs and worship of this people are much the same as that of any other sun worshippers . . . , and their degradation the same as the degradation brought on by polytheism and ignorance in any land."[40]

Officials were particularly concerned with Native dances, which they saw as sexually immoral, secretive, heathen ceremonies that happened out of their control, and that threatened to undo their attempts to civilize and Christianize the Indian. In the 1921 Circular No. 1665, Charles H. Burke, commissioner of Indian affairs, tried to draw a distinction between "the dance per se," which "is not condemned" and is "a medium through which elevated minds may happily unite art, refinement, and healthful exercise," and the "dance . . . under most primitive and pagan conditions," which "is apt to be harmful." Burke argued for the need to guard against such harmful practices: "When found to be so among the Indians we should control it by educational processes as far as possible, but if necessary, by punitive measures when its degrading tendencies persist." Burke further elaborated on which dances required "corrective penalties": "Any dance which involves acts of self-torture, immoral relations between the sexes, the sacrificial destruction of clothing or other useful articles, the reckless giving away of property, the use of injurious drugs or intoxicants, and frequent and or prolonged periods of celebration which bring the Indians together from remote points to the neglect of their crops, livestock, and home interests; in fact any disorderly or plainly excessive performances that promote superstitious cruelty, licentiousness, idleness, danger to health, and shiftless indifference to family welfare." The list identified as dangerous those dances that were destructive to lands (neglect of crops, et cetera) and to lives (danger to health), referencing the well-established trope of the heathen's inability to properly care for person and property.[41]

"The Heathen Dance House and Drum Are Always Opposed to the Church." In "A Well-Invested Life and Its Rewards," by William Hobart Hare, obituary for Rev. Joseph Witherspoon Cook, *Spirit of Missions*, 1902 (detail). In Charlotte Everett [Cook] Webster Scrapbook, mssHM 48551 (9). Huntington Library, San Marino, California.

Heathens on Probation

At the same time that politicians were debating, enacting, and enforcing Chinese exclusion, annexation of Hawai'i and the Philippines, and Native American detribalization and citizenship, liberalizing theologians were arguing over whether the heathen might also be included in the life after death. These were not unrelated developments. Just as inclusion in the American empire was on White Protestant civilizational terms, so also was inclusion in heaven. Heathenness had to become domesticated in order for the heathen to be included in the body politic and the life after death.

Debates over the heathen's potential for salvation were, of course, nothing new. As we have seen, medieval and eighteenth-century Euro-Americans wondered whether the Greco-Roman pagans might have had enough virtue to be saved. But deistic hopes about the law of nature as salvific were overshadowed by the idea that the heathen had just enough natural light to know that they were flagrantly disobeying it. The conviction that the heathen were damned without Christian intervention lent urgency to nineteenth-century missions. Chinese missionary William Speer acknowledged that the heathen "see the dim light of nature" and "hear the still small voice of natural conscience; but they are without the clear light of the revelation which we enjoy."[42] The "dim light of nature" was enough to convict them and sentence them to eternal hell. "Is it possible that such persons can go to heaven?" medical missionary John Scudder asked in his 1849 children's book. "How could such ever relish its pure joys? What would they do, could they be admitted there? My dear children, it is a charity which has no foundation, to suppose that the heathen can go to heaven. I have preached the Gospel to tens of thousands of them, but I never saw one who had the least atom of a qualification for that holy place."[43]

That hundreds of millions of their forebears were already writhing in the flames of hell furthered the othering of the impure heathen as unsuited for heaven. The heathen Europeans of yore were purportedly there as well in the evangelical view of things. Scudder acknowledged as much when he wrote, "Perhaps you know that our Saxon fathers, before they had the Bible, were as great idolaters as are this people. They worshipped Thor and Woden and other similar idols, and they were in the habit of offering up human sacrifices." But "God's gift of the Bible" had long ago lifted them from their heathen idolatry into Christian civilization. Since then, in Scudder's view, these Europeans and Euro-Americans had continued to progress and develop (though of course individuals could still end up in hell for a host of reasons), while the contemporaneous heathen peoples of the world remained mired in stagnating and damnable superstition.[44]

The notion that those of Saxon descent were not inherently different from the heathen, just historically different, suggested that all that separated them was the passage of time, and all the heathen had to do was receive and voluntarily accept the gospel to join the forward-charging path of history toward individual salvation and the redemption of the world.[45] This jibed with the biblical assurance that God had created all the nations "of one blood." But since, as a whole, Europeans and their descendants had received the gospel centuries earlier, it was not hard for them to reach the conclusion that hell was now overwhelmingly populated by the non-European-origin heathen peoples of the world. The instant these heathen bodies hit the afterlife was the instant "of one blood" failed to mean anything, as the damned became irrevocably and unchangeably different from the saved. The Bible describes the saved and the damned in such terms as the wheat and the chaff, the sheep and the goats—different species, even.[46] This eternal othering could color perceptions of the heathen in this life, too. Even if, theoretically, most American Christians maintained that the heathen could be saved, the idea that their natural, unsaved destination was hell made them seem like the very damned on earth. Hence the glowing eyes and sulphurous smell of the satirical kahuna in Cleveland's "SECRET MEMO."

The dubious fairness of this proposition did not go unnoticed, not least by the so-called heathen themselves, who were "often horrified by the claim that their ancestors were condemned to hell."[47] The question of why God would allow so many millions in historically non-Christian nations to be damned became more pressing over the course of the nineteenth century, as more Americans became aware of distant non-Christian people through the writings and translations of travelers, missionaries, and Transcendentalists.[48] By the 1880s, discomfort with the prospect of widespread heathen damnation even spread to the halls of America's bastion of Calvinist orthodoxy, where the foreign mission movement had taken flight: Andover Theological Seminary. By this time, the ravages of the American Civil War, Darwinism, and increasing American awareness of German biblical criticism were forcing reconsiderations of traditionally accepted doctrines.[49] The views of two brothers, Revs. Newman and Egbert Smyth, provoked an outcry over the question of heathen salvation at the seminary. In 1882 the thirty-eight-year-old Newman was chosen as professor of Christian theology. His appointment delighted some but terrified others because he had, in a series of published sermons, suggested that "if any person or any class of persons has not had a fair and sufficient probation before death they will have it after death, prior to the day of judgment."[50] Newman's second-chances theory struck some as a blatant attack against the Calvinistic creed Andover had been founded to defend, and which its professors were required to affirm. Rev. E. B. Webb called Newman's views on future probation "monstrous." Death was now just another moment in an ever-evolving life, undoing the urgency of missions and the necessity of repentance and conversion.[51]

The professors who had unanimously recommended Newman's appointment held that "the questionings of today in Christian hearts respecting the doctrine of eternal punishment are a consequence of the elevating and spiritualizing power of the gospel."[52] At stake was whether human understanding of scripture could and should evolve, or whether unraveling one thread might destroy the entire fabric of the tradition. Also at stake was the question of whether human pity for the heathen might mean that God should also feel the same, or whether human sentiment was an unreliable measure of God. The Board of Visitors rejected Newman's candidacy, criticizing him for "seem[ing] to conceive of the truth sentimentally and practically, rather than speculatively or philosophically." They "fear[ed] that his pupils would be 'turned more or less adrift on the sea of sentiment, where one loses all guidance except the bent of his own feelings or will.'"[53] Newman instead took up the ministry of the First Church of Christ in New Haven, Connecticut.

Five years later, his older brother Egbert, chair of ecclesiastical history at Andover since 1863, also found himself before the Board of Visitors for holding similar views. He was one of five faculty members who had spearheaded the creation of the *Andover Review,* a progressive journal that defended the possibility of a second chance after death. In 1886 Egbert and the other coeditors of the *Review* were charged with heresy by the Board of Visitors, and in 1887 Egbert was dismissed from his chair. For Egbert, "the question about the heathen has a deep interest to us because they are men," he wrote; "a deeper interest because they are men for whom Christ died, each and every one; the deepest interest because they are children of the same God on whom all our personal hopes depend and in whom all our lives are lived."[54] Was this God just? Should Christians even place their hope in this God, much less the heathen? Egbert claimed that it was the question of the "ethical character of God," more than the question of future probation, that was the fundamental issue at stake. The flesh-and-blood peoples of the world served as a conduit to this issue, much as the Greco-Roman heathen of yore had opened up questions about God and good works in the eighteenth century. As a November 1887 article in the *Andover Review* put it, the "'case of the heathen' is now the largest factor in determining one's belief in the doctrine of judgment. Its practical effect is seen, not in the preaching to the heathen, but upon the preaching at home. The most serious intellectual obstacle to the success of the gospel is any sense of inequality in the application of the gospel. The endeavor to meet this difficulty has led to the advocacy of a Christian probation for all men."[55]

The doctrine of second chances made God seem more fair and heaven more inclusive, but it still set the heathen behind the Christian on a religio-racial ladder that now simply extended to the life to come. At the same time that the brothers Smyth were advancing these propositions, other theologians were suggesting that heaven might not just be a stagnant realm where the blessed sang hymns of praise to God ad nauseum, but that it might actually be a state for the eternal development and improvement of humans.[56] In this view, which became dominant among mainstream Protestants in the late nineteenth century, those who had already converted in this life would have a head start over the heathen in the life to come, as the latter waited for their opportunity to receive the gospel. The heathen still needed to realize that Christ was the culmination of their longings, whether in this life or after death, in order to be saved. And even if and when they did accept Jesus as their savior, the heathen would still be second-class citi-

zens of a dynamic and progressive heaven, requiring remedial afterlife instruction as multitudes of the earlier saved reveled in mind-expanding
knowledge and bliss as soon as they hit the grave.

"Virtues of the Heathen"

The Andover controversy and debates over heathen salvation reverberated
in newspapers and magazines across the United States. In 1886, one year
before it printed Wong Chin Foo's "Why Am I a Heathen?," the *North
American Review* published a piece by Gail Hamilton, "Heathendom and
Christendom under Test," which lampooned the traditional perspective of
Andover's old guard: that the heathen were damned because they had
enough natural light to save them but ignored it. Hamilton was the pen name
of Mary Abigail Dodge, a liberal Congregationalist from New England.
"The reasoning which establishes the sufficiency of heathen knowledge
would hardly hold in every-day affairs," she wrote. "If a queen mother
should decide and decree that one pair of woolen stockings should be ample
provision for each child during the winter," and if such stockings were to
wear out such that "the great majority of little feet became frost-bitten,
sore, useless, and finally had to be amputated, we should not infer that it
was the children's fault in not keeping their stockings whole. We should
say that the queen had fallen into an error of judgment." By comparing
the old guard's God to a parsimonious and unfeeling queen, Dodge echoed
Egbert Smyth's claim that the assumption of heathen damnation raised
an ethical problem about the nature of God.[57]

Dodge connected the question of heathen salvation to American greed
and Chinese exclusion. "We see nation after nation struggling up into light
only to perish into darkness," she lamented. And meanwhile, rather than
helping them, "we see Christian nations stealing, gambling, robbing, mur-
dering, slandering, beating wives, rearing children to crime." Dodge was
sympathetic to the liberal view that heathenness was not inherently damnable, and professed dismay that Andover's old guard claimed to find
nothing of redeeming value in any save the Christian. To these tradition-
ists, "Heathen, Moslems, Greek, and Armenian apostates are all embarked
in the same boat, rowing toward the same Dead Sea." If only they had
asked me, said Dodge; I could have supplied better evidence of heathen
virtue. The evidence she had in mind came from a petition to the Senate
presented by a Mrs. S. L. Baldwin, a former Methodist missionary in China.
Baldwin had asked the Senate for allowance to "import a heathen to this
country, because of his great superiority to the Christians here; because the

private virtues of the heathen showed far stronger signs of thrift than our own." Baldwin wanted this "heathen" for a servant. She had grown "accustomed to Chinese servants" during her time as a missionary and had learned "the peace and comfort possible with them." Upon returning to the States, she had had difficulty finding similar service from impertinent Euro-Americans: "Not one has seemed to feel under the slightest obligation to give any fair return for wages received, or to have the slightest regard to my interests." By contrast, "in China our servants loved us and left our employ reluctantly."[58]

Dodge interpreted Baldwin's petition to "import a heathen" as evidence that "in this Christian country private virtues are so submerged beneath ingratitude, selfishness, dishonesty, extravagance, impertinence, disobedience, that we fly for refuge to the peace, comfort, fidelity, love, found only in heathen character and heathen service." Concluded she, "These are high qualities. They are Scripturally stamped as a preparatory course for the kingdom of Heaven."[59] That Dodge chose this case as her evidence for heathen inclusion—on earth as in heaven—suggests the significant price for entry that White Protestant Americans, liberals very much included, expected from the heathen. Heathens were acceptable only to the extent that they were subservient, peaceable, and faithful to White people. And it was their cheerful labor that ultimately proved them worthy of inclusion and demonstrated their ability to learn and walk the path of righteousness. Viewing the theological pressures of the Andover controversy side by side with the imperial ambitions that defanged heathenness by forcefully annexing, detribalizing, or excluding the people characterized as such thus reveals how each worked to police heathen character while assessing what White Americans could gain from selective heathen admission to the body politic.

PART III

Inheritances

The theme of happy and useful heathens offering something of value to White people hit the academic mainstream in a mid-twentieth-century publication, William White Howells's *The Heathens: Primitive Man and His Religions* (1948). *Kirkus Reviews* noted early on that the book, soon after publication, had already "sold over 27,000 copies, which may indicate that the market for this may go beyond the academic and scientific field." *The Heathens* was reprinted in 1962 and again in 1986 and acquired the status of a classic. Even as late as 2010, a cultural anthropology textbook cited *The Heathens* as "a good place to start for an overview of human religious diversity," as long as one keeps "the date of its first publication in mind."[1]

Howells (1908–2005) was the grandson of *Atlantic Monthly* editor and "Dean of American Letters" William Dean Howells. He trained as a physical anthropologist, receiving his PhD from, and then becoming a professor at, Harvard University. Howells made a "lasting contribution to anthropology in the mid-1960s" with a study of skull sizes that he completed with the assistance of his wife, Muriel. Measuring "thousands of skulls at dozens of sites in Europe, Africa, Asia and the Pacific," they determined, contra the popular nineteenth-century work of Samuel George Morton in *Crania Americana,* that "variations within these groups far exceeded the variations distinguishing group from group." This finding supported "the proposition that all modern humans are of one homogeneous species" rather than "evolving in separate regions of earth."[2]

The Heathens predated Howells's work on skull sizes but spoke to his interest in human evolution, the interplay between biological and cultural anthropology, and the shared origins of modern humans. His avowed object was to "forget our own familiar religious ideas and look through sympathetic eyes, from a little distance, at some different ones." "Naïve" scholars had too easily dismissed the "real nature" of "primitive religion" as they scurried about and "collected curios." But now that the "museums are pretty full," Howells said, we can "grasp some of the meaning" of the things they preserved. The kind of meaning anthropologists sought, he explained, was like that of "bird watchers." Howells created a stark dividing line between observer and observed, the one distinctly human and scientific, the other animal and wild. The anthropologists' "first duty is toward unliterate people," said he, who "are unable to keep their own history, and thus to hoist themselves up into the realm of self-criticism. Anthropology must do this for them." Howells figured the White observer as singularly able to rescue other people's history and folkways from oblivion. (He himself had worked at the American Museum of Natural History after receiving his PhD, and served as a curator at Harvard's Peabody Museum for many years.) A sense of White Christian superiority also suffuses the volume, as Howells affirmed "that we know their gods do not exist and their magic is hollow." He further instructed his readers—"we (the European Whites)"—to take "immense pride in [our civilization] and be endlessly loyal to it."[3]

On the other hand, Howells told his readers that "we ourselves, as individuals, as Christians, or as Occidentals," should not "take any special credit for the great civilization, system of knowledge, and religion which have gradually accumulated in thirty or forty centuries on the continent of Europe and in the Near East." For it is only because "we are lucky," due to "fortunate historical and geographical incidents," that "we" have received such benefits. Our own ancestors, he admitted, were doing just what the present-day heathen are doing now, speaking to his belief in the unity of human origins. As much as we might currently be the birdwatchers and they the birds, the difference between "us" and "them" was not biological but temporal. "Look now at the practitioners of heathenism: Eskimos, Apaches, Basutos, Yaghans, Botocudos, Dravidians, Igorots, Truk Islanders. Our brains and theirs have the same structure, are fed by the same amount and kind of blood, are conditioned by the same hormones and titillated by the same senses."[4] Howells attributed to luck, and "fortunate historical and geographical incidents," the ever-vexing problem of inequality (as perceived by White Christians who believed themselves to be superior to and the envy of the heathen).

But Howells also maintained that White Christians might not actually be that lucky after all, for they had forgotten or lost something that "the heathens" had retained. Not only were White Christians useful to "unliterates," usefulness also went the other way. Howells promised to demonstrate for readers in "what ways religious needs may be fulfilled," and claimed that "the only people who can show us that are heathens and pagans." For the "Wild Man," the "Noble Savage," and the "primitive people"—all terms that Howells used interchangeably with his titular "heathens"—knew how to be happy, and their religions were to no small extent responsible for that knowledge. "My point is this," Howells emphasized: "a savage tribe searching for an earthly salvation in its own religious resources usually finds it; poor people are not necessarily unhappy, and neither are rain makers and ancestor worshippers." Indeed, he claimed, "your chances of being psychotic would be less in many primitive tribes than right where you are, surrounded though you may be by sanitation, law, psychiatry, uplifting literature, and good advice on every hand. Primitive people have long ago put into practical religious forms many things that your countrymen are trying to find for themselves in lectures and books on the good society, or on how to find happiness, or on what is wrong with them. This is not because the Noble Savage is so exceedingly noble; it is just that his religions are meaningful, and we can learn something from them."[5]

What Howells wanted his readers to see was the satisfaction and usefulness that heathens and pagans found in their own supposedly simple religions, in contrast to the dissatisfaction and angst that turned Americans into a nation of near-psychotic strivers. Like the anthropologist Bronislaw Malinowski, who explained that the point of myth is not its truth or falsity but how it provides a charter for a community's social life, so Howells contended that heathen "religious ideas help in the struggle for existence as verily as a bow and arrow," and that "the usefulness of religious belief has no relation to its accuracy or absurdity in physics, geology, or astronomy."[6] Heathens as happy; heathenism as useful: even as Howells sought to associate positive connotations with the heathen world, his volume continued to describe the heathen as a necessary foil for White Christians both to mark their civilizational superiority and to worry over their own overdeveloped inadequacies.

The view of heathens as offering something of value to White Americans contributed to the term's decline as well as to its resilience in some circles. As we will see in Part III, the term's decline coincided with Americans' growing appreciation of other world religions that had their own names and eloquent representatives, several of whom toured the States and became well known in the years after the 1893 World's Parliament of Religions. As Americans increasingly referred to Buddhism, Hinduism, Sikhism, Jainism, and more by those names, the specific label of "heathen" shrank to primarily apply to those traditions considered to be "primitive," "folk," and "ethnic." Even as uses of the term diminished in the public sphere, though, the ideas that had built up around the figure of the heathen and the heathen world remained ubiquitous, surfacing in surprising places like Howells's popular academic text and in less surprising venues like large-scale humanitarian mission organizations. The heathen barometer also continued to be of use to people on the receiving end of American paternalistic racism, while others followed in Wong Chin Foo's footsteps to adopt the label of "heathen" as a moniker of resistance against White Christianity.

8

PRESERVATION AND
PUSHBACK

In 1907 sixty-eight-year-old Nathaniel Bright Emerson took a moment to wax poetic about bygone days on the islands of Hawai'i. After vehemently advocating for Hawaiian annexation on the grounds that its rulers were heathen and its people incompetent, Emerson in his older age ironically became an indefatigable preserver of the islands' legends, history, language, and culture. As he reflected in an unpublished manuscript in 1907, "It goes without saying, that the reservoir from which this almost forgotten lore has been drawn has run nearly dry: what the earth has not swallowed up has mostly evaporated into very thin air. So much the more are thanks due to dear old men and women of Hawaiian stock—whose names I shall ever preserve—who have shared with me the remainder biscuit of life's voyage—race-memories of far-off, sweet, pagan days."[1] For Emerson after annexation, Hawai'i's heathen history—its "race-memories"—was worth preserving, even celebrating, because it seemed on the verge of disappearing.

Yet Emerson's turn to preservation may not have been so ironic after all. Indeed, it can be read as of a piece with his paternalistic stance during annexation: having fancied himself Hawai'i's rescuer from heathen leaders, he now fancied himself the rescuer from oblivion of Hawaiian folkways. Like Emerson after annexation, other Americans at the turn of the century were becoming nostalgic about the people whose lives, livelihoods, and lands they had been trampling for centuries. Historians have noted how late nineteenth-century worries about the effeteness of white-collar men led to attempts like Theodore Roosevelt's to prove White masculinity by traveling west, volunteering for the Rough Riders, or even just participating in rough-and-tumble sports at the local YMCA. Such worries also led to the valorization of "barbarian virtues" and attempts to preserve and learn from cultures that seemed to be disappearing.[2]

It was only after specific heathens were safely policed and domesticated, and their practices relegated to "bygone days," that preservation of their ways became popular.[3] The continued liberalization of mainline Protestantism is important to this history, for it matters what the preservationists thought they were preserving: dangerous, demonic, stultifying superstitions, or partial truths instructive of the religious progress and development of humanity. As we saw in Part I of this book, earlier preservers like José de Acosta and Joseph-François Lafitau had sought to demonstrate the former, explaining to European audiences how the devil mimicked true Christianity. This mimicry was supposed to make heathens easier to convert (their practices are inversions of ours; all we need to do is redefine them). It also excused Christians who tried but failed to convert heathens (they are in the clutches of the devil; what could we do?). The preservers of the late nineteenth and twentieth centuries had different objectives in mind, adopting instead a stance of paternalistic preservation for the benefit of humanity's memory. Heathenness, in their view, was no longer a live threat but rather a vestige of the past, pointing to and bound to retreat before the superiority of Western Christian civilization.

White preservers like Emerson fancied themselves responsible for determining what in the heathen past was worth preserving and how. But the move toward the preservation and romanticization of heathenism also swung open the door to pushback from the people dubbed "heathen" themselves. Pushback was nothing new, of course, but the turn to preservation meant that it found more receptive audiences than in the past. The people labeled "heathens" adopted a variety of strategies to counter White Protestants' superiority complex, proudly claiming the label for themselves, asserting the superiority of so-called heathenism over Christianity, or arguing against use of the term, which was increasingly seen in polite circles as an embarrassing holdover of an unenlightened Christian worldview. Their efforts helped to galvanize a shift in mainline twentieth-century approaches toward the heathen world, whereby conversion of damned souls took a back seat to humanitarian aid in the here and now.

From "Heathen" to "Ethnic" Religions

The idea that heathenness was an embarrassing, outdated concept began to spread by the second half of the nineteenth century, even as anti-Chinese demagogues, Hawaiian annexationists, and others were using the term with abandon. Barely four decades separated the publication of the fourth edition of Hannah Adams's *Dictionary of All Religions* and Lydia Maria Child's 1855 *The Progress of Religious Ideas, through Successive Ages*. Where Adams had used the idea of heathenness uncritically, Child's text explicitly disavowed the term "heathen" as an embarrassment. "While my mind was in its youth," Child wrote, "I was offended by the manner in which Christian writers usually describe other religions. . . . The one-sidedness of the representation troubled my strong sense of justice." To correct these biases, Child endeavored to "[treat] all religions with reverence" and "[show] no more favour to one than to another." She continued, "I have not declared that any system was true, or that any one was false. I have even avoided the use of the word heathen; for though harmless in its original signification, it is used in a way that implies condescension, or contempt; and such a tone is inconsistent with the perfect impartiality I have wished to observe."[4] Less than two decades later, James Freeman Clarke, in his 1871 *Ten Great Religions: An Essay in Comparative Theology,* similarly wrote of the "error into which most of the Christian apologists of the last century fell, in speaking of ethnic or heathen religions. In order to show the need of Christianity, they thought it necessary to disparage all other religions." Like Child, Clarke claimed to set religions on an equal footing, examining them side by side through the method of "comparative theology," which he described as a "positive science."[5] Child's and Clarke's volumes were intended for broad audiences; Child explained, "I have written for the popular mind, not for the learned," while chapters of Clarke's manuscript were published in the *Atlantic* before the book's publication.[6] Both were also reprinted numerous times.

And yet, despite their claims to impartiality and their criticisms of Christian narrow-mindedness, Child's and Clarke's accounts did not hold the people formerly known as heathen to be on a par with Protestants. Protestantism remained, for them as for the vast majority of other liberals, the most advanced form of religious expression, even if it, too, was still evolving.[7] Child wrote, "I place great reliance on sincerity, and have strong faith in the power of genuine Christianity to stand on its own internal merits, unaided by concealment."[8] Child's own religious views were far from the Calvinism of Andover, as she was close to her brother Convers, a Unitarian minister, and enjoyed the company of Transcendentalists like Theodore Parker and Margaret Fuller. These New England–based women and men "constructed taxonomies of comparative religion to identify and compare religions in hopes of discovering a universal core of Mind, Truth, or Religion that could unite mankind."[9] But they saw a purified Christianity, drawing from the wisdom of ancient traditions, as the closest to that universal core. The traditions once lumped under the category of heathen became, in this view, imperfect stepping-stones on the path to more sophisticated religious forms, which would in turn continue to develop as humans became more enlightened.

This teleological view of religious development reversed the degeneration theory of previous taxonomists, whereby heathens took the original, pure light of revelation and corrupted it. Instead, heathenness offered premature glimmers of useful truth toward the development of Christianity. As Child put it, "All the nations added some gems to [Jesus's] crown of righteousness."[10] Clarke, a Unitarian minister, explained that the common view of heathen religions as solely "teach[ing] degeneracy and failure" "contradicts the law of progress which alone gives meaning and unity to history." Instead of revealing humanity's fallen nature, said he, "heathen religions are a step, a preparation for Christianity," and "the effort of man to feel after God." The table of contents of Clarke's *Ten Great Religions* demonstrates how he viewed Christianity as the universal religion toward which everything else was imperfectly evolving. In his first chapter alone, "Ethnic and Catholic Religions," he promised to "show that, while most of the Religions of the World are Ethnic, or the Religions of Races, Christianity is Catholic, or adapted to become the Religion of all Races"; "that Ethnic Religions are partial, Christianity universal"; and "that Ethnic Religions are arrested, but that Christianity is steadily progressive."[11] Clarke used "ethnic religions" as a synonym for "heathen religions." In doing so, he drew on a long history of similar usage. The *Oxford English Dictionary* explains that the term "ethnic" derives both from the "post-classical Latin *ethnicus* (adjective and noun) heathen, pagan," and from the "Hellenistic Greek ἐθνικός, national, foreign, Gentile." The King James Version of the Bible translated the Greek *panta ta ethne* into "all nations," as in the Great Commission's "Go ye therefore, and teach all nations." *Ethne* was also translated into the English Bible as "gentile," "pagan," and "heathen." By the fifteenth century, "ethnic" was used interchangeably with "pagan" or "heathen," a usage that continued into the early twentieth century.[12]

To have "ethnicity" meant to be partial, incomplete, confined to one part of the world, and stagnant. Ethnic or heathen religions could not hope to gain adherents beyond a regionally and racially specific nation group; the main reason to study them was to see how they helped to prepare people for Christianity, the only truly universal religion. Such preparation could take the form of proto-truths taught by proto-prophets, but all would eventually and inevitably lead to and be superseded by the raceless, regionless religion of pure Christianity. This assertion of universality forged the racial imagination of White Christians themselves. Their very identity was rooted in their claim to supersede the Jewish people as God's new universal template for the salvation of the world, the new normative whom all other heathen/ethnic/raced peoples should aspire to emulate.[13]

Preservation

The view of heathenness as a stepstool to universal Christianity rather than a chute to hell sheds light on Euro-Americans' growing impulse to preserve and understand, rather than eradicate, the practices, myths, and artifacts of the vast regions they clumped into the heathen world. In the Hawaiian context, Native Hawaiians had always recounted and sustained their own *moʻolelo* (histories and stories), whether through oral tradition or in Hawaiian-language newspapers and books after the creation of the Hawaiian alphabet in the 1820s.[14] In texts that continue to be reprinted and revered, Davida Malo (1795–1853), Samuel Manaiākalani Kamakau (1815–1876), John Papa Iʻi (1800–1870), and Kepelino Keauokalani (ca. 1830–1878) countered the "official" histories offered by the missionaries and their descendants, which tended to focus on missionary success and transformations of Hawaiian society and landscapes. As we saw, Kamakau had helped to found the Hawaiian Historical Society in 1841; some two decades later he noted the reasons for its founding in a newspaper article: "As the people of Albion had their British history yet read about the Saxons and William, so the Hawaiians should read their history."[15] King David Kalākaua also published his own *Legends and Myths of Hawaiʻi*, which worried White onlookers had complained—before annexation—was a guidebook to heathenism. In addition to recording time-honored tales, the *Legends and Myths* presented a distinctly Hawaiian interpretation of the violence wrought by the missionaries' arrival, from the overthrow of the kapu system to the last stand of its defenders.[16] Hawaiians refused to let the ways of the "people of old" (ka poʻe kahiko) be forgotten. In lively newspaper debates over the meaning of their moʻolelo, they engaged in active cultural maintenance and affirmed the presence of the past: "'I ka wā mamua, ka wā mahope,' goes a familiar ʻōlelo noʻeau (proverb): 'In the future is the past.'"[17]

And yet White people nevertheless fancied themselves necessary to the accurate preservation of "heathen" Hawaiian history. This had been the case for Hiram Bingham, who sniffed in his memoir, "How imperfectly, then, were those stupid, unlettered, unsanctified heathen tribes furnished for making out a trustworthy history of their country for ages back or even for a single generation!" For Bingham, the Hawaiians' lack of a written language doomed them to a murky past of "obscure oral traditions" and "rude narratives." Their heathen idolatry rendered them "reprobate" and "destitute of high moral principle," and hence left them incapable of "forming in their own minds, or conveying to others by language, just conceptions of facts."[18] Years later, missionary son Emerson made strikingly similar claims. He alleged that the Hawaiian language was inadequate to the task of telling its own history: its vocabulary had no terms for "abstract ideas," while its grammar lacked any forward direction, instead proffering circular sentences that had no beginning, middle, or end, and therefore no "notion of cause and effect." To Emerson, these supposed language defects signaled a primitive "mental condition" or "[^rotatory] action of mind" that rendered the Hawaiians historyless without White intervention. Even "one so exceptionally intelligent as David Malo" could not move beyond these limitations of language, Emerson alleged. "The prose style of Malo if his manner of writing can be said to have had any style, was lacking in all of these respects." And so Emerson anointed himself the critic, interpreter, and translator of Malo's moʻolelo.[19]

In another essay, Emerson explained why, and for whom, he thought such preservation was important. Titled "Ethnic Factors in Civilization," the essay was completed in December 1905, just a handful of years after Hawaiʻi became a US territory under Governor Sanford Dole. In an about-face from his preannexation stance, in which he had called for the extermination of heathen practices, Emerson now bemoaned "the full list of man's wholesale slaughtering of the lower races and of the animal tribes," which in his words, "makes a ghastly tale." He was not primarily interested in actual violence against "ethnic" bodies, but rather in the loss of the "ethnic factors" they possessed, and the benefits such factors could accrue to "civilization." The affinity between "ethnic" and "heathen" is significant here: though Emerson stopped using the latter term in this essay, paralleling the growing discomfort with the label signaled in Child's and Clarke's volumes and the Andover controversy, his use of "ethnic" served the same purpose of differentiating White Christian civilizers (universal) from everyone else (ethnic). As the people leading humanity into the future, they alone could see what needed to be preserved and why: to inject the natural, primitive, and childlike into White society so that it did not become over-civilized.[20]

Just as most theologians affirmed that the heathen were "of one blood" with the Christian, so Emerson said that the ethnic—the "savage, the semi-primitive man"—is "physically . . . bone of our bone, flesh of our flesh, patterned after the same image with ourselves." The key difference was psychological and developmental: "Psychologically he is a child. . . . Through no fault of his own, he has for many generations been an outcast in the wilderness, like Romulus, denied the milk and cream of the mother breast, left to the rude suckling of the wolf." The familiar motif of the heathen wandering in the heath, becoming ever more animal-like when left to the whims of nature, resonated in Emerson's "ethnic" man. The developmental stunting that supposedly resulted was not final; now that the ethnic had come in contact with the civilized, it could potentially be saved.[21] Said Emerson, repeating a point others had made before him, "Only a few generations ago, we, in our ancestors, were as degraded as the savages of to-day," and therefore "shall we vaunt ourselves and hold them in contempt and abhorrence?" Heathenness had long been conceived as a marker of flawed understanding that could be immediately changed through conversion, thus setting into motion the miraculous transformation of entire societies, bodily habits, and disorderly landscapes. But heathenness qua ethnicity extended the trend promoted by the liberalizing theologians in the Andover controversy. Difference became something to be shed gradually over time as the world's childlike people got carried out of their nondevelopment into the forward-charging course of Anglo-driven history, graduating from childhood to adolescence and, finally, adulthood.

Educational and psychological research supported this trend, parsing out the various stages of human life rather than assuming that children were simply mini-adults and, as such, responsible for converting as much as any full-grown human. In the nineteenth century, theologian and minister Horace Bushnell began arguing against the immediate conversion model of evangelical revivalists in favor of "Christian nurture," in which children were lovingly and patiently raised in the Christian life. Similarly, physicians and psychiatrists like Amariah Brigham, one of the forefathers of the American Psychiatric Association, argued that the evangelical emphasis on immediate conversion at risk of hell was psychologically detrimental and that, instead, the precepts of Christian living should be more gently conveyed.[22]

By the turn of the century, the idea that gradual nurture was essential to the proper development of the civilized adult took firm hold with the 1904 publication of G. Stanley Hall's two-volume *Adolescence: Its Psychology and Relations to Physiology, Anthropology, Sociology, Sex, Crime, Religion, and Education*. Hall warned that "our urbanized hothouse life" tended to "ripen everything before its time," and that educators needed to take care not to snuff out the youthful vigor, love of nature, and normal sexual development of the adolescent.[23] Hall was familiar with the work of William Byron Forbush, whose 1900 "The Social Pedagogy of Boyhood" and 1901 *The Boy Problem* (with an introduction by Hall himself) encouraged special attention to the transitional teenage years and advocated distinct educational strategies for adolescents. Forbush claimed that these strategies would be useful for missions, too, since "the so-called heathen peoples are, whatever their age, all in the adolescent period of life."[24] In his chapter "Adolescent Races and Their Treatment," Hall elaborated on the idea that "so-called heathen peoples" needed to be treated much as the teenage boy: sexually mature but intellectually childlike, the "adolescent races" demanded patience and careful study in order to help them develop into full-fledged adults. "The proper attitude toward heathen customs and religions is one of the gravest questions," said Hall, but "the heart of the educator sinks to see how small consideration these seem entitled to receive even at the hands of the most liberal and enlightened writers." Criticizing those who sought to eradicate "heathen" traditions and "exterminate them root and branch," Hall claimed that "this is psycho-pedagogic barbarism and brutality. Only the most ignorant and bigoted do not now recognize the sympathy of religions or realize that there are many psychic and ethical roots, trunks, and even branches that should be preserved and grafted on to." Christianity, after all, came from "an alien stock" that had borrowed extensively from these other traditions.[25]

According to Hall, there were three reasons why the older method of cultural extermination and quick conversion was flawed. First, it robbed Christianity of its roots and of sources of primitive renewal. Hall believed that the essence of conversion to true religion, and from child to adult, was a gradual shift wherein "self-love merges in resignation and renunciation into love of man." The Christian "Gospel story" offered the "most adequate and classic, dramatic representation" of this shift, but that did not make other cultures morally bankrupt or unimportant. Hall criticized the "bibliolatry" of biblical literalists and suggested that close study of heathen religions and peoples might actually reinvigorate Christianity. "As Jesus praised the beautiful teeth of the carcass of a dead dog," said he, "so we must begin by learning the good in other faiths."[26]

Second, the older method robbed heathens of the opportunity to experience the authentic, gradual conversion that was "the philosophy of history and religion and the germ of all educational systems." Just as premature ripening in the urban hothouses of turn-of-the-century America might permanently damage the teenage boy, so too could overly rapid Christianization and civilization in the mission fields of the heathen world impede heathens' survival and historical development. After all, "our pagan ancestors were won by having their heathen practices sanctified and not ridiculed." Hall even went so far as to suggest that the best way to eventually bring the unbeliever over to Christianity might be to train him to be a "good heathen" first, rather than a "bad Christian." For "is there any barbarism that equals that caused by premature and forced civilization"? Forced civilization had caused the demise of too many "adolescent races," Hall explained; unable to fend off the temptations of civilization, they had sunk into oblivion.[27]

And why did this matter? For Hall, the heathen, "adolescent races" were important because they offered diversion and diversity to a world quickly threatening to become one in its sameness. This was the third reason in a nutshell: if every culture came to look like the colonizers, how boring a world it would be. Hall essentially anticipated the multicultural arguments of the twentieth century, with their paternalistic protection of the quaint and nonthreatening in other traditions for the amusement, cosmopolitan improvement, consumption, and humanitarian concern of the cultivated Anglo-American. Hence the need for careful preservation of select difference alongside gradual, gentle change toward sameness.

Emerson was likely aware of Hall's opus, which had been published the year before he sat down to pen his "Ethnic Factors in Civilization." Emerson's primary interest in preserving the ways of the "primitive" was not so much for the sake of the "ethnic man" but more for the sake of the "civilized," to help him know himself and from whence he came. For "the choicest gift which the primitive man has to bestow on his cultivated brother is his very primitiveness, by virtue of which he has an infant's nearness to that morning time of the human race." Studying the "primitive" thus "benefits and enriches mankind by enlarging man's acquaintance with himself." Continuing with the gift and goods language, Emerson affirmed that "every new race that civilized man has become acquainted with is to the ethnologist, philosopher and psychologist a rich-pay gold-mine."[28] While the Anglo-Saxon was a "world-conquering, dominant race" whose "ethnic contribution" to the "wealth of the human family" "embraces vast territories of thought and philosophy, literature and poetry, invention and achievements in every domain of science and art," this did not mean that the "isolated tribe" had nothing to offer. For—and here commodities talk again loomed large—the tribal man "has adapted the economies of his life to the order of nature about him," and "to specify the contributions which the backward brother—backward because long isolated—has given to us, or has yet to give, would be, in the first place, to enumerate many thousands of objects that fill our museums of ethnology, besides a host of unpatented articles, devices and methods that find useful and necessary employ in our daily life." But most important, said Emerson, were not the material but the psychological commodities the ethnic could provide to the Anglo: "Our need for the primitive is greater than his need for us. We need him for the same reason that the father needs his child, that we may learn of him lessons of humility, of self-restraint, of kindliness and altruistic love, lessons which Heaven can impress in no other way: 'Lest we forget, lest we forget.'"[29]

Emerson worried about the dangers of over-civilization and the consequences of American imperial ambition. He was attuned to arguments such as those Congregationalist minister Josiah Strong had made in the widely read *Our Country: Its Possible Future and Its Present Crisis,* published by the American Home Missionary Society in 1885. Strong lauded Anglo-Saxons as a "race of unequaled energy" and "the representative, let us hope, of the largest liberty, the purest Christianity, the highest civilization," which made him, by divine intent, "his brother's keeper." But Strong also warned of the dangers they faced from immigrants, Catholics, Mormons, and alcohol. He described Anglo-Saxons as a race that had "developed peculiarly aggressive traits calculated to impress its institutions among mankind," and that was destined to "spread itself over the earth."[30]

Strong's perspective on the heathen shows how different views of race—as inherent, hierarchical, and influenced by Darwinism; and as changeable, binary, and rooted in Christianity—could coexist with and support each other. To Strong, each race had its own flaws that could either be speedily exacerbated by wrong religion or gradually eased through the "salt of Christianity." This applied to the Anglo-Saxon as well as to the heathen. "Bring savages into contact with our civilization," he wrote, "and its destructive forces become operative at once, while years are necessary to render effective the saving influences of Christian instruction." Given the "years" it took for Christian influences to build, Strong drew on Charles Darwin's "survival of the fittest" theory to claim that the "extinction of inferior races before the advancing Anglo-Saxon" was "probable," given the "out-populating power of the Christian stock." This, he said, was "God's final and complete solution of the dark problem of heathenism among many inferior peoples." But he also thought that "some of the stronger races" might survive, "forced to adopt the [Anglo-Saxon's] methods and instruments, his civilization and his religion." Strong maintained that "there is taking place among the nations a widespread intellectual revolt against traditional beliefs," and that "the contact of Christian with heathen nations is awakening the latter to new life."[31]

In his annexationist days, Emerson had agreed on the need to swiftly impress Anglo institutions on the heathen world lest heathens convert Anglo-Saxons to their ways first. But now he worried that Anglos might be becoming too brutal and destructive. Preservation of "ethnic" ways promised not just the valuable commodities and skills they could provide but also to keep the arrogance and violence of the Anglo in check. Indeed, if conversion was, as Hall defined it, the shift from self-love to the love of man, then the heathen/ethnic was essential to the process for Anglos, since the heathen's continued existence as needy "children" spurred their "fathers" to "kindliness and altruistic love."[32] In Emerson's preservationist impulse, we can clearly see that the real people in need are White Americans: they need the needy heathen in order to activate their own compassion, a compassion necessary for their self-understanding and self-presentation as loving parents to the world, rather than as rapacious imperialists.

"Christians Must Always Be Ready for Good Criticism"

How fortunate, then, that the spread of print media and photography in the late nineteenth and early twentieth centuries provided ordinary Americans with more access to the needy overseas than ever before. As scholar Heather Curtis has shown, at the turn of the twentieth century, Christian publishing magnates Louis Klopsch and William Talmage used vivid reporting on and images from global humanitarian crises to unify a Protestant base that was fracturing over issues of biblical inerrancy, evolution, race relations, and women's suffrage. Just as a suffering and dying heathen world had encouraged Europeans, and then Americans, to feel grateful for their own relative comfort and prospective salvation, so global crises in an age of expanded imperial ambitions gave Americans a welcome and unifying distraction from their own problems.[33]

David Hollinger has argued that the twentieth-century rise in global humanitarian projects originated with missionary-connected Americans in the mainline denominations. Their experiences overseas made them reconsider the narrow, provincial outlook with which they had originally entered the mission field, hoping to convert and "civilize" the heathen. Finding that other people had their own rich religious systems and cultures, these missionaries—or, more frequently, their children—moved, over the course of the twentieth century, from the "Christ over culture" emphasis of Rufus Anderson to a model in which the amelioration of human suffering took precedence over the imperative to save lost souls. As agricultural and medical technologies improved, these missionary-connected Americans came to see the preservation of suffering bodies as more pressing, and indeed more important, than their conversion.[34]

This became especially the case as more mainliners adopted the liberal Protestant perspective that other religions might have value as preparatory steps to salvation and that God might work through different means to lead people to salvation, rather than necessitating that everyone believe in Jesus Christ. But where Hollinger attributes the shift to White missionaries and their children, who moved in countercultural directions as they realized they were not the only people on the planet, we should not also overlook the agency of missionized people who pushed back against White Protestant superiority and vigorously defended so-called heathenism, and the religions formerly known as heathen, to increasingly receptive audiences.

Turn-of-the-century Americans famously learned about religions once dubbed "heathen" from ambassadors to the World's Parliament of Religions in 1893. The Parliament has rightfully been viewed by recent scholars as a celebration of the kind of liberal Protestantism that animated Lydia Maria Child and James Freeman Clarke. "Its true purpose was to highlight the superiority of Protestant Christianity," explains scholar David Mislin. "The eloquent contributions of nonwhite participants from both the United States and abroad did little to shake the organizers' faith in the superiority of white, Anglo-Saxon, Protestant civilization." And yet, even if the speeches did not dethrone the regnant notion of Anglo-Protestant superiority, the Parliament did "rais[e] some disquieting issues" around the truthfulness of Christianity vis-à-vis other religions. Moreover, the speeches were widely covered in local and national newspapers and reprinted in an illustrated tome soon after the Parliament ended, thus extending their influence beyond the organizers and immediate attendees. Some of the Parliament's non-Christian representatives also became minor celebrities after the event, hitting the lecture circuit and spreading their perspectives still farther. Like others called heathens who used the label as a barometer to critique White hypocrisy, they turned the table on Christians and proclaimed the superiority of their own traditions.[35]

Kinza Riuge M. Hirai, a lay Buddhist preacher from Kyoto, lamented that "there are very few countries in the world so misunderstood as Japan. Among innumerable unfair judgments, the religious thought of our countrymen is especially misrepresented, and the whole nation is condemned as heathen. Be they heathen, pagan or something else, it is a fact that from the beginning of our history, Japan has received all teachings with open mind."[36] Hirai characterized the Christianity from which Japanese Buddhists "revolt" "as cruel injustice to the weaker with the apparent assumption that heathen and idolaters (falsely so-called) have no rights to life, liberty and happiness which Christians are bound to respect."[37] Here, Japanese "religious thought," ignorantly called "heathenism," was tolerant; Christianity was intolerant.

For his part, Indian theosophist C. N. Chakravarti from Allahabad stroked the egos of his audience when he announced to his predominantly White American listeners (and readers), "You have acted worthily of the race that is in the van-guard of civilization—a civilization, the chief characteristic of which, to my mind, is widening toleration, breadth of heart and liberality toward all the different religions of the world." He professed gratitude to the Parliament's organizers for "even allowing me, who, I confess, am a heathen, as you call me," to speak from the "same platform" as the other invited guests. Chakravarti then swiftly put them in their place by averring, "You have acted in a manner worthy of the motherland of the society which I have come to represent to-day." In other words, the standard by which he was measuring White Americans—and not vice versa—was his own, more ancient motherland's, and not a Western one. Chakravarti put White Americans under his own "heathen, as you call me," gaze. In India, he said, "universal tolerance" had long preceded the emergence of the same in America. India had been around for eons, while America was as yet "in the first flutter of life." Chakravarti even turned the tables on White American color expectations, explaining, "From time immemorial spirit has been represented by white, and matter has been represented by black." Spirit, he claimed, was the province of the ancient and wise (and white, by implication) East, where heathens had "been taught for ages after ages and centuries after centuries to turn our gaze inward toward realms that are not those which are reached by the help of the physical senses." By contrast, matter was the province of the materialistic and youthful (and black, by implication) West.[38]

Chakravarti's speech signaled how much the West needed to learn from so-called heathens in the East. For although "in the West you have evolved such a stupendous energy on the physical plane . . . I can discern beneath this thickness of material luxury, a secret and mystic aspiration to something spiritual. I can see that even you are getting tired of your steam, of your electricity, and the thousand different material comforts that follow these two great powers." Spoken in the shadow of the Chicago World's Fair, which celebrated and signaled to the world America's technological accomplishments at the turn of the century, Chakravarti's words would have carried extra weight. All this pomp and circumstance is impressive, he admitted. Yet the vaunted "White City" was not really "white" at all in Chakravarti's spiritual sense. For all the technological advances in the world were nothing without that "something which is beyond matter"—that "something greater within man, underneath the universe, that is to be longed for and striven after."[39]

Chakravarti acknowledged the material deficits India seemed to face vis-à-vis America but implied that they were by choice. In a context in which many Americans would have thought of India as impoverished and on the continual edge of famine, he explained that "we have in India, even to this day, thousands of people who give up as trash, as nothing, all the material comforts and luxuries of life" in order to pursue this "something greater within man."[40] The idea that heathens simply might not want or need all the luxuries Americans had created, because they were pursuing higher, spiritual concerns, mirrors Wong Chin Foo's critique of Americans' busy striving for bigger and better machines that would eventually create more suffering by putting human workers out of business.

Chakravarti's division of the "East" and "West" also resonates with Edward Said's famous description of the Orientalist imagination, in which the East is held up as a mystical, spiritual, ancient, and exotic realm that promises to infuse the mechanistic West with the mystery that it has lost. This Orientalist vision relies on a notion of the modern West as secularized, scientific, and disenchanted. Having abandoned its religious soul in its quest for scientific mastery of the world, the West needs the Orient to balance its overly secular orientation.[41] As Chakravarti's speech suggests, the ideas underlying Orientalism have never simply been expounded by White people in the West but have also been used by people of color to argue for their relevance, much as Wong used the notion of heathenism to promote rather than denigrate Confucianism.

But for all their similarities in this context, heathenism and Orientalism are not synonymous. While both are imagined constructions of a world beyond, and in opposition to, the West, the "heathen world" is a more capacious umbrella than the "Orient." It has folded under its heading not only the Middle East and Asia but also Africa, the Pacific Islands, and the Americas. Furthermore, the Orientalist idea that the West is scientific and that the East is spiritual overlooks the ways in which technology undergirded religion and vice versa in industrial America. As we have seen, the capacity for significant technological development was denied to the heathen, because they were thought to misunderstand the nature of nature and of humans as God's designated dominators of the same. American technological advances, by contrast, were heralded as providential and progressive. Orientalism separated "Oriental" from other so-called heathens, but the notion of the heathen world wove them together as one and the same in their pagan stagnation.

If Orientalism was on display at the Parliament, the heathen world was visible at the Midway Plaisance, a mile-long stretch of living dioramas, carnival entertainment, and food. The over two million visitors who attended the Chicago World's Fair saw live displays of people arranged in hierarchical orientation, with the most "civilized"—the peasant, village peoples of Catholic Europe (long thought to be practically pagan)—closest to, but still outside, the technological marvels of the White City.[42] The Midway was not the first such ethnological display of humans the world over. P. T. Barnum's Ethnological Congress opened a decade earlier and anticipated the ways in which the Midway "reif[ied] the common nonwhiteness of the representatives into a single racialized category." In Barnum's shows, this

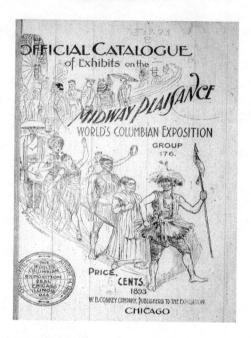

Cover of the *Official Catalogue of Exhibits on the Midway Plaisance* (Chicago: W. B. Conkey, 1893). From Center for Research Libraries, Global Resources Network.

The Barnum and Bailey Greatest Show on Earth. Poster from the Great Ethnological Congress of Curious People from All Parts of the World, the Strobridge Lith. Co., ca. 1895. Library of Congress, Prints and Photographs Division, LC-DIG-ppmsca-54802.

single category was variously labeled as "Heathens and Barbarians" and "Strange and Heathen Types of Human Beings."[43] The similarities between Barnum's Ethnological Congress and the Midway Plaisance were manifestly clear in the promotional materials used to advertise each. The cover of the Midway's *Official Catalogue of Exhibits* depicts a line of bodies arrayed in stereotypical attire, marching down an S-shaped path. Here, representatives of the "Orient" are of a piece with other heathens; none of them belongs in the White City because none of them has innovated.[44] Likewise, an 1895 circus poster for Barnum's Ethnological Congress clumps together a line of exoticized ethnic people following an S-shaped path, parading for the edification and entertainment of White audiences.[45]

The contrast between the staid World's Parliament, which celebrated Eastern religions, and the circus-like Midway Plaisance, which lumped all non-White people together, anticipated what would happen to the category of "heathen" in the twentieth century. On the one hand, some traditions came to be classified as part of the "world religions," and the names Hinduism, Buddhism, Jainism, Taoism, Confucianism, and Shinto came to replace "heathen" virtually for good, at least in polite and public parlance. Meanwhile, Indigenous traditions have continued to be classified as "ethnic," "folk," "primitive," and, yes, even "heathen," well into the twentieth century. On the other hand, all of these traditions—"Oriental" and otherwise— also continued to be grouped together as materially backwards relative to the West. This material backwardness could be read in two ways: as a sign of their pitiful and sorry ignorance, requiring Western educational, agricultural, and medical intervention; and as a sign of their greater mystical absorption in spiritual things. These two ways were not necessarily mutually exclusive. Humanitarianism could provide the heathen with the material benefits of the West, while time spent overseas could teach Westerners the ancient spiritual wisdom of the heathen. Swami Vivekananda, who became one of the celebrities of the Parliament with his impassioned and vivid explications of Hindu philosophy, simultaneously argued for the superiority of Vedanta and appealed for humanitarian aid. "Christians must always be ready for good criticism, and I hardly think that you will care if I make a little criticism," he said. "You Christians who are so fond of sending out missionaries to save the souls of the heathen, why do you not try to save their bodies from starvation? In India during the terrible famines thousands died from hunger, yet you Christians did nothing. . . . I came here to seek aid for my impoverished people, and I fully realized how difficult it was to get help for heathens from Christians in a Christian land."[46] Western Christianity was so spiritually impoverished, Vivekananda and others suggested, that its exemplars failed to react to the real suffering of others. Fortunately, this moral bankruptcy could be assuaged by learning from those maligned as heathen, who could then materially benefit from the empathy newly sparked in the West: a win-win situation.

"I Never Forsook the Blanket"

While the Parliament gave Asian representatives of the "World's Religions" a platform from which to critique the West, African Americans and Native Americans did not receive the same opportunities. African Americans were only minimally included in the Parliament. The "African Methodist Episcopal Church was the sole black religious organization represented," and only two of the Parliament's major speakers were African Americans: Frederick Douglass and Fannie Barrier Williams. Both called out American racism in their speeches, with Douglass referring to the White City as a "whited sepulcher" for "the colored people of America," and Williams asking, "Can religion help the American people to be consistent and to live up to all they profess and believe in their government and religion?"[47]

Native Americans were absent from the Parliament entirely and their traditions excluded from the status accorded the "world religions" represented there. Native people were instead displayed on the Midway. The Parliament had taken place a mere three years after "Chief Sitting Bull had been arrested and killed, the Ghost Dance had been suppressed, and 350 Sioux had been massacred at Wounded Knee Creek."[48] Native authors turned to other outlets to make their resistance heard. In 1902 Zitkála-Šá (1876–1938) published a piece in the *Atlantic Monthly*, "Why I Am a Pagan," that echoed Wong Chin Foo's "Why Am I a Heathen?" Zitkála-Šá was born on the Yankton Sioux (Ihanktonwan Dakota Oyate) reservation and educated at White's Indiana Manual Labor Institute; a Quaker boarding school for Native American children; Earlham College; and the New England Conservatory of Music. In the years before publishing this piece, she taught at Carlisle Indian Industrial School and had already begun to gain national recognition as a writer for the *Atlantic Monthly* and *Harper's Monthly*, detailing the trauma of her boarding school experiences at a time when others were touting their benefits for "saving" and "civilizing" the Indian.

In "Why I Am a Pagan," Zitkála-Šá's preacher cousin tells her that missionaries convinced him of the "folly of our old beliefs" and that she had better also renounce them lest she face "the after-doom of hell-fire!" But Zitkála-Šá rhetorically turns the tables on her cousin by calling Christianity "the new superstition" and giving her own worldview the imprimatur of the ancient and authentic. "A wee child toddling in a wonder world, I prefer to their dogma my excursions into the natural gardens where the voice of the Great Spirit is heard in the twittering of birds, the rippling of mighty waters, and the sweet breathing of flowers. If this is Paganism, then at present, at least, I am a Pagan."[49] Zitkála-Šá's piece found a receptive audience among those preservationists who maintained that ancient and authentic "pagan" ways could infuse the effete West with hearty vigor, closeness to nature, and essential survival skills.

Another survivor of a residential school and a contemporary of Zitkála-Šá was Ota Kte (Plenty Kill), also known as Luther Standing Bear (Sicangu and Oglala Lakota). Born in Dakota Territory in 1868, Standing Bear was raised in Lakota tradition, writing later of the joyous and free days of his "Indian boyhood." At the age of eleven, he was sent to Carlisle Indian Industrial School in Pennsylvania, a drastic shock and devastating experience. In his 1933 *Land of the Spotted Eagle,* published six years before his passing at the age of seventy-nine, Standing Bear provided an account of the before and after that he had experienced, as well as the through-line that he felt had sustained him amid the upheaval of Euro-American attempts to change him and his people. He claimed for himself the pejorative term "blanket Indian," which missionaries and reservation administrators had used to refer to Native people who resisted White ways, and proudly proclaimed, "Though my hair had been cut and I wore civilian clothes, I never forsook the blanket."[50]

Land of the Spotted Eagle explained why. In his preface, Standing Bear laid out the stereotypes against which he framed the book as a whole. The "Caucasian" perceives the "native American as a savage," he wrote, "meaning that he is low in thought and feeling, and cruel in acts," and believes "that he is a heathen, meaning that he is incapable, therefore void, of high philosophical thought concerning life and life's relations."[51] To these slanders, Standing Bear provided retorts that went beyond defense to offense, inverting the charges laid against Native people and applying them to White society instead.

Where White Americans saw wilderness wandering as a quality of heathenness, Standing Bear argued that "only to the white man was nature a 'wilderness' and only to him was the land 'infested' with 'wild' animals and 'savage' people. To us it was tame." Standing Bear depicted his people as truly indigenous to the land—engaged in kin relationships with its flora and fauna and the "Great Mystery" that created all—while White invaders lusted after but could never achieve this sense of rootedness. The reason for this was not only that they had invaded the land recently but also that their attitude toward it was one of exploitation and fear rather than conservation and appreciation.[52] These divergent attitudes toward nature manifested in different philosophical and religious outlooks. Speaking back to the allegation that the Indian "is a heathen" lacking "high philosophical thought," Standing Bear contended that the White man's alienation from nature rendered him incapable of perceiving that the Indian had a principled outlook on life: "The white man finds Indian philosophy obscure—wrapped, as he says, in a maze of ideas and symbols which he does not understand." But not only did the Indian have a philosophy; theirs was superior to the White man's. Since the Lakota had nothing to fear in the natural world, Standing Bear said, their "philosophy was healthy—free from fear and dogmatism," and their "religion was sane, normal, and human." "The Lakota was not a 'heathen' of many gods, nor was he a fearer of devils." Satisfied, indeed delighted, with the natural world the "Great Mystery" had created and of which they were a part, the Lakota found no need to change themselves or it. By contrast, the "white man's vindictive religion" was punishing. White people experienced the world as "a place of sin and ugliness to be endured until he went to another world, there to become a creature of wings, half-man and half-bird." "Forever" this man "directed his Mystery to change the world He had made; forever this man pleaded with Him to chastise His wicked ones; and forever he implored his Wakan Tanka to send His light to earth. Small wonder this man could not understand the other."[53] By calling Lakota religion "sane," Standing Bear implied that the "vindictive religion" of the White man was insane by contrast.

Similarly, where White Americans called Native people "savages," Standing Bear called into question their "humaneness" instead. Because Indians had a "welling kindness for all living, growing things" and a healthier view of the life to come, they were more humane toward each other and the earth than the "white man," who, "it seems to me . . . has come to fear nearly everything on earth—even his fellow being." Refusing to believe that there was anything of value in Native culture worth learning from, the White man had lost his own humanity instead. The only way he could regain it was to recognize humanity in the people he called "savages" and "heathens." Said Standing Bear, "Let him look upon the Indian world as a human world; then let him see to it that human rights be accorded to the Indians. And this for the purpose of retaining for his own order of society a measure of humanity."[54]

Recognizing humanity in Native people did not mean trying to change them. Where White humanitarians claimed that Christianization would bring the so-called heathen into the progressive march of history and raise their quality of life, Standing Bear told a starkly different story. Things had

John Nicholas Choate, "Luther Standing Bear and his father, George Standing Bear, at Carlisle Indian School, Carlisle, PA," ca. 1880. Photo number: 0321.f.0021. Courtesy of the Museum of Ethnography, Stockholm, The National Museums of World Culture, Sweden.

certainly changed since the advent of the White man, but decidedly for the worse: "True, the white man brought great change. But the varied fruits of his civilization, though highly colored and inviting, are sickening and deadening. And if it be the part of civilization to maim, rob, and thwart, then what is progress?" Standing Bear spoke from his own experience at Carlisle, where, in the name of Christianization and civilization, he and his fellow students had been forced into uncomfortable clothes, had their hair cut, been "forbidden to speak our mother tongue," and fed an "injurious" diet. These changes, "combined with lonesomeness was too much," Standing Bear mourned, "and in three years nearly one half of the children

"Chief Standing Bear in Full Regalia." Reproduced from *Land of the Spotted Eagle*, by Luther Standing Bear, by permission of the University of Nebraska Press. Copyright 1933 by Luther Standing Bear. Copyright renewed 1960 by May Jones.

from the Plains were dead and through with all earthly schools." Even as Standing Bear acknowledged that "the white people had much to teach us," he argued that "we had much to teach them, and what a school could have been established upon that idea!" And yet "this was not the attitude of the day. . . . We were 'savages,' and all who had not come under the influence of the missionary were 'heathen.'. . . Should we not have been justified in thinking them heathen? And so the 'civilizing' process went on, killing us as it went."[55]

Recognizing the power accorded to writing in White society ("the written word became established as a criterion of the superior man"), Standing Bear used the education he received at Carlisle to give the lie to their claims. "Regarding the 'civilization' that has been thrust upon me since the days of reservation," he scoffed, "it has not added one whit to my sense of justice; to my reverence for the rights of life; to my love for truth, honesty, and generosity; nor to my faith in Wakan Tanka—God of the Lakotas." Standing Bear would not forsake Lakota ways. Where White missionaries lauded before-and-after pictures of Native people forced into Western attire and hairstyles, the images in *Land of the Spotted Eagle* tell the opposite story. Buried in the text, in a closing chapter on "later days," is an image of him at Carlisle, hair shorn, standing next to his father, who had come to visit him there. Both are in Western suits and pocket chains, but his father has long hair still. Neither smiles. On the frontispiece, by contrast, occupying pride of place in the book, we see a much older "Chief Standing Bear in full regalia," an unmistakable grin on his face, despite the graininess of the image. "According to the white man, the Indian, choosing to return to his tribal manners and dress, 'goes back to the blanket,'" he explained. But if the White man saw this as a reversion to heathenness, that was not Standing Bear's problem. For "'going back to the blanket' is the factor that has saved [the Indian] from, or at least stayed, his final destruction." Wearing his regalia with pride, Standing Bear editorialized that "the Indian blanket or buffalo robe, a true American garment, and worn with the significance of language, covered beneath it, in the prototype of the American Indian, one of the bravest attempts ever made by man on this continent to rise to heights of true humanity" in devastating circumstances. And so, just as Zitkála-Šá maintained with pride that she was a pagan, and Wong Chin Foo a heathen Confucian, so Standing Bear concluded, "If today I had a young mind to direct, . . . I would, for its welfare, unhesitatingly set that child's feet in the path of my forefathers. I would raise him to be an Indian!"[56]

Rethinking Missions

The critiques that so-called heathens were leveling against Christianity found increasingly receptive ears. A booklet published around 1909 by the Woman's Baptist Foreign Missionary Society of the West, *Our Need of the Heathen*, echoed pleas about the complementary, or even saving, value that other traditions could provide to a spiritually impoverished West. Written by L. W. Cronkhite, a longtime missionary to Burma, the piece argued that "we need the heathen, not simply for the discipline and the enlargement of love that we get out of trying to do for them"—the familiar trope of the heathen world as crucial outlet for the exercise of American humanity— "but we need them for their own intrinsic worth." What did this mean? Cronkhite simultaneously affirmed the idea of a multifarious world of heathens while also celebrating an umbrella heathen world as a boon to the West: "The Chinaman with his mystic insight will make his contribution to our knowledge of God. The man of India with his understanding of spiritual things will make his. The African will teach us how to love." For Cronkhite, the diversity of the world reflected the diversity of God, "and together, *but never separately*, mankind will come to see God."[57] Cronkhite offered an Orientalist complementarian theology for how the feminized heathen world (mystical, spiritual, loving) could support the masculine West (scientific and prosperous, but in sore need of a heart).

By the 1930s, such views spread to the very center of mainline missions theory. As the landmark 1932 *Re-Thinking Missions: A Laymen's Inquiry after One Hundred Years* put it, "Western Christianity has in the main shifted its stress from the negative to the affirmative side of its message." Where the brothers Newman and Egbert Smyth had faced censure for their overly "sentimental" views of heathen salvation, now *Re-Thinking Missions* affirmed that "whatever [Christianity's] present conception of the future life, there is little disposition to believe that sincere and aspiring seekers after God in other religions are to be damned." *Re-Thinking Missions* was the joint effort of "fifteen ecumenical leaders" who spent nine months investigating missions in "India, Burma, China, and Japan," financed by the deep pockets of John D. Rockefeller Jr. A Harvard philosopher, William Ernest Hocking, compiled their findings. According to the report, "These changes will immediately alter that view of the perils of the soul which gave to the original motive of Protestant missions much of its poignant urgency."[58]

In contrast to nineteenth-century missions manuals that were liberally sprinkled with the terminology of heathenness and heathendom, *Re-Thinking Missions* used the terms "heathen" and "pagan[ism]" only once each.[59] The manual's shift in terminology importantly signaled a shift in mind-set. Hocking laid out a series of side-by-side transformations in thinking about missions in the early twentieth century. So, for instance, "expounding single-mindedly the Christianity and culture of the West" was to be replaced with "trying to preserve what is valuable in the past of the people." Furthermore, "carrying on educational and medical work primarily as a means of evangelizing" should be replaced with humanitarian work that was aimed "primarily in view of the emerging needs of the foreign land."[60]

But even as the mainliners signaled a shift in rhetoric, the concept of the heathen remained vital for conservative missiologists well into the twentieth century. Reborn under different names, the idea of a world "out there" that needs saving has also continued to reverberate outside the missions realm, reinforcing a racial binary that elevates the White humanitarian over the deluded and degraded Other, and undergirding American exceptionalism over the "developing" world.

9

RESONANCES

Carl McIntire (1906–2002), dubbed the "Fighting Fundamentalist" and "Founding Father of the Religious Right" by later biographers, accused everyone from the Presbyterian Church USA (PCUSA) to the Methodists of capitulating to modernism and spreading paganism in the land. McIntire had been a student at Princeton Theological Seminary during the fundamentalist-modernist controversy of the 1920s. Feeling that the seminary was moving in too liberal a direction, not least in its approach to missions, McIntire had departed with New Testament teacher J. Gresham Machen to the new Westminster Theological Seminary, from which he graduated in 1931. He had similarly severed ties with the mainline PCUSA, joining with Machen to form the Presbyterian Church of America in 1936, rebranded later as the Orthodox Presbyterian Church. In 1937, the year of Machen's death, he left the Orthodox Presbyterian Church to form the Bible Presbyterian Church. At the heart of Machen's and McIntire's problem with the PCUSA was its stance on foreign missions. They were appalled that the PCUSA "failed to utter any ringing disapproval" of Re-Thinking Missions. Machen wrote that the volume "constitutes from beginning to end an attack upon the historic Christian faith," "present[ing] as the aim of missions that of *seeking* truth together with adherents of other religions rather than that of *presenting* the truth which God has supernaturally recorded in the Bible. . . . It deprecates the distinction between Christians and non-Christians."[1] Machen, McIntire, and likeminded fundamentalists doubled down on the idea of a heathen world of damned unbelievers overseas, even as they also found plenty of pagans at home, not least in their liberalizing peers who seemed to want to hold hands with the heathen rather than try to save their eternal souls.

In an article titled "A Christian America vs. a Pagan America," featured in the newsletter that accompanied his popular *Twentieth-Century Reformation Hour* radio show, McIntire railed that "the Presbyterian Church is leading the retreat" from Christian nationhood "in order that a paganistic,

A CHRISTIAN AMERICA vs. A PAGAN AMERICA

Header on Carl McIntire, *A Christian America vs. a Pagan America* (Collingswood, NJ: distributed by 20th Century Reformation Hour; sponsored by Christian Beacon, 1963). Carl [Charles Curtis, Jr.] McIntire Manuscript Collection, SCM 222 Series 3: Christian Beacon and 20th Century Reformation, Box 449, Special Collections, Princeton Theological Seminary.

materialistic, so-called 'pluralistic society' may be the order of the day in the United States of America." (The font used for "Pagan" in the article title is distinctly "Oriental," the kind of stereotyped lettering one might expect from a Chinese restaurant catering to a White clientele.) McIntire listed a series of wrongs that paved the way to a "pagan America": removing the Bible as a source of moral authority from schools, abandoning school prayers, and treating the Bible as a historical document.[2] The Methodists were like the United Presbyterians in capitulating to modernism and historicism, mingling with unbelievers, and "using their church and their publication to introduce their young people to a whole world of darkness where unregenerate men live." Indeed, they "present a pagan religion to youth," the essence of which consisted of dialoging with others in a Hegelian sense, coming to a blended synthesis with those of different faiths rather than holding firm to their own Christian convictions. By contrast, argued McIntire, "the Christian is called to go out and separate men from the world of darkness. . . . Let us have churches where dialogue will be rebuked."[3] For McIntire and other fundamentalists, interfaith dialogue was an invitation to an Old Testament sort of paganism where God's chosen people disappointingly consorted with the idols and deities of surrounding tribes rather than living holy and apart. McIntire feared a kind of religious miscegenation, paralleling White conservatives' fear of racial miscegenation.

In the face of challenges leveraged against a conversionist and imperialist Christianity in the late nineteenth century and leading into the twentieth, conservative Christians on both sides of the Atlantic rallied in defense of a worldview that continued to use the term "heathen" and to conceive of the heathen as damned and dangerous. The Edinburgh World Missionary Conference of 1910 had represented the apex of Protestant missions in the long nineteenth century, as attendees optimistically projected the "evangelization of the world in this generation." But in the years after that, fundamentalists withdrew from joint missionary efforts and created their own agencies, chagrined by what they saw as the mainliners' neglect of salvation in favor of social issues.[4]

While McIntire and likeminded conservative evangelicals referred to "heathens" and "pagans" well into the twentieth century, others continued the trends we saw earlier and abandoned the labels. Still, the euphemistic synonyms they adopted—the "unreached people," the "hungry world," the "developing" nations—reveal the deep resonances of the concept from the mid-twentieth century into the present day, not only in the realm of Christian missions but also in glossy mainstream media, US politics, and technological humanitarian ventures. Named or (more often) not, the heathen continues to inform race-making in America and to stalk Americans' attitudes toward each other and the world at large.

"But Yet a Genuine Heathenism"

Published in Chicago between 1910 and 1915, *The Fundamentals: A Testimony to the Truth* united conservatives on both sides of the Anglo-Atlantic behind shared principles of biblical inerrancy and literalism against the incursions of theological liberalizers. Authors in *The Fundamentals* continued to call people who did not believe in biblical revelation "heathens" and "pagans," even as they acknowledged growing critiques of the terms. William Caven of Knox College in Toronto allowed that "there is nothing, indeed, in the Lord's teaching which forbids us to recognize anything that is good in ethnic religions—any of those elements of spiritual truth which . . . were not completely lost in the night of heathenism." Yet he maintained that it is "abundantly evident" that the "Testimony of Christ to the Old Testament" set it apart and that the scriptures simply "cannot be shared with the sacred books of other peoples."[5] Similarly, Rev. G. Campbell Morgan of Westminster Chapel in London acknowledged that "we have had such remarkable teachers as Zoroaster, Buddha, Confucius; men speaking many true things, flashing with light." But "notwithstanding these things a perpetual failure in morals and a uniform degradation of religion has been universal. The failure has ever been due to a lack of final knowledge concerning God."[6] Fundamentalists did not want to appear entirely disparaging of other people's cultures as knowledge of and interest in them spread. They allowed for some truth to have made its way into the heathen world, but declared that only with Christ's revelation could this truth find fulfillment.

Fundamentalists were not insensitive to the problem of what to do with the heathen who never had access to the gospel. Sir Robert Anderson, in an essay titled "Sin and Judgment to Come," posed the problem directly: "What of the heathen who have never heard at all?" Would they be destined for eternal hell if no one evangelized them? Preferring to leave the question unanswered, he said, "No one can claim to solve these problems without seeming profanely to assume the role of umpire between God and men." Instead of worrying that a God who could damn the far-off heathen might be unjust, Anderson instead rested in the conviction that a "God of perfect justice and infinite love" decides all such matters: "Unhesitating faith is our right attitude in presence of divine revelation, but where Scripture is silent let us keep silence."[7]

This stance of modesty before a sovereign God contrasted with the heathenish hubris of modern-day philosophy and higher criticism as taught in universities, claimed other authors in *The Fundamentals*. There were two major problems with education in the twentieth century, they lamented: first, it put Eastern, "heathen" philosophies on an equal level with Christianity, and second, it elevated humans to the level of God in promising them knowledge beyond where scripture would go. In a piece titled "Modern Philosophy," Philip Mauro, counselor-at-law in New York City, echoed eighteenth century debates over the classics in education. Where eighteenth-century Protestants had worried about Greco-Roman philosophy, Mauro worried about Hinduism and Buddhism. As he put it, "Our present-day teachers of philosophy appear to say" that "our ancestors" erred "when they chose, and founded great universities to preserve, the doctrines taught by Jesus Christ and His apostles, rather than . . . the doctrines associated with the name of Buddha." But "twentieth-century man" would do well to remember that "whatever there may be of superiority in the social order of Christianized England and America over that of pantheistic India is due to the choice which our forefathers made when they accepted the teaching of the Gospel of Christ." Mauro explained that Eastern philosophy was a trick of the devil, who bewitched humans into thinking that they were "truly one in substance and being" with God, urging them to rely on their own fallen intellects rather than on God. Allured by these teachings, the present generation had strayed, and now, Mauro catastrophized, "we are living under the dark shadow of the *greatest national apostasy that has ever taken place. During all the history of mankind there has never been such a wholesale turning away from the Source of national blessings, in order to take up with the gods of the heathen."[8]

Meanwhile, Professor J. J. Reeve of Southwestern Baptist Theological Seminary in Fort Worth, Texas, explained how he had once adopted and then rejected higher criticism because of its similar overemphasis on the human intellect. According to Reeve, evolution was the fundamental hypothesis underlying higher criticism, and it effectively locked God into one way of working: the "state of change, of flux, or of becoming." The effect of this was too destabilizing for Reeve to abide, for even God Himself became subject to the law of change, ultimately leading to a time when "the Bible and Christ will be outgrown, Christianity itself will be left behind." Where mainliners trumpeted progress as the hallmark of Christian civilization contra the stagnating pagan, Reeve worried that they were deifying progress. With no more biblical authority on which to rely, a dangerous moral relativism would take hold, he warned, where "there is no *absolute* truth, nothing in the moral religious world is fixed or certain. All truth is in solution." Every man would become his own philosopher, relying on "his own reason," which becomes "his lord." Jesus Christ would be "bowed out" as humans became glibly and dangerously self-reliant. Warned Reeve, "Such a religion is the very negation of Christianity, is a distinct reversion to heathenism. It may be a cultured and refined heathenism with a Christian veneer, but yet a genuine heathenism."[9] As Reeve's problem with higher criticism signals, the heathen barometer continued to be deployed against White Americans who seemed to have abandoned Christianity (as the accuser would define it), used to diagnose problems within White American Protestantism itself, particularly as it succumbed to outside pressures, whether of the intellectual order (like higher criticism and moral relativism) or in the realm of popular culture.

"Why All the Urgency?"

Organizations like Basil Miller's World-Wide Missions and Bob Pierce's World Vision, both founded in 1950, grew from the conservative side of the fundamentalist-modernist divide. Although conservative missiologists had retrenched in the wake of the 1910 Edinburgh World Missionary Conference, they reemerged on the public stage after World War II.[10] The war itself had given rise to familiar rhetoric deployed against America's enemies. Just as heathenness had been used to support late nineteenth-century American interests of exclusion and inclusion, so allegations that Japanese Shinto and Buddhism were heathen swirled around Japanese Americans in the leadup to internment and, after the war, justified American occupation to institute "real" religious freedom in Japan.[11] Even as America emerged as a superpower after the war, the imminent threat of nuclear apocalypse and the spread of "atheistic" Communism galvanized conservatives to action.

They called on Americans to save the free world and spread a "gospel of freedom and power" by joining and contributing to organizations like Youth for Christ, Navigators, the Billy Graham Evangelistic Association, World Vision, and World-Wide Missions.[12] By 1955 these conservative missionary organizations outnumbered the mainline associations. Reiterating the hope of Edinburgh, and armed with a heady mix of self-confident optimism and dire pessimism, they believed that they could—and should—bring about the evangelization of the world in their generation.

Postwar evangelical humanitarian organizations adopted a two-pronged approach to missions, prioritizing the salvation of souls but not at the expense of starving bellies. Missionaries like Pierce and Miller believed that it was easier to convert people who weren't starving, and that conversion could lead "to material benefits, helping to alleviate poverty and ward off communism." Missionaries had long linked the supposed inadequacies of heathen bodies and societies to their wrong beliefs, as we have seen. The idea that conversion could combat poverty reveals how midcentury conservative evangelicals understood the causes of suffering: they focused on "individual needs over structural issues."[13]

Just as earlier missionaries had used new print and photographic technologies to publicize the plight of the poor heathen overseas, so postwar agencies also took advantage of new mass technologies like radio, glossy color printing, and television to dramatize the plight of suffering sinners abroad.[14] Pierce believed that "once American Christians saw the severity of humanitarian needs through a personal face, they would act." He brought the "sights and sounds" of "pagan" China to Americans in travelogues like *China Challenge, The Red Plague,* and *Cry in the Night,* contrasting depictions of deformed and starving bodies living in putrid conditions with images of Christian churches and tales of evangelistic success. Once China "fell" to Communism in 1949, Pierce turned to Korea, where he established World Vision in 1950 and continued to produce film exposés. He explicitly "labeled non-Christian religions as 'heathen' and 'backwards'"; as scholar David King puts it, he "made Asians seem exotic, and he demonized aspects of their 'heathen' cultures," like their "pagan" dances and temples, "as symbols of their 'otherness.'" At the same time, Pierce affirmed that the "heathen" could be redeemed if Americans would share their wealth and feed the souls and stomachs of the spiritually and somatically starving overseas.[15]

The productions of World-Wide Missions similarly used visual media to encourage Americans to open their wallets to the cause of heathen uplift around the world. Brochures conflated different regions and people as lying in critical need—of food, shelter, and transportation; of Jesus; and of the

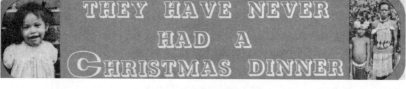

"Share Christmas with Them," 1965. Collection 143: Material from World-Wide Faith Mission, 1950–1985 Collection. David Allan Hubbard Library at Fuller Theological Seminary. Photo made available by Fuller Theological Seminary.

White people to bring Him to them. A 1965 pamphlet, "Share Christmas with Them," presents black-and-white images of children from different parts of the world with the plaintive captions, "Share your Christmas with these orphans," and "They have never had a Christmas dinner." These images serve to visually clump the children together. The middle spread of the pamphlet makes this clumping even clearer, as it provides snapshots from Southeast Asia, South America, West Africa, and the Twin Wells reservation, all of which need the help of "you, dear friends," to "meet Christ" and share a "happy Christmas." The brochure explicitly refers to these needy people as heathen, and to their habitations as the heathen world. A young Christian girl in Alaska suggests donating money saved from a simple Christmas meal to "some other child or family in the heathen world." Meanwhile, the "chief of a heathen village in West Africa" speaks of the "dark superstition" of his people and complains, "We have never had a Christmas." "Precious friends," the pamphlet editorializes, "this is typical of the heathen world in many, many nations."[16]

Basil Miller and his wife, Esther, conclude the pamphlet with a letter to their "fellow Americans," testifying to the sadness of the heathen world and telling Americans how to interpret the images presented in the pamphlet: "I've been to heathen countries. I've seen these sunken-eyed children, bloated-bellied little children. I've seen beggar boys. I've seen Hong Kong's children scratching in garbage. I've seen war refugees. I've seen the outcasts. They all ask one question: 'Do you love us enough to care for us now?'"[17] Even where children were smiling, in other words, the Millers' letter trained readers to see them as sunken-eyed; even where their bellies seemed full, readers should view them as bloated from starvation. This was the heathen world, and this was what Americans still needed to save.

To do so required urgency. Here, World-Wide Missions tapped into familiar tropes of the perishing heathen to urge Americans to open their wallets. The cover of a brochure from 1984, six years after Basil Miller's death, featured an unsmiling child, rendered in black on red, with the stark words, "Do it now!" emblazoned on the front. Inside, readers could find an article titled "Why All the Urgency?" rendered in the same color scheme but with the child's image cropped to just the eyes, which glow red above the white lettering. Red glowing eyes is a time-honored way of depicting the devil and evil, and the implication is startling and unsettling: here is a child who is bound for hell without your immediate intervention. These heathens are all on the verge of death without American medical, food, or disaster relief. And not only did that mean their bodies were imperiled: their "souls are in jeopardy," the article concluded. And "that is why there is such urgency."[18]

"A Garment of Semireligious Nationalism"

Persistent stereotypes about the heathen did not stay confined to the realm of religious humanitarianism. Midcentury photographic magazines like *Life* and *National Geographic* popularized images and ideas of the world beyond the United States that had clear roots in the heathen world. To take just one paradigmatic example, the May 4, 1953 special issue of *Life* promised an "exciting 10,000 mile trip through Africa: a continent in ferment," offering articles and photographs saturated with clichés about the heathen world. *Life,* published by missionary son Henry Luce, aimed to help American readers "to see and be amazed; to see and be instructed." Luce "conceived *Life* as an ambitious and even messianic news magazine aimed at shaping citizenship, defining class, and regulating national identity among readers." By the 1940s the magazine reached roughly 22.5 million people, helping to form their sense of what it meant to be American in a changing global context.[19]

The special issue's opening essay framed Africa as a continent in transition. Describing the state out of which Africa was transitioning, the essay's author, Alexander Campbell, head of Time-Life's Africa, India, Korea, Japan, and Middle Eastern bureaus (quite the sweeping-together of the world), tapped into familiar characterizations of the heathen world as stagnant, inhabited by "wandering nomads" subject to environmental whims, and in the sway of tyrants who promised protection from evil forces. Campbell wrote, "For centuries the rhythm of Africa remained unchanged. It was not slow, as in lands where the sun swings wide, but sharp and savage as a tom-tom beat. But it had no meaning. . . . Men's activities were molded by environment. Life was dominated by the witch doctor prancing in his devil mask and swaying headdress; peace was abruptly stopped by the stabbing spear."[20] European colonizers had now turned the continent into a place "where some five million whites rule some 175 million brown and black people on a quarter of the earth's surface." But their rule had recently been threatened by the "flames of nationalism," which "scorched into wakefulness the native African's long lost pride" and "licked at the flimsy framework of white mastery." Campbell alleged that the Bible "has been often responsible for fanning the flames of African nationalism and anti-white feeling" as, "in the past year, from Kenya to the Cape, African nationalist sects have joined in anti-white fronts, concocting from the Old Testament a garment of semireligious nationalism." Campbell described one such "sect," the Dini ya Msambwa—founded by Elijah Masinde, a student of the Kenyan Friends of Africa Mission—as preaching "mumbo-jumbo" later inherited by the Mau Mau. Campbell warned that "these aroused Negroes, linking hands with their brothers all over the continent, may yet blow all hopes for Africa sky-high. There is still time to avert this, but not too much time. In Africa, both white and black stand today at a fateful crossroads. Working together, they can pass from darkness to light. If they clash, Africa will pass back into jungle night." Campbell depicted Africa as on a knife's edge between regression to a "dark" past of "mumbo-jumbo" and a promising and prosperous future, but only if Native Africans would cooperate with White oversight.[21]

Other essays in the special issue picked up on the themes Campbell raised. One article was tellingly titled "History's Impact upon Africa" in the magazine's table of contents, but "The White Impact upon Africa" in the article itself. This conflation of Whiteness with history was set against the "no recorded history" and "primitive isolation" in which Africa supposedly languished "before the white man came in."[22] The special issue concluded with an editorial directly aimed at Americans and their relationship to and interest in Africa. Titled "Americans and Africa: We Need an Attitude That Is True to Our Own Best Lights," the editorial characterized Americans as "ignoran[t]" of the situation in Africa, even as "the problems of Africa first invite, then mock, comparisons with our own experience, whether the problem be that of subduing the wilderness, uplifting the backward, mingling races or proclaiming freedom."[23] In this context, the special issue itself might be understood as a salvo in overcoming American "ignorance." Its editors likely understood that middle-class readers might go looking for an outlet to send their dollars to Africa after reading the issue. The White readership of Life overlapped with the audience for World Vision, World-Wide Missions, and other similar humanitarian organizations' brochures and publications. But before Americans haphazardly invested their money, Life's editors wanted to be sure they knew to what end.

They warned that "American ignorance of Africa appalls its European rulers. They therefore hope that American money and technical aid, which they skittishly invite to help build an African future, will arrive unaccompanied by American political attitudes. But even non-intervention is an attitude." The editors intimated that Americans' lack of interest in "Europe's carving up of Africa" into "meaningless boundaries" might be particularly concerning to European powers invested in those boundaries. But this disinterest in European politicking was, for Life's editors, a net positive that served to differentiate America as a better kind of world power that was less interested in political than in economic intervention.

The advertisements littering the pages of the magazine, for everything from deodorant and Listerine to DeBeers diamonds, spoke volumes about the hygienic products and material luxuries American-style development promised to both bring to and reap from Africa in what Luce called the "American century."[24]

The closing editorial suggested that, despite their "ignorance" about Africa, Americans might "help [Europeans] avert" the problems that a number of articles in the issue had raised, of a continent in transition and turmoil. Though the American context was very different, the editorial suggested that the "American Negro" might have some lessons to offer Africa, for "in all his various quests for status, [he] has returned always to white models whenever they were worth copying."[25] Leaning wholeheartedly into the fantasy of the White man's burden, the editorial proclaimed that "in working toward decent race relations in America, therefore, the white man's problem has been to remain true to his own best lights, such as the Golden Rule and the Declaration of Independence, acceptable to whites and blacks alike. By the same token, no white definition of African civilization will come true without a universal idea that commands black assent." The editors made a classic secularist move here, framing Western Christian ideals as universals even as, in the words of scholar Peter Coviello, these ideals "(freedom, agency, reason, autonomy) come down to us bloodied, steeped in the history of their use as tools for racialized subjugation." Secularism is, as Coviello explains, a "*theodicy*: a sacralized vindication of the world—colonial, racially stratified, authorizing itself in the exclusions it pledges one day to redeem—as it is."[26] This is precisely how the *Life* editorial functions, justifying American intervention in Africa in order to eventually "redeem" it by the "universal" values Americans espouse that are "acceptable to whites and blacks alike." Conclude the editors, "That certainly implies racial equity and, on the long path to it, mutual respect. One does not show respect for the African by pretending to believe in his rain makers; nor by denying him what he has earned, whether a Gramophone or the vote; nor by withholding what he needs and desires, notably education."[27] The end goal of "racial equity" is, here, the transformation of the Native African from dupe who believes in "rain makers" and deserves no "respect" as such, to secular subject who wants nothing more than to exercise free choice in the liberal marketplace of commodities, politics, and education. Racial equity is achieved, in this fantasy, when the pagan turns paragon, and racial othering functions here not through reference to the unchangeable body but through reference to the still influential idea of changeable heathens to whom respect is due only if they respect and adopt the White man's ways.

Christopaganism or Indigenous Christianity?

Much as the *Life* special issue warned against a "mumbo-jumbo" of pagan rites clothed in a Christian veneer, so American missiologists in the latter part of the twentieth century worried about their evangelization efforts leading in unanticipated and (to them) alarming directions justified in the name of Christianity. They took it as an imperative to suss out where evangelizing led to "true" Christianization and where it instead seemed to meld with heathenism, emboldening anticolonial struggles against Western powers. Even as Bob Pierce and Basil Miller continued to freely invoke the language and imagery of heathen damnation for American audiences, other missiologists found themselves increasingly defensive over the same. They realized that, in the midst of anticolonial movements for independence, they could no longer hope to win approbation, much less change hearts, for overhauling cultures they denigrated as heathen. Instead, they sought to determine what was "safe" and what was "satanic" in the cultures they were trying to evangelize. They also sought to determine what (in their view) was narrowly Western and what was universal in the gospel they were trying to export.

An April 1974 conference, the William S. Carter Symposium on Church Growth held at Milligan College in East Tennessee, focused on parsing "legitimate accommodation from illegitimate syncretism." In a series of lectures, later collected and published as a book, a half-dozen professors of missiology discussed and defended "indigenous Christianity" while denigrating what they called "Christopaganism," a syncretistic corruption of the gospel. According to Alan Tippett, professor of missionary anthropology at Fuller Theological Seminary, "The basic problem . . . would seem to be how to communicate the essential *supracultural* core of the gospel to new believers in other cultures without having it contaminated by the non-Christian forms with which it must be communicated and shared." Heathen contamination remained an essential fear of these missiologists. They drew a distinction between the "distortion of Christian theology by mixing it with pagan myth" (not acceptable) and the "singing of, say, a western Calvinist theology in an unfamiliar chant to a drumbeat previously used only for pagan dances" (acceptable).[28] The former had to do with content, while the latter (they thought) was merely about form. Heathen ideas were still dangerous, but now the modes of their expression were deemed by and large problem-free. The notion that the two could be separated reflected a Protestant view of religion as primarily a matter of the mind and its beliefs rather than of the body and its actions.

The example Tippett chose to illustrate Christopaganism was a familiar Protestant foe: Latin Catholicism. "My data base is the case study of a real character, one Juan, a small peasant village official, who considered himself a Christian," Tippett wrote. Clearly Tippett did not consider Juan as such. "In point of fact," he opined, Juan's life, as told in his autobiography, was "so thoroughly Christopagan as to be hardly Christian at all." Tippett outlined four reasons why Juan's professed Christianity was (in his eyes) a sorry heathen sham. First was the survival of "cohesive animistic units" embedded within Juan's belief system, most egregiously, "sheer nature worship." Second was a misunderstanding of biblical stories that resulted in "completely confused" and "appalling" mythical thinking. Third was the continuation of "shamanistic" rites with "pagan overtones," as communities looked beyond Christianity for help in sickness and adversity. Last was ancestral veneration, or the "notion of the living dead," who "still must eat the produce of the land and receive the services of the present occupants of their lands." Tippett extrapolated outward from the autobiography of one lone individual—Juan—to the rest of the "Christopagan" world, past and present: "I want to point out that none of these is confined to Latin America or to the present day."[29] Here we see again the long-lived idea of the heathen world as a geographically and temporally elastic realm.

In July of the same year, a much larger gathering of evangelicals from 150 countries convened in Lausanne, Switzerland, for the Billy Graham–initiated First International Congress on World Evangelization. The Lausanne Congress grappled with many of the same questions as the professors at the William S. Carter Symposium, about how to distinguish between seemingly innocuous and dangerous cultural practices, and the pitfalls of Western ethnocentrism for missionary work. These questions were brought into even sharper relief by the fact that half the delegates at the Congress hailed from countries in the Global South that had historically been seen as part of the heathen world and on the receiving end of world missionizing. In his opening plenary address, Graham celebrated these delegates and the spread of Christianity across the globe. But he cautioned that "with the promise, there are many dangers." Naming inflation, famine, the occult, breakdown of the nuclear family, and loss of the fear of God, Graham told delegates that "the world may be standing at the very brink of Armageddon." What he wanted to come out of the Congress was "the Spirit of Lausanne," a sense of united purpose and urgency among evangelicals worldwide as they sought to proclaim to as much of the world as possible the saving power of Jesus Christ before it was too late. Graham took issue with those who "have openly taught that there are many ways to God and that ultimately no one is lost." "To this," he said, "evangelicals must return a resounding *no.*" Despite the long history of Christians made uncomfortable by the damnation of the heathen, Graham did not concede an inch to those who hoped that God might have mercy. Given his conviction in a hell awaiting unbelievers, Graham's utmost priority was "*evangelism* and the *salvation of souls.*" Although he acknowledged the importance of social responsibility and humanitarian aid to the needy, he drew attention to the vastness of what he called the "*unevangelized world,*" which "consists of large 'unreached' populations which can be found in almost every country." It is not difficult to see resonances of the heathen world in Graham's "*unevangelized world.*" He told the delegates that "there are tens of millions who live in areas that never hear the Gospel. . . . . We should give a great deal of thought and prayer to ways and means of reaching these lost millions. . . . This Congress will be shocked to learn of the magnitude of the unreached populations on every continent."[30]

In reality, many delegates were likely not shocked, but already shared Graham's convictions and sense of the urgency of world evangelization. In the months leading up to the Congress, a number of them had already been hard at work drafting a statement, spurred by Graham, that encapsulated these sentiments. The drafting committee circulated a sketch of the statement among Congress attendees, who sent in hundreds of amendments and suggestions. The final product, the Lausanne Covenant, was adopted by the 2,300 delegates in attendance and became one of the most significant evangelical productions of the twentieth century.[31] The Covenant took on many of the same pressing issues around the salvation of the unevangelized with which Christians had long grappled. Could the unreached be saved if they had no access to the Bible? If not, how was that fair?

The Covenant affirmed that "everyone has some knowledge of God through his general revelation in nature." God did not, in other words, leave people high and dry even if they had no knowledge of Christianity. Why, then, was evangelization necessary? Said the Covenant, despite such natural light, "we deny that this can save, for people suppress the truth by their unrighteousness. We also reject as derogatory to Christ and the gospel every kind of syncretism and dialogue which implies that Christ speaks equally through all religions and ideologies."[32] The Covenant made the familiar move to protect the goodness of God by blaming humans for their own damnation, even if they lived out of reach of the gospel, because of their own "unrighteousness." On the question of how much to accommodate churches to local, Indigenous cultures (essentially Christopaganism or Indigenous Christianity), the Covenant declared, "Culture must always be tested and judged by Scripture. Because men and women are God's creatures, some of their culture is rich in beauty and goodness. Because they

are fallen, all of it is tainted with sin and some of it is demonic." Evange-
lizers had to guard against their own cultural imperialism while also warding
off the "demonic" in the cultures they sought to save. In the battle between
Christ and Satan, now was the time to reach the "more than 2,700 million
people, which is more than two-thirds of all humanity," who "have yet to
be evangelized." The unreached world stood as a "standing rebuke to us
and to the whole Church."[33]

It was significant that the drafters and signers of the statement styled it
a *covenant*. John Stott, the chairman of the Drafting Committee, explained
that the signatories viewed the statement as a "binding contract" and not
merely a "declaration," "to commit ourselves to the task of world evangelization." Reaching the unreached, to "let the earth hear his voice," would
become the rallying cry of Lausanne.

"Euricans" and "Latfricasians"

The notion of the "unreached" would also become one of the most influential concepts in twentieth-century evangelical missiology and a term often
used as an updated (read: politically correct) replacement for the "heathen
world." It was popularized by the Church Growth Movement spearheaded
by Donald McGavran, founding dean of the School of World Mission at
Fuller Seminary. In his own address at Lausanne, "The Dimensions of
World Evangelization," McGavran acknowledged the changed world in
which missionaries were operating and the need for new strategies to reach
the "huge numbers of men and women [who] will never be reached by
Christian neighbors." Using the terms "Eurican" and "Latfricasian" as
shorthand for Europe/North America (the West) and Latin America/Af-
rica/Asia (the rest), McGavran explained that the "unreached" overwhelmingly came from the latter regions, but that their evangelization was ham-
pered by a sense that the former was insufferably and ruinously overbearing.
Lausanne delegates needed to counter the "pernicious notion that world
evangelism is a concealed form of European imperialism and will destroy
the beautiful cultures of Asia, Africa, and Latin America." This notion, he
insisted, was "false and must be cleared out of the way. . . . This Congress
does not believe that Eurican culture is God's chosen culture." After all,
said McGavran, God accepted "the wealth and splendor" of all "nations"
into the "Holy City."[34] But—and this was a big but—"there is one condition." McGavran cited Revelation 21:27 to explain that "nothing unclean
shall enter." This meant, in his words, "no oppression, no injustice, no por-
nography, no idolatry, no corruption, no lust, no drunkenness, no lies, no

racial arrogance." Euricans needed to get off their (racial) high horse and cleanse themselves for the kingdom of heaven, while Latfricasians—quite a euphemism for the heathen—needed to purge their forms and objects of worship, sexual mores, and political structures to qualify for the Holy City.[35]

How best to encourage Latfricasians toward the City of God? For Mc-Gavran, aiming for conversions one soul at a time was not the answer. Spurred by critiques of Western missions as too individualistic, McGavran instead advocated for the data-driven analysis and division of the unreached world into "people groups" with shared languages, cultures, and kin structures that could be evangelized corporately.[36] The Christianization of Europe had occurred in such a manner, he claimed. Some people "bewailed" this fact and believed that "after these rough tribal conversions, Christians were little better than baptized heathen, and the Christian faith had more affinity with the worship of Thor than with that of the Prince of Peace." But McGavran countered that "it was tribal conversions or nothing. Had tribal conversions not been allowed by the Christian churches there might well have been very little Christianization at all, and our Christian leaders today might be leading war dances around the Sacred Oak. The emergence of a Christian-scientific civilization might still today be eons away."[37] History—development over time—is again what separates the stagnant heathen from the scientifically advanced Christian. And right religion is what spurs a people group to join the march of history.

McGavran's insistence that Christians exhaustively research the "unreached" in order to divide them into people groups represents both a continuation of missionaries' attention to on-the-ground specifics and a persistent view of "Latfricasia" as a teeming mass of "voiceless multitudes" who need Christianity to tame their revolutionary impulses amid an "irreversible tide" of anticolonial struggle. "The Christian church has good news for the awakening masses," he proclaimed: "that God the Father Almighty is just and intends to have a just world. . . . Contrary to paternalistic thinking, the greatest need of the masses is neither aid nor kindness. Their greatest need is neither handouts nor social action; but a religion which gives them a bedrock on which to stand as they battle for justice."[38] Read charitably, McGavran suggests that Christianity can empower the "masses" because of its insistence that all humans are equal in the eyes of God. (Of course, the notion that no other religion offers this foundation for justice is paternalistic, despite McGavran's denial.) Read less charitably, he expresses a barely contained anxiety about the "illiterate peasants, country serfs, factory laborers, poverty-stricken miners, cannon fodder, the poor, the hewers of wood and drawers of water [who] have been given the vote in nation after nation." Would they exercise their vote in a manner deemed by the West to be responsible? Or would the newly empowered and "awakening" masses in Latfricasia degenerate once more into the anarchy and tyrannical governance that had characterized the heathen world before colonization? The "roar of their demands," he said, "testifies eloquently to the titanic force of the revolutionary dynamic." But while their demands might be legitimate, for McGavran they must be channeled through Christianity.[39]

The biblical allusion McGavran makes to the "hewers of wood and drawers of water" would have been understood by the delegates at Lausanne to indicate heathens excluded from God's peoplehood. The reference is to the Gibeonites, a Canaanite people who were supposed to be exterminated by the Israelites for their idolatry and inhabitation of the promised land that the Israelites were to occupy. The Gibeonites tricked the Israelites into thinking they were not local Canaanites but ambassadors from afar. Joshua enters into a covenant with them, but once he realizes their deception, he condemns them to servitude as "hewers of wood and drawers of water" in perpetuity. The Gibeonites are idolaters who escape one quintessential consequence of heathenism—extermination—only to suffer another: enslavement.[40]

Rich Christians and the Hungry World

That McGavran delivered such an address at Lausanne suggests the extent to which, as scholar David King puts it, "Western leaders still set much of the agenda" there. But also at Lausanne were delegates from Latin America, Asia, and Africa who criticized the "evangelicalism" Western leaders espoused as "'a cultural Christianity' that equated faith with the American way of life." Challenged by the critiques of Third World theologians, which we will see in Chapter 10, the movement for Civil Rights, and America's embarrassing failures in Vietnam, a younger generation of White American evangelicals began to "rethin[k] their approach to missions." They shifted emphasis from Graham's laser-beam focus on evangelization toward the amelioration of social woes like poverty, hunger, illiteracy, racism, and gender inequality.[41] One of the leaders of this newer generation of evangelicals, Ronald J. Sider, was Graham's junior by twenty years. Trained in history at Yale, Sider had planned a career in academia teaching European history. But his first job, at Messiah College in Philadelphia, inspired him to instead dedicate himself to evangelical solutions to social problems.

At first glance, Sider's *Rich Christians in an Age of Hunger: Moving from Affluence to Generosity,* published in 1978 when Sider was not yet forty, might seem to have moved far from the persistent heathen world paradigm of World-Wide Missions and its ilk. *Rich Christians* has received wide acclaim as one of the most "influential religious books of the twentieth century" and has gone through six reprints. In its most recent (2015) iteration, it calls for "structural change," asks Americans and Europeans to abjure their "absurd" addiction to material goods, decries environmental devastation, and tells multinational corporations to stop their "aggressive advertising campaigns"—of cigarettes, makeup products, sodas, and infant formula—to "poor nations." Sider calls out European colonialism for "foster[ing] injustice" and calls US lands "stolen."[42] One of the reasons Sider's work has been so popular is that he "finds himself agreeing with both" liberals and conservatives—the former of whom blame "constrictive social and economic policy" and the latter "morally reprehensible individual choices" for poverty.[43] Both perspectives find a sympathetic voice in his text.

Even as he calls for redistribution of wealth, Sider is neither a Marxist nor a trickle-down capitalist. He criticizes "democratic capitalism" as much as Communism for their attitudes toward money and envisions a radical overhaul of the global economy. He acknowledges that asking people to "consume less" would most likely lead to "declining demand" and "declining production," which could in turn lead to "a decline in the need for workers" or even "severe unemployment." His initial solution to this problem is for Americans and Europeans to channel money that they would otherwise spend on themselves into Christian aid agencies. By raising the standard of living in poor nations, Sider says, these agencies send money back to industrialized nations in order to purchase the goods needed "to create wealth and attain an adequate level of material well-being."[44] Much as nineteenth-century missionaries celebrated the creation of new markets for new desires among their missionees (for cloth and buttons and needles, for farming and gardening tools), so here the industrialized nations get to keep producing while also cutting their consumption and virtuously helping the rest of the world. But Sider doesn't stop here. "Even if we reached the biblical norm of distributional justice," he says, we should not "again pursue the same sort of economic growth we formerly did." Sounding uncannily like Wong Chin Foo, he does not advocate the creation of more wealth—to what end?—but instead suggests that Americans need to "reexamine priorities at a still deeper level." Is "quality family life . . . more important than economic growth and more gadgets? Or do we prefer to absolutize the material world and the things that scientific technology can produce?" Ultimately he suggests that Americans "work fewer hours at their jobs, and in their new leisure . . . do volunteer work in their community or spend more time with their families or in constructive hobbies."[45]

So how—if at all—do conceptions of heathenness manifest in *Rich Christians*? One clear way Sider draws on older tropes is by flipping the stigma of paganism and attaching it to White Americans rather than to the "poor nations." Like others before him, he uses the heathen barometer to diagnose problems at the very heart of American Christian practice. The churches are full of rich Christians who believe that they have a right to do with their private property as they see fit (which usually means spending it on themselves). Sider claims that this is a "pagan view" of possessions that runs contrary to a "biblical" understanding in which "Yahweh is Lord of all things. . . . Economics is not a neutral, secular sphere," for "God alone has an absolute right to property." Sider repeatedly uses the words "idol" and "idolatry" to refer to "rich Christians" and their addiction to wealth. "Possessions are the most common idol for rich Christians today," he says. "Covetousness, a striving for more and more material possessions, has become a cardinal vice of modern civilization. . . . In its essence, it is idolatry."[46]

But this does not mean that Sider lets the "hungry world" off the hook for its own hunger or that continuing ideas about the heathen world as a needy realm separate from our own do not also creep into his book. Indeed, they underlie it. Sider bifurcates the world into "rich Christians" and their "billion hungry neighbors" who live in "what used to be called the Third World." These poor are subjected to "illiteracy, inadequate medical care, disease, and stunting." Famine stalks their dwelling-places, and "children's brains vegetate and their bodies succumb prematurely to disease."[47] Such language is reminiscent of earlier tropes about damaged and dying heathen bodies. In those earlier tropes, heathen bodies are made such by their very heathenness: wrong belief leads to harmful practices and backwards or no technologies, which lead to adverse health effects. Sider does not link religious cause and bodily effect so directly since he devotes much space to blaming rapacious colonialism and Christian greed for harming the world's poor. But in his explanations for "poverty's complex causes," he also indicts "misguided cultural values and non-Christian worldviews." As a primary example, Sider uses India, long a stand-in for the heathen world, as we have seen. "Hinduism's complex theology and practice of the caste system is a major cause of poverty in India," he alleges. "The Hindu worldview teaches that people in the higher castes are there because of good choices in previous incarnations, and those in the lowest castes are there because of evil choices in earlier incarnations. . . . What India needs is a worldview that rightly names the gaping disparity as sinful and unjust. . . .

In short, India's untouchables need the Gospel." Sider also links technological development (or apparent lack thereof) to religious orientation.
Sounding like nineteenth-century missionary William Speer, he writes,
"Those who think, as animists do, that the rivers and trees are living spirits,
will not dam rivers to create hydroelectric power or cut forests to manu-
facture paper. Those who think, as some Eastern monists do, that the material world is an illusion to be escaped, will not waste much time creating
material abundance." Sider taps into the stagnating pagan motif, too, when
he names "Confucian culture" for "perceiv[ing] innovation and technology
as a threat rather than an opportunity." Sider uses the terms "Hindu,"
"animist," and "Confucian" rather than "heathen" but nevertheless
echoes earlier missionaries in connecting these "non-Christian worldviews"
to lack of development, inequality, and poverty.[48]

Finally, *Rich Christians* is undergirded with persisting ideas about the
blighted and hungry world out there as an outlet for rich Christians to exercise and exorcise their wealth. Rich Christians have the power to save the
rest of the world—the only question is whether they are "generous enough
to save these lives." (Benjamin Wisner's "Have you the feelings of humanity?
I wait for your reply" echoes still.[49]) The hungry world also holds the key to
true happiness for Christians. "It is tragic that so many rich Christians are
missing Jesus' path to joy and self-fulfillment," Sider laments. "Millions of
North Americans, Western Europeans, and increasingly rich people everywhere are in despair as they seek in vain for happiness through ever-greater
material abundance." The cure? Comparing ourselves with "the poorest
one-third of the world's people" rather than always trying in vain to measure up to "our affluent neighbors," and following "Jesus' paradoxical
teaching that it is better to give than to receive." Just as with Basil Miller,
who has a newfound appreciation for his tired divan following a trip to the
heathen world, so with Sider, the world of hunger frees rich Christians from
the "idolatrous materialism of the economic rat race." Giving creates a win-
win situation: "By spending less on ourselves," we can find "genuine joy
and enduring happiness" while also "transform[ing] the lives of neighbors
who will die unless we care." *We* hold the power to save lives; *they* harbor
the hunger to give our lives purpose and meaning.[50]

THUMB(S) People

With the advent of the internet, new technologies of communication have
enabled older trends to blossom with renewed vigor. Webpages saturated
with color and sound are just a click away. Older missionary maps that

colored the heathen world in drab browns or grays have found new life in interactive web maps where a visitor can hover over a country and find out just how much of its population is "unreached." Joshua Project, for instance, a ministry of Frontier Ventures, links to no fewer than a dozen maps that are updated as evangelists make "progress toward engaging unreached peoples." Founded by evangelists Ralph and Roberta Winter, Frontier Ventures grew directly out of the Lausanne Congress, where Ralph had given a "watershed speech" about the need to reach the "thousands of distinct people groups who were cut off from any forms of traditional evangelistic outreach." In 1976 the Winters purchased seventeen acres in Pasadena to build "the largest single property in the world dedicated to the cause of the unreached peoples." The campus continues to this day as the Venture Center.[51]

Joshua Project joined Frontier Ventures in 2006, eleven years after its own founding. It describes itself as a "research initiative seeking to highlight the ethnic people groups of the world with the fewest followers of Christ."[52] Joshua Project's "People Groups of the World" map attempts a finer-tuned color coding than earlier maps of the heathen world, using dots to represent people groups at varying stages of evangelization rather than filling in entire swaths of the world with a single color for "heathen." The coding of the dots nevertheless still relies on the same assumptions of danger and urgent need that we have been seeing all along. Red stands for "unreached," orange for "minimally reached," yellow for "superficially reached," light green for "partially reached," and dark green for "significantly reached."[53] The colors unmistakably coordinate not only with traffic signals but also with the Homeland Security Advisory System, wherein red stands for "severe," orange for "high" alert, and green for "low" risk.

Joshua Project is the offspring of the Enlightenment impulse to gather data and classify, wedded to the older, sweeping concept of the benighted heathen world. Its motto, "Bringing definition to the unfinished task," enacts McGavran's call to research the human "mosaic" in order to best evangelize it. Joshua Project's understanding of "people groups" draws from a definition generated by the 1982 meeting of the Lausanne Committee in Chicago. A "people group" is a cohesive ethnic entity united by language and "local ethnic issues" such as "caste, religious tradition, location, common histories and traditions, and other subtle cultural distinctives." It is supposed to be the "largest group within which the Gospel can spread as a church planting movement without encountering barriers of understanding or acceptance."[54] Joshua Project confidently states that when Jesus issued the Great Commission to make disciples of all nations—*panta ta ethne*—the "ethne" was "referring to people groups."[55]

That "ethne" and "ethnic" originally carried the meaning of "pagan" or "heathen" is evident in the easy slide between "ethnic" and "unreached" in Joshua Project's productions, and in the data sources on which it relies. "Joshua Project is not a formal research organization," its website claims, "but rather seeks to compile and integrate ethnic peoples information from various global, regional, and national researchers and workers into a composite whole." The project aspires to a data-driven, formulaic accuracy in its determination of people groups, updating its "viewable data" "approximately every two weeks," while acknowledging that "the margin of error may vary from data point to data point."[56] One of its sources, Etnopedia, is a Wikipedia-esque database whose "purpose is to inform Evangelical Protestant Christians taking the Gospel of Jesus Christ to unreached people groups." Like Wikipedia, Etnopedia relies on the contributions of community members who "consul[t] all of the worlds major Christian sources of Ethnic peoples." Drilling down into the content of Etnopedia, one can find information on nearly three thousand "people profiles in English," as well as on the countries where these "ethnic" people groups can be found. Each "classified" group is color-coded on a scale from "totally unreached" (black) to "unreached" (red) to "some progress" (yellow) to "reached" (green), echoing Joshua Project's Homeland Security–style map of the world.[57]

Western nations like the United States, Canada, and the United Kingdom have profiles, but within those profiles the "unreached people group" categories are of primarily non-Western "ethnics" who are understood to be immigrants or refugees within a host nation. In the United States, for example, we find the Gujarati, Han Chinese (Xiang), Iu Mien, Kashmiri Muslim, Lao, Parsi, and Urdu, among others.[58] Jews are included as non-Christians who "have a wonderful understanding of their connection with the Abrahamic covenant" but also a "history of rejecting Jesus Christ as Messiah." Readers are asked to "pray that the Gospel will be shared with them, and that it will not be viewed as anti-Semitic."[59] According to Joshua Project, unchurched White Americans do not count in the category of "unreached": "Just because someone does not believe the gospel does not mean they are unreached. 'Unreached peoples' are actually those who have no opportunity to hear the gospel at all."[60] Within the category of "unreached" are the "frontier peoples," who are understood to be in even direr straits, defined as those peoples "that are less than or equal to 0.1% Christian."[61]

All of this data-driven differentiation, represented in tables, charts, and graphs, might suggest that evangelicals have moved beyond the blanket classification entailed in the concept of the heathen world. But nineteenth-century missionaries also provided on-the-ground specificity in their reports on different mission fields, often serving as the first conduits of local information to the White American public.[62] The heathen world has long been a site for both differentiation and homogenization, understood to house the sensorily and sensually exotic under the broad umbrella of the unsaved.

Just as visuals and lectures by returned missionaries reinforced both the apparent differences and underlying similarities of the heathen for earlier Americans, so Joshua Project's audiovisual media conveys both the specificity and similarity of the world's "unreached peoples" for contemporary audiences. The homepage of Joshua Project's website features a scrolling bar of Brown faces in unmistakably "ethnic" clothing (or no clothing at all). These are the unreached people: Burmese, Chamar, Java Banyumasan, Teli, Azerbaijani . . . and the list goes on. One can embed a widget from Joshua Project "to any website" that shows a business card–size snapshot of the "Unreached of the Day," featuring a representative "people group" face along with brief data about the population, language, religion, and status, and a button and counter to let others know "I am Praying."[63]

The "Unreached of the Day" is also available on Twitter, and in podcast, daily email, and app form. The podcast summarizes, with a smattering of "ethnic" background music, what the email and app convey (all in precisely a minute and one second per day).[64] The app similarly offers a headshot of a new Brown face per day, along with more detailed information about the people group it represents, the specific prayer requests needed by this group, and a map showing where the group is located. The group of the day for January 30, 2020, for instance, was the Kagoro of Mali, whose religion is "ethnic" and whose status is "unreached." The majority are "animists," the app explains, who "believe that sometimes their ancestors may take the form of animals or even vegetables!" "Pray the Kagoro will be set free from the bondage of worshiping created things," the app implores, with a scripture focus for meditation: "The people who walk in darkness, will see a great light; Those who live in a dark land, the light will shine on them" (Isaiah 9:2). The impact of seeing and hearing about a new "people group" in need of Christian prayer day after day is incalculable. Despite the specificities offered by Joshua Project's data, the guess-who's-next interchangeability of the "unreached of the day," the sameness of their presentation, and the ethnic exoticism of their pictures serve to classify them all in the same bucket of the "unreached" living far from the salutary gospel.[65]

Of all the euphemisms for the heathen world that have caught on in its decline, perhaps the most specifically descriptive one is an acronym— THUMB or THUMBS—that organizations like Joshua Project use to help

Listen

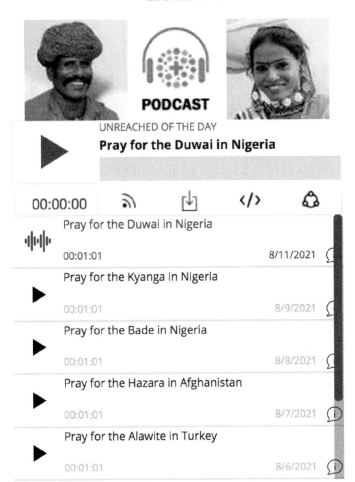

Unreached of the Day, Joshua Project podcast, August 10, 2021. Joshua Project, https://joshuaproject.net/pray/unreachedoftheday/podcast.

evangelicals remember whom they are trying to reach and for whom they are supposed to regularly pray. The THUMB(S) people include

- · T—Tribal groups (90 Million)
- · H—Hindu (771 Million)
- · U—Unreligious/Chinese (161 Million)
- · M—Muslim (1.18 Billion)
- · B—Buddhist (273 Million)
- · S—Sikh (30 Million)[66]

The THUMB(S) people are understood to live primarily in the 10/40 window, the area between 10 and 40 degrees latitude that "is home to some of the largest unreached people groups of the world."[67] They "believe in spirits that live all around us," in "hundreds or thousands of gods," or in no "god at all."[68] That all of these "world religions" can be swept under the diminutive acronym THUMBS testifies to the ongoing, infantilizing power of the heathen world.

The Heathen Reborn

Outside the missions realm, twenty-first-century Americans no longer look at maps of the world and see large swaths of heathens (or unreached, or frontier, or THUMBS people). And yet they do continue to look at the world and clump vastly different people and places together under the rubrics of the "Third World" and "developing countries." In "Secular Coloniality: The Afterlife of Religious and Racial Tropes," William D. Hart explores "the reproduction in secular discourse of colonial tropes that are common in both scholarly and popular accounts of religion." He looks at how "fetishism, voodoo, and frenzy are colonial, religious, and racial tropes that pass over and are reborn within secular discourse."[69] Contemporary maps that color-code the world in the "secular discourse" of development are strikingly similar to nineteenth-century missionary maps of the world color-coded by religion, the "developing" zones replicating the "heathen" regions of the past. The idea of the heathen world underlies such coding and helps to explain how Euro-Americans can see different regions of the world as capable of being grouped together under the same heading. Economic development has never, after all, been neutral, but has been tied to people's supposed inability to make good use of the land and take good care of their bodies. The heathen were to blame for their own backwardness; the heathen world has been reborn as the forty-fifth US president's "shithole countries."

The historical weight of "wrong" religion also continues to be used as an excuse for the exclusion of those thought to be culturally incapable of adaptation. Contemporary Islamophobia illustrates the point. Islam was long considered a form of heathenism by ordinary Europeans and Americans who saw the Muslim God as different from the Judeo-Christian one and believed Muhammad to be a false prophet. Nineteenth-century rhetoric about heathenism resonates in today's Islamophobia, explicitly and extremely so in a June 2017 Facebook post by US representative Clay Higgins of Louisiana. The post, coming on the heels of the London Bridge attack, made the national news. "The free world . . . all of Christendom . . . is at war with Islamic horror," Higgins wrote. "Not one penny of American treasure should be granted to any nation who harbors these heathen animals. . . . Hunt them, identify them, and kill them. Kill them all. For the sake of all that is good and righteous."[70] Here we can see the continuity of the idea that cultures of wrong religion—of heathenism—can be so strong as to turn the very bodies of their followers into "animals" over time. As Étienne Balibar writes in "Is There a 'Neo-Racism'?," "Current racism . . . is a racism whose dominant theme is not biological heredity but the insurmountability of cultural differences." Where George Fredrickson, in *Racism: A Short History,* does not see cultural differentiation as fully racist because it is not innate, Balibar notes that *"culture can also function like a nature, and it can in particular function as a way of locking individuals and groups a priori into a genealogy, into a determination that is immutable and intangible in origin."*[71] Along the lines of Balibar's diagnosis, Higgins's post suggests how quickly historically "heathen" people can be seen as dispensable once they reject the prospect of conversion to the ways of the Western Christian humanitarian. The humanitarian turns hunter; the heathenness of the "animal" justifies the kill; and the humanity of the hunter is preserved in the name of "all that is good and righteous."

Admittedly, such extreme and explicit rhetoric about "heathen animals" is less commonly seen now than in the past; today, the rebirth of the heathen concept in "secular discourse" is more readily apparent in the swarms of do-gooders who aim to save the world (and make money) through the power of technology. By way of example, the Tech for Global Good, an initiative of San Jose's Tech Museum, honors "innovators" who use technology to solve the world's problems.[72] An annual ceremony lauds each year's laureates. Videos about the laureates premiere at the ceremony for later year-round viewing at the museum. They are geared at students, who are the museum's primary visitors, and they follow a pattern. First, a problem is presented, typically one that affects the "developing world." Suffering people, animals, or landscapes are shown. They need help with basic health care, poaching, deforestation. The narrator asks, "How would *you* solve this problem?" A brief pause and blank screen are followed by upbeat music and the stories of the laureates and their solutions. Smiling people, living animals, and lush forests show the happy results of their innovations. Finally, a map of the world highlights how widely the laureates' technologies have been adopted.

The videos are followed by a fund-raising text-a-thon, suggesting that they are also aimed at Silicon Valley donors in attendance. Earnest high school students plead for donations to develop their "problem-solving power," presumably so that they, too, can become world-changing laureates one day. Audience names flash on a giant screen that shows contributions in real time. "$500—thanks, mom!" "$10,000—wow, thank you, Hunt family!" The roots of today's technological humanitarianism lie in the heathen world and in Euro-Americans' attempts to save it. The heathen were supposed to lack technology, leaving them exposed to the elements, starvation, and disease. Nineteenth-century missionaries were technologists as much as conversionists, who desired to change the ways people lived on the land and cared for their bodies. And today's humanitarians have been conversionists as much as technologists, believing that the suffering world needs to be converted to a right understanding of what they should desire; requires the technology to achieve these new desires; and will profit their beneficent Western providers once they adopt these desires and technologies.

Just as the Tech videos display a pattern, so too did nineteenth-century stories about converted heathens and their transformations. Missionaries identified a problem and made that problem manifest to the heathen. They brought the requisite technologies to solve it, such as printing, sewing, and irrigating. That such technologies could profit not only heathen bodies but also the pockets of European traders (as when Mary Moffat's South African sewing school created a new demand for "European produce") was the icing on the cake that every good Silicon Valley social entrepreneur is also trying to achieve: money for themselves in the service of the global good. Like the maps at the end of the Tech videos, so missionary publications also featured maps showing the spread of evangelization efforts across the globe. And just as the Tech Awards include a fund-raising drive, so nineteenth-century missionary tacticians used tales about the needy heathen to raise money for their efforts. These stories inspired readers to feel grateful that they did not live in the heathen world, but also to feel guilty that they were not doing more to help. Just as the Tech videos ask, "What would *you* do to solve this problem?" so missionary publications asked readers what *they* would do to save the suffering overseas. These patterns also continue to be replicated in the global outreach programs of contemporary mission organizations. Pray for the unreached THUMBS people. Save your money; send it to the starving overseas. Subscribe to our magazines; watch our films. Read about heroic missionaries and one day you might become one. You can do it too.

10

CONTINUING
COUNTERSCRIPTS

Two years after Lausanne, in Dar es Salaam, a group disaffected by the Western bias of Lausanne's leaders formed their own Ecumenical Association of Third World Theologians (EATWOT). The group's first president, Russell Chandran, admitted that the acronym "sounds like Eat What." He leaned into it. "This is quite significant because the association is concerned with theologies from the regions of the world where for considerable sections of the people the primary question is what shall we eat?"[1] The members of EATWOT aimed to "address the specific concerns of Third World contexts," "realizing that traditional theology with its European origination and Westernized context failed to sufficiently meet the needs of the Third World."[2] These self-professed Third World theologians walked a line between Christian conviction and the radicalism of anticolonial theorists like Aimé Césaire and Frantz Fanon, who saw Christianity as the colonizers' religion, and who themselves engaged with the deep history of anti-heathen sentiment that we have been tracking.[3]

A poem written by Sun Ai Park, "The Poor Shall Rise," illustrates the orientation of EATWOT's members.[4] An ordained minister of the Disciples of Christ, Park opened by referencing the "millions of immobile creatures" who were "doomed in poverty" in the Third World. Her description resonates with the tropes of heathen stagnation and despair, even as it also echoes descriptions of the colonized by Césaire and Fanon:

As if devoid of all human marks
as if life were only a nightmare
they wander as in a sleepwalk
they lie still, crushed,
shrunk in size as if dead
under a broad daylight.

Park wrote the poem "after a poignant experience of India's villages and Delhi's streets." Where White Christian observers of such poverty had historically attributed it to heathen ignorance, Park suggested that it was externally imposed on a

> nation
> so rich in culture
> where great sages and warriors reigned . . .
> What a scandal.
> What a violence.

Park closed the poem with a reference to Fanon's most famous book. But where Fanon called for violent resistance, Park concluded with hope in Christ:

> But the wretched of the earth shall rise.
> Oh, the multitudes of the poor of India shall rise.
> Oh, the poor of the Third World shall rise.
> And you will rejoice
> with the risen Christ.

Park's Christ was not the same as the God foisted on the "irrupting millions" by Christian evangelists over the centuries. EATWOT's God did not specially favor the wealthy West but was "in solidarity with the poor and oppressed," "in solidarity with the poor of other peoples, of despised races and ethnic minorities," and "in solidarity with women."[5]

This chapter loops back to consider EATWOT's pushback against the scripts generated at Lausanne, alongside mid-twentieth-century and more contemporary counterscripts offered by people once considered to be part of the heathen world. Even as the concept of the heathen world has continued to inform humanitarian ventures to the "Third World" and "THUMBS people," the people classified in those groups have also continued to engage with, lambaste, and adapt the underlying notion of something shared among them to resist a colonizing, hegemonic "West." In *How Race Is Made in America: Immigration, Citizenship, and the Historical Power of Racial Scripts*, scholar Natalia Molina offers the concepts of scripts and counterscripts to analyze race-making in the United States. She "coin[s] the term *racial scripts* to highlight the ways in which the lives of racialized groups are linked across time and space and thereby affect one another, even when they do not directly cross paths." These scripts "endure" over time, and "no matter how discredited racial scripts become in any era, they are always available for use in new rounds of dehumanization and demonization in the next generation or even the next debate."[6]

The heathen world has operated as an enduring religio-racial script that has linked different groups together as essentially similar, even as other racial scripts have separated groups into hierarchies based on socially constructed differences that are supposedly innate. Racial hierarchies emphasize differences in a divide-and-conquer strategy of rule. Any such differences always hit the heathen ceiling, though, which works to keep all members of the former heathen world in a position of inferiority vis-à-vis the White Christian West. The script of the changeable Other who needs help coexists with racial scripts of inherent difference, the latter used to provide cover when the European fails to remake the Other in their image.

Molina also offers the possibility of "counterscripts" put forward by "racialized groups," for "just as racial scripts have a seeming persuasiveness, resistance too has a long fetch." Like racial scripts, counterscripts can also arc over time and space, as "the process of racialization can be more important than the identity of who is being racialized, therefore enabling seemingly unlikely antiracist alliances to form based on similar, but not identical, experiences of racialization when groups recognize the similarity of their stories in the collective experiences of others."[7] Along these lines, counterscripts to the heathen world have sometimes recognized the similarities—and potential for solidarities—in the ways so-called heathen peoples have been lumped together by White Christians.

The "Dishonest Equations"

Counterscripts from the mid-twentieth century and beyond not only resonated with the claims of earlier resistors—people like Wong Chin Foo, Zitkála-Šá, and others—but also contributed to and derived inspiration from anticolonial movements. Martinique poet and politician Aimé Césaire penned one of the most famous of these, his 1950 *Discourse on Colonialism*. Césaire was a member of the Communist Party at the time he wrote the *Discourse* and served as a deputy for the party from 1946 to 1956. He spurned Christianity as "the religion of colonialism" and "identif[ied] himself with colonized Africans." In his *Notebook*, he "assumed the posture of an animist,"[8] writing,

> I declare my crimes and that there is nothing to say in my defense.
> Dances. Idols. An apostate. I too

I have assassinated God with my laziness with my words with my gestures with my obscene songs

I have worn parrot plumes musk cat skins
I have exhausted the missionaries' patience
insulted the benefactors of mankind.[9]

Césaire exulted, "The extent of my perversity overwhelms me!"[10] Given his stance, it is not surprising that the *Discourse* took up and summarily dismissed the supposed "paganism" of the Third World as justification for colonization.

The *Discourse* joined a "'tidal wave' of anticolonial literature" published after World War II, in the wake of European infighting and in the midst of Cold War competition over the Third World.[11] For Western democracies, led by an emboldened United States, Communism loomed as a heretical faith that threatened to spread to the weak and vulnerable states if not stopped in its tracks. It featured unscrupulous leaders who duped the masses into laboring for them; neglected the bodily needs of the people, leading to famine and starvation; and asked for cringing allegiance to worldly idols and departed ancestors (Joseph Stalin, Mao Zedong, Vladimir Lenin, and their embalmed bodies). But even as Western democracies claimed to be fighting Communism to save the Third World from its heresies, Césaire vehemently denounced such justification as mere cover for the rapacious profit motive underlying the Western European and American colonizing impulse from its very beginnings. "What, fundamentally," he asked, "is colonization?" It is "neither evangelization, nor philanthropic enterprise, nor a desire to push back the frontiers of ignorance, disease, and tyranny, nor a project undertaken for the greater glory of God, nor an attempt to extend the rule of law." The main actors in colonization were not the missionary of Christ or of democracy, but rather the "pirate" and the "gold digger." Colonization was about stretching the reach of capitalism across the globe.[12]

For Césaire, the category of the "pagan" or "heathen" was a smokescreen that covered the true economic motives behind colonization. This was a "hypocrisy" of "recent" origin: Hernán Cortez, Francisco Pizarro, and Marco Polo never claimed to be "the harbinger of a superior order" but killed in the open and without apology. The "slavering apologists came later" and "the chief culprit in this domain is Christian pedantry, which laid down the dishonest equations *Christianity = civilization, paganism = savagery,* from which there could not but ensue abominable colonialist and racist consequences, whose victims were to be the Indians, the Yellow peoples,

and the Negroes"—the heathen world.[13] The idea that "abominable colonialist and racist consequences" ensued from the "dishonest equations"
suggested that, even if disingenuous, they were not merely a cover for the
real issues at stake, of money and profit: the "dishonest equations" were
in fact central to racial othering and governance. Césaire carefully threaded
the needle here, giving explanatory power to greedy capitalism for colonization, while not discounting the significance of religious rationalization,
however hypocritical he believed it to be.

Much of the *Discourse* convicts Europeans themselves of a savagery that
results from colonization. Colonization "works to *decivilize* the colonizer,
to *brutalize* him in the truest sense of the word," Césaire argued, sounding
like Mary Church Terrell on the effects of slavery on slaveholders and their
descendants. Flipping the familiar trope of the animalized heathen on its
head, Césaire said that colonization animalized the European instead,
"dehumaniz[ing] even the most civilized man." Césaire explained, "The
colonizer, who in order to ease his conscience gets into the habit of seeing
the other man as *an animal,* accustoms himself to treating him like an animal, and tends objectively to transform *himself* into an animal." This
"boomerang effect" meant that everything the colonizer projected onto the
"pagan = savage" redounded back onto Europeans themselves. Even as the
horrors of World War II revealed the European animal to be "anemic" now,
"losing its hair, its hide . . . no longer glossy," its "ferocity has remained,
barely mixed with sadism."[14] And so the Third World must, even as it gathered strength and fostered solidarity, be ever cautious.

Césaire offered a special warning to those who hoped the United States
might prove helpful in the liberation struggle. Despite all its rhetoric about
spreading *"aid to the disinherited countries"*—after all, Americans loved
the "dishonest equations"—the United States was perhaps more dangerous
still than Europe. Swayed by the "bulldozers! the massive investments of
capital! the roads! the ports!" Césaire knew that some of his readers might
be willing to overlook "American racism," "inured" as they were to "European racism in the colonies." But "be careful!" he cautioned. "American
domination" is "the only domination from which one never recovers. I
mean from which one never recovers unscarred." What made American
domination different from—and worse than—European? Césaire's reasoning extended the kind of argument Wong Chin Foo had made about
America in the 1880s. Wong had argued against Americans' relentless drive
to mechanize, which enriched factory owners while impoverishing ordinary
people, whose labor was cheapened and whose jobs were lost to machines.
By 1950 American mechanization had grown exponentially. To those who
saw liberation in American industry, Césaire asked, "Since you are talking

about factories and industries, do you not see the tremendous factory hysterically spitting out its cinders in the heart of our forests or deep in the bush, the factory for the production of lackeys; do you not see the prodigious mechanization, the mechanization of man; the gigantic rape of everything intimate, undamaged, undefiled that, despoiled as we are, our human spirit has still managed to preserve; the machine, yes, have you never seen it, the machine for crushing, for grinding, for degrading peoples?" American machines could not help the liberation struggle, as they were responsible for much of the oppression against which the Third World fought, turning men into machines rather than empowering them, and devastating their lands rather than cultivating them. Bodies and lands subjected to American machines did not thrive or blossom as the rose—they became violated and ruined instead. Concluded Césaire, "So that the danger is immense."[15]

Césaire's "third world manifesto" was more a poetic rallying cry than a "blueprint for revolution,"[16] but one of his students, mentees, and friends, Frantz Fanon, would be inspired by the themes he raised and apply them to his own manifesto, the hugely influential 1961 *The Wretched of the Earth*, which laid out a bold vision of "anti-colonial struggle, revolutionary action, and post-colonial statecraft and imagination."[17] Fanon was Césaire's junior by twelve years and, like him, was born in the French colony of Martinique. *The Wretched of the Earth* is Fanon's most famous work, written while he was dying of leukemia in his mid-thirties. As one of his close friends later described it, "The Wretched of the Earth should be read like an urgent message, delivered in a raw state, uncorrected—we did not dare question certain passages in front of a man who was reading his text to the close friends that we were, while pacing up and down in his room in Tunis, sick and aware that he was condemned, desiring with all his force, in a superb language, to say what he had to say."[18]

"The Wretched" is an English translation of *Les Damnés* in Fanon's original French. "The Damned" carries more pointed religious overtones than "The Wretched" and bears recovery in English, as traces of the heathen world reverberate in *The Wretched of the Earth*. Fanon's "colonized sector" was both an invention and a reality. "It is the colonist who *fabricated* and *continues to fabricate* the colonized subject," he maintained. The colonist asserts a Manichaean dichotomy between his (always gender-specific) world and the world of the colonized, which "sometimes . . . reaches its logical conclusion and dehumanizes the colonized subject. . . . Allusion is made to the slithery movements of the yellow race, the odors from the 'native' quarters, to the hordes, the stink, the swarming, the seething, and the gesticulations." The roots of such animalization trace back to the notion that the heathen turned themselves into no better than the creeping and crawling things that they worshiped. Knowing better of themselves and understanding the fabricated nature of the Manichaean divide between themselves and the colonizers, the colonized "roar with laughter every time they hear themselves called an animal by the other."[19]

And yet Fanon's "colonized sector" was subject to a very real "spiral of domination, exploitation and looting" by the West. It was the "colonist" who "makes history," while the "Third World is abandoned and condemned to regression, in any case stagnation, through the selfishness and immorality of the West." Nor was stagnation just a side effect of selfishness and immorality: it was a deliberate and "perverted" policy of colonialism that, "not content merely to impose its law on the colonized country's present and future," also "turns its attention to the past of the colonized people and distorts it, disfigures it, destroys it." Echoing Césaire's "dishonest equations," Fanon explained, "For centuries Europe has brought the progress of other men to a halt and enslaved them for its own purposes and glory; for centuries it has stifled virtually the whole of humanity in the name of a so-called 'spiritual adventure.' Look at it now teetering between atomic destruction and spiritual disintegration." Christianity did not equal civilization; Christianity *threatened* civilization.[20]

But Fanon did not only blame the West for the Third World's supposed stagnation. He also blamed the colonized subject's religion for his "petrifaction," recalling the notion of heathen historylessness. Fanon depicted the colonized subject as a "coiled" mass of potential but thwarted energy, "more dead than alive" as he "crouches for ever in the same old dream." While the colonizers stormed through history, pillaging and plundering, the colonized diverted his energy toward "terrifying myths that are so prolific in underdeveloped societies as inhibitions for his aggressiveness." These myths reduced European colonizers to a position of utter insignificance vis-à-vis the "far more terrifying" fantastic and phantasmagoric mythical monsters. For Fanon, the myths' ability to render the colonizers impotent was not empowering: rather, in Marxist fashion, he argued that the myths "drained" the colonized subjects' "energy" in useless "hallucinatory dreams" and "the ecstasy of dance."[21]

Unlike the colonizers, Fanon did not hold that the dances of the colonized were demonic and sexually immoral. Still, Fanon's perception of the colonized subjects' religious habits was not far afield from the colonizers' own view of backwards heathen ways that stultified societies and kept them from joining the providential movement of history. Like the colonizers, Fanon wanted the colonized to leave their traditional religions behind, arguing that their myths and rituals detracted from what was really real.

Where Western colonizers wanted the colonized to turn to Christianity, though, Fanon wanted them to abandon religious "unreality" entirely and confront the true demon: colonialism. Christianity, to him, was no better than the myths it sought to replace: it was a handmaiden of colonialism, serving as its "DDT, which destroys parasites, carriers of disease," and clears a path "to the ways of the white man, to the ways of the master, the ways of the oppressor."[22]

Casting aside the myths, Fanon believed, would happen in the "struggle for liberation," when there would be a "singular loss of interest in these rituals":

> With his back to the wall, the knife at his throat, or to be more exact the electrode on his genitals, the colonized subject is bound to stop telling stories.
>
> After years of unreality, after wallowing in the most extraordinary phantasms, the colonized subject, machine gun at the ready, finally confronts the only force which challenges his very being: colonialism.[23]

In Fanon's view, it was not just credulous followers of "chiefs, *kaids*, and witch doctors" who needed to wake up to reality: it was also "colonized intellectuals." They were becoming aware of how much their brains had been formed by Western education and values, which they had once "accepted" as "eternal." But they had overcorrected. Zealous to find a "national culture prior to the colonial era," they tried to rescue and rehabilitate the colonized's past. Fanon had no patience for this preservationist impulse, which was also shared by White "metropolitan specialists," as we have seen in figures like Nathaniel Bright Emerson. According to Fanon, the intellectual's "painful, forced search seems but a banal quest for the exotic."[24]

Fanon instead called for a radical break with the past, achieved through violence by the damnés, which would both shock colonizers into the realization that the damnés were human and rouse the damnés to a sense of their own potential energy. Like Henry Highland Garnet in the nineteenth century, Fanon argued that the damned needed to save themselves. And just as Césaire had warned, so too did Fanon accuse the United States of being no better than Europe—indeed, of having "become a monster where the flaws, sickness, and inhumanity of Europe have reached frightening proportions." The European model that the United States had followed with such gusto was pathetic, having "lost control and reason," "heading at dizzying speed towards the brink" of destruction and, as such, hardly worthy of emulation. "We no longer have reason to fear it, let us stop then envying

it," Fanon entreated. "The Third World is today facing Europe as one colossal mass whose project must be to try and solve the problems this Europe was incapable of finding the answers to." As "one colossal mass," the
Third World could draw a strategic and powerful solidarity from the blanket
othering that Europeans had long drawn across the heathen world.[25]

The problems the Third World needed to solve were not about "profit-
ability," "productivity," or "production rates." Rather, "it is the very basic
question of not dragging man in directions which mutilate him, of not imposing on his brain tempos that rapidly obliterate and unhinge it. The
notion of catching up must not be used as a pretext to brutalize man, to
tear him from himself and his inner consciousness, to break him, to kill
him." Fanon's counterscript was clear: "No, we do not want to catch up
with anyone." The "notion of catching up" that Europeans used to colo-
nize and dehumanize the Third World can be traced back to a religious dynamic of othering, and the pretext, believed or not, that the heathen can
and should change. It functions as a binarizing racial script that is less focused on inherent difference than on that which needs to be shaped (or, in
Fanon's words, mutilated and brutalized) through European tutelage and
governance. Fanon rejected this script, arguing instead that, "for Europe,
for ourselves and for humanity, comrades, we must make a new start, develop a new way of thinking, and endeavor to create a new man."[26]

Irruption: Theological Counterscripts

Fanon's view of the Third World as a realm impoverished by Western exploitation that should be jolted out of its "petrifaction" to "create a new
man" found receptive ears across the globe. At the Bandung Conference in
1955, formerly colonized nations from Africa and Asia heard from President Ahmed Sukarno of Indonesia that "the Third World's historic turn was
directed at 'the liberation of man from his bonds of fear, his bonds of poverty, the liberation of man from the physical, spiritual and intellectual bonds
which have for long stunted the development of humanity's majority.'"[27]
In the US context, American students of color found solidarity with the
Third World. At San Francisco State College in 1968, they created the Third
World Liberation Front; across the Bay, students at Berkeley formed an-
other such coalition in 1969. Demanding the creation of a Third World
Studies curriculum, the students proclaimed, "We adhere to the struggles in
Asia, Africa, and Latin America, ideologically, spiritually, and culturally. . . .
We have decided to fuse ourselves with the masses of Third World people,
which are a majority of the world's peoples, to create, through struggles,

a new humanity, a new humanism, a New World Consciousness, and within the text collectively control our own destinies."[28]

Self-professed Third World theologians heeded the call for a new world consciousness. They rejected Fanon's rejection of Christianity and Indigenous religions, though, instead holding that collaboration between the two was of the utmost urgency and most likely to produce real liberation. They sought to rescue Christianity from its co-option by colonizers, and Indigenous religions from their dismissal by the same. In August 1981 members of EATWOT convened in New Delhi. In their conference papers, published as *Irruption of the Third World: Challenge to Theology,* they considered the "layers of meaning" that had built up around the term "Third World," which "vary from the purely geographic ('the South') to the socioeconomic ('poor, underdeveloped') to the political ('non-aligned') and even the theological ('from the underside of history'). To those who met in Delhi, Third Worldness is characterized by massive poverty and oppression." There are striking similarities in this list to those qualities that had characterized the heathen world. The areas marked "heathen" on nineteenth-century maps had likewise been understood to be in a perilous state of nonalignment, waiting to fall to Catholicism or Islam, or to be rescued by Protestantism. Like Fanon, EATWOT also understood the "Third World" to be a "growing historical force" just beginning to realize its potential. The Third World operates here as the afterlife of the heathen world, reborn from a long, deathlike state of oppression and stagnation and sparked into action. Members of EATWOT turned the unnuanced ways in which they had been swept together into an opportunity for real solidarity and collaboration with each other. For Virginia Fabella, editor of the conference proceedings and a Maryknoll sister born in the Philippines, the "irruption of the Third World mark[ed] the dawning of a new era and the setting of an old one," a "new stage in human history that is evincing the resistance to, and decline of, the dominance of North Atlantic countries and of Western civilizations."[29]

In his contribution to the conference, Sri Lankan Jesuit priest Aloysius Pieris elaborated on the up-and-coming significance of the Third World, making a move similar to that of the people once designated "heathens" who had worn the term with pride. "The phrase 'Third World,'" he said, "is a theological neologism for God's own people." While the heathen had been understood by White Christians to be excluded from God's peoplehood, Pieris insisted that the Third World was special to God. "It stands for the starving sons of Jacob—of all places and all times—who go in search of bread to a rich country, only to become its slaves." Just as African Americans read themselves into the Exodus narrative, so Pieris read the Third

World into the story of an oppressed "peoplehood announcing the liberating presence of a God who claims to humanize this cruel world." Both Fabella and Pieris also stressed another critical characteristic of the Third World that lays bare its status as heir to the category of "heathen": the "irruption of the Third World is also the irruption of the non-Christian world." For "the vast majority of God's poor perceive their ultimate concern and symbolize their struggle for liberation in the idiom of non-Christian religions and culture. . . . We need a theology of religions that will expand the existing boundaries of orthodoxy as we enter into the liberative streams of other religions and cultures."[30] Where White evangelical missiologists anxiously sought to ensure that Indigenous Christianity remain unsullied by heathen influences lest it slide into "Christopaganism," Third World theologians embraced dialogue, cooperation, reinterpretation, and expansion.

Many of EATWOT's members were Catholics. In their openness to dialogue, they referenced Vatican II's revision of the historical Catholic stance toward other religions. Just as Protestants reconsidered their approach to missions in the twentieth century—finding synonyms for "heathen" even as they continued to tap into its resonant meanings—so Catholics also reconsidered their relationship with other religions. *Nostra Aetate,* the "Declaration on the Relation of the Church to Non-Christian Religions," passed in 1965 by a vote of 2,221 to 88 bishops. It proclaimed, "From ancient times down to the present, there is found among various peoples a certain perception of that hidden power which hovers over the course of things and over the events of human history." Naming the "ascetical practices" of Hinduism, the Buddhist "way by which men" seek "liberation," and the "teachings, rules of life, and sacred rites" in "other religions found everywhere," the Declaration assured that "the Catholic Church rejects nothing that is true and holy in these religions. She regards with sincere reverence those ways of conduct and of life, those precepts and teachings which, though differing in many aspects from the ones she holds and sets forth, nonetheless often reflect a ray of that Truth which enlightens all men." Of course, to merely acknowledge a "ray of Truth" in those religions once dubbed "heathen" was not too far a step from Enlightenment-era affirmations of the natural light available to all humanity.[31]

The Catholic members of EATWOT turned the step into a leap—or at least, they stressed the need to do so. In New Delhi, delegates from Latin America, whose Catholicism marked them as part of the West but who also identified as members of the Third World, were particularly taken by "what was for us a strange world." Touring New Delhi in the August monsoon season, they—like many generations of Christian tourists before them—

found themselves disoriented by its sights, sounds, and smells. "In India," they explained, "we saw another religious expression and it challenged us by its difference." The smell of incense, the sound of street singing, the sight of "tiny images of Krishna, Shiva, Buddha, and others," the "color and flowers of religious ceremonies," all "awakened us. At one blow, we became aware that in the end 'our truth' is only a part of the Truth." This awareness galvanized the group to conclude that "the logic of either . . . or"—so often expressed as Christian *or* heathen, saved *or* damned—"does not find much expression in India. For this world, wisdom seeks complementarity rather than exclusivity."[32]

The "Final Statement" of EATWOT's August 1981 conference elaborated on how Christian theologians might learn from and speak through other religions that they had historically denigrated, providing a counterscript in constant conversation with the heathen concept's historical valences.

On the question of salvation: EATWOT urged Christians to recognize that the "sacred scriptures and traditions" of other faiths "are also a source of revelation for us." Instead of holding that other religions led to hell, EATWOT affirmed that "the concept of the 'people of God'" should "be widened to include not only believers of other faiths but the whole of humanity." In light of the long history of heathenness as exclusion from God's peoplehood, this was a significant claim that rendered the question of salvation, which so vexed White evangelicals, moot. If non-Christians were God's people, there was no point wasting time dialoguing "on an intellectual level about God, salvation, human fulfillment, or other such concepts." Everyone would be fine in the afterlife, and Christians and adherents of other religions needed to engage in direct "collaborative action" *now*, "for the integral liberation of the oppressed, not only action to change unjust and oppressive social structures but also attempts to regain our identity and life-giving values."[33]

On the land: EATWOT flipped the script on Westerners who believed that heathenness implied wildness and wilderness. Perhaps the Third World had not exploited the land to the fullest. But this was for the best, since the "wasteful lifestyle of the affluent in the capitalist countries" was "leading to an escalating despoliation of nature and depletion of natural resources, dangerously threatening the future of nature and human life itself." By contrast, the Third World offered the wisdom of ancestral religions that could serve as "powerful antidotes to capitalist consumerism and to the worship of mammon." The "irruption of a world that is not Christian" would teach the capitalist West "freedom from greed as well as from overattachment to material or mental possessions and to one's private self." Nature and humanity would flourish as a result.[34]

On the body: EATWOT argued that it was in the West that bodies suffered premature harm. The exhausting rat race of capitalism led to "youth unrest, exaggerated individualism, alcoholism, drug addiction, violence, loneliness, [and an] increasing suicide rate." That said, EATWOT also echoed earlier descriptions of the dying heathen world, explaining that "poverty and oppression" created "not just a situation of deprivation" but also "unjust and untimely death to millions of women, men, and children through hunger, disease, and repression." Moreover, the theologians said, "death in the Third World is not only physical. Countless persons are degraded and have suffered the loss of their identity, dignity, and personhood. Not only individual persons are killed, but also entire cultures and religious traditions have been annihilated by colonialism and by more modern forms of repression." EATWOT's mission was to recapture what colonialism had tried to quash: "our own appreciation of our indigenous cultures."[35]

On idolatry: EATWOT argued that "to proclaim a God who does not see the plight of the poor and does not act in their favor is to preach a God of death, a dead God. When the forces of death are free to kill, God's reality is not recognized. When life is ignored or cruelly crushed, false Gods are set up. This is idolatry."[36] For EATWOT, the true God was on the side of the oppressed, and to proclaim anything else was to worship false idols.

The spread of Christianity in the Global South at least partly reflects the success of Third World theologians in indigenizing it and holding it back up to Americans and Europeans as a measure of how far they have fallen from the truth. Evangelists from the Global South now often see America and Europe as reverse mission fields, needing to be drawn back to Christianity.[37]

"The Buck Stops with Us": Academic Counterscripts

Even as EATWOT recognized that some residents of the "so-called free world" or "first world" were "subjected to conditions of third worldness, such as Black Americans, Hispanics, and Native Americans," they initially excluded them from membership in the association, limiting such membership to "theologians from the three continents of Africa, Asia, and Latin America." EATWOT's members "saw US theologians as people who enjoyed greater privileges that were, in objective terms, the fruits of the organized exploitation and plunder of third world peoples and their resources," despite the racial discrimination they faced.[38] But Black and Native American theologians and scholars (among others) have seen the situation of racial minorities in the United States as part of the greater colonizing frame.

By way of example, four influential academics in the United States—Vine Deloria Jr., Charles H. Long, Sylvia Wynter, and Sylvester Johnson—all understand themselves to be writing from the "underside of history," and all engage with the problem of the Other in both racial and religious terms.

Vine Deloria Jr. was a member of the Standing Rock Sioux Tribe (Hunkpapa Lakota) and the great-grandson of Francis Deloria; he trained and taught as a lawyer and theologian, and helped to establish the field of American Indian Studies. Deloria authored more than twenty books, including *God Is Red: A Native View of Religion* (1973), which earned him a notice from *Time* magazine as "one of the 'primary movers and shapers' of Christian faith and theology."[39] Writing *God Is Red* at a fraught time—the "collapse of the Civil Rights movement, the concern with Vietnam and the war, the escape to drugs, the rise of power movements, and the return to Mother Earth"—Deloria diagnosed White America as "fragmented," alienated, and bereft of meaning; in desperate search of "authenticity" wherever it might be found. "The present theological vacuum is being filled to a great degree by efforts to establish exotic religions in America," he wrote. At the top of the list of "authentic" alternatives for White American appropriators was Native religion. Just as preservationists in the earlier part of the century had idealized "far off, sweet pagan days," so in the 1970s Deloria saw that "for many people the stoic, heroic, and noble Indian who had lived an idyllic existence prior to contact with whites seemed to hold the key to survival and promised to provide new meanings for American life." But the Americans who flocked to tourist sweat lodges and found shamans for hire rarely cared to understand what Native religion was actually about. If they did, they would have to drastically change their relationship to the land on which they lived and how they made the money to hire those shamans in the first place. Deloria lambasted the West's "propensity to judge a society or civilization by its technology and to see in society's effort to subdue and control nature as the fulfillment of divine intent." He sounded the same theme as Césaire, Fanon, and the members of EATWOT when he accused the West's adulation of technology of despoiling the land: "If we factor in the environmental damage created by technology the argument falls flat. In less than two centuries American whites have virtually destroyed a whole continent and large areas of the United States are now almost uninhabitable."[40]

Charles H. Long similarly described America as alienated and destructive, though he focused less on the environmental damage Americans wreaked than on the psychic damage they inflicted and sustained. Long was born in the Jim Crow South, in Little Rock, Arkansas, and became a leading scholar of the history of religions at the University of Chicago, with a particular focus on "American and Black Religions."[41] "The center does not hold," he wrote in his classic *Significations: Signs, Symbols, and Images in the Interpretation of Religion* (1986). "There is no longer that privileged position which is the West or America. There is only the bricolage of America and the West, the flotsam and jetsam of bits and pieces of a reality that once was thought to be an order and a unity, possibly dreamed of in an illusory age when these things were thought to be real." But Americans are in denial about this, said Long. Unwilling to confront the gaping void at the center of their identity, they have kept moving, finding more lands and lives to renovate so as not to have to think about anything for too long. As Long put it, "The American has for one reason or another never taken time to contemplate the ambiguity of act and value, the horror and the evil which is synonymous with the conquest of this new land." But just because Americans have never slowed down to think about their actions does not exonerate them from responsibility. If Americans have believed themselves innocent, "this innocence is gained only through an intense suppression of the deeper and more subtle dimension of American *experience.*" Such suppression has been enabled by the "religion of the American people," which "centers around the telling and retelling of the mighty deeds of the white conquerors." By ignoring the experiences of "Indians and blacks," White Americans reveal a "void or deeper invisibility within [their own] consciousness. . . . The ordinate fear they have of minorities is an expression of the fear they have when they contemplate the possibility of seeing themselves as they really are."[42]

Long is less invested in generating a new "theology opaque"—the term he coins to describe Deloria's Native-centered work and other liberation theologies connected to specific groups—than he is in deepening how Americans conceive of themselves, their history, and humanity more broadly. Without grappling with the "horror and the evil" that underlay the conquest, he says, "any future will be an escapism sustained only by the physical and psychological repression" of self and other. Long says that such grappling is also necessary in the academy. The "science of the human" that developed under the rubric of "civilization" has purported to maintain a stance of "rationality and objectivity" toward the religions of "foreign and exotic cultures"—the religions once known as heathen—but, says Long, scholars "failed to grasp" that "our rational Western intellectual tradition . . . has blinded us to an adequate appreciation of the diversity of the human." The recognition that the "very intellectual religious task is framed within a racist context," Long notes, has understandably given rise to the "theologies opaque" by Black and Native theologians like James Cone and Deloria.[43]

Jamaican cultural theorist and Stanford professor emerita Sylvia Wynter similarly speaks to an impoverishment in thinking that she connects to the emergence of race in her widely cited 2003 essay, "Unsettling the Coloniality of Being/Power/Truth/Freedom: Towards the Human, After Man, Its Over-representation—An Argument." Wynter, like Long and others, asks about the implications of colonization, or the "'Big Bang' processes that were to lead to a contemporary modernity defined by the 'rise of the West' and the 'subjugation of the rest of us.'"[44] Wynter offers a narrative that is attentive to both continuity and discontinuity, and in which the "pagan-idolator" plays an important though receding role. She both joins a lineage of people formerly known as heathens talking back and challenges them/us to do *more* than talk back. Wynter explains the rise of race as a "transumed formulation" of the older "Judeo-Christian Grand Narrative," where the raced subject "reoccupies," rather than replaces, the position of the "pagan-idolator."[45] The Big Bang emergence of race, per Wynter, fragmented the human from a single bifurcated category (saved/damned, Christian/non-Christian) into an explosion of categories, some more and some less "human," and all defined by their level of rationality and closeness to or distance from "the lower natures of brutes." Despite this sudden proliferation of imagined categories, though, there was also a certain narrowing of thought that accompanied the emergence of race. Once the genre of "human" was transformed from an inclusive category where all bore the burden of Original Sin (though only some were redeemed) into the apex of a Chain of Being where Westerners figured themselves as the "only, universally applicable mode of being human," then the idea that other people could have their own ways of being human, including ways of being religious, no longer had purchase. Wynter's point here mirrors Long's on Westerners' inability to appreciate the full "diversity of the human" and the human's religious expression because the West so worships objectivity and rationality.[46]

In her characteristically dense, rich prose, Wynter also suggests that "'native' intellectuals (and postcolonially speaking, the intellectuals of the subordinated and economically impoverished world)" face another kind of impoverishment, too, an impoverishment of language. Because the "genre of human" has been so "overdetermined" by the parochially Western Man that represents itself as universal, Native intellectuals can now "only 'echo.'" That is, [they] must think, write, and prescribe policies, however oppositionally so, in the terms of the very biocentric paradigms that prescribe the subordination and impoverishment of the vast majority of the worlds to which they/we belong." Wynter here offers a version of Gayatri Spivak's famous question, "Can the subaltern speak?" Are counterscripts possible? Can the otherized do more than echo?[47]

A final, contemporary case study that offers a counterscript in the lineage not only of Long and Wynter but also of Zitkála-Šá and Wong Chin Foo is Sylvester Johnson, a scholar of religion at Virginia Tech who takes the concept of heathenness very seriously as a historical and continued mode of othering in the United States. Johnson's *Myth of Ham in Nineteenth-Century American Christianity: Race, Heathens, and the People of God* (2004) is an award-winning intervention into the lasting pain caused by the concept of the heathen. For Johnson, African Americans have been signified as the ultimate heathens in the United States, and heathenness is at the root of anti-Blackness. Not only were Black people subject to forced Christianization that was too often used to justify enslavement, but they also faced an existential dilemma: "What . . . did it mean for black American Christians to share in a self-understanding as people of God while also 'remembering' an evil past and experiencing an evil identity as Ham's descendants?"[48]

Johnson shows how African American Christian leaders in the late nineteenth century turned to Ethiopianism to make sense of this problem, as we saw earlier. But Johnson does not merely end with the promise that "Ethiopia shall soon stretch out her hands unto God" as the empowering pushback of erstwhile heathens against their denigration and maltreatment. Instead, he critiques other scholars who have ended their own investigations on this seemingly uplifting premise. While some are "quick to point out that the language of being people of God has been a steadfast source of strength" for oppressed people, Johnson insists that oppressed people who turn to this source of strength must acknowledge that "their very identity as people of God is made possible because they tread upon the bodies and blood—the identities and selves—of those on the underside of Christian narrative knowledge."[49] That is to say, they gain their strength through the oppression of others. Rather than celebrate this, Johnson calls for a wholesale reformation of American Christianity in light of the problem of the heathen.

The Myth of Ham is not just history but also a normative intervention against the pernicious power of the heathen concept. Johnson situates himself as an insider-outsider who was raised in the church and was filled with a missionary zeal for spreading Christianity. He experienced a kind of conversion away from Christianity in college—a *metanoia*, as he puts it—that increased his interest in the academic study of religion even as he "realize[d] that [he] did not want to be a Christian." This realization was met with a searing and "intimate rejection" by friends and family. As "ugly" and "illegitimate" as the rejection made him feel, Johnson recognized it because he "had done the same thing to and believed the same thing about others.

It mattered not how sincere they were or who they were; if they were not Christian, they lacked the most important, overriding quality. They had rejected God, and I would never affirm that rejection. I would never accept them. Now the shoe was on the other foot, so to speak."[50]

While Johnson found graduate school to be a "wonderful change," allowing him to study and converse with others about Christianity from an academic standpoint, he also felt more deeply the entanglement of Christianity with Black identity. "On the one hand, I was treated amiably and was well respected" by African American colleagues, he explains. "On the other hand, it was very clear to me that Christianity was regarded as normative. And those who were not Christians (such as I) were something ominously other than normal." It was Johnson's intimate experience of "radical alterity" that led him to research and write *The Myth of Ham*.[51]

All four scholars, then, diagnose deep problems at the heart of America's ecological, psychological, spiritual, and academic life that stem from Americans' treatment of the racial and religious Other. The remedies they suggest align with the problems on which they focus. Deloria devotes much of *God Is Red* to an exposition of the differences between Christian and Native religious perspectives, offering the latter as the only way to prevent the "imminent and expected destruction of the life cycle of world ecology." Where Fanon called for a radical break with the past and the creation of a "new man," and where EATWOT called for an "irruption" of the Third World that newly combined Indigenous religions with Christianity, Deloria does not need to look to the future for new answers to the problems of the present. Instead, the "radical shift" he proposes necessitates respect for and acceptance of traditional Native beliefs that had historically been denigrated as heathen: "Many thoughtful and useful systems of belief of ancient peoples have been simply rejected a priori by Western religious thinkers. This attitude has intruded into Western science and then emerged as the intellectual criteria by which the world of our experience is judged, condemned, and too often sentenced to death." Dismissing others' "religious experiences" of "a multitude of gods," Westerners held up "monotheism . . . as the highest form of religious knowledge" and assumed that polytheistic religions were "cruel delusions perpetrated against primitive societies by religious leaders, shamans, and medicine people seeking personal gain or additional powers, or people forced into trickery to preserve their place in society." This was a familiar trope leveled against heathen priests and rulers; Deloria contends that the real costs of such denigration redound to Westerners themselves, as their bias renders them incapable of learning from others, a point Luther Standing Bear had also made. "We cannot conclude that other peoples spent centuries in a state of delusion simply because their experiences of God were radically different from those of Western peoples," Deloria maintains. "That their experiences could not be either described accurately by Westerners or understood in western categories of thought does not make them false."[52]

Indeed, not only are they not false, they also hold the last hope for the "redemption" of the "lands of the planet. . . . Who will find peace with the lands? The future of humankind lies waiting for those who will come to understand their lives and take up their responsibilities to all living things." Where White Westerners had historically denigrated so-called heathens for believing that spirits resided in the land, Deloria's counterscript depicts Westerners as disconnected and pitiable for ignoring the "voices of the places of the land." Deloria calls on the "long-forgotten people of the respective continents"—the erstwhile heathen world—to recapture their traditional inheritance and save their lands from ravage. As they "rise and begin to reclaim their ancient heritage, they will discover the meaning of the lands of their ancestors" and the "invaders of the North American continent will finally discover that for this land, God is red."[53]

For his part, Long urges Americans to face head-on the fear that results from ignoring past and present evils and from flattening the Other into a superficial caricature.[54] He entreats Americans to open themselves to the "*mysterium tremendum,* that experience which establishes the *otherness* and mystery of the holy," and "which is so familiar in my background." At multiple junctures in *Significations,* and in full to close out the volume, Long quotes James Weldon Johnson's "Lift Every Voice and Sing" to offer a different God from the superficial, patriotic one White Americans have worshiped. Long describes the latter as "the god of American history," who celebrates the "saga of the mighty outward acts" and who is only made possible by suppressing the devastation these acts leave in their wake. Long says that the African American "community from which [he] come[s] expressed *an-other* attitude" that confronted reality head-on: "a reality so agonizing that it forced us to give up our innocence while at the same time it sustained us in humor, joy, and promise. I am speaking of a quality of the American experience which through its harsh discipline destroyed forever a naive innocence, revealing a god of creation—a god of our silent tears—a god of our weary years." If "there may indeed be an authentic god of time and history in the American experience," Long says, it must be this God who has presided over it and who will see it into the future.[55]

The "reorientation of America is contingent upon a recognition of the otherness within and the otherness without" that might, Long hopes, foster among "both sides the possibility for a kind of humility—the humility to reflect on their common creaturehood, and, I may add, an invitation to participate in both the tragedy and the comedy of human existence." America is not separate from what used to be called the heathen world or, in Long's terminology, the world of the "primitives." It is built on the backs and lands of people White Westerners clumped together, whose otherness is of a piece with colonized people around the world. These Others are actively calling White Americans to account for the depths and devastation of their shared history and countering White Americans' jingoistic false God—a mirror image of themselves, and hence an idol of narcissism—with an "authentic god of time and history." Redemption lies in recognition of "common creaturehood" under a God who understands and shares in pain and suffering.[56]

Johnson, for his part, prefers to identify with heathens. He calls for this identification not as a backdoor into a celebratory biblical narrative but as an alternative to the American—including African American—desire to see themselves as God's favored Israelites. He asserts that "American Christianity and its religious and racial implications cannot be rightly understood without an interpretive perspective (hermeneutics) that takes seriously the *problem* of violently constructing the heathen as illegitimate." Dubbing this a "Canaanite perspective," he turns on its head the notion that it is the Israelites whose suffering in bondage deserves our attention; instead, "the most victimized characters in biblical narrative are those who are not the people of God." For Johnson, it is the "heathens, the non-Christians . . . who must be valued as legitimate existents." Due to his own firsthand experience, Johnson recognizes how alive the concept of the heathen remains. Even if "few would invoke the legends of Ham, Shem, or Japheth today," yet "in the twenty-first century," he maintains, "the Bible is *still* a weapon, and the battle of divine identity has not abated." It is not enough to draw attention to the "history of vilifying non-Christian identities and cultures"; rather, Johnson argues that a real "commitment to end Christian expansionism (i.e., Christian missions)" is crucially necessary as a "first step in a sort of nonmaterial reparations, without which the histories of Christianity's constructing the heathen would merely pass uncorrected."[57] This is no small recommendation: in essence, Johnson advocates that a conversionist religion that excludes those who fail to join the fold stop converting and excluding. Adopting a Canaanite perspective—a quintessentially *heathen* perspective—reclaims the pejorative concept to critique American Christianity.

Finally, since Wynter calls into question the very possibility of speaking back, she is less interested in reoccupying and resignifying pejorative concepts; instead, she calls for a complete and radical break with the Western mode of being human. To do more than echo, she says, "native" intellectuals must create another Big Bang, so to speak: a "new science of the Word," as called for by Césaire; "introducing invention into existence," as urged by Fanon. Concludes Wynter, "The buck stops with us."[58]

"Into Our Light I Will Go Forever"

The story that Euro-Americans have generated about the heathen world is, in the words of scholar Eve Tuck (Unangax̂), a "damage-centered" one. To varying extents, the counterscripts presented here both recapitulate the "damage" and call for a wholly different orientation to the world, whether that means drawing from past wisdom or creating an unprecedented future. They also draw on the radical potential of the underside of history, whether described as the Third World, the damnés, or the Canaanites, to revise the religio-racist heathen world, with its homogenizing force, into a liberating potential for solidarity. In so doing they move toward what Tuck calls "Desire," a "thirding of the dichotomized categories of reproduction and resistance" that "more closely matches the experiences of people who, at different points in a single day, reproduce, resist, are complicit in, rage against, celebrate, throw up hands/fists/towels, and withdraw and participate in uneven social structures—that is, everybody."[59] The call to recapture the complexity of humanness within the commonalities that link the colonized is a move of both desire and rage against the flattening that happens when people are cast as part of the heathen world and its successors.

In her 2002 collection of poetry, *Night Is a Sharkskin Drum,* Hawaiian activist and scholar Haunani-Kay Trask undulates between damage and desire. She minces no words in detailing the damage Native Hawaiians faced from "the waxy smell of missionary lies" and the "flaunting foreigners" parading their wealth as they tour the islands, giving off the "stench of empire."[60] She laments the changes on the islands, both spiritual and somatic:

> How is it now
>> you are gone,
>>> our *ali'i* dismembered,
>>>> their *mana* lost,
> we are left
>> with broken bodies, blinded
>>> children, infected winds
>>>> from across the sea.[61]

Yet although Hawaiians have been left "in the morass of Paradise," over-taken by tourists with no respect for the sacred, Trask concludes her slim volume with an anthem of sovereign resistance and desire that draws strength from the living gods. The poem "Into Our Light I Will Go Forever" is a resounding counterscript to the devastation wrought on the lands and lives of people marked as "heathen" by the Western Christian world. Without explicitly naming it as such, Trask inverts the equations of light = Christian, darkness = heathen. She invokes Kane and Hina. She rhapsodizes on the beauty of Hawaiian places, all of them sacred no matter how the *haole* might desecrate them: the "sanctuaries of hushed bamboo, awash in amber," the "spangled, blue-leafed *taro*, flooded with *wai*," the "wet-lands of He'eia, bubbling black mud." The mana—Divine power—is still alive. And

> Into our light
> > I will go forever . . .
> > > Into our sovereign suns,
> > > > drunk on the *mana*
> > > > > of Hawai'i.[62]

EPILOGUE

"The Aforesaid Heathen Peoples"

In her 2020 collection of poetry, *All Heathens*, Marianne Chan meditates on the Italian explorer Antonio Pigafetta's *Magellan's Voyage: A Narrative Account of the First Circumnavigation*. Pigafetta was Magellan's assistant on his journey to the Philippines, in which capacity he kept a detailed log and later produced the first translation of the Cebuano language, known as Bisaya to Native speakers. Pigafetta titled this translation "Some Words of the Aforesaid Heathen Peoples." Chan highlights what is missing from his list. Pigafetta "translates the Bisaya word for 'mother-of-pearl,' but not the Bisaya word for 'mother.'" Chan "wonder[s] if his readers— Europeans—found this strange, the exclusion. Perhaps they thought: These heathen peoples did not have a word for 'mother.'"[1] "Most likely," Chan surmises, "Pigafetta's list of heathen words excluded the word for 'mother' because the items he named were limited to merchandise, that is, objects or elements that could be exported":

Mana	Cinnamon
Boloto	Boats
Pilla	Silver
Tipai	Mothers-of-pearl

Why then did he include

Camat	Hand
Illoc	Armpits
Boto	Genitals
Dila	Tongue[2]

Pigafetta's list as rendered through Chan's poetry resonates with the salivating descriptions of Jedidiah Morse's geographies, the exploratory excursions of missionaries to Hawaiʻi, and the keen attentiveness to the land's richness by agents in Sierra Leone. Pigafetta is attuned to what the land can produce, and he is attuned to the bodies of the "aforesaid heathen peoples" as laborers on that land. And he sees their language as useful. Language facilitates governance. Says Chan, "Pigafetta sold my mother's tongue in the form of his book all over Europe. He said the language was more valuable than cloves."[3]

Chan, born in the Philippines and raised in Stuttgart, Germany, and Lansing, Michigan, has lost her mother's tongue. She understands when her mother talks to her in Bisaya but she "can't speak it. These are words I forget until I hear them."[4] Her book of poetry writes back to Pigafetta and reclaims the words he left out. In looking at people he deemed to be heathens and in hearing them talk, Pigafetta reduced them to the spoils of their lands and the parts of their bodies. But Chan shows how much more there is to hear, how much more there is to say: "When I ask my mother questions about her childhood, her answers tumble onto shore. . . . She overflows, overflowers. Discovers new feelings she can't express eloquently in English. . . . She awakens with leaves in her throat, Bisaya in her teeth, a belly full of her mother tongue." These are the words Chan writes down so she won't forget them:

When I think about my lola, my mother, myself—I recognize all the things that have been and will be forgotten, so I'm writing this down,

like Pigafetta, alongside his list of words, all of them ours, all of them heathen.[5]

Chan's is a proudly heathen inheritance.

But most Americans live with a different kind of heathen inheritance, one that draws more from Pigafetta and his reduction of the Other to the spoils and spoilage of their lands and bodies than from Chan and her attempt to bring overflowing, overflowering complexity back to the "words of the aforesaid heathen peoples." The stakes of this reduction are high. By claiming the power to tell the story of the heathen world as one of blight and despair, Americans have placed themselves in a paternalistic position of dominance over much of the world, like the "new Christian" Hugo resting his rump on the globe in *The Mission Connection*, the musical I was in as a child.

In a 2009 TED Talk, Nigerian author Chimamanda Ngozi Adichie describes this reductive view of the world as "the danger of a single story."

She recounts how, when she came to the United States for college, her "American roommate was shocked" by her. She continues, "What struck me was this: She had felt sorry for me even before she saw me. Her default position toward me, as an African, was a kind of patronizing, well-meaning pity. In this single story, there was no possibility of Africans being similar to her in any way, no possibility of feelings more complex than pity, no possibility of a connection as human equals." Adichie explains that "power is the ability not just to tell the story of another person, but to make it the definitive story of that person," such that anyone encountering that person thinks they know everything about her before hearing anything she has to say.[6] The heathen world operates as just such a "single story" that has called forth European and American intervention in order to rescue heathen histories from stagnation, save diseased heathen bodies from themselves, and make heathen lands blossom as the rose.

This book narrates the roots, resonances, reproductions, resistance to, and rage against this single story, and yet I grapple with the implications of telling it, not only because it is a damaging story but also because the idea that there is a world of sufferers "out there" and that Americans can do something to materially ameliorate their suffering has done some good. It has spurred clean water initiatives, the development of low-priced baby incubators, vaccination campaigns, and the like. How can such well-meaning and often salubrious humanitarian activity be reconciled with the knowledge that it emerges not just from an immediate (albeit paternalistic) desire to help but also from a long history of viewing the heathen world as an expansive domain in need of help in the first place, to extract the wealth of the land for the good of heathen bodies (and Americans' own pockets)?

I am, again, the "us" and the "them" in wrestling with these questions. As an academic, I am steeped in the mode of critique. But critique is, in some ways, easy. It is harder to ask what we should do about this, a question that students often put to me when I share my research with them. Many are eagerly looking forward to humanitarian work after they graduate. Who am I to throw cold water on their eagerness to help? And what good, after all, is critique when people are dying because they don't have access to vaccines? The academic critiquing from a comfortable office chair is not morally superior to the volunteer bringing medicine—far from it. I offer this history, then, not as definitive prescription but in the hopes that it might help foster conversation about religion, race, and the ethics of aid. I have no doubt that the majority of humanitarians working in and for the so-called heathen world, both now and in the past, have been firmly convinced about the righteousness and helpfulness of their work. But racism is about more than people's feelings and intentions: it is about the structural inequities that privilege one group over others. The figure of the heathen and the vast realm of the heathen world are part of the very sinews that have conflated and upheld Whiteness, Protestantism, and Americanness as superior to the world at large, and only by recognizing this continued power of the concept of heathenness can we talk about where to go from here.[7]

Americans have long constituted the heathen world as a realm to both feel pity for and shudder over. The heathen world is an imagined space of suffering that parents use to shame their children into eating that last bite of food ("Think of the poor and starving children overseas!"), a region beyond America's comfortable borders that allows Americans to realize how fortunate they are, and a realm that provides an outlet for exercising the guilt that might accrue over luxuriating in that good fortune.[8] Of course not every American luxuriates in good fortune. But that is precisely the point. Constituting the heathen world as a place that lies, for the most part, "out there" has led to the extension of aid abroad while the same issues Americans see in the heathen world are denied or ignored at home. *They* are wallowing in poverty, starvation, and disease, not us. *They* are ignoramuses enslaved to tyrants and false gods, not us. *They* keep their women in positions of subservience and servitude, not us.

In her TED Talk, Adichie says that the way to "create a single story" is to "show a people as one thing, as only one thing, over and over again."[9] The single story of the heathen world is nothing if not resonant in this way. As we have seen, heathens were repeatedly described as people who had stalled in time while White Christians leapfrogged them into the future. Christians were thought to be forward-looking and inventive like their Creator God; heathens regressive and repetitive in their obeisance to false idols. Christian history moved from the Fall to the Second Coming; heathen history hardly merited the name since it unfolded in endless cycles of lethargic sameness. But the very extent to which Europeans and Americans reiterated this story about the heathen world in fact reveals their own repetitive anxieties in facing the world-out-there.

Attentive to continuities and resonances, *Heathen* is a history attuned to the ironies of the discipline as constructed against the stagnating figure of the heathen. The idea that history should be linear and charge ever forward underlay the development of the modern historical profession, which is founded on the notion that history moves "chronologically from A to B" and changes over time.[10] This book is my attempt to suggest that it doesn't, always. Continuities matter as much as change, and this is adamantly as true for Euro-Americans as for the people they deemed heathen. Repeating the "single story" about a blighted and stagnating heathen world contra their own forward momentum served as a ritualistic and racist incantation reassuring Euro-Americans of their own superiority and justifying their interventions in the world. In "Postcoloniality and the Artifice of History," Dipesh Chakrabarty "ask[s] for a history that deliberately makes visible, within the very structure of its narrative forms, its own repressive strategies and practices." Chakrabarty explains that "European" assumptions about history have come to seem universal and, in being foisted on "modern third-world histories," have held them to a "transition narrative" that has marked them for their failures to achieve "development, modernization, capitalism."[11] In arguing for and organizing this book around continuity as well as change in American attitudes toward the heathen world, I have tried to "provincialize 'Europe[an]'" historical method by subjecting it to the same lens of stagnation and repetition that historians of European descent so often claimed for the heathen. Chakrabarty's "transition narrative" resonates with the replacement narrative that I have also tried to complicate. As I hope should be clear by now, the heathen was not replaced by the racialized subject, but formed and continues to inform both it and the identity of the White Protestant American as human and humanitarian.

There have always been critics who have pointed out that this identity is a sham and that the United States has not only never been immune to the woes Americans have so pityingly pointed out in others, but has been actively responsible for creating them in the US and the world. These critics, such as Wong Chin Foo, David Walker, Mary Church Terrell, and Uchimura Kanzō, have excoriated the hypocrisy of sending money and missionaries overseas while perpetuating misery at home. They have used the heathen barometer to reveal plenty of heathens at home, in the very same White Christian Americans who professed such pity over the heathen world abroad.

A final example of just such a counterscript comes from a 2020 independent presidential contender, Mark Charles, in collaboration with Soong-Chan Rah, professor of evangelism at Fuller Theological Seminary. Charles is the child of a Dutch American mother and Diné father, while Rah is the son of Korean immigrants. Together, they take on the doctrine of discovery in their 2019 *Unsettling Truths*, arguing that its justification for the invasion of Indigenous lands—that they are inhabited by "pagan" people—has long undergirded White American exceptionalism and triumphalism. The only reason the United States has come across as a beacon of freedom is simply that "we have just won our wars. And therefore, for centuries, we wrote our own history." In other words, the United States has bulldozed over other people, justifying violence and land theft in the name of the doctrine of discovery, and then whitewashed history (literally) to make White Americans appear righteous and godly in the aftermath of devastation and destruction. As Christians of Diné and Korean descent, Charles and Rah claim a God who sides with the oppressed and adamantly assert that the United States is not "the chosen people of Israel," but rather, "in the Old Testament narrative, Americans would be the citizens of the pagan nations."[12] White Americans are the heathens, and the doctrine of discovery is founded on a lie.

Charles and Rah do not stop there; writing for a primarily Christian audience, they seek to bring White Christians into "racial conciliation," stressing that there is nothing yet to *re*concile. They do this by returning the gaze on White Americans and seeing them "from a fresh perspective": not merely as oppressors but as themselves "a traumatized people." Like soldiers who feel tremendous guilt over deaths they have caused but suppress their guilt and cover it with patriotic justifications, White Americans are aware that their past is not pure but are in deep "denial" about it. As much as White Americans called heathen histories unreliable and designated themselves the preservers of other people's pasts, Charles and Rah, echoing Charles H. Long, hold them "unable to even publish accurate history" because of their own "unresolved trauma" and festering shame, resulting in historical censorship in favor of purely "patriotic history." (This charge reverberates even more profoundly as recent attacks on critical race theory demonstrate ignorance of what it even is, alongside a deep protectiveness of "patriotic history.") Charles and Rah assert that viewing White people as traumatized allows "people of color" to "maintain their own agency and humanity." They call for White Americans to join with people of color in "the healing power of lament," a lament that necessitates "humility" and "truth telling."[13]

The Mission Connection closes with a pairing of songs that encapsulates the tensions at play in Americans' conception of the "heathen" or "Third World." The first is called "Humble Yourself" and features a plaintive solo of subservience to "the mighty God." Charles and Rah might have agreed with such a message, of the need for White American Christians to humble themselves before a just and mighty Lord.[14] But immediately after this, the choir launches into "The Mission Connection," a "lively" tune that evinces none of the humility and all of the confidence that "we're bound for happiness!" (repeated three times for good measure, to close out the production). The heathen world, whether it is the "mountain peak," "jungle land," or "prairie"—all interchangeable and all ripe for volunteering—promises the transformation of humility into happiness. The riders on the Jesus Express find their own humanity affirmed in their humanitarianism; find their own happiness in the heathen world.[15]

But at what cost? In *The Origin of Others,* Toni Morrison writes that "there are no strangers. There are only versions of ourselves, many of which we have not embraced, most of which we wish to protect ourselves from. . . . That makes us reject the figure and the emotions it provokes—especially when these emotions are profound. It is also what makes us want to own, govern, and administrate the Other. To romance her, if we can, back into our own mirrors. In either instance (of alarm or false reverence), we deny her personhood, the specific individuality we insist upon for ourselves."[16] The heathen world is precisely this: an elastic realm of individual-less Others who reflect back to Americans, as in a fun-house mirror, the selves they wish to deny, pity, control, or romance behind closed doors. Americans find their happiness in the heathen world by having their individuality affirmed vis-à-vis the global, fungible masses whose essential neediness reflects back Americans' supposed prosperity and positive agency. As long as Americans are not the interchangeable child starving overseas—as long as they are the ones putting money in the offering plates for the poor heathen in Africa or Asia, they tell themselves that they are blessed.

POSTSCRIPT

The More Things Change . . .

Or not. The COVID-19 pandemic that began in late 2019 has laid bare not only latent and long-lasting fears about diseased and contagious foreign (formerly heathen) bodies but also fears that the United States' chaotic and uncoordinated response to the crisis might reveal it to be on a par with the countries it has long dismissed as heathen/Third World.

When rumors of a strange new pneumonia-like illness began filtering out of Wuhan in late December 2019, many were quick to lay the blame squarely at the feet of the Chinese. Their wet markets are "quite unsanitary," wrote Therese Shaheen in the *National Review,* "with blood, entrails, excrement, and other waste creating the conditions for disease that migrates from animals to people through virus, bacteria, and other forms of transmission." These wet markets feature the sale of "wild animals not only for consumption but as the supposedly magic ingredients in tonics and alternative medicines." Shaheen's use of "supposedly magic" here signals clear disbelief and skepticism, echoing nineteenth-century discourse against Chinese medicine as heathen superstition rather than empirically validated pharmaceuticals. The "commingling with wild animals" at wet markets, Shaheen wrote disapprovingly, has "created much misery for the Chinese and for the world."[1] While Chinese markets do feature meats that are uncommon and unfamiliar in the West, Shaheen's phrasing goes beyond reporting to recall earlier disapproving stereotypes about the heathen: for being too close to the wilderness; for "commingling" with it, eating it, endowing it with "magic."

The notion that COVID-19 is a Chinese disease caused by strange and unsanitary Chinese eating practices informed the Trump administration's initial reaction to the novel coronavirus. Donald Trump issued a China travel ban and then reassured Americans that, with the unhealthy foreign element safely excluded, they had little to worry about. Even as it became increasingly apparent that the administration's favored border control policy could not keep a hardy virus out, Trump continued to claim that it was working: "We pretty much shut it down coming in from China," he trumpeted on February 2, 2020.[2] When it became clear that the virus had been silently spreading on US soil for weeks and that the United States was woefully unprepared, Trump repeatedly passed responsibility back onto China, referring to COVID-19 as the "Chinese virus" and denying any allegations of racism in the label because "it comes from China, that's why. It comes from China. I want to be accurate." As historian Gordon Chang has put it, using such language is "an effective political way to rally people, deflect the attention away from his administration's response to this crisis, [and] find a scapegoat."[3] Anti-Asian hate crimes have risen in the wake of this scapegoating, calling to mind earlier waves of violence.[4]

The embarrassingly ineffectual US response to the pandemic in 2020— not enough test kits, not enough ventilators, not enough hospital beds, not enough masks, not enough hand sanitizer—uncovered a familiar worry: that the United States might actually be no better than the diseased heathen/Third World peoples it was trying to exclude. Even as Trump was publicly deflecting blame onto China and insisting that "America will never be a supplicant nation" and "should never be reliant on a foreign country for the means of our own survival," his own administration was soliciting aid from "other countries"—including China—"for everything from hand sanitizer to ventilators to help fight the coronavirus."[5]

Many reacted to the shortage of essential medical equipment in the United States with shock and dismay. That the United States could be faced with a situation of dire need was incomprehensible to those who expected the nation to be at the head of the world in science and technology and who believed in a national mythology of plenty, in which *we* are the givers and *they* are the receivers. "We don't have the machines, we don't have the beds," an anonymous New York City doctor said to CNN: "To think that we're in New York City and this is happening. It's like a third-world country type of scenario. It's mind-blowing."[6] The idea that the United States is no better than a Third World country was repeated again and again by doctors and nurses forced to wear plastic trash bags and bandannas because their hospitals had no more personal protective equipment; by journalists appalled at the situations on which they were reporting; and by the American public sheltering in place and looking on in horror.[7] Others, though, were less than shocked at what the COVID-19 crisis revealed about America. Applying a Third World barometer, so to speak, digital content creator Jasmine Tyon tweeted on March 22, 2020, that "America is a third world country in a Gucci belt." "In a stolen Gucci belt," replied Gary Poleman. Chimed in Jaimie Seaton, "This is the most perfect thing ever written about this God-forsaken country."[8]

Social critics blamed rapacious capitalism for America's missteps. As we have seen, critics from the erstwhile heathen world had long lambasted Americans' individualistic pursuit of money at the expense of social welfare, urging instead what they named as a heathen/non-Christian ethic of care for others without excessive concern for the Almighty Dollar. They flipped the script on American Christians who stereotyped the heathen as people who did not have the "least ounce of charity" for others, instead arguing that White Americans were the ones who were selfish and uncaring in their idolatry of the market. In the age of COVID-19, a *New York Times* article about people who bought up hand sanitizer and other essential supplies in order to resell them at a huge markup garnered fiery scorn and anger at the harmful greediness of such profiteering.[9] This is "your brain on capitalism," tweeted historian Andrew Hartman about the story.[10] When mandatory social distancing policies threatened the economy, Republicans who were worried about another Great Depression claimed that they would be willing to die in order to save the country (and implied that others should come out of isolation and be willing to die for the economy as well). Critics likewise piled on with numerous "This is your brain on capitalism" tweets, arguing that to end social distancing too early would be to sacrifice the vulnerable to the idol of the American economy.[11]

The idea that capitalism functions as a kind of religion that can warp the brain recalls nineteenth-century thinking about how heathenism could stymie the brain development of heathens. That Trump initially wanted to reopen the American economy on Easter 2020—a "beautiful timeline"—cements the connection between the market and Christianity that self-professed heathens criticized harshly. "I would love to have the country opened up and just raring to go by Easter," said Trump. "Wouldn't it be great to have all the churches full? You'll have packed churches all over our country. I think it'll be a beautiful time." Trump connected the symbolism of Easter—a time of resurrection—to the resurrection of America ("It's such an important day for other reasons, but I'll make it an important day for this too").[12] As many doctors urgently warned, packing the churches on Easter would have resulted in death, not resurrection.[13]

In the Euro-American imagination, the heathen were supposed to be the ones subject to premature death because their "wrong" religion created unhealthy attitudes toward the body and disease. The Third World inheritors of heathen mentalities were supposed to be languishing in the consequences of such wrongheadedness, not Americans. In laying bare the reality of widespread disease and death on US soil, COVID-19 may finally compel Americans to see the nation as part and parcel of the suffering world; as just as in need of help as the helpers of others.

And yet COVID-19 is a disease that has also exacerbated long-lived inequalities within the United States and between the US and the world. From the beginning, the pandemic has hit communities of color with disproportionate force, preying on health conditions that are often associated with poor access to health care and nutritious food. The creation of powerful vaccines has helped those Americans willing and able to take them but has intensified global inequalities. Americans looked with horror at the rise of the Delta variant and the catastrophic toll it wreaked on India, even as they celebrated, with relief, their own access to cutting-edge mRNA vaccines and a return to pre-pandemic normalcy (until Delta, and then Omicron, surged in the still undervaccinated United States). The vaccine nationalism of the United States has manifested in the country's purchasing of "1.3 billion doses, enough to fully vaccinate more than three times its adult population,"[14] while the vaccine hesitant require incentives like lotteries and free donuts and beer to consider getting the shot. To the vaccinated, the unvaccinated-by-choice have become the new intransigents within the nation, offered the chance of salvation but refusing to take it. Meanwhile, Americans are back to pitying the world, donating unused and unwanted vaccines, and reinforcing the old narrative of the chosen nation as grateful and guilty for its special benefits vis-à-vis the suffering heathens.

And so, even as COVID-19 has seemed to upend the world as we know it, even still, even now—so much has changed, and yet so much remains the same.

NOTES

ACKNOWLEDGMENTS

INDEX

NOTES

Prologue

1. Declan Leary, "The Meaning of the Native Graves," *American Conservative*, July 8, 2021, https://www.theamericanconservative.com/articles/the-meaning-of-the-native-graves/, italics in original.

2. "Paganism" and "heathenism" have often, though not always, been used synonymously. "Heathen" appears with much more frequency than "pagan" in books written in "American English" and published in (what became) the United States for much of the period between 1500 and 1950, when a rise in use of the term "pagan" likely reflected the growth of Contemporary Paganism, also known as Modern Paganism or Neopaganism, in the 1960s and beyond. This analysis draws on data from Google's Ngram viewer, which shows the percentage of single words in books written in American English and published in the United States that are "heathen" and "pagan," between the years 1500 and 2019. Both terms reach a high point in the mid-nineteenth century, but the frequency of "heathen" at its high (~0.002 percent) is 500 percent the frequency of "pagan" at its high (~0.0004 percent). The related—though in key ways importantly different—terms "savage" and "barbarian" can also be compared with "heathen." "Savage" also reaches a high of roughly 0.002 percent in the mid-nineteenth century, while "barbarian" lags behind at a high of 0.0002 percent at the same time.

3. For more on this subject, see Jefferson F. Calico, *Being Viking: Heathenism in Contemporary America* (Sheffield, UK: Equinox, 2018); Jennifer Snook, *American Heathens: The Politics of Identity in a Pagan Religious Movement* (Philadelphia: Temple University Press, 2015); and Mattias Gardell, *Gods of the Blood: The Pagan Revival and White Separatism* (Durham, NC: Duke University Press, 2003).

4. Tyler Huckabee, "The American Conservative Does the Unthinkable and Defends the Unmarked Indigenous Graves as 'Good, Actually,'" *RELEVANT*, July 9, 2021, https://www.relevantmagazine.com/faith/church/the-american-conservative-does-the-unthinkable-and-defends-the-unmarked-indigenous-graves-as-good-actually/.

5. Christian millennials are especially divided on this issue; another article from *RELEVANT* cites a study that found that 47 percent "agree at least somewhat that it is wrong to share one's personal beliefs with someone of a different faith

in hopes that they will one day share the same faith." "Report: 47% of Christian Millennials Believe Evangelism Is Wrong," *RELEVANT,* February 6, 2019, https://www.relevantmagazine.com/faith/report-47-of-christian-millennials -believe-evangelism-is-wrong/.

6. "About Us," *RELEVANT,* accessed September 27, 2021, https://www.relevant magazine.com/about/.

7. *RELEVANT* Staff, "Exclusive: Check Out This Excellent Short Documentary about 'Heathen,' GAWVI's Upcoming Album," *RELEVANT,* March 27, 2020, https://www.relevantmagazine.com/culture/music/exclusive-check-out-this -excellent-short-documentary-about-heathen-gawvis-upcoming-album/.

8. "Foreword and Synopsis," in Eric Rainwater and Fred Judkins, arr. Phil Shackleton, *The Mission Connection* (Tarzana, CA: Fred Bock Music, 1992), 2.

9. Phil Shackleton (arr.) and Eric Rainwater (words and music), "Miss Shunary," in *Mission Connection,* 41–43.

10. Phil Shackleton ("awwanged") and "Ewic Wainwatew" (words and music), "Wigwam Wobble," in *Mission Connection,* 44–48; "Foreword and Synopsis," 2–3.

11. *Mission Connection,* 25, 49–50.

12. On American displays of heathenism, see Hillary Kaell, *Christian Globalism at Home: Child Sponsorship in the United States* (Princeton, NJ: Princeton University Press, 2020). Kaell looks not only at the letters, print material, and money that circulated around child sponsorship but also at the "participatory techniques" that helped engender emotional responses to the world's suffering. In performances for Christian audiences, White children dressed in "native" garb; White adults read aloud the conversion narratives of "heathens" who had become Christians. See Kaell, chap. 2, "Systems and Statistics: Aggregate Numbers and Particular Objects," esp. 66–67.

13. Jim Herron Zamora, "Wilbur Victor Holt—Lutheran Pastor in China and S.F.," *SFGATE,* August 24, 2003. The article spells Holt's first name differently in the title and text. The church Holt founded renders his name "Wilbert," not "Wilbur."

14. "Frequently Asked Questions—Doctrine," Lutheran Church Missouri Synod, accessed June 2021, https://www.lcms.org/about/beliefs/faqs/doctrine.

15. Dipesh Chakrabarty, "Postcoloniality and the Artifice of History: Who Speaks for 'Indian' Pasts?," *Representations,* no. 37 (Winter 1992): 3.

Introduction

1. Basil Miller, *Arms around the World: Missions World Wide* (Pasadena, CA: World-Wide Missions, 1971), 92, 95, in Collection 0143: Material from World-Wide Faith Mission, 1950–1985, Fuller Seminary Archives and Special Collections, Pasadena, CA. Miller first founded the Basil Miller Foundation in 1950 (the same year that Bob Pierce founded World Vision); its name was changed to World-Wide Missions in 1960. "A Brief History of World-Wide Missions," Collection 0143, Fuller Seminary, n.d.

2. Miller, *Arms around the World,* 79, 80.

3. Miller, 79–81, 101, 104, 107, 84.

4. George Fredrickson, *Racism: A Short History* (2002; repr., Princeton, NJ: Princeton University Press, 2015), 7, 9.

5. On monogenesis, see Colin Kidd, *The Forging of Races: Race and Scripture in the Protestant Atlantic World, 1600–2000* (Cambridge: Cambridge University Press, 2006). Kidd does not claim to "advance any grand overarching thesis about the relationship of race and theology" (272) but nevertheless suggests that monogenesis inhibited extreme racialist thought, whereas the dethroning of scripture from its dominance in Western intellectual life opened the door to "the uninhibited articulation of racialist sentiments" (19). See also Paul Goodman, *Of One Blood: Abolitionism and the Origins of Racial Equality* (Berkeley: University of California Press, 1998).

6. Michael Omi and Howard Winant, *Racial Formation in the United States: From the 1960s to the 1990s*, 2nd. ed. (New York: Routledge, 1994), 55, 113. In addition to Fredrickson, *Racism,* see, for instance, Tanya Golash-Boza's popular textbook, *Race and Racisms: A Critical Approach,* 2nd ed. (New York: Oxford University Press, 2017), which explains that "before the rise of science, Westerners understood the world primarily in biblical terms," and that in the eighteenth century, "the question of human difference began to move from the realms of religion and folk ideas to that of science," marking the emergence of race as a "modern invention" that is "distinct from previous ways of thinking about human difference" (chap. 1, "The Origins of Race," esp. 27, 32). See also Rebecca Goetz, *The Baptism of Early Virginia: How Christianity Created Race* (Baltimore: Johns Hopkins University Press, 2012), which argues for the creation of race in the seventeenth century; and Roxann Wheeler, *The Complexion of Race: Categories of Difference in Eighteenth-Century British Culture* (Philadelphia: University of Pennsylvania Press, 2000), which "detects a moment when the older order, based primarily on the division between Christian and heathen, gives way to a new division between black and white" (back cover).

7. Fredrickson, *Racism,* 61. This assessment is based on a Google Ngram graph of the frequency of the term "heathen" in American English publications between 1500 and 2019. See n. 2 in the Prologue.

8. Ussama Makdisi shows a similar monolithicizing dynamic in his study of American missionaries in the Middle East, *Artillery of Heaven: American Missionaries and the Failed Conversion of the Middle East* (Ithaca, NY: Cornell University Press, 2008): "From a presumably Christian center, missionaries saw themselves enlightening the darker areas of the world. For the chroniclers of mission, the setting might just as well have been the Sandwich Islands as Syria; the Maronite As'ad Shidyaq might just as well have been the Cherokee Catherine Brown, and the Ottoman sultan, the Hawaiian queen Keopuolani" (7). Makdisi points out the "remarkable similarity of [missionary] writings on 'the' heathen, whatever the locale" (9).

9. Emily Conroy-Krutz, *Christian Imperialism: Converting the World in the Early American Republic* (Ithaca, NY: Cornell University Press, 2015), Chapter 1, "Hierarchies of Heathenism."

10. On a binary of "European versus non-European" that "underlay" a "graduated hierarchy of peoples and races," see also David A. Chang, *The World and All the Things upon It: Native Hawaiian Geographies of Exploration* (Minneapolis: University of Minnesota Press, 2016), esp. 69–70.

11. Henry Goldschmidt, "Introduction: Race, Nation, and Religion," in *Race, Nation, and Religion in the Americas,* ed. Henry Goldschmidt and Elizabeth McAlister (New York: Oxford University Press, 2004), 3.

12. Terence Keel, *Divine Variations: How Christian Thought Became Racial Science* (Stanford, CA: Stanford University Press, 2018), 150n32, 14. See also Peter Coviello, *Make Yourselves Gods: Mormons and the Unfinished Business of American Secularism* (Chicago: University of Chicago Press, 2019), esp. "Introduction: What We Talk about When We Talk about Secularism"; Vincent Lloyd and Jonathon Kahn, eds., *Race and Secularism in America* (New York: Columbia University Press, 2016); and Talal Asad, *Genealogies of Religion: Discipline and Reasons of Power in Christianity and Islam* (Baltimore: Johns Hopkins University Press, 1993).

13. In addition to the works discussed in the text, see (among many others) Anthea Butler, *White Evangelical Racism: The Politics of Morality in America* (Chapel Hill: University of North Carolina Press, 2021); Khyati Joshi, *White Christian Privilege: The Illusion of Religious Equality in America* (New York: New York University Press, 2020); Jemar Tisby, *The Color of Compromise: The Truth about the American Church's Complicity in Racism* (Grand Rapids: Zondervan, 2019); Judith Weisenfeld, *New World A-Coming: Black Religion and Racial Identity during the Great Migration* (New York: New York University Press, 2017); Paul Harvey, *Bounds of Their Habitation: Race and Religion in American History* (Lanham, MD: Rowman and Littlefield, 2016); Willie James Jennings, *The Christian Imagination: Theology and the Origins of Race* (New Haven, CT: Yale University Press, 2011); J. Kameron Carter, *Race: A Theological Account* (New York: Oxford University Press, 2008); Barnor Hesse, "Racialized Modernity: An Analytics of White Mythologies," *Ethnic and Racial Studies* 30, no. 4 (July 2007): 643–663; Kidd, *Forging of Races;* Goldschmidt and McAlister, *Race, Nation, and Religion;* and Forrest Wood, *The Arrogance of Faith: Christianity and Race in America* (New York: Knopf, 1990).

14. Geraldine Heng, "The Invention of Race in the European Middle Ages I," *Literature Compass* 8, no. 5 (May 2011): 315–331, esp. 325. See also the book version, Heng, *The Invention of Race in the European Middle Ages* (Cambridge: Cambridge University Press, 2018); Cord Whitaker, *Black Metaphors: How Modern Racism Emerged from Medieval Race-Thinking* (Philadelphia: University of Pennsylvania Press, 2019); and Whitaker's review of Heng (*Critical Inquiry,* July 1, 2020) for further scholarship treating "religious race" in the Middle Ages. María Elena Martínez makes a similar claim about the relationship between religion and race in colonial Mexico. She pushes back against Fredrickson's characterization of Spain as the birthplace of race and racism and refuses to draw a clear line between religious and racial othering: "To elevate 'race as biology' to an ideal type is to set up a false dichotomy—to ignore that racial discourses have proven to be remarkably flexible, invoking nature or bi-

ology more at one point, culture more at another." *Genealogical Fictions: Limpieza de Sangre, Religion, and Gender in Colonial Mexico* (Stanford, CA: Stanford University Press, 2008), 11. Jorge Cañizares-Esguerra similarly de-exceptionalizes the Iberian colonies as particularly racist in *Puritan Conquistadors: Iberianizing the Atlantic, 1550–1700* (Stanford, CA: Stanford University Press, 2006), which bemoans the Black Legend's continued influence on scholarship about the emergence of race.

15. Heng, "Invention of Race," 322, 323, italics in the original.

16. Scholarly resistance to Heng's and others' work on race in the European Middle Ages shows just how powerful the replacement narrative continues to be. Though Heng's book won four major prizes, some have critiqued her for making a "sustained argument for the existence of race and racisms in the deep European past," preferring to see the emergence of race later. Heng writes back to one particular "hatchet job" of a review in order to "tell young medievalists of color . . . *not to be intimidated into fearing to attempt new work on race just because they, too, might be savaged.*" Heng, "Why the Hate? *The Invention of Race in the European Middle Ages,* and Race, Racism, and Premodern Critical Race Studies Today," *In the Middle,* December 21, 2020, https://www.inthemedievalmiddle.com/2020/12/why-hate-invention-of-race-in-european.html, italics in the original.

17. Sylvester Johnson, *African American Religions, 1500–2000: Colonialism, Democracy, and Freedom* (Cambridge: Cambridge University Press, 2015), 392, emphasis in original.

18. King James Version. Updated versions (the New International Version, the English Standard Version, and the New King James Version, among others) translate "heathen" as "nations."

19. Beverly Daniel Tatum, *Why Are All the Black Kids Sitting together in the Cafeteria? And Other Conversations about Race,* rev. ed. (New York: Basic Books, 2017), 87. See also Ibram Kendi's popular *Stamped from the Beginning: The Definitive History of Racist Ideas in America* (New York: Nation Books, 2016). Kendi divides "racist ideas" into two categories: segregationist and assimilationist. This book nuances how these categories have operated in the concept of the heathen: while it might seem to be an assimilationist concept because of the possibility of conversion, it has also given rise to segregationist policies.

20. For a comprehensive history of racisms, see Francisco Bethencourt, *Racisms: From the Crusades to the Twentieth Century* (Princeton, NJ: Princeton University Press, 2013). Bethencourt defines racism as "prejudice concerning ethnic descent coupled with discriminatory action" (1, and throughout), focusing on inherited essentialisms as the basis for prejudice and discrimination. Bethencourt does not draw a bright line between religious and racial othering, arguing against Fredrickson and others that a modern scientific notion of "race" does not precede racism, but that different historically contingent racisms preceded the emergence of modern race.

21. See Lisa Lowe, *The Intimacies of Four Continents* (Durham, NC: Duke University Press, 2015), on the racial division of groups not only in colonial governance

but also in the archive: "The repeated injunctions that different groups must be divided and boundaries kept distinct indicate that colonial administrators imagined as dangerous the sexual, laboring, and intellectual contacts among enslaved and indentured nonwhite peoples. The racial classifications in the archive arrive, thus, in this context of the colonial need to prevent these unspoken 'intimacies' among the colonized" (35).

22. See, for instance, Tisby, *Color of Compromise,* and Butler, *White Evangelical Racism,* both important works of public scholarship that focus primarily on, as Tisby puts it, "the black-white racial divide in American Christianity" (17).

23. Judith Weisenfeld, "The House We Live In: Religio-Racial Theories and the Study of Religion," *Journal of the American Academy of Religion* 88, no. 2 (June 2020): 440–459, esp. 446.

24. On binaries and "Blackness" as itself a clumping category, see again Chang, *The World and All the Things upon It,* 69–70, and esp. 190: "In the Kanaka Maoli diasporic experience of racial construction in the mid-nineteenth-century United States, despite the differences among Kānaka and American Indians and African Americans and Fijians and others, all of these could situationally belong to one category. In the 1850 census, that category is called 'black' . . . . Today we might choose a different term than 'black.' We might instead term all of these as people whose racialization made them variously liable to colonization, enslavement, and labor exploitation." *Heathen* contends that the broad concept of the heathen also informed the wide net cast around the different people racialized as "Black" in the nineteenth century.

25. Benjamin Wisner, *The Moral Condition and Prospects of the Heathen. A Sermon, Delivered at the Old South Church in Boston, before the Foreign Mission Society of Boston and the Vicinity, at their Annual Meeting, Jan. 1, 1824* (Boston: printed by Crocker and Brewster, 1824), 36. See also reprints of Wisner's sermon in *The Monitor: Designed to Improve the Taste, the Understanding, and the Heart,* vol. 2 (Boston: Cummings, Hilliard, 1824) and *The Missionary Herald,* vol. 20 (Boston: published for the American Board of Commissioners for Foreign Missions by Samuel T. Armstrong, 1824).

26. Butler explains the conflation of Whiteness, Americanness, and Christianity like this: "For evangelicals, 'Christian race,' America, and belief are synonymous. Christianity is whiteness as well as belief" (*White Evangelical Racism,* 9).

27. W. E. B. Du Bois, "The Souls of White Folk," in *W. E. B. Du Bois: Writings* (New York: Library of America, 1987), 925. Originally published in the *Independent,* August 10, 1910, and revised for *Darkwater: Voices from within the Veil* (1920).

28. Du Bois, 927, 936.

29. On scripts and counterscripts, see Natalia Molina, *How Race Is Made in America: Immigration, Citizenship, and the Historical Power of Racial Scripts* (Berkeley: University of California Press, 2014), discussed further in Chapter 10.

30. Kathryn Lofton, "Religious History as Religious Studies," *Religion* 42 (July 2012): 387, 391; Linda Tuhiwai Smith, *Decolonizing Methodologies: Research and Indigenous Peoples* (London: Zed Books, 2002), 30. See also Jean Comaroff and John Comaroff's classic *Of Revelation and Revolution,* vol. 2,

The Dialectics of Modernity on a South African Frontier (Chicago: University of Chicago Press, 1997): "Important continuities emerge from histories like the one we recount here. . . . To conclude that the colonial age is over, or that modernity ended with it, is premature. It is crucial not to move on too quickly" (13–14).

31. William Swinton, *Outlines of the World's History, Ancient, Mediaeval, and Modern, with Special Relation to the History of Civilization and the Progress of Mankind: For Use in the Higher Classes in Public Schools, and in High Schools, Academies, Seminaries, etc.* (New York: Ivison, Blakeman, Taylor, 1874), 1–2, italics in original. See Kathryn Gin Lum, "The Historyless Heathen and the Stagnating Pagan: History as Non-Native Category?," *Religion and American Culture* 28, no. 1 (Winter 2018): esp. 52–56; Edward Said, *Orientalism*, 25th anniversary ed. (New York: Vintage Books, 2003); Asad, *Genealogies of Religion;* Eric Wolf, *Europe and the People without History* (Berkeley: University of California Press, 1982); Kerwin Klein, *Frontiers of Historical Imagination: Narrating the European Conquest of Native America, 1890–1990* (Berkeley: University of California Press, 1997); and Bernard McGrane, *Beyond Anthropology: Society and the Other* (New York: Columbia University Press, 1989).

32. On the "religio-racial," see Weisenfeld, *New World A-Coming*. Weisenfeld puts religion and race together not just for the sake of casual convenience, but to indicate a causal and mutually constitutive relationship where religious orientations shape racial identities, and vice versa. Weisenfeld's focus is on the agency of Black people who redefined their racialization by the American nation-state and crafted alternative religio-racial identities. This book looks at how the concept of the "heathen" shored up the religio-racial identity of White Protestant Americans, not only racializing the Other as deficient due to wrong religion, but also racializing its deployers as people who believed themselves to be saviors of the vast majority of the world. As such, the heathen ought to be understood as an essential component in the construction and maintenance of White supremacy. In making this claim I am inspired by Laura McTighe's charge in a roundtable on Weisenfeld's *New World A-Coming:* "Although increasingly attentive to colonialism and racism, scholars too often treat race as pertaining solely to people of color. This leaves the taxonomies of whiteness unchecked and unchallenged, reinscribing the spatial and temporal logics of white supremacy." Laura McTighe, "Introduction to Roundtable: 'Religio-Racial Identity' as Challenge and Critique," *Journal of the American Academy of Religion* 88, no. 2 (June 2020): 299–303, esp. 301.

33. See Susan M. Ryan, *The Grammar of Good Intentions: Race and the Antebellum Culture of Benevolence* (Ithaca, NY: Cornell University Press, 2003), which similarly shows how benevolence provided middle-class Americans with "a way to feel morally comfortable with their selfishness" (88) and assuage their feelings of guilt over the enslavement of African Americans and removal of Native Americans from their homelands. Ryan tells a primarily domestic, antebellum story focused on published literature; this book draws from her insights but looks through a wider lens at a longer chronology and geography.

Part I. Imagining the Heathen World

1. *Missionary Society of the Methodist Episcopal Church,* certificate, mezzotint, 20.25×16 in., Philadelphia, [ca. 1835], African Americana Prints and Watercolors and Drawings, Print Department of the Library Company of Philadelphia. At least four slightly different versions of this lithograph exist, with varying levels of detail and shading. Two are anonymous, and two are inscribed with the name John Sartain, a British engraver and artist who immigrated to the United States in 1830. American Edward Williams Clay is also identified as artist/contributor to the print; he was known for a series of racist and political cartoons, *Life in Philadelphia* (1828–1830).

2. "Missionary Society of the Methodist Episcopal Church [certificate] [graphic] / Clay, del.; Sartain, sculpt.," Library Company of Philadelphia, accessed September 28, 2021, https://digital.librarycompany.org/islandora/object/digitool%3A129970. The Library Company's catalog identifies the temple in the background as "probably the Vatican," but I am indebted to Adeana McNicholl for her expertise in reading the image alternately. The many possible interpretations of the image suggest precisely the blurred conflation of symbols that creates the heathen world as an elastic realm stretching from past to present and across the globe.

3. Emily Conroy-Krutz and David Hollinger argue that missionaries conveyed specific and detailed on-the-ground knowledge about foreign places and people to Americans at home. See Conroy-Krutz, "Missionary Intelligence and Americans' Mental Map of the World," S-USIH blog, July 2017, https://s-usih.org/2017/07/roundtable-missionary-intelligence-and-americans-mental-map-of-the-world/; and Hollinger, *Protestants Abroad: How Missionaries Tried to Change the World but Changed America* (Princeton, NJ: Princeton University Press, 2017). But as this book shows, missionaries also glossed over the differences between people and places in order to solicit pity, funds, and volunteers to help save the heathen world as a whole.

4. Per the Library Company catalog, "the Missionary Society, officially organized in New York in 1820, worked first to convert Native Americans and enslaved people before extending their missions to the Black inhabitants of Liberia in 1823" ("Missionary Society of the Methodist Episcopal Church").

5. "Annual Meeting," *Life and Light for Heathen Women* 1, no. 5 (1870): 165–166.

6. "Annual Meeting," 165–166.

7. On European views of Islam, see John Marenbon, *Pagans and Philosophers: The Problem of Paganism from Augustine to Leibniz* (Princeton, NJ: Princeton University Press, 2015). On nineteenth-century American views, see Ussama Makdisi, *Artillery of Heaven: American Missionaries and the Failed Conversion of the Middle East* (Ithaca, NY: Cornell University Press, 2008). The American Board of Commissioners for Foreign Missions, founded in 1810, largely wrapped the Middle East into the heathen world and trained its missionaries to Palestine and Syria in the same way that it prepared missionaries to Hawai'i and other so-called heathen mission fields. It was not until later in the nineteenth century, in the context of "imperial globalization," that Islam became separated from the heathen world and the notion of a distinct and essentialized "Muslim world" "achieved full flower," as Cemil Aydin puts it, advanced by both "pan-Islamists and Islamophobes . . . to advance political agendas." Aydin, *The Idea of the Muslim World: A Global Intellectual History* (Cambridge, MA: Harvard University Press, 2017), 5.

1. Precedents

1. Gerald MacLean, *The Rise of Oriental Travel: English Visitors to the Ottoman Empire, 1580–1720* (New York: Palgrave Macmillan, 2004), chap. 5, esp. 52.

2. Theophilus Lavender [William Biddulph], *The Travels of Foure English Men and a Preacher into Africa, Asia, Troy, Bythinia, Thracia, and to the Blacke Sea: and into Syria, Cicilia, Pisidia, Mesopotamia, Damascus, Canaan, Galile, Samaria, Iudea, Palestina, Ierusalem, Iericho, and to the Red Sea: and to sundry other places. Beginne in the Yeere of Iubile, 1600. and by some of them finished the yeere 1611. The others not yet returned. Very profitable for the helpe of Trauellers, and no lesse delightfull to all persons who take pleasure to heare of the Manners, Gouernment, Religion, and Customes of Forraine and Heathen Countries* (London: imprinted by Felix Kyngston, for William Aspley, 1612).

3. Lavender, preface to *Travels of Foure English Men*, n.p.

4. Lavender, n.p.

5. Anthony Pagden, *The Fall of Natural Man: The American Indian and the Origins of Comparative Ethnology* (Cambridge: Cambridge University Press, 1982), chap. 2, esp. 16, 20.

6. Pagden, 18, 22.

7. Pagden, 20.

8. *Oxford English Dictionary Online* (Oxford University Press, 2021), s.v. "pagan, n. and adj." See also Owen Davies, *Paganism: A Very Short Introduction* (New York: Oxford University Press, 2001), 2–3.

9. *Oxford English Dictionary Online* (Oxford University Press, 2021), s.v. "heathen, adj. and n.1." While some have disputed this etymology, the understanding of the "heathen" as heath- or wilderness-dwellers was held by most Americans as well, as their dictionaries and missionary publications attest. See also Davies, *Paganism*, 3.

10. *Century Dictionary* (1897), s.vv. "pagan," "heathen," cited in *Online Etymology Dictionary*, accessed September 2016, http://www.etymonline.com/index.php?term=pagan.

11. Olive Dickason, *The Myth of the Savage and the Beginnings of French Colonialism in the Americas* (Edmonton: University of Alberta Press, 1987), 64 and chap. 4, "L'Homme Sauvage."

12. On the "problem of paganism," see John Marenbon, *Pagans and Philosophers: The Problem of Paganism from Augustine to Leibniz* (Princeton, NJ: Princeton University Press, 2015).

13. Acts 17:23–26, King James Version.

14. Marenbon, *Pagans and Philosophers*, 20.

15. Romans 1:20–25, King James Version.

16. Davies, *Paganism*, 13–24, 17, 25–26.

17. Robin Lane Fox, *Pagans and Christians* (New York: Alfred A. Knopf, 1987), 22.

18. Marenbon, *Pagans and Philosophers*, 21.

19. Plutarch, *De Iside et Osiride*, 65, quoted by J. Reville, *La Religion à Rome sous les Sévères* (Paris, 1886), 114, in Marcel Simon, "Early Christianity and

Pagan Thought: Confluences and Conflicts," *Religious Studies* 9, no. 4 (December 1973): 385–399, esp. 394.

20. Marenbon, *Pagans and Philosophers*, 21.

21. Marenbon, 28–29.

22. Augustine, *On the Trinity* 4.15.20, quoted in Marenbon, *Pagans and Philosophers*, 31.

23. Davies, *Paganism*, 36.

24. Peter Abelard, *Problemata Heloissae* (PL 178, 696A), quoted in Marenbon, *Pagans and Philosophers*, 92.

25. Marenbon, *Pagans and Philosophers*, 138, 139.

26. Tamarah Kohanski and C. David Benson, introduction to *The Book of John Mandeville*, ed. (Kalamazoo, MI: Medieval Institute Publications, 2007), 1, 8.

27. John Mandeville (2000), bk. 19, p. 328, quoted in Marenbon, *Pagans and Philosophers*, 122.

28. Mandeville (2000), bk. 32, pp. 459–460, quoted in Marenbon, *Pagans and Philosophers*, 125.

29. Marenbon, *Pagans and Philosophers*, 126.

30. Pagden, *Fall of Natural Man*, 42–43.

31. Marenbon, *Pagans and Philosophers*, 110; David Brion Davis, *Inhuman Bondage: The Rise and Fall of Slavery in the New World* (New York: Oxford University Press, 2006), 60–61; María Elena Martínez, "The Black Blood of New Spain: Limpieza de Sangre, Racial Violence, and Gendered Power in Colonial Mexico," *William and Mary Quarterly* 61, no. 3 (July 2004): 479–520, esp. 485.

32. Papal bull, *Inter Caetera*, May 4, 1493, in *A Documentary History of Religion in America to the Civil War*, ed. Edwin Gaustad (Grand Rapids: Wm. B. Eerdmans, 1982, 1993), 22–23.

33. Pagden, *Fall of Natural Man*, 38.

34. See María Elena Martínez, *Genealogical Fictions: Limpieza de Sangre, Religion, and Gender in Colonial Mexico* (Stanford, CA: Stanford University Press, 2008) and "Black Blood of New Spain"; and Jessica L. Delgado and Kelsey C. Moss, "Religion and Race in the Early Modern Iberian Atlantic," in *The Oxford Handbook of Religion and Race in American History*, ed. Paul Harvey and Kathryn Gin Lum (New York: Oxford University Press, 2018), 40–60.

35. See Jonathan Z. Smith, "Religion, Religions, Religious," in *Critical Terms for Religious Studies*, ed. Mark C. Taylor (Chicago: University of Chicago Press, 1998), 269–284. Though "religion" was a term applied or withheld based on how a people's practices and beliefs compared with those of the colonizers, the label of paganism was applied with abandon. To be "religious" was something colonizers said of themselves; to be a "pagan" was the opposite of what they were supposed to be.

36. Acosta, *De procuranda*, quoted in Pagden, *Fall of Natural Man*, 162.

37. Pagden, *Fall of Natural Man*, 109.

38. Juan Ginés de Sepúlveda, excerpt from *The Second Democrates* (1547), *Digital History*, accessed October 2021, https://www.digitalhistory.uh.edu/active _learning/explorations/spain/spain_sepulveda.cfm.

39. Pagden, *Fall of Natural Man,* 159.
40. Bartolomé de las Casas, *The Destruction of the Indies* (1542), ed, and trans. Nigel Griffin (New York: Penguin Books, 1992), 11, 9.
41. Martínez, "Black Blood of New Spain," 485–486.
42. Martínez, 489.
43. Pagden, *Fall of Natural Man,* 100, 99.
44. José de Acosta, *De natura novi orbis libris duo* (Cologne, 1596), quoted in Pagden, *Fall of Natural Man,* 160.
45. Hakluyt to Ralegh, quoted in John Patrick Montaño, *The Roots of English Colonialism in Ireland* (Cambridge: Cambridge University Press, 2011), 49. I am grateful to John Smolenski for sharing the sources in this section with me.
46. Lord Deputy to Henry, November 14, 1540, State Papers, Henry VIII, 1:266–270, quoted in Montaño, *Roots of English Colonialism,* 1.
47. Davies, *Historical Tracts,* 95–96, quoted in Montaño, *Roots of English Colonialism,* 2.
48. Montaño, *Roots of English Colonialism,* 339–340.
49. Edmund Spenser, *A View of the State of Ireland,* from the first printed edition (1633), ed. Andrew Hadfield and Willy Maley (Oxford: Blackwell Publishers, 1997), 54, 61. On Spenser in Ireland, see Hadfield and Maley's introduction, and Ethan Shagan, *The Rule of Moderation: Violence, Religion, and the Politics of Restraint in Early Modern England* (Cambridge: Cambridge University Press, 2011), 52.
50. Spenser, *View of the State of Ireland,* 67.
51. Shagan, *Rule of Moderation,* 52.
52. Marenbon, *Pagans and Philosophers,* 294.
53. On Protestant concern over salvation, see Jacques Le Goff, *The Birth of Purgatory* (Chicago: University of Chicago Press, 1984); Peter Marshall, *Beliefs and the Dead in Reformation England* (Oxford: Oxford University Press, 2002); and David Stannard, *The Puritan Way of Death: A Study in Religion, Culture, and Social Change* (New York: Oxford University Press, 1977).
54. Sir Walter Ralegh, "Of the Voyage for Guiana," in Robert Schomburgk, ed., *The Discovery of the Large, Rich, and Beautiful Empire of Guiana . . . by Sir W. Ralegh* (n.d.; reprint, New York: Burt Franklin, 1970), 143, and Richard Hakluyt, "Discourse on Western Planting" (1584), in Jack P. Greene, ed., *Settlements to Society, 1607–1763: A Documentary History of Colonial America* (New York: W. W. Norton & Co., 1975), 7–8, both quoted in Jill Lepore, *The Name of War: King Philip's War and the Origins of American Identity* (New York: Vintage Books, 1999), 9. On English identity forged in triangulation see Lepore, *The Name of War;* on English versus French colonial practices and societies, see James Axtell, *The Invasion Within: The Contest of Cultures in Colonial North America* (New York: Oxford University Press, 1985).
55. On English respect for Native technologies, see Joyce Chaplin, *Subject Matter: Technology, the Body, and Science on the Anglo-American Frontier, 1500–1676* (Cambridge, MA: Harvard University Press, 2001).

56. Paul Hulton, "Introduction to the Dover Edition," in *A Briefe and True Report of the New Found Land of Virginia: The Complete 1690 Theodor de Bry Edition*, by Thomas Hariot (New York: Dover, 1972), viii.

57. Hariot, *Briefe and True Report*, 68, 66.

58. Hariot, 24, 27.

59. Hariot, 41, 75, 76.

60. On the trajectory from hopefulness to condemnation and violence, see Lepore, *Name of War*; Rebecca Goetz, *The Baptism of Early Virginia: How Christianity Created Race* (Baltimore: Johns Hopkins University Press, 2012); and Richard Bailey, *Race and Redemption in Puritan New England* (New York: Oxford University Press, 2011). For newer histories of King Philip's War that decenter Euro-Americans and are attentive to Native peoples' continued struggles for sovereignty in New England, see Christine DeLucia, *Memory Lands: King Philip's War and the Place of Violence in the Northeast* (New Haven, CT: Yale University Press, 2018); and Lisa Brooks, *Our Beloved Kin: A New History of King Philip's War* (New Haven, CT: Yale University Press, 2018). On colonists' views of Indigenous bodies, see Chaplin, *Subject Matter*; and Heather Miyano Kopelson, *Faithful Bodies: Performing Religion and Race in the Puritan Atlantic* (New York: New York University Press, 2014).

61. Edward Waterhouse, *A Declaration of the State of the Colony and Affaires in Virginia*, quoted in Goetz, *Baptism of Early Virginia*, 57–58.

62. Goetz, *Baptism of Early Virginia*, 58.

63. Todd Romero, *Making War and Minting Christians: Masculinity, Religion, and Colonialism in Early New England* (Amherst: University of Massachusetts Press, 2011), 18.

64. *An Act For the promoting and propagating the Gospel of Jesus Christ in New England. Die Veneris, 27 Julii, 1649. Ordered by the Commons assembled in Parliament, That this Act be forthwith printed and published. Hen: Scobell, Cleric. Parliament* (London: printed for Edward Husband, 1649), 407, 411–412.

65. *Strength out of Weaknesse; Or a Glorious Manifestation of the further Progresse of the Gospel among the Indians in New-England. Held forth in Sundry Letters from divers Ministers and others to the Corporation established by Parliament for promoting the Gospel among the Heathen in New-England; and to particular Members thereof since the last Treatise to that effect, formerly set forth by Mr Henry Whitfield late Pastor of Gilford in New-England. Published by the aforesaid Corporation* (London: printed by M. Simmons for John Blague and Samuel Howes, 1652), n.p. See Chapter 3 on the significance of this passage for nineteenth-century missions as well.

66. John Endecott, Boston, August 28, 1651, in *Strength out of Weaknesse*, 34.

67. See William Cronon, *Changes in the Land: Indians, Colonists, and the Ecology of New England* (New York: Hill and Wang, 1983).

68. Increase Mather, *A Brief History of the Warr with the Indians in New-England. (From June 24, 1675 when the first English-man was murdered by the Indians,*

to *August 12 1676 when Philip, alias Metacomet, the principal Author and Beginner of the Warr, was slain.) Wherein the Grounds, Beginning, and Progress of the Warr, is summarily expressed. Together with a Serious Exhortation to the Inhabitants of that Land* (Boston: printed and sold by John Foster, 1676), 29, 77, italics in original.

69. Linford D. Fisher, "'Why Shall Wee Have Peace to Bee Made Slaves': Indian Surrenderers during and after King Philip's War," *Ethnohistory* 64, no. 1 (2017): 91–114, esp. 92.

70. Neal Salisbury, introduction to *The Sovereignty and Goodness of God, together with the Faithfulness of His Promises Displayed: Being a Narrative of the Captivity and Restoration of Mrs. Mary Rowlandson and Related Documents,* by Mary Rowlandson (Boston: Bedford/St. Martin's, 1997), 48–49.

71. Rowlandson, *Sovereignty and Goodness of God,* 69, 70, 78, 80, 107.

72. Rowlandson, *Sovereignty and Goodness of God,* 94.

73. Rowlandson, 71, 89, 79, 107.

74. Cotton Mather, *India Christiana. A Discourse, Delivered unto the Commissioners, for the Propagation of the Gospel among the American Indians which is Accompanied with several instruments relating to the Glorious design of Propagating our Holy religion, in the eastern as well as the western, Indies. An Entertainment which they that are Waiting for the Kingdom of god will receive as Good News from a far Country. By Cotton Mather, D. D. and F. R. S.* (Boston: printed by B. Green, 1721), 28–29.

75. See, in particular, Goetz, *Baptism of Early Virginia;* see also Bailey, *Race and Redemption;* and Katharine Gerbner, *Christian Slavery: Conversion and Race in the Protestant Atlantic World* (Philadelphia: University of Pennsylvania Press, 2018).

76. Thomas Blake, *The Birth Priviledge, or Covenant-holinesse of Beleevers and their Issue* (London, 1644), and Increase Mather, *Pray for the Rising Generation: A Sermon Wherein Godly Parents are Encouraged to Pray and Believe for their Children* (Cambridge, 1678), both quoted in Goetz, *Baptism of Early Virginia,* 63.

77. Goetz notes that Christian universalism continued to operate against the notion of hereditary heathenism, especially when enslaved people took matters into their own hands (*Baptism of Early Virginia,* epilogue). She emphasizes "how hard colonial planters had to work to undermine the idea of potential Christianity and to construct hereditary heathenism" (173).

78. Here I draw on the definition of race in Sylvester Johnson, *African American Religions, 1500–2000: Colonialism, Democracy, and Freedom* (Cambridge: Cambridge University Press, 2015), as quoted in the Introduction.

2. Origin Stories

1. Nicholas Noyes, *New-Englands Duty and Interest, To be an Habitation of justice, and Mountain of holiness. Containing Doctrine, Caution & Comfort with Something relating to the restaurations, reformations and benedictions Promised to the Church and World in the latter dayes; With grounds of*

Hope, that America in General, & New-England in Particular, may have a Part therein. Preached to the General Assembly of the Province of the Massachusetts-Bay, at the Anniversary Election. May, 25. 1698. By Nicholas Noyes, Teacher of the Church at Salem. Published by Order of Authority (Boston: printed by Bartholomew Green, and John Allen, 1698), 69.

2. Noyes, 69–70, 74.
3. Noyes, 72–73.
4. On scientific racism as a secular reoccupation of Christian ideas, see Terence Keel, *Divine Variations: How Christian Thought Became Racial Science* (Stanford, CA: Stanford University Press, 2018).
5. This summary is drawn from Gary Okihiro, *Third World Studies: Theorizing Liberation* (Durham, NC: Duke University Press, 2016), chap. 3.
6. Brent Nongbri, *Before Religion: A History of a Modern Concept* (New Haven, CT: Yale University Press, 2013), 56–57.
7. Colin Kidd, *British Identities before Nationalism: Ethnicity and Nationhood in the Atlantic World, 1600–1800* (Cambridge: Cambridge University Press, 2004), 10. On the synchronization of multiple times into "the homogeneous, linear, and teleological time of progress," achieved over the eighteenth century through "universal histories, encyclopedias, novels, [and] world maps," see Helge Jordheim, "Introduction: Multiple Times and the Work of Synchronization," in "Forum: Multiple Temporalities," *History and Theory* 53, no. 4 (December 2014): 498–518, esp. 502, 514. See also Shahzad Bashir, "On Islamic Time: Rethinking Chronology in the Historiography of Muslim Societies," in "Forum: Multiple Temporalities," *History and Theory* 53, no. 4 (December 2014): 519–544, on the origins of and problems with a universal timeline. Bashir advocates paying more attention to "the role of human agency in creating 'time'" (521) and to consideration of multiple timelines instead of a single chronology.
8. Kidd, *British Identities before Nationalism,* 12.
9. Sylvester Johnson, *The Myth of Ham in Nineteenth-Century American Christianity: Race, Heathens, and the People of God* (New York: Palgrave Macmillan, 2004), esp. 4.
10. Colin Kidd, *The Forging of Races: Race and Scripture in the Protestant Atlantic World, 1600–2000* (Cambridge: Cambridge University Press, 2006), 35–36; Kidd, *British Identities before Nationalism,* 12–14.
11. Kidd, *British Identities before Nationalism,* 15.
12. José de Acosta, *Natural and Moral History of the Indies,* ed. Jane E. Mangan, trans. Frances M. López Morillas (Durham, NC: Duke University Press, 2002), 51.
13. Acosta, 71–72.
14. Acosta, 254, 256, 261.
15. Acosta, *De Procuranda* (1596), 108, quoted in Anthony Pagden, *The Fall of Natural Man: The American Indian and the Origins of Comparative Ethnology* (Cambridge: Cambridge University Press, 1982), 164. See also Pagden chap. 7, "A Programme for Comparative Ethnology (2)—Jose de Acosta."

16. Acosta, *Natural and Moral History*, 254–256.

17. Acosta, 300, 306.

18. On the four-stages theory, see Roxann Wheeler, *The Complexion of Race: Categories of Difference in Eighteenth-Century British Culture* (Philadelphia: University of Pennsylvania Press, 2000), 35.

19. Kidd, *British Identities before Nationalism*, 16; Kidd, *Forging of Races*, 62.

20. Matthew Binney, "Joseph-François Lafitau's *Customs of American Indians* and Edmund Burke: Historical Process and Cultural Difference," *Clio* 41, no. 3 (2012): 311.

21. Joseph François Lafitau, *Customs of the American Indians Compared with the Customs of Primitive Times*, Vol. I, ed. and trans. William N. Fenton and Elizabeth L. Moore (Toronto: The Champlain Society, 1974), 26.

22. David Allen Harvey, "Living Antiquity: Lafitau's *Moeurs des sauvages américains* and the Religious Roots of the Enlightenment Science of Man," *Journal of the Western Society for French History* 36 (2008): 75–92, esp. 85.

23. Acosta, *Natural and Moral History*, 71; Lafitau, *Customs*, 79–80.

24. Lafitau, *Customs*, 42, 34, 47. See also Binney, "Joseph-François Lafitau's *Customs*," 313–314.

25. Lafitau, *Customs*, 35. For an analysis of Lafitau's comparative or "analogical approach" in *Moeurs*, particularly his idea of the "conformity" of Indigenous religions with pagan antiquity, see Mary Helen McMurran, "Rethinking Superstition: Pagan Ritual in Lafitau's *Moeurs des sauvages*," in *Mind, Body, Motion, Matter: Eighteenth-Century British and French Literary Perspectives*, ed. Mary Helen McMurran and Alison Conway (Toronto: University of Toronto Press, 2016), esp. 118–119, 120–121, 128.

26. Lafitau, dedication, in *Customs*, 3–4.

27. Lafitau, *Customs*, 28.

28. Lynn Hunt, Margaret C. Jacob, and Wijnand Mijnhardt, *The Book That Changed Europe: Picart and Bernard's Religious Ceremonies of the World* (Cambridge, MA: Belknap Press of Harvard University Press, 2010), 10.

29. Lafitau, *Customs*, 29.

30. Lafitau, 81–84.

31. Lafitau, "Explanation of the Plates and Figures in Volume I," in *Customs*, 7.

32. Winthrop Jordan, *The White Man's Burden: Historical Origins of Racism in the United States* (New York: Oxford University Press, 1974), 8–9.

33. Lafitau, *Customs*, 89, 44.

34. Hunt, Jacob, and Mijnhardt, *Book That Changed Europe*, 7, 9.

35. See Jonathan Sheehan, review of *Bernard Picart and the First Global Vision of Religion*, ed. Lynn Hunt, Margaret Jacob, and Wijnand Mijnhardt (Los Angeles: Getty Research Institute, 2010) and Hunt, Jacob, and Mijnhardt, *Book That Changed Europe*, in *The Journal of Modern History* Vol. 83 No. 4 (December 2011): 897–901, esp. 900. Hunt, Jacob, and Mijnhardt speak to the tolerance and open-mindedness of Bernard and Picart; various essays in *Bernard Picart and the First Global Vision of Religion* contest that view.

36. Hunt, Jacob, and Mijnhardt, *Book That Changed Europe*, 11.

37. Jean Frédéric Bernard and Bernard Picart, *The Ceremonies and Religious Customs of the Various Nations of the Known World, Together with Historical Annotations, and several Curious Discourses Equally Instructive and Entertaining,* vol. 1, *Containing the Ceremonies of the Jews, and the Roman Catholicks. Written originally in French, and illustrated with a large Number of Folio Copper Plates, all beautifully Designed By Mr. Bernard Picart, And curiously Engraved by most of the Best Hands in Europe. Faithfully translated into English, by a Gentleman, some Time since of St. John's College in Oxford* (London: printed by William Jackson, for Claude Du Bosc, 1733), 2.

38. Bernard and Picart, 2, 7, 3, 4, 5.

39. Bernard and Picart, 20, 24.

40. Hunt, Jacob, and Mijnhardt, *Book That Changed Europe,* 10–11.

41. Caption translation in Hunt, Jacob, and Mijnhardt, *Book That Changed Europe,* 13, emphases in original.

42. Caption translation in Hunt, Jacob, and Mijnhardt, 13, emphases in original.

43. On the Protestantization of the populace see Jon Butler, *Awash in a Sea of Faith: Christianizing the American People* (Cambridge, MA: Harvard University Press, 1990).

44. Charles Goodrich, *Religious Ceremonies and Customs, or, The Forms of Worship Practised by the Several Nations of the Known World, from the Earliest Records to the Present Time. On the Basis of the Celebrated and Splendid Work of Bernard Picart. To which Is Added, a Brief View of Minor Sects, which Exist at the Present Day; Designed Especially for the Use of Families; not only as Entertaining and Instructive, but of Great Importance as a Work of Reference. By Charles A. Goodrich. Accompanied with a large map of the world, and embellished with elegant engravings* (Hartford, CT: published by Hutchison and Dwier, 1834), 15.

45. David Hume, *The Natural History of Religion* (1757), 1.1, in *A Dissertation on the Passions; The Natural History of Religion: A Critical Edition,* ed. T. L. Beauchamp (Oxford: Clarendon, 2007).

46. Paul Russell and Anders Kraal, "Hume on Religion," in *The Stanford Encyclopedia of Philosophy,* Summer 2017 ed., ed. Edward N. Zalta, https://plato .stanford.edu/archives/sum2017/entries/hume-religion/.

47. Hume, *Natural History of Religion,* 15.5.

48. Thomas Paine, *Common Sense,* in *Political Works of Thomas Paine* (Springfield, MA: Peter Raynolds, 1826), 147–148.

49. Thomas Paine, *The Age of Reason* (1794; repr., Holyoake, 1864), 3.

50. See Amanda Porterfield, *Conceived in Doubt: Religion and Politics in the New American Nation* (Chicago: University of Chicago Press, 2012).

51. See Caroline Winterer, *American Enlightenments: Pursuing Happiness in the Age of Reason* (New Haven, CT: Yale University Press, 2016), chap. 6, "Religion in the Age of Reason."

52. Frank E. Manuel, *The Eighteenth Century Confronts the Gods* (New York: Atheneum, 1967), 3. See also Caroline Winterer, *The Culture of Classicism: Ancient Greece and Rome in American Intellectual Life, 1780–1910* (Baltimore: Johns Hopkins University Press, 2002) and *The Mirror of Antiquity:*

American Women and the Classical Tradition, 1750–1900 (Ithaca, NY: Cornell University Press, 2007).

53. "Of the Law of Nature, and State of the Heathen," *London Magazine: or, Gentleman's Monthly Intelligencer,* November 1732.

54. Y. Z., "Heathen Virtues Condemned by the Church Articles," *London Magazine: or, Gentleman's Monthly Intelligencer,* July 1772.

55. Winterer, *American Enlightenments,* chap. 6.

56. Quoted in Winterer, *Culture of Classicism,* 15.

57. Gerald McDermott, *Jonathan Edwards Confronts the Gods: Christian Theology, Enlightenment Religion, and Non-Christian Faiths* (New York: Oxford University Press, 2000), 93–95.

58. McDermott, 108, 133. See also Rachel Wheeler, "Friends to Your Souls: Jonathan Edwards' Indian Pastorate and the Doctrine of Original Sin," *Church History* 72, no. 4 (December 2003): 736–765. Wheeler shows how the idea of original sin could have an "egalitarian" effect when preached to Native audiences, as Edwards assured his Stockbridge congregation that "we are no better than you" (737).

59. See Kathryn Gin Lum, *Damned Nation: Hell in America from the Revolution to Reconstruction* (New York: Oxford University Press, 2014), esp. chap 1; and Porterfield, *Conceived in Doubt.*

60. Thomas Tweed, "An American Pioneer in the Study of Religion: Hannah Adams (1755–1831) and Her 'Dictionary of All Religions,'" *Journal of the American Academy of Religion* 60, no. 3 (Autumn 1992): 437–464, esp. 442.

61. Hannah Adams, *A Memoir of Miss Hannah Adams, Written by Herself, with Additional Notices by a Friend* (Boston: Gray and Bowen, 1832), 3, 4.

62. Adams, 8, 10, 11.

63. Hannah Adams, *A Dictionary of All Religions and Religious Denominations, Jewish, Heathen, Mahometan, and Christian, Ancient and Modern. With an Appendix, containing a sketch of the present state of the world, as to population, religion, toleration, missions, etc. and the articles in which all christian denominations agree. Fourth edition, with corrections and large additions* (New York: James Eastburn, 1817), "Advertisement" and "Preface," n.p.

64. Tweed, "American Pioneer," 437. Gary Schmidt, in *A Passionate Usefulness: The Life and Literary Labors of Hannah Adams* (Charlottesville: University of Virginia Press, 2004), also views Adams's work as more than just compilation, but compilation with a point of view rooted in a rationalist understanding of religion.

65. Adams, *Memoir,* 14–15, 43.

66. Adams, 28.

67. See Chapter 8 of this book on Lydia Maria Child's and James Freeman Clarke's abnegation of the term.

68. Adams, *Dictionary,* 104, 213.

69. Adams, 213.

70. Adams, 225.

71. Adams, 6–7, 8–9, 11.

72. Adams, 55, 107. On Adams's treatment of "Gentoo" and then "Hindoo" religion see Michael J. Altman, *Heathen, Hindoo, Hindu: American Representations of India, 1721–1893* (New York: Oxford University Press, 2017), 11–21.

73. Adams, *Dictionary*, 195–198.

74. Benjamin Tucker Tanner, *The Descent of the Negro* (1898), quoted in Johnson, *Myth of Ham*, 8.

75. See Johnson, *Myth of Ham*, esp. chap. 3, "Ham, History, and the Problem of Illegitimacy."

76. Adams, *Dictionary*, 138–142.

77. Elias Boudinot, *A Star in the West; or, a Humble Attempt to Discover the Long Lost Ten Tribes of Israel, Preparatory to Their Return to Their Beloved City, Jerusalem* (Trenton, NJ: D. Fenton, S. Hutchinson, and J. Dunham, 1816), iii, 68–74.

78. Adams, *Dictionary*, 138–139.

79. Adams, 11.

80. Tomoko Masuzawa has shown how the vaunted rise of world religions still masked a residual European universalism. See Masuzawa, *The Invention of World Religions: Or, How European Universalism Was Preserved in the Language of Pluralism* (Chicago: University of Chicago Press, 2005). See also Nongbri, *Before Religion*; and Jonathan Z. Smith, "Religion, Religions, Religious," in *Critical Terms for Religious Studies*, ed. Mark C. Taylor (Chicago: University of Chicago Press, 1998), 269–284.

81. Benjamin Wisner, *The Moral Condition and Prospects of the Heathen: A Sermon, Delivered at the Old South Church in Boston, before the Foreign Mission Society of Boston and the Vicinity, at Their Annual Meeting, Jan. 1, 1824* (Boston: printed by Crocker and Brewster, 1824), 33.

82. Wisner, 34.

3. Landscapes

1. Thomas Smith Grimké, *Address on the Power and Value of the Sunday School System in Evangelizing Heathen and Re-constructing Christian Communitys, by an Improvement of the Religion and Morals, the Education and Literature, and the Social, Civil, and Political Institutions of Evry [sic] People: and on the Southern Enterprise of the American Sunday School Union. Delivered in the Lutheran Church, City of Charleston, on Monday Evening, March 17, 1834, by Thomas Smith Grimké* (Philadelphia, 1834), 6.

2. Grimké, 7–8.

3. Grimké, 8.

4. "HEATHEN," in *Fessenden & Co.'s Encyclopedia of Religious Knowledge*, ed. John Newton Brown (Brattleboro, VT: Fessenden, 1836), 604.

5. Isaiah 35, King James Version.

6. Isaiah 34, King James Version.

7. See David Paul Nord, *Faith in Reading: Religious Publishing and the Birth of Mass Media in America* (New York: Oxford University Press, 2004); and Candy Gunther Brown, *The Word in the World: Evangelical Writing, Publishing, and*

Reading in America, 1789–1880 (Chapel Hill: University of North Carolina Press, 2004). "Protestant" is of course a blanket term encompassing multiple denominations and affiliations, but for the most part this chapter's purpose is not to parse denominational differences but rather to survey the global outlook with which the ecumenical ABCFM and likeminded organizations blanketed the nation's readers.

8. Amy DeRogatis shows how home missionaries made similar assumptions about how orderly landscapes, preferably mapped onto a grid, reflected the state of White inhabitants on the frontier. DeRogatis, *Moral Geography: Maps, Missionaries, and the American Frontier* (New York: Columbia University Press, 2003).

9. Willie James Jennings, *The Christian Imagination: Theology and the Origins of Race* (New Haven, CT: Yale University Press, 2011), 24, 39.

10. Jennings, 43.

11. Pope Alexander VI, "Demarcation Bull Granting Spain Possession of Lands Discovered by Columbus," Rome, May 4, 1493, Gilder Lehrman Collection, https://www.gilderlehrman.org/sites/default/files/inline-pdfs/T-04093.pdf.

12. Johnson & Graham's Lessee v. M'Intosh, 21 U.S. 543, 576–577 (1823).

13. Steven T. Newcomb, *Pagans in the Promised Land: Decoding the Doctrine of Christian Discovery* (Golden, CO: Fulcrum, 2008), xxv.

14. Winnifred Fallers Sullivan, "Comments on *Johnson v M'Intosh*," in "Theologies of American Exceptionalism: Marshall and Morgan," Immanent Frame, February 17, 2017, https://tif.ssrc.org/2017/02/17/marshall-and-morgan/.

15. See Martin Brückner, *The Geographic Revolution in Early America: Maps, Literacy, and National Identity* (Chapel Hill: published for the Omohundro Institute of Early American History and Culture by the University of North Carolina Press, 2006).

16. Elizabeth Noble Shor, "Jedidiah Morse," in *American National Biography Online* (New York: Oxford University Press, 1999 [print], 2000 [online]), http://www.anb.org/articles/13/13-01182.html?a=1&n=jedidiah%20morse&d=10&ss=0&q=1.

17. Jedidiah Morse, *The American Universal Geography: or a View of the Present State of All the Empires, Kingdoms, States and Republicks in the Known World, and of the United States of America in Particular. In Two Parts. Part First. Fifth Edition Corrected and Improved* (Boston: printed by J. T. Buckingham for Thomas and Andrews, 1805), 9–10.

18. On climate theory, particularly in the eighteenth century, see Roxann Wheeler, *The Complexion of Race: Categories of Difference in Eighteenth-Century British Culture* (Philadelphia: University of Pennsylvania Press, 2000), esp. 21–28.

19. Morse, *American Universal Geography*, 13–14.

20. Morse, 14–15.

21. Jedidiah Morse, *A Sermon, Delivered Before the American Board of Commissioners for Foreign Missions, at Their Annual Meeting in Springfield, Massachusetts, September 19, 1821* (Boston: printed for the Board of Commissioners by George Clark, 1821), 6, 3, 4.

22. Morse, 5, 6.

23. Morse, 24, 25, 26.

24. On how missionaries attempted "cultural genocide," see also Jennifer Graber, *The Gods of Indian Country: Religion and the Struggle for the American West* (New York: Oxford University Press, 2018).

25. On Hawaiians' experience of missionary incursions in the broader context of Hawaiian unification and the codification of oral law into writing, see Noelani Arista, *The Kingdom and the Republic: Sovereign Hawai'i and the United States* (Philadelphia: University of Pennsylvania Press, 2019).

26. On 'Ōpūkaha'ia, see David A. Chang, *The World and All the Things upon It: Native Hawaiian Geographies of Exploration* (Minneapolis: University of Minnesota Press, 2016), 82–92; on missionaries desacralizing the Hawaiian landscape, see Chang, 204–208.

27. Hiram Bingham, *A Residence of Twenty-One Years in the Sandwich Islands* (Hartford, CT: Hezekiah Huntington, 1848), 94.

28. Bingham, 98. On the significance of gifts as a language communicating relative status to both recipients and other onlookers, see Chang, *World*, 74.

29. Bingham, *Residence of Twenty-One Years*, 115–116.

30. *The Heathen Nations: Or, Duty of the Present Generation to Evangelize the World. By the Missionaries at the Sandwich Islands*, 3rd ed. (Oberlin, OH: James M. Fitch, 1849), 34–38.

31. Titus Coan, *Life in Hawaii: An Autobiographic Sketch of Mission Life and Labors (1835–1881)* (New York: Anson D. F. Randolph, 1882), 255.

32. "Hale Pa'i / Printing Museum: House of Printing First Hawaiian Language Newspaper," Lahaina Restoration Foundation, accessed August 2017, http://lahainarestoration.org/hale-pai-museum/.

33. David W. Forbes, *Engraved at Lahainaluna: A History of Printmaking by Hawaiians at the Lahainaluna Seminary, 1834 to 1844 with a Descriptive Catalogue of All Known Views, Maps, and Portraits* (Honolulu: Hawaiian Mission Children's Society, 2012), 108.

34. On the idyllic New England village as a nineteenth-century creation, see Joseph Wood, *The New England Village* (Baltimore: Johns Hopkins University Press, 1997). I am grateful to Douglas Winiarski for alerting me to this source and to Barber's sketch of Cornwall.

35. See John Demos, *The Heathen School: A Story of Hope and Betrayal in the Age of the Early Republic* (New York: Alfred A. Knopf, 2014); and Chang's critique in *World*, 83.

36. *Pacific Commercial Advertiser* (1866), quoted in Ronald Williams Jr., "Peerless and Alone," *Hana Hou!* 15, no. 3 (June / July 2012), https://hanahou.com /15.3/peerless-and-alone.

37. Chang, *World*, 209–212.

38. Lilikala Kame'eleihiwa, introduction to *Ruling Chiefs of Hawaii*, by Samuel M. Kamakau, rev. ed. (1961; Honolulu: Kamehameha Schools Press, 1992), iv.

39. Samuel Kamakau, *The Works of the People of Old* (1869–1870; Honolulu: Bishop Museum Press, 2006), 23.

40. Hokulani Aikau, *A Chosen People, a Promised Land: Mormonism and Race in Hawai'i* (Minneapolis: University of Minnesota Press, 2012), 58.

41. On how Hawaiians also identified themselves as cultivators in contrast to Native Americans, who were presented in Hawaiian textbooks as hunters and wanderers, see Chang, *World*, 229–236.
42. Kamakau, *Works of the People*, 29–30.
43. Kepelino, *Kepelino's Traditions of Hawaii* (1868; Honolulu: Bishop Museum Press, 2007), 154.
44. American Sunday-School Union, *The Gospel among the Bechuanas, and other Tribes of Southern Africa. Prepared for the American Sunday-School Union, and Revised by the Committee of Publication* (Philadelphia: American Sunday-School Union, 1846), 23–24, 27.
45. American Sunday-School Union, 126; 116–117.
46. American Sunday-School Union, 126–127.
47. Emma Pitman, *Heroines of the Mission Field. Biographical Sketches of Female Missionaries Who Have Laboured in Various Lands among the Heathen* (New York: Anson D. F. Randolph, [1880?]), 58, 55–56, italics in original.
48. Ephraim Bacon, *Abstract of a Journal of E. Bacon, Assistant Agent of the United States, to Africa: with an Appendix, containing interesting accounts of the effects of the Gospel among the Native Africans. With Cuts, showing a contrast between two Native towns, One of which is Christianized and the other Heathen. Second Edition. Published for the Benefit of Africa* (Philadelphia: Clark and Raser, printers, 1822).
49. Bacon, 37.
50. Bacon, 38–39.
51. Bacon, 39–40.
52. Bacon, 42.
53. Morse, *American Universal Geography*, 381.
54. Morse, 416, 419.
55. Morse, 432.
56. Charles Lloyd, *Travels at Home, and Voyages by the Fire-Side, for the Instruction and Entertainment of Young Persons*, vol. 1, *Europe and Asia* (Philadelphia: Edward Earle, T. and G. Palmer, printers, 1816), xiii, xv.
57. Lloyd, 39, 61, 58–59.
58. Lloyd, 58–59, 60.
59. See Michael J. Altman, *Heathen, Hindoo, Hindu: American Representations of India, 1721–1893* (New York: Oxford University Press, 2017).
60. Lloyd, *Travels at Home*, 8.
61. Lloyd, 9.
62. "Rude Farming," *Child's World* 2, no. 9 (May 9, 1863): 3.
63. Kathleen A. Brosnan and Jacob Blackwell, "Agriculture, Food, and the Environment," in *Oxford Research Encyclopedia of American History Online*, April 2016, http://americanhistory.oxfordre.com/view/10.1093/acrefore/9780199329175.001.0001/acrefore-9780199329175-e-179.
64. On machines as a sign of civilizational development (or lack thereof), see Michael Adas, *Machines as the Measure of Men: Science, Technology, and Ideologies of Western Dominance* (Ithaca, NY: Cornell University Press, 1989).

65. See DeRogatis, *Moral Geography;* and Laurie Maffly-Kipp, *Religion and Society in Frontier California* (New Haven, CT: Yale University Press, 1994).
66. Aikau, *Chosen People,* 59–60.
67. Coan, *Life in Hawaii,* 124.
68. Sarah Lyman, Hilo, to Sister M., February 5, 1852 [written by her husband], Sarah Joiner Lyman Letters, Hawaiian Mission Children's Society Library, Hawaiian Mission Houses Historic Sites and Archives, Honolulu.
69. Sarah Lyman, Hilo, to Sister Melissa, June 13, 1851, Sarah Joiner Lyman Letters.
70. Coan, *Life in Hawaii,* 234–235.
71. Coan, 123.
72. Seth Archer, "Remedial Agents: Missionary Physicians and the Depopulation of Hawaii," *Pacific Historical Review* 79, no. 4 (November 2010): 516.
73. Kepelino, *Kepelino's Traditions of Hawaii,* 150.

4. Bodies

1. Lyman Beecher, *The Bible a Code of Laws. A Sermon, Delivered in Park Street Church, Boston, September 3, 1817, at the Ordination of Mr. Sereno Edwards Dwight, as Pastor of that Church; and of Messrs. Elisha P. Swift, Allen Graves, John Nichols, Levi Parsons, & Daniel Buttrick, As Missionaries to the Heathen. By Lyman Beecher, A. M. Pastor of a Church of Christ in Litchfield, Conn.* (Andover, MA: Mark Newman, 1827), 40.
2. Beecher, 41.
3. Beecher, 41.
4. For the continued significance of the notion of monogenesis, see Colin Kidd, *The Forging of Races: Race and Scripture in the Protestant Atlantic World, 1600–2000* (Cambridge: Cambridge University Press, 2006).
5. Beecher, *Bible a Code,* 42.
6. Benjamin Wisner, *The Moral Condition and Prospects of the Heathen: A Sermon, Delivered at the Old South Church in Boston, before the Foreign Mission Society of Boston and the Vicinity, at Their Annual Meeting, Jan. 1, 1824* (Boston: printed by Crocker and Brewster, 1824), 16, 17, 26.
7. Wisner, 26, 34.
8. *What Will Become of the Baby? With Three Other Stories about Children in Heathen Lands* (New York: Carlton and Porter for the Sunday School Union, [1855?]), 8–9. Italics in original.
9. *Aunt Margaret's Twelve Stories, to Illustrate and Impress Important Truths* (1856; Philadelphia: American Sunday-School Union, 1893), 63.
10. Charles S. Stewart, *Private Journal of a Voyage to the Pacific Ocean, and Residence at the Sandwich Islands, in the Years 1822, 1823, 1824, and 1825* (New York: John P. Haven, 1828), 251. Italics in original.
11. Stewart, 251–252.
12. Stewart, 253.
13. Introduction to "Betsey Stockton's Journal," in *African-American Religion: A Historical Interpretation with Representative Documents,* ed. David W. Wills

and Albert J. Raboteau (Chicago: University of Chicago Press, 2006), excerpted at African-American Religion: A Documentary History Project, accessed July 2, 2020, https://aardoc.sites.amherst.edu/Betsey_Stockton_Journal_1.html.

14. Betsey Stockton, journal entry, April 4, 1823, in "Betsey Stockton's Journal," Wills and Raboteau, *African-American Religion,* https://aardoc.sites.amherst.edu/Betsey_Stockton_Journal_1.html.

15. See Gregory Nobles, "Betsey Stockton," Princeton and Slavery, accessed July 2, 2020, https://slavery.princeton.edu/stories/betsey-stockton.

16. Emma Pitman, *Heroines of the Mission Field. Biographical Sketches of Female Missionaries Who Have Laboured in Various Lands among the Heathen* (New York: Anson D. F. Randolph, [1880?]), 21–22.

17. *Condition and Character of Females in Pagan and Mohammedan Countries* (New York: American Tract Society, 183[?]), 1, 4, 15.

18. Ussama Makdisi, *Artillery of Heaven: American Missionaries and the Failed Conversion of the Middle East* (Ithaca, NY: Cornell University Press, 2008), 65.

19. American Board of Commissioners for Foreign Missions, minutes of Prudential Committee, September 24, 1818, American Board Archives, Congregational House, Boston, quoted in Makdisi, *Artillery of Heaven,* 65.

20. Makdisi, *Artillery of Heaven,* 64.

21. *Condition and Character,* 16, 7.

22. *Condition and Character,* 8.

23. *Condition and Character,* 15, 16.

24. *What Will Become of the Baby?,* 10.

25. Rufus Anderson, *The Theory of Missions to the Heathen. A Sermon at the Ordination of Mr. Edward Webb, as a Missionary to the Heathen. Ware, Mass., Oct. 23, 1845* (Boston: Crocker and Brewster, 1845), 12.

26. *Condition and Character,* 4.

27. Ross C. Houghton, *Women of the Orient: An Account of the Religious, Intellectual, and Social Condition of Women in Japan, China, India, Egypt, Syria, and Turkey* (Cincinnati: Walden and Stowe, 1877), 415.

28. See Karen Halttunen, *Confidence Men and Painted Women: A Study of Middle-Class Culture in America, 1830–1870* (New Haven, CT: Yale University Press, 1982).

29. *Condition and Character,* 12–13, emphasis in original.

30. Quoted in Houghton, *Women of the Orient,* 414.

31. *What Will Become of the Baby?,* 13.

32. *What Will Become of the Baby?,* 13.

33. "The Heathen," in *Aunt Margaret's Twelve Stories,* 61.

34. *What Will Become of the Baby?,* 13, 11.

35. American Sunday-School Union, *The Gospel among the Bechuanas, and other Tribes of Southern Africa. Prepared for the American Sunday-School Union, and Revised by the Committee of Publication* (Philadelphia: American Sunday-School Union, 1846), 73, 81, 87.

36. On Anderson's view, see Paul William Harris, *Nothing but Christ: Rufus Anderson and the Ideology of Protestant Foreign Missions* (New York: Oxford University Press, 2000).

37. Richard Marley, *Medical Missionaries; Or, Medical Agency Cooperative with Christian Missions to the Heathen* (London: James Blackwood, 1860), 20, 22.
38. Daniel Macgowan, *Claims of the Missionary Enterprise on the Medical Profession: An Address Delivered before the Temperance Society of the College of Physicians and Surgeons of the University of the State of New-York, October 28, 1842* (New York: printed by William Osborn, 1842), 5, 10.
39. Macgowan, 11–12.
40. Macgowan, 12, 10.
41. Macgowan, 10–11.
42. Kate C. Bushnell, "Competing with an Idol," *Heathen Woman's Friend* 13, no. 5 (November 1881): 102–103.
43. Bushnell: 103.
44. Bushnell: 103–104.
45. *What Will Become of the Baby?*, 13.
46. *What Will Become of the Baby?*, 14–15.
47. Joseph Witherspoon Cook, "Death of Francis Deloria, a Yankton Chief," in *The Church and the Indians* (New York: Office of the Indian Commission, Protestant Episcopal Church, October 1876), 4, Charlotte Everett Webster [Cook] Scrapbook 1863–1961, Box 3, Folder 40, Joseph Witherspoon Cook Papers, Collection of Samuel Derrick Webster, 1771–1966, Huntington Library.
48. Cook, 4.
49. Cook, 1.
50. Vine Deloria Jr., *Singing for a Spirit: A Portrait of the Dakota Sioux* (Santa Fe, 2000), 35–36, quoted in Jeffrey Ostler, *The Plains Sioux and U.S. Colonialism from Lewis and Clark to Wounded Knee* (Cambridge: Cambridge University Press, 2004), 190.
51. Ostler, *Plains Sioux*, 189–190.
52. Deloria, Jr., *Singing for a Spirit*, 35–36.
53. Ostler, *Plains Sioux*, 190.
54. Rufus Anderson, *Memoir of Catharine Brown, a Christian Indian of the Cherokee Nation* (Boston: Crocker and Brewster, 1825), 123–124. See also Julius Rubin's *Perishing Heathens: Stories of Protestant Missionaries and Christian Indians in Antebellum America* (Lincoln: University of Nebraska Press, 2017), esp. chap. 5, which focuses on Catharine Brown. Rubin psychologizes missionaries as a melancholy and idealistic lot, focusing on the shared evangelical worldview that developed between them and Native converts, and devoting less attention to White chauvinism and Native resistance.
55. Anderson, *Memoir of Catharine Brown*, 28–30, 83.
56. William Taylor, *Story of My Life. An Account of what I have thought and said and done in my ministry of more than fifty-three years in Christian lands and among the heathen* (New York: Hunt and Eaton, 1896), 402–403.
57. Stewart, *Private Journal*, 246–248.
58. Titus Coan, *Life in Hawaii: An Autobiographic Sketch of Mission Life and Labors (1835–1881)* (New York: Anson D. F. Randolph, 1882), 255.
59. Stewart, *Private Journal*, 247.
60. Pitman, *Heroines of the Mission Field*, 54–55.

Part II. The Body Politic

1. Richard H. Drummond, "Uchimura, Kanzō (1861–1930)," in *Biographical Dictionary of Christian Missions,* ed. Gerald H. Anderson (New York: Macmillan Reference USA, 1998), 687, http://www.bu.edu/missiology/missionary-biography/t-u-v/uchimura-kanzo-1861-1930/.
2. Uchimura Kanzō, *The Diary of a Japanese Convert* (New York: Fleming H. Revell, 1895), front matter "Note," n.p.
3. On the complexities of conversion, including an Indigenous understanding of conversion as "affiliation," see Linford Fisher, *The Indian Great Awakening: Religion and the Shaping of Native Cultures in Early America* (New York: Oxford University Press, 2012); see also David A. Chang, *The World and All the Things upon It: Native Hawaiian Geographies of Exploration* (Minneapolis: University of Minnesota Press, 2016), on Native Hawaiian reasons for affiliation with Christianity.
4. Uchimura, *Diary,* 9, 5–6, 11–12.
5. Uchimura, 13, 15.
6. Uchimura, 20–21, 16–17, 24–25.
7. Uchimura, 117, 102, 146–147.
8. Uchimura, 149, 148.
9. Uchimura, chap. 6, "The First Impressions of Christendom," esp. 114–115, 107.

5. Barometer

1. Uchimura Kanzō, *The Diary of a Japanese Convert* (New York: Fleming H. Revell, 1895), 107–108.
2. David Walker, *Walker's Appeal, in Four Articles: Together with a Preamble, to the Coloured Citizens of the World, but in Particular, and Very Expressly, to Those of the United States of America, Written in Boston, State of Massachusetts, September 28, 1829* (Boston: David Walker, 1830), title page verso image, 3.
3. "Black laws of Louisiana," passed on March 16–17, 1830, quoted in "Stuart's Three Years in North America," *Eclectic Review,* 3rd ser., 9 (January–June 1833): 255.0.
4. "David Walker, the Black Harriet Beecher Stowe," New England Historical Society, updated 2021, https://www.newenglandhistoricalsociety.com/david-walker-the-black-harriet-beecher-stowe/.
5. On the use of the "perishing soul trope" in proslavery and abolitionist arguments, see Kathryn Gin Lum, *Damned Nation: Hell in America from the Revolution to Reconstruction* (New York: Oxford University Press, 2014), chap. 5.
6. See Rebecca Goetz, *The Baptism of Early Virginia: How Christianity Created Race* (Baltimore: Johns Hopkins University Press, 2012); Katharine Gerbner, *Christian Slavery: Conversion and Race in the Protestant Atlantic World* (Philadelphia: University of Pennsylvania Press, 2018); and Travis Glasson, *Mastering Christianity: Missionary Anglicanism and Slavery in the Atlantic World* (New York: Oxford University Press, 2012).

7. On proslavery Christianity, in addition to Goetz, Glasson, and Gerbner, see Charles Irons, *The Origins of Proslavery Christianity: White and Black Evangelicals in Colonial and Antebellum Virginia* (Chapel Hill: University of North Carolina Press 2008); and Elizabeth Fox-Genovese and Eugene Genovese, *The Mind of the Master Class: History and Faith in the Southern Slaveholders' Worldview* (Cambridge: Cambridge University Press, 2005).

8. Bryan LaPointe, "A Southern Family at Princeton College," Princeton and Slavery Project, accessed February 20, 2021, https://slavery.princeton.edu /stories/a-southern-family-at-princeton-college. For more on Jones, see also Erskine Clark, *Dwelling Place: A Plantation Epic* (New Haven, CT: Yale University Press, 2005).

9. Charles Colcock Jones, *The Religious Instruction of the Negroes* (Savannah: Thomas Purse, 1842), 100, 153, emphasis in original.

10. Jones, 125, 127–128, 134, 153.

11. Jones, 163, 165.

12. Jones, 165, emphasis in original.

13. Benjamin Wisner, *The Moral Condition and Prospects of the Heathen: A Sermon, Delivered at the Old South Church in Boston, before the Foreign Mission Society of Boston and the Vicinity, at Their Annual Meeting, Jan. 1, 1824* (Boston: printed by Crocker and Brewster, 1824), 36.

14. Jones, 165–167.

15. Henry Highland Garnet, "Garnet's Address to the Slaves of the United States of America," in *Walker's Appeal, with a Brief Sketch of His Life. By Henry Highland Garnet. And also Garnet's Address to the Slaves of the United States of America* (New-York: Printed by J. H. Tobitt, 1848), 93.

16. Garnet, 93.

17. Joel Schor, "The Rivalry between Frederick Douglass and Henry Highland Garnet," *Journal of Negro History* 64, no. 1 (Winter 1979): 30–38.

18. Frederick Douglass, *Narrative of the Life of Frederick Douglass, an American Slave, Written by Himself* (Boston: Anti-slavery Office, 1845), 119, 122.

19. On African American religion after emancipation, see, for example, Nicole Myers Turner, *Soul Liberty: The Evolution of Black Religious Politics in Postemancipation Virginia* (Chapel Hill: University of North Carolina Press, 2020); Elizabeth Jemison, *Christian Citizens: Reading the Bible in Black and White in the Postemancipation South* (Chapel Hill: University of North Carolina Press, 2020); Kathryn Gin, "'The Heavenization of Earth': African American Visions and Uses of the Afterlife, 1863–1901," *Slavery and Abolition* 31, no. 2 (June 2010): 207–231; Edward J. Blum and W. Scott Poole, eds., *Vale of Tears: New Essays on Religion and Reconstruction* (Macon, GA: Mercer University Press, 2005); Paul Harvey, *Redeeming the South: Religious Cultures and Racial Identities among Southern Baptists, 1865–1925* (Chapel Hill: University of North Carolina Press, 1997); Evelyn Brooks Higginbotham, *Righteous Discontent: The Women's Movement in the Black Baptist Church, 1880–1920* (Cambridge, MA: Harvard University Press, 1993); William E. Montgomery, *Under Their Own Vine and Fig Tree: The African-American Church in the South, 1865–1900* (Baton Rouge: Louisiana State

University Press, 1993); and Stephen W. Angell, *Bishop Henry McNeal Turner and African-American Religion in the South* (Knoxville: University of Tennessee Press, 1992). On African American missions to Africa, see James T. Campbell, *Middle Passages: African American Journeys to Africa, 1787–2005* (New York: Penguin, 2006).

20. Sylvester Johnson, *The Myth of Ham in Nineteenth-Century American Christianity: Race, Heathens, and the People of God* (New York: Palgrave Macmillan, 2004), 75. See also Timothy Fulop, "'The Future Golden Day of the Race': Millennialism and Black Americans in the Nadir, 1877–1901," *Harvard Theological Review* 84, no. 1 (1991): 75–99.

21. On how this freedom-oriented view of African American religions is grounded in Christian settler colonialism, see Sylvester Johnson, *African American Religions, 1500–2000: Colonialism, Democracy, and Freedom* (Cambridge: Cambridge University Press, 2015), esp. Chapter 4, "Stateless Bodies, African Missions, and the Black Christian Settler Colony."

22. Daniel Alexander Payne, "To the Colored People of the United States" (1862), quoted in Wilson Jeremiah Moses, *The Golden Age of Black Nationalism, 1850–1925* (New York: Oxford University Press, 1978, reprint 1988), 158.

23. Daniel Alexander Payne, *Recollections of Seventy Years* (Nashville: AME Sunday School Union, 1888), 253.

24. Payne, 253–254.

25. Payne, 255–256.

26. Payne, 333–334, 313.

27. Thomas Johnson, *Africa for Christ. Twenty-Eight Years a Slave* (London: Alexander and Shepheard, 1892), 15–16, 21, 31–32. I am grateful to Laurie Maffly-Kipp for sharing Johnson's work with me.

28. Johnson, 27.

29. Johnson, 48–49, 52, 61. The image reproduced here is from pg. 116 of a later edition of the book under a slightly different title (see caption) and is used for its higher resolution.

30. Johnson, 61.

31. Johnson, 60.

32. See Wilson Jeremiah Moses, *Alexander Crummell: A Study of Civilization and Discontent* (New York: Oxford University Press, 1989).

33. Alexander Crummell, "The Regeneration of Africa. A Discourse before the Pennsylvania Colonization Society; Church of the Epiphany, Philadelphia, Pa., October, 1865," in *Africa and America: Addresses and Discourses* (Springfield, MA: Willey, 1891), 433–434.

34. Crummell, 435–442.

35. Booker T. Washington, "The Standard Printed Version of the Atlanta Exposition Address," September 18, 1895, in *The Booker T. Washington Papers Digital Edition*, ed. Louis R. Harlan and Raymond W. Smock (Charlottesville: University of Virginia Press, Rotunda, 2021), https://rotunda.upress.virginia.edu/founders/BTWN-01-02-03-0439, accessed October 2021.

36. Alexander Crummell, "Civilization the Primal Need of the Race, the Inaugural Address, March 5, 1897," and "The Attitude of the American Mind toward

the Negro Intellect, First Annual Address, December 28, 1897," *American Negro Academy Occasional Papers,* no. 3 (Washington, DC: published by the Academy, 1898), 4, 6, 7. On the idea of America as a "caste-tainted country," see Isabel Wilkerson, *Caste: The Origins of Our Discontents* (New York: Random House, 2020).

37. Crummell, "Attitude," 8–10.

38. See Alison M. Parker, *Unceasing Militant: The Life of Mary Church Terrell* (Chapel Hill: University of North Carolina Press, 2020).

39. Damon Mitchell, "The People's Grocery Lynching, Memphis, Tennessee," *JSTOR Daily,* January 24, 2018, https://daily.jstor.org/peoples-grocery -lynching/.

40. Mary Church Terrell, "Lynching from a Negro's Point of View," *North American Review* 178, no. 571 (June 1904): 853–868, esp. 858, 860–862.

41. See Chad Seales, *The Secular Spectacle: Performing Religion in a Southern Town* (New York: Oxford University Press, 2014).

42. Terrell, "Lynching," 859.

43. Terrell, 865.

44. Terrell, 866.

45. John Scudder, *Dr. Scudder's Tales for Little Readers, about the Heathen* (New York: American Tract Society, 1849), 177.

46. Edwin Long, *The Union Tabernacle; or, Movable Tent-Church: Showing in Its Rise and Success a New Department of Christian Enterprise* (Philadelphia: Parry and McMillan, 1859), 35–36, 57–58.

47. See Jana Riess, "'Heathen in Our Fair Land': Presbyterian Women Missionaries in Utah, 1870–1890," *Journal of Mormon History* 26, no. 1 (Spring 2000): 165–195; W. Paul Reeve, *Religion of a Different Color: Race and the Mormon Struggle for Whiteness* (New York: Oxford University Press, 2015); Max Perry Mueller, *Race and the Making of the Mormon People* (Chapel Hill: University of North Carolina Press, 2017); and Peter Coviello, *Make Yourselves Gods: Mormons and the Unfinished Business of American Secularism* (Chicago: University of Chicago Press, 2019).

48. Dudley C. Haskell, "Mormonism: An Address," June 8, 1881, Sheldon Jackson Collection 161, Presbyterian Church History Department, quoted in Riess, "'Heathen in Our Fair Land,'" 170.

49. "Topics of the Times: By the Editor [George Q. Cannon]," *Juvenile Instructor* 22, no. 19 (October 1, 1887): 290–291.

50. George Augustus Lofton, "Modern Paganism," n.d. (majority of collection dates from 1875 to 1900). Insertion is Lofton's own. Papers of George Augustus Lofton, Collection RL.00818, David M. Rubenstein Rare Book and Manuscript Library, Duke University.

51. Joshua Paddison, *American Heathens: Religion, Race, and Reconstruction in California* (Berkeley: published for the Huntington-USC Institute on California and the West by University of California Press, 2012), 12. See also Edlie Wong, *Racial Reconstruction: Black Inclusion, Chinese Exclusion, and the Fictions of Citizenship* (New York: New York University Press, 2015).

52. Uchimura, *Diary,* 108, 112.

6. Exclusion

1. Calvin Colton, *A Lecture on the Railroad to the Pacific. Delivered, August 12, 1850, at the Smithsonian Institute, Washington, at the Request of Numerous Members of both Houses of Congress* (New York: A. S. Barnes, 1850), 11.

2. See, for instance, Alexander Saxton, *The Indispensable Enemy: Labor and the Anti-Chinese Movement in California* (Berkeley: University of California Press, 1971); David Roediger, *The Wages of Whiteness: Race and the Making of the American Working Class* (London: Verso, 1991); and Ronald Takaki, *Iron Cages: Race and Culture in 19th-Century America* (New York: Alfred A. Knopf, 1979). For a definitive recent take, see Beth Lew-Williams, *The Chinese Must Go: Violence, Exclusion, and the Making of the Alien in America* (Cambridge, MA: Harvard University Press, 2018). Lew-Williams nods to the stereotype of the "heathen coolie" as "the primary rationale for exclusion" (31), but her focus is not primarily on "why the whites found the Chinese undesirable beyond the traditional anti-labor argument." Diana Ahmad, review of *The Chinese Must Go: Violence, Exclusion, and the Making of the Alien in America*, by Beth Lew-Williams, *American Historical Review* 124, no. 3 (June 2019): 1089–1090. For scholarship that centers religion, see Joshua Paddison, *American Heathens: Religion, Race, and Reconstruction in California* (Berkeley: published for the Huntington-USC Institute on California and the West by University of California Press, 2012). Paddison argues that two religio-racial visions competed with each other—one emphasizing "Christian white male supremacy" and the other "anti-Catholicism and paternalistic racial uplift" (9). This chapter builds on Paddison's work by further interrogating the meanings of the term "heathen" as applied to the Chinese.

3. Takaki essentially credits Harte's poem for the popularity of the stereotype. See Takaki, *Iron Cages,* chap. 10, "The Heathen Chinee and American Technology."

4. See Gordon Chang, *Fateful Ties: A History of America's Preoccupation with China* (Cambridge, MA: Harvard University Press, 2015); and Jack Kuo-Wei Tchen, *New York before Chinatown: Orientalism and the Shaping of American Culture, 1776–1882* (Baltimore: Johns Hopkins University Press, 1999).

5. John R. Peters Jr., *Guide to, or Descriptive Catalogue of the Chinese Museum, in the Marlboro' Chapel, Boston, with Miscellaneous Remarks upon the Government, History, Religions, Literature, Agriculture, Arts, Trades, Manners and Customs of the Chinese* (Boston: Eastburn's, 1845), 44–45, 152.

6. Tchen, *New York before Chinatown,* xvi.

7. Peters, *Guide,* 150.

8. Laurie Maffly-Kipp, "Engaging Habits and Besotted Idolatry: Viewing Chinese Religions in the American West," *Material Religion* 1, no. 1 (March 2005): 72–97.

9. See Takaki, *Iron Cages,* 228: "He is able to render impotent white superiority in technology."

10. See Paddison, *American Heathens,* 38–44; and Wesley Woo, "Protestant Work among the Chinese in the San Francisco Bay Area, 1850–1920" (PhD diss., Graduate Theological Union, 1983).

11. Daniel Cleveland, "The Chinese in California," manuscript, 1868–1869, M 72175–72177, Huntington Library, San Marino, CA. Quote comes from smaller pages titled "The Heathen among Us," 1–2, stapled into unnumbered chapter titled "Missionary Labor among the Chinese in California."

12. "Can the Chinese Be Converted?," *Oriental,* February 1856.

13. Cleveland, "Chinese in California," chap. 11, "Religion and Temples of the Chinese in California," 2.

14. John Archbald, *On the Contact of Races: Considered Especially with Relation to the Chinese Question* (San Francisco: Towne and Bacon, 1860), 30–31.

15. Quoted in William Speer, *The Oldest and the Newest Empire: China and the United States* (Hartford, CT: S. S. Scranton, 1870), 580–581. On how Native Americans and African Americans also protested against being clumped with the Chinese and each other, and how some White women protested at being clumped with heathens in their inability to vote, see Paddison, *American Heathens,* chap. 1, "A New Vision of Citizenship, 1861–1870."

16. See Michael C. Coleman, "Presbyterian Missionary Attitudes toward China and the Chinese, 1837–1900," *Journal of Presbyterian History* 56, no. 3 (1978): 198.

17. Others have noted how the Chinese fell in esteem from a "great empire" to despicable "coolies," but typically base the explanation on the racialization or "negroization" of the Chinese, as Takaki puts it in *Iron Cages* (219). Paddison, by contrast, explains that the Chinese were more often differentiated from African Americans in debates over their immigration, since African Americans had become Christianized while the Chinese had by and large not.

18. William Mungen, *The Heathen Chinese. Speech of the Hon. William Mungen of Ohio, Delivered in the House of Representatives, January 7, 1871* (Washington, DC: F. and J. Rives and Geo. A. Bailey, 1870), 13.

19. Speer, *Oldest and the Newest,* 80–81.

20. Michael Adas, *Machines as the Measure of Men: Science, Technology, and Ideologies of Western Dominance* (Ithaca, NY: Cornell University Press, 1989).

21. James Haggerty, Diaries and Sketchbook of James Haggerty, 1870–1927, HM 70394–70396, Diary #1, 7–8, Huntington Library.

22. Alfred Trumble, *"The Heathen Chinee" at Home and Abroad. Who He Is; What He Looks Like; How He Works and Lives; His Virtues, Vices and Crimes. A Complete Panorama of the Chinese in America. By an old Californian* (New York: Richard K. Fox, 1882), 19.

23. Arthur B. Stout, *Chinese Immigration and the Physiological Causes of the Decay of a Nation* (San Francisco: Agnew & Deffebach, Printers, 1862), 17.

24. "A Chinese Miracle, From the S. F. Chronicle, A Strange Scene in a Joss House—A Reporter Takes a Peep Behind the Altar," in *The Chinese Invasion; Revealing the Habits, Manners and Customs of the Chinese, Political, Social and Religious, on the Pacific Coast, Coming in contact with the free and enlightened citizens of America. Containing careful selections from The San Francisco Press,* by H. J. West (San Francisco: Excelsior Office, Bacon, 1873).

25. "Sacramento City, California," *Missionary News,* April 1, 1867, 41.

26. M. B. Starr, *The Coming Struggle; or What the People on the Pacific Coast Think of the Coolie Invasion* (San Francisco: Excelsior Office, Bacon, 1873), frontispiece.
27. Trumble, *"Heathen Chinee,"* 20, 51, 47, 20.
28. Starr, *Coming Struggle*, 79, italics in original. On Starr as "Grand Lecturer" see West, *The Chinese Invasion*, 15. On the People's Protective Alliance see Edlie L. Wong, *Racial Reconstruction: Black Inclusion, Chinese Exclusion, and the Fictions of Citizenship* (New York: New York University Press, 2015), 265n99. On Chinese bodies as diseased see Nayan Shah, *Contagious Divides: Epidemics and Race in San Francisco's Chinatown* (Berkeley: University of California Press, 2001); and Larissa Heinrich, *The Afterlife of Images: Translating the Pathological Body between China and the West* (Durham, NC: Duke University Press, 2008). For a comparison of how British Protestant missionaries viewed Chinese bodies as proxies for their beliefs (since they did not always understand their language), see Eric Reinders, *Borrowed Gods and Foreign Bodies: Christian Missionaries Imagine Chinese Religion* (Berkeley: University of California Press, 2004).
29. Starr, *Coming Struggle*, 9.
30. "Address of Rev. S. V. Blakeslee," in *Chinese Immigration; Its Social, Moral, and Political Effect. Report to the California State Senate of Its Special Committee on Chinese Immigration,* by Special Committee on Chinese Immigration, California State Senate (Sacramento: State Office, 1878), 245.
31. "Address of Hon. Edwin R. Meade, before the Social Science Association of America, Held at Saratoga, New York, September 7th, 1877," in Special Committee on Chinese Immigration, California State Senate, *Chinese Immigration*, 296, 295.
32. Starr, *Coming Struggle*, 87.
33. Maffly-Kipp, "Engaging Habits," 80.
34. Augustus Ward Loomis, "Chinese 'Funeral Baked Meats,'" *Overland Monthly* 3, no. 1 (July 1869): 26.
35. Augustus Ward Loomis, "Occult Science in the Chinese Quarter," *Overland Monthly* 3, no. 2 (August 1869): 160.
36. Loomis, "Chinese 'Funeral Baked Meats,'" 22, 24, 29.
37. Loomis, 29.
38. Speer, *Oldest and the Newest*, 647, 669–670.
39. Mungen, *Heathen Chinese*, 4–5.
40. Mungen, 3.
41. W. Lobscheid, *The Chinese: What They Are, and What They Are Doing* (San Francisco: A. L. Bancroft, 1873), 13.
42. Benjamin Wisner, *The Moral Condition and Prospects of the Heathen: A Sermon, Delivered at the Old South Church in Boston, before the Foreign Mission Society of Boston and the Vicinity, at Their Annual Meeting, Jan. 1, 1824* (Boston: printed by Crocker and Brewster, 1824), 29.
43. Lobscheid, *Chinese*, 20.
44. "A Dark Picture. From the Morning Call, May 19, 1873. What We May Expect as Results of Chinese Immigration—A Missionary's Opinion of the Chinaman," in West, *Chinese Invasion*, 59.

45. "The Chinese Question. A Paper Read by John H. Boalt, before the Berkeley Club, August, 1877," in Special Committee on Chinese Immigration, California State Senate, *Chinese Immigration,* 261–262.

46. "Address of Rev. S. V. Blakeslee," 244.

47. "Chinese Question," 261.

48. Starr, *Coming Struggle,* 14.

49. On the clumping of "heathens" with Catholics, see Reinders, *Borrowed Gods;* and Paddison, *American Heathens,* 82–83. On the clumping of missionaries with capitalists, see Paddison, 90.

50. Starr, *Coming Struggle,* 25.

51. "The Great Problem: From the Morning Call, May 27, 1873," in West, *Chinese Invasion,* 50; "White Labor Employed Exclusively," in advertisement for "C. Jas. King of Wm. & Co., manufacturers of HERMETICALLY SEALED GOODS, San Francisco," in West, *Chinese Invasion,* n.p.

52. Mungen, *Heathen Chinese,* 6.

53. Starr, *Coming Struggle,* 71–72.

54. "Address of Hon. Edwin R. Meade," 297.

55. "Address of Rev. S. V. Blakeslee," 245.

56. "Address of Rev. S. V. Blakeslee," 245–246, emphasis in original. On boomtowns in the West see Laurie Maffly-Kipp, *Religion and Society in Frontier California* (New Haven, CT: Yale University Press, 1994).

57. Starr, *Coming Struggle,* 11.

58. See Paddison, *American Heathens,* 77–78: "Buchard had been born and raised on a Delaware Indian reserve in present-day Kansas. The son of a Delaware father and a French mother who had been adopted by Comanches as a girl, Buchard was known as Watomika until his baptism in 1847. Although some of Buchard's fellow Jesuits knew of his religious and racial background, he kept it hidden from the California audiences who turned out for his sermons and speeches."

59. "Father Buchard's Lecture. 'Chinaman or White Man—Which?,'" in West, *Chinese Invasion,* 142.

60. Otis Gibson, *"Chinaman or White Man, Which?" Reply to Father Buchard by Rev. O. Gibson, Delivered in Platt's Hall, San Francisco, Friday Evening Mar. 14, 1873. Published at the request of the "San Francisco Methodist Preachers' Meeting"* (San Francisco: Alta California, 1873), 21.

61. American Board of Commissioners for Foreign Missions, *Appeal for the Heathen* ([Boston?], [1865?]), 7, 10.

62. Starr, *Coming Struggle,* 11, 13–14.

63. Starr, 20–21, 106.

64. Starr, 17, 13–14, 25, 17.

65. "Resolutions Adopted by the General Association of Congregational Churches of California, and Address of Rev. S. V. Blakeslee, Delivered before the General Association, held in Sacramento from the 9th to the 13th of October, 1877," in Special Committee on Chinese Immigration, California State Senate, *Chinese Immigration,* 240. See also Paddison, *American Heathens,* chap. 5.

66. Special Committee on Chinese Immigration, California State Senate, *Chinese Immigration*, 39–40. On how ministers began to see exclusion as a way to "actually aid evangelism because anti-Chinese hostility would diminish, and those Chinese men and women in California would be more likely to convert to Christianity once cut off from pagan influences from China," see Paddison, *American Heathens*, 147–148.

67. See Takaki, *Iron Cages*, 248.

68. "The Consequence of the Completion of the U.P.R.R.—a New Sect Is Added to Those Already in Existence," *Frank Leslie's Illustrated Newspaper*, July 3, 1869. I am grateful to Peter Blodgett for sharing this image with me.

69. See also journalist Pierton Dooner's *The Last Days of the Republic* (San Francisco: Alta California, 1880), which featured on its cover a similar image of a bloated master, "THE RULER OF ALL LANDS." The book presents a nightmarish depiction of a future war if America's gates remained open to the Chinese.

70. Scott D. Seligman, *The First Chinese American: The Remarkable Life of Wong Chin Foo* (Hong Kong: Hong Kong University Press, 2013), esp. "Wong Chin Foo Chronology," xxi–xxvi.

71. Wong Chin Foo, "Why Am I a Heathen?," *North American Review* 145, no. 369 (August 1887): 173, 176.

72. Wong, 178, 171–172, 179.

73. Mark Alden Branch, "Neither Here Nor There," *Yale Alumni Magazine*, May/June 2021, https://yalealumnimagazine.com/articles/5324-yan-phou-lee.

74. Yan Phou Lee, "Why I Am Not a Heathen: A Rejoinder to Wong Chin Foo," *North American Review* 145, no. 370 (September 1887): 306–312, esp. 309, 307.

75. Lee, 311, 312, 308.

7. Inclusion

1. Nathaniel Bright Emerson, "A Page from Hawaiian History," essay, January 31, 1893, 8, Box 3: Emerson's Research Material, Hawaiian Rebellions of 1893 and 1895, Nathaniel Bright Emerson Papers, mssEMR 1-1323, Huntington Library, San Marino, CA.

2. The archive does not note this. I draw this conclusion from the absurdity of the text and from Richard Lightner, comp., *Hawaiian History: An Annotated Bibliography* (Westport, CT: Praeger, 2004), 90: "apparently done in jest toward Cleveland as part of an Annexationist meeting."

3. "Cleveland, Grover, 1837–1908: Broadside regarding Hawaiian-U.S. Relations," 1893, Box 3: Emerson's Research Material, Nathaniel Bright Emerson Papers.

4. "Cleveland, Grover."

5. "Cleveland, Grover."

6. Mark Twain, *Extract from Captain Stormfield's Visit to Heaven* (New York: Harper and Brothers, 1909), 87.

7. Rufus Anderson, *A Heathen Nation Evangelized. History of the Sandwich Islands Mission* (Boston: Congregational Publishing Society, 1870), ix.

8. Emerson, "Page from Hawaiian History," 5–8. Emerson's edits are represented in the text with strikeouts and "[^]" to indicate his handwritten insertions.
9. Emerson, 16, 17.
10. James Bicknell, "On the State of the Hawaiian Churches" (handwritten, n.d.), 1–4, in "Idolatry, Assoc. of Christian Workers for the Suppression of. Rev. James Bicknell 1890–92," Hawaiian Mission Children's Society Library, Honolulu. Strikeout in original.
11. Bicknell, 6, 2.
12. James Bicknell, "Hoomanamana—Idolatry," (pamphlet, n.d.), 2, Hawaiian Mission Children's Society Library, Honolulu. Valerio Valeri, in *Kingship and Sacrifice: Ritual and Society in Ancient Hawaii* (Chicago: University of Chicago Press, 1985), 102, notes that "hoʻomanamana is defined as 'to impart mana, as to idols or objects; superstitious.'"
13. *Laws of His Majesty, Kamehameha V, King of the Hawaiian Islands, Passed by the Legislative Assembly at Its Session, 1864–65* (Honolulu: printed by order of the government, 1865), 85.
14. "Constitution Granted by Kalakaua, July 6, 1887," available at "The 1887 Bayonet Constitution: The Beginning of the Insurgency," *Hawaiian Kingdom Blog*, accessed June 2017, https://hawaiiankingdom.org/pdf/Bayonet_Constitution .pdf.
15. On how "religious freedom" talk privileges Whiteness and Protestant Christianity, see Tisa Wenger, *Religious Freedom: The Contested History of an American Ideal* (Chapel Hill: University of North Carolina Press, 2017).
16. Included in *The Penal Laws of the Hawaiian Islands, 1897. Compiled from the Penal Code of 1869 and the Session Laws of 1870 to 1896 Inclusive* (Honolulu: Hawaiian Gazette Print, 1897), 1.
17. *The Penal Code of the Hawaiian Islands, passed by the House of Nobles and Representatives on the 21st of June, A.D. 1850, to which are appended the Other Acts Passed by the House of Nobles and Representatives During Their General Session for 1850* (Honolulu: printed by Henry M. Whitney, government press, 1850), 91–92.
18. *Penal Code of the Hawaiian Kingdom, Compiled from the Penal Code of 1850: And the Various Penal Enactments Since Made, Pursuant to Act of the Legislative Assembly, June 22d, 1868, compiled by Robert G. Davis and Richard H. Stanley* (Honolulu: printed at the government press, 1869), 142.
19. S. N. Haleole, "History of the Hawaiian Priesthood in Olden Times, Called Hoomanamana," Honolulu, June 13, 1863, in Abraham Fornander and Thomas George Thrum, *Fornander Collection of Hawaiian Antiquities and Folk-lore* (Honolulu: Bishop Museum Press, 1919–1920), 68.
20. In addition to the penal codes cited earlier, see *Revised Laws of Hawaii: Comprising the Statutes of the Territory, Consolidated, Revised and Annotated* (Honolulu: Hawaiian Gazette, 1905), esp. 1151–1152.
21. See Noenoe K. Silva, *Aloha Betrayed* (Durham, NC: Duke University Press, 2004).
22. Carol Silva, trans., *Hale Naua Society, 1886–1891: Translation of Documents at the Hawaiʻi State Archives and Hawaiian Mission Children's Society Library*, with an introduction by Frank J. Karpiel (Honolulu: Hawaiian Historical So-

ciety with a preservation grant from the Hawai'i Committee for the Humanities, 1999), 126.

23. Silva, 3.

24. David Kalakaua [?], *Constitution and By-Laws of the Hale Naua or . . . Temple of Science. Ancient Secret Society of the Order of Nauas, or Order of the Temple of Science* (San Francisco: Bancroft, 1890).

25. Silva, *Hale Naua*, 87, 97.

26. Bicknell, "On the State," 5.

27. Nathaniel Bright Emerson, "Notes regarding Hawaiian Annexation" [between 1893 and 1895], Box 3: Emerson's Research Material, Nathaniel Bright Emerson Papers. Underlines and edits are Emerson's own.

28. Lili'uokalani to William McKinley, June 17, 1897, University of Hawai'i at Manoa Library, http://libweb.hawaii.edu/digicoll/annexation/protest/liliu5 .php.

29. Murat Halstead, *The Story of the Philippines and Our New Possessions, Including The Ladrones, Hawaii, Cuba, and Porto Rico* (H. L. Barber, Chicago, 1898), 100.

30. Jeffrey Wheatley, "US Colonial Governance of Superstition and Fanaticism in the Philippines," *Method and Theory in the Study of Religion* 30 (2018): 22.

31. Wheatley, 22–23.

32. *Congressional Record: Containing the Proceedings and Debates of the Fifty-Seventh Congress, First Session; Also Special Session of the Senate*, vol. 35 (Washington, DC: Government Printing Office, 1902), 290–291, italics in original.

33. William H. Taft, *Outlook*, May 31, 1902, quoted in *Congressional Record*, 7479.

34. See Jennifer Graber, *The Gods of Indian Country: Religion and the Struggle for the American West* (New York: Oxford University Press, 2018).

35. "Dawes Severalty Act," in *The Oxford Companion to United States History*, ed. Paul S. Boyer (Oxford: Oxford University Press, 2001), 173–174.

36. "St. Paul's Indian Boarding-School, Yankton Agency, Dakota," (n.d.), in Charlotte Everett [Cook] Webster, Scrapbook, 1863–1961, Box 3, Folder 20, Joseph Witherspoon Cook Papers, Collection of Samuel Derrick Webster, 1771–1966, mssHM 48531–48557, Huntington Library.

37. William Hobart Hare, "A Well-Invested Life and Its Rewards," in Charlotte Everett [Cook] Webster Scrapbook, Box 3, Folder 9. At the top of the obituary someone has handwritten "From 'The Spirit of Missions' April 1902."

38. David Wallace Adams, *Education for Extinction: American Indians and the Boarding School Experience, 1875–1928* (Lawrence: University Press of Kansas, 1995). See also K Tsianina Lomawaima, *They Called It Prairie Light: The Story of Chilocco Indian School* (Lincoln: University of Nebraska Press, 1994), which shows how some children at the boarding schools found opportunities for mutual support and pan-Indian alliances amid the hardships they faced.

39. Dorchester quotes from US Office of Indian Affairs, *Sixty-First Annual Report of the Commissioner of Indian Affairs to the Secretary of the Interior*, 540–549, quoted in Tisa Wenger, *We Have a Religion: The 1920s Pueblo Indian Dance*

Controversy and American Religious Freedom (Chapel Hill: University of North Carolina Press, 2009), 29, 40.

40. John Menaul, "Characteristics of Pueblo Indians," *Home Missions Monthly* 6, no. 4 (February 1892): 80, quoted in Wenger, *We Have a Religion*, 40.

41. Department of the Interior Office of Indian Affairs, *Segments from the Circular No. 1665 and Supplement to Circular No. 1665* (Washington, DC: April 26, 1921, and February 14, 1923), http://www.webpages.uidaho.edu/~rfrey/PDF /329/IndianDances.pdf. On the religious freedom claims made by the Pueblo people who supported and opposed the dances, see Wenger, *We Have a Religion*. On Circular No. 1665 and the Pueblo Dance Controversy see also Michael McNally, *Defend the Sacred: Native American Religious Freedom beyond the First Amendment* (Princeton: Princeton University Press, 2020), 57–61.

42. William Speer, *The Oldest and the Newest Empire: China and the United States* (Hartford, CT: S. S. Scranton, 1870), 605–606.

43. John Scudder, *Dr. Scudder's Tales for Little Readers, about the Heathen* (New York: American Tract Society, 1849), 111.

44. Scudder, 46.

45. On time as the key separator between peoples, see Bernard McGrane, *Beyond Anthropology: Society and the Other* (New York: Columbia University Press, 1989); and Kathryn Gin Lum, "The Historyless Heathen and the Stagnating Pagan: History as Non-Native Category?," *Religion and American Culture* 28, no. 1 (Winter 2018): 52–91.

46. Matthew 3:12; Matthew 25:32–33.

47. Quoted in Gary Dorrien, *The Making of American Liberal Theology: Imagining Progressive Religion, 1805–1900* (Louisville, KY: Westminster John Knox, 2001), 1:305. For responses of missionized people to the claim that they were condemned to hell without conversion, see Kathryn Gin Lum, *Damned Nation: Hell in America from the Revolution to Reconstruction* (New York: Oxford University Press, 2014), chaps. 3 and 4.

48. The New England Transcendentalists, who found much of value in Buddhist and Hindu thought, were responsible for bringing texts like the Lotus Sutra to the attention of other Euro-Americans in publications like the *Dial*. See Thomas Tweed, *The American Encounter with Buddhism, 1844–1912: Victorian Culture and the Limits of Dissent* (Bloomington: Indiana University Press, 1992); and Michael J. Altman, *Heathen, Hindoo, Hindu: American Representations of India, 1721–1893* (New York: Oxford University Press, 2017). On eighteenth- and nineteenth-century skeptics and doubters in the eternal damnation of the "heathen," see Lum, *Damned Nation*, chaps. 1 and 4; and Christopher Grasso, *Skepticism and American Faith from the Revolution to the Civil War* (New York: Oxford University Press, 2018).

49. See Gary Scott Smith, "Changing Conceptions of Hell in Gilded Age America," *Fides et Historia*, Winter / Spring 2015. See also James Moorhead, *World without End: Mainstream American Protestant Visions of the Last Things, 1880–1925* (Bloomington: Indiana University Press, 1999).

50. "The Andover Controversy," *Cincinnati Daily Gazette*, April 20, 1882, 4.

51. "Sunday Services: Rev. Dr. Webb on Recent Events in the Congregational Order," *Boston Journal,* October 16, 1882, 4.

52. "The Andover Election: Progress Made in Congregational Theology: A Sermon Preached by Rev. C. Van Norden in the Congregational Church, St. Albans, April 23," *St. Albans Daily Messenger,* April 24, 1882, 2.

53. "Andover Controversy," 4.

54. *The Andover heresy: in the matter of the complaint against Egbert C. Smyth and others* (Boston: Cupples, Upham, 1887), 36–37.

55. "The Doctrinal Appeal to the Churches," editorial, *Andover Review,* November 1887, 535.

56. See Moorhead, *World without End.*

57. Gail Hamilton [Mary Abigail Dodge], "Heathendom and Christendom under Test," *North American Review* 143, no. 361 (December 1886): 541. On Dodge, see David Mislin, *Saving Faith: Making Religious Pluralism and American Value at the Dawn of the Secular Age* (Ithaca, NY: Cornell University Press, 2015), 52.

58. Hamilton, "Heathendom," 541, 543, 544.

59. Hamilton, 545.

Part III. Inheritances

1. "Religion and World View: Suggested Readings," in *Essentials of Cultural Anthropology,* by Garrick Bailey and James Peoples, 2nd ed. (Belmont, CA: Cengage Learning, 2010), 226. Notably, the third edition of this textbook (2013) has removed Howells from the list of suggested readings.

2. Wolfgang Saxon, "William W. Howells, Leading Anthropologist, Is Dead at 97," *New York Times,* December 30, 2005. See also "William White Howells," *Harvard Gazette,* April 26, 2007.

3. William W. Howells, *The Heathens: Primitive Man and His Religions* (Garden City, NY: Doubleday, 1948), 1, 3, 6, 8. I am grateful to Daniel Tuzzeo for sharing this source with me.

4. Howells, 7–8.

5. Howells, 4, 9, 2.

6. Howells, 1, 7; Bronislaw Malinowski, "Myth in Primitive Psychology," in *Magic, Science, and Religion and Other Essays* (1926; Garden City, NY: Doubleday, 1954), 100–126.

8. Preservation and Pushback

1. Nathaniel Bright Emerson, "A Hawaiian Chap Book," monograph, second and third drafts, September 2–14, 1907, Box 13: Manuscripts, Nathaniel Bright Emerson Papers, mssEMR 1-1323, Huntington Library, San Marino, CA.

2. See Matthew Jacobson, *Barbarian Virtues: The United States Encounters Foreign Peoples at Home and Abroad, 1876–1917* (New York: Hill and Wang, 2001); and Clifford Putney, *Muscular Christianity: Manhood and Sports in Protestant America, 1880–1920* (Cambridge, MA: Harvard University Press, 2003).

3. On a similar move, from denigrating Africans as having "no religion," to the postconquest quest to taxonomize African traditions to better police them, see David Chidester, *Savage Systems: Colonialism and Comparative Religion in Southern Africa* (Charlottesville: University Press of Virginia, 1996).

4. Lydia Maria Child, *The Progress of Religious Ideas, through Successive Ages* (New York: C. S. Francis, 1855), 1:viii.

5. James Freeman Clarke, *Ten Great Religions: An Essay in Comparative Theology* (Boston: Houghton Mifflin, 1871), 4.

6. Child, *Progress of Religious Ideas,* 1:ix.

7. On how White Protestant liberals simultaneously embraced the notion of comparative religions and the partial truths that other religions contained but continued to maintain the superiority of Anglo-Protestantism, see David Mislin, *Saving Faith: Making Religious Pluralism and American Value at the Dawn of the Secular Age* (Ithaca, NY: Cornell University Press, 2015), chap. 2, "Correcting Elijah's Mistake."

8. Child, *Progress of Religious Ideas,* 1:xi.

9. Michael J. Altman, *Heathen, Hindoo, Hindu: American Representations of India, 1721–1893* (New York: Oxford University Press, 2017), 91.

10. Child, *Progress of Religious Ideas,* 3:420.

11. Clarke, *Ten Great Religions,* 8–9, and table of contents.

12. *Oxford English Dictionary Online,* 3rd ed. (Oxford University Press, 2014), s.v. "ethnic, n. and adj." See also Colin Kidd, *British Identities before Nationalism: Ethnicity and Nationhood in the Atlantic World, 1600–1800* (Cambridge: Cambridge University Press, 2004), 11.

13. Willie James Jennings, *The Christian Imagination: Theology and the Origins of Race* (New Haven, CT: Yale University Press, 2011); Tomoko Masuzawa, *The Invention of World Religions: Or, How European Universalism Was Preserved in the Language of Pluralism* (Chicago: University of Chicago Press, 2005). See also Chidester, *Savage Systems;* the colonial project of comparative religions led some to see "the light of religious truth even in the most remote and savage forms of religious life," in the words of Rev. John Colenso (171).

14. See Marvin Puakea Nogelmeier, *Mai Pa'a I Ka Leo: Historical Voice in Hawaiian Primary Materials, Looking Forward and Listening Back* (Honolulu: Bishop Museum Press, 2010); and David A. Chang, "The Good Written Word of Life: The Native Hawaiian Appropriation of Textuality," *William and Mary Quarterly* 75, no. 3 (April 2018): 237–258.

15. "Pela ka poe Alebiona, ka poe nona ka aina o Beretania mamua, aka, o ka moolelo o ka poe Saxonia me ka William ka moolelo no Beretania, he poe malihini lakou, he poe puapuakaulei, no hai ka punana." Quoted and translated in Ronald Williams Jr., "Peerless and Alone," *Hana Hou!* 15, no. 3 (June/July 2012), https://hanahou.com/15.3/peerless-and-alone.

16. David Kalakaua, *The Legends and Myths of Hawaii by His Hawaiian Majesty Kalakaua* (Honolulu: Mutual, 1990).

17. Williams, "Peerless and Alone."

18. Hiram Bingham, *A Residence of Twenty-One Years in the Sandwich Islands* (Hartford, CT: Hezekiah Huntington, 1848), 17–18.

19. Nathaniel Bright Emerson, "Biographical Information regarding Davida Malo, 1795–1853," n.d., Box 2: Emerson's Research Material, Hawaiian Antiquities, Nathaniel Bright Emerson Papers.

20. Nathaniel Bright Emerson, "Ethnic Factors in Civilization," essay, December 12, 1905, 22, Box 12: Manuscripts, Nathaniel Bright Emerson Papers.

21. On the paternalism/maternalism in this view—and the ways in which it tore families apart as self-professed "civilizers" separated children from their parents in order to "educate" them—see Margaret D. Jacobs, *White Mother to a Dark Race: Settler Colonialism, Maternalism, and the Removal of Indigenous Children in the American West and Australia, 1880–1940* (Lincoln: University of Nebraska Press, 2009). See also Patrick Brantlinger, *Dark Vanishings: Discourse on the Extinction of Primitive Races, 1800–1930* (Ithaca, NY: Cornell University Press, 2003), on the assumption that contact with civilization would lead to extinction.

22. See Kathryn Gin Lum, *Damned Nation: Hell in America from the Revolution to Reconstruction* (New York: Oxford University Press, 2014), chap. 4.

23. G. Stanley Hall, *Adolescence: Its Psychology and Its Relations to Physiology, Anthropology, Sociology, Sex, Crime, Religion, and Education* (New York: D. Appleton, 1904), 1:xi.

24. William Byron Forbush, "The Social Pedagogy of Boyhood," in *The Pedagogical Seminary*, ed. G. Stanley Hall (Worcester, MA: Louis N. Wilson, 1900), 7:344. The same quote appears in Forbush, *The Boy Problem: A Study in Social Pedagogy*, with an introduction by G. Stanley Hall (Boston, 1901), 157. *The Boy Problem* was popular; it saw eight reprints from its publication to 1913. See Kenneth B. Kidd, *Making American Boys: Boyology and the Feral Tale* (Minneapolis: University of Minnesota Press, 2004), 67.

25. Hall, *Adolescence*, 2:735, 736, 321.

26. Hall, 304, 337, 321, 744.

27. Hall, 351, 743, 747–748.

28. Emerson, "Ethnic Factors in Civilization," 21.

29. Emerson, 14–16, 22.

30. Josiah Strong, *Our Country: Its Possible Future and Its Present Crisis* (New York: American Home Missionary Society, 1885), 175, 161.

31. Strong, 176–178.

32. Emerson, "Ethnic Factors in Civilization," 22.

33. Heather Curtis, *Holy Humanitarians: American Evangelicals and Global Aid* (Cambridge, MA: Harvard University Press, 2018). David King similarly shows how a pattern of humanitarian distraction continued to smooth over evangelical differences from 1950 to 2010 in "The New Internationalists: World Vision and the Revival of American Evangelical Humanitarianism, 1950–2010," *Religions* 3, no. 4 (2012): 922–949. On technologies for bringing the world's suffering to Americans, see also Hillary Kaell, *Christian Globalism at Home: Child Sponsorship in the United States* (Princeton, NJ: Princeton University Press, 2020), esp. chap. 3: "Food and Famine: The Visual/Visceral Production of Humanitarianism."

34. David Hollinger, *Protestants Abroad: How Missionaries Tried to Change the World but Changed America* (Princeton, NJ: Princeton University Press, 2017).

35. Mislin, *Saving Faith*, 57, 59. See also Michael J. Altman, *Heathen, Hindoo, Hindu: American Representations of India, 1721–1893* (New York: Oxford University Press, 2017), Chapter 6.

36. Kinza Riuge M. Hirai, "The Real Position of Japan toward Christianity," in *The World's Parliament of Religions: An Illustrated and Popular Story of the World's First Parliament of Religions, Held in Chicago in Connection with the Columbian Exposition of 1893*, ed. John Henry Barrows (London: "Review of Reviews" Office, 1893), 1:444.

37. "Hopes for the Religious Union of the Whole Human Family," in Barrows, *World's Parliament of Religions*, 244.

38. "Speech of Prof. Chakravarti," in "The Assembling of the Parliament—Words of Welcome and Fellowship," in Barrows, *World's Parliament of Religions*, 98–99.

39. "Speech of Prof. Chakravarti," 99–100.

40. "Speech of Prof. Chakravarti," 99.

41. Edward Said, *Orientalism*, 25th anniversary ed. (New York: Vintage Books, 2003). See also Bluford Adams, "'A Stupendous Mirror of Departed Empires': The Barnum Hippodromes and Circuses, 1874–1891," *American Literary History* 8, no. 1 (Spring 1996): esp. 49–50.

42. Richard Hughes Seager, *The World's Parliament of Religions: The East / West Encounter, Chicago, 1893* (Bloomington: Indiana University Press, 1995), chap. 2, "The Midway Plaisance and the Magic of the White City."

43. Adams, "'Stupendous Mirror,'" 45.

44. *Official Catalogue of Exhibits on the Midway Plaisance* (Chicago: W. B. Conkey, 1893).

45. *The Barnum and Bailey Greatest Show on Earth—The World's Grandest, Largest, Best Amusement Institution—The Great Ethnological Congress of Curious People*, photograph, ca. 1895, Library of Congress, https://www.loc.gov /item/97514559/.

46. "The Chronicle of the Parliament from the Second Day to the Sixteenth—Social Receptions," in Barrows, *World's Parliament of Religions*, 128–129.

47. D. Keith Naylor, "The Black Presence at the World's Parliament of Religions, 1893," *Religion* 26 (1996): 249–259, esp. 254, 253, 252.

48. "Parliament of Religions, 1893," Pluralism Project, Harvard University, accessed October 5, 2021, https://pluralism.org/parliament-of-religions-1893.

49. Zitkála-Šá, "Why I Am a Pagan," *Atlantic Monthly*, December 1902, 801–803.

50. Luther Standing Bear, *Land of the Spotted Eagle*, new ed. (1933; Lincoln: University of Nebraska Press, 2006), 237.

51. Standing Bear, xxi.

52. Standing Bear, 38, 166.

53. Standing Bear, 196, 193, 198, 212, 197.

54. Standing Bear, 45, 56, 251.

55. Standing Bear, 249, 234, 236.

56. Standing Bear, 249, 258, 191, 259.

57. L. W. Cronkhite, *Our Need of the Heathen* (Chicago: Woman's Baptist Foreign Missionary Society of the West, [1909?]), 4, 14, italics in original.

58. William Ernest Hocking, *Re-Thinking Missions: A Laymen's Inquiry after One Hundred Years* (New York: Harper and Brothers, 1932), 19; Hollinger, *Protestants Abroad*, 69.

59. Reference to "heathen lands" in Hocking, 313; to "paganism" in Hocking, 25.

60. Hocking, 28.

9. Resonances

1. Ned Bernard Stonehouse, *J. Gresham Machen: A Biographical Memoir* (Grand Rapids, MI: Wm. B. Eerdmans, 1954), 474–475. I am grateful to Austin Steelman for sharing this source with me.

2. Carl McIntire, "A Christian America vs. A Pagan America" (Collingswood, NJ: distributed by 20th Century Reformation Hour; sponsored by Christian Beacon, 1963), Carl [Charles Curtis, Jr.] McIntire Manuscript Collection, SCM 222 Series 3: Christian Beacon and 20th Century Reformation, Box 449, Special Collections, Princeton Theological Seminary.

3. Carl McIntire, "The Methodists Present a Pagan Religion to Youth" (Collingswood, NJ: distributed by 20th Century Reformation Hour; sponsored by Christian Beacon, 1963), Carl [Charles Curtis, Jr.] McIntire Manuscript Collection, Box 451.

4. See Brian Stanley, *The World Missionary Conference, Edinburgh 1910* (Grand Rapids, MI: William B. Eerdmans, 2009), esp. 88; David King, *God's Internationalists: World Vision and the Age of Evangelical Humanitarianism* (Philadelphia: University of Pennsylvania Press, 2019).

5. William Caven, "The Testimony of Christ to the Old Testament," in *The Fundamentals: A Testimony to the Truth: Compliments of Two Christian Laymen* (Chicago: Testimony, 1910–1915), 4:52.

6. G. Campbell Morgan, "The Purposes of the Incarnation," in *Fundamentals,* 1:32.

7. Robert Anderson, "Sin and Judgment to Come," in *Fundamentals,* 4:49.

8. Philip Mauro, "Modern Philosophy," in *Fundamentals,* 2:97–98, 105, 100 (emphasis in original).

9. J. J. Reeve, "My Personal Experience with the Higher Criticism," in *Fundamentals,* 3:113–114.

10. See King, *God's Internationalists.*

11. See Jolyon Baraka Thomas, *Faking Liberties: Religious Freedom in American-Occupied Japan* (Chicago: University of Chicago Press, 2019); and Duncan Ryūken Williams, *American Sutra: A Story of Faith and Freedom in the Second World War* (Cambridge, MA: Belknap Press of Harvard University Press, 2019).

12. See Sarah Ruble, *The Gospel of Freedom and Power: Protestant Missionaries in American Culture after World War II* (Chapel Hill: University of North Carolina Press, 2012).

13. King, *God's Internationalists,* 62.

14. On earlier missionaries, see Heather Curtis, *Holy Humanitarians: American Evangelicals and Global Aid* (Cambridge, MA: Harvard University Press,

2018). On postwar agencies, see King, *God's Internationalists,* 63. On earlier and later manifestations of American interest in the suffering world, focusing on child sponsorship programs, see Hillary Kaell, *Christian Globalism at Home: Child Sponsorship in the United States* (Princeton, NJ: Princeton University Press, 2020). On how American evangelicals in the second half of the twentieth century fostered "victim identification," see Melani McAlister, *The Kingdom of God Has No Borders: A Global History of American Evangelicals* (New York: Oxford University Press, 2018). McAlister discusses how American evangelicals have engaged in "enchanted internationalism," a posture toward world Christianity in the Global South that craves the emotionalism and perceived authenticity of its worship styles in contrast to the "stale and dry" West (9). This posture resonates with the preservationist and complementarian attitude toward "heathen" ways as offering what the West lacks.

15. King, *God's Internationalists,* 38–39, 59, 56, 88.

16. "Share Christmas with Them," 1965, Collection 0143: Material from World-Wide Faith Mission, 1950–1985, Fuller Seminary Archives and Special Collections, Pasadena, CA.

17. "Share Christmas with Them," underlining in original.

18. "Do It Now!," January/February 1984, Collection 0143: Material from World-Wide Faith Mission, 1950–1985.

19. "Creating a Visual Culture through Print Media: In the Beginning: A Brief History of *Life Magazine,*" in *Constructing a Culture,* by Maureen Kudlik et al., last updated March 8, 2016, https://scalar.usc.edu/works/constructing-a-culture /life-magazine. Also see Aida Amoako, "Life Magazine: The Photos That Defined the US," BBC Culture, March 11, 2020, https://www.bbc.com/culture /article/20200311-life-magazine-the-photos-that-defined-the-us; and Erika Doss, "*Life*'s Circulation: Circumventing the ABC with 'Pass-Along' Stats," *Circulating American Magazines: Visualization Tools for U.S. Magazine History,* February 20, 2020, https://sites.lib.jmu.edu/circulating/2020/02/20/lifes -circulation-circumventing-the-abc-with-pass-along-statsby-erika-doss/. For more on Luce, see David Hollinger, *Protestants Abroad: How Missionaries Tried to Change the World but Changed America* (Princeton, NJ: Princeton University Press, 2017), esp. chap. 2.

20. Alexander Campbell, "Africa: A Continent in Ferment," *Life,* May 4, 1953, 9. I am grateful to Eden Consenstein for sharing this issue with me.

21. Campbell, 9–10.

22. "The White Impact upon Africa," *Life,* May 4, 1953, 19.

23. "Americans and Africa: We Need an Attitude That Is True to Our Own Best Lights," editorial, *Life,* May 4, 1953, 178.

24. "Americans and Africa," 178.

25. "Americans and Africa," 178. Homi Bhabha has discussed the subversive potential of what he calls "mimicry"; by adopting "white models," colonized subjects can hold White colonizers to standards they profess but fail to practice. The heathen barometer might be seen as such an adoption. See Bhabha, "Of Mimicry and Man: The Ambivalence of Colonial Discourse," *October* 28 (1984): 125–133.

26. "Americans and Africa," 178; Peter Coviello, *Make Yourselves Gods: Mormons and the Unfinished Business of American Secularism* (Chicago: University of Chicago Press, 2019), 44–45. See also Lisa Lowe, *The Intimacies of Four Continents* (Durham: Duke University Press), esp. 41.

27. "Americans and Africa," 178.

28. Alan R. Tippett, "Christopaganism or Indigenous Christianity," in *Christopaganism or Indigenous Christianity?*, ed. Tetsunao Yamamori and Charles R. Taber (South Pasadena, CA: William Carey Library, 1975), 14, 17.

29. Tippett, 19–25.

30. Billy Graham, "Why Lausanne?," opening plenary address, in *Let the Earth Hear His Voice: International Congress on World Evangelization, Lausanne, Switzerland: Official Reference Volume: Papers and Responses,* ed. J. D. Douglas (Minneapolis: World Wide, 1975), 23, 25, 28–29, 31–32, italics in original.

31. Tom Houston, "The Story of the Lausanne Covenant: Case Study in Cooperation," Lausanne Movement, accessed February 2020, https://www.lausanne .org/gatherings/related/the-story-of-the-lausanne-covenant-case-study-in -cooperation. On how evangelicals from the Global South "spoke back" to Western evangelicals, placing pressure on them to rewrite the Lausanne Declaration, see David R. Swartz, *Facing West: American Evangelicals in an Age of World Christianity* (New York: Oxford University Press, 2020).

32. "Lausanne Covenant," in Douglas, *Let the Earth,* 3–4.

33. "Lausanne Covenant," 6.

34. Donald McGavran, "The Dimensions of World Evangelization," in Douglas, *Let the Earth,* 99, 94–96.

35. McGavran, 96.

36. As David King puts it, "Church growth required the latest anthropological and sociological research as well as the technology to process data. . . . World Vision's leaders believed the latest management and scientific tools complemented rather than replaced the Spirit." *God's Internationalists,* 106.

37. Donald McGavran, *The Bridges of God: A Study in the Strategy of Missions* (New York: Friendship, 1955), 39–41.

38. McGavran, "Dimensions," 103.

39. McGavran, 102–103.

40. Joshua chapter 9.

41. King, *God's Internationalists,* 149, 110.

42. Ronald J. Sider, *Rich Christians in an Age of Hunger: Moving from Affluence to Generosity* (1997; Nashville: W Publishing, 2015), 165, 139, 138.

43. "*Rich Christians in an Age of Hunger,*" Thomas Nelson, accessed January 2020, https://www.thomasnelson.com/9780718037048/rich-christians-in-an-age-of -hunger/.

44. Sider, *Rich Christians,* 243.

45. Sider, 244.

46. Sider, 98–99, 183, 104.

47. Sider, 8, 14.

48. Sider, 130–131.

49. Benjamin Wisner, *The Moral Condition and Prospects of the Heathen. A Sermon, Delivered at the Old South Church in Boston, before the Foreign Mission Society of Boston and the Vicinity, at their Annual Meeting, Jan. 1, 1824* (Boston: printed by Crocker and Brewster, 1824), 36.
50. Sider, *Rich Christians*, 12, xvi, 1.
51. "History," Frontier Ventures, accessed July 20201, https://www.frontierventures .org/about/history.
52. "About," Joshua Project, accessed January 2020, https://joshuaproject.net /about/details.
53. "People Groups of the World," Joshua Project, accessed January 2020, https:// joshuaproject.net/assets/media/maps/progress-scale-map-plain.pdf.
54. "What Is a People Group?," Joshua Project, accessed January 2020, https:// joshuaproject.net/resources/articles/what_is_a_people_group.
55. "What Defines a People Group?," Joshua Project, accessed January 2020, https://joshuaproject.net/assets/media/handouts/what-defines-a-people-group.pdf.
56. "Data Sources," Joshua Project, accessed January 2020, https://joshuaproject .net/help/data_sources.
57. "Main Page: Welcome to Etnopedia," Etnopedia, last edited 2019, https://en .etnopedia.org/wiki/index.php/Main_Page.
58. "Category: United States' unreached peoples," Etnopedia, last edited 2008, https://en.etnopedia.org/wiki/index.php/Category:United_States%27 _unreached_peoples.
59. "Jews," Etnopedia, last edited 2020, https://en.etnopedia.org/wiki/index.php ?title=Jews.
60. "Reclaiming the Meaning of Unreached," Joshua Project, accessed January 2020, https://joshuaproject.net/resources/articles/reclaiming_unreached. Jesse Curtis shows how Donald McGavran's Church Growth Movement actually defined White evangelicals as a "people" in the 1970s in "White Evangelicals as a 'People': The Church Growth Movement from India to the United States," *Religion and American Culture* 30, no. 1 (Winter 2020): 108–146.
61. Robby Butler, "Frontier Peoples: An Introduction," Joshua Project, accessed January 2020, https://joshuaproject.net/resources/articles/frontier_peoples_intro.
62. See Emily Conroy-Krutz, "Missionary Intelligence and Americans' Mental Map of the World," S-USIH blog, July 2017, https://s-usih.org/2017/07/roundtable -missionary-intelligence-and-americans-mental-map-of-the-world/.
63. "Joshua Project: Bringing Definition to the Unfinished Task," *Joshua Project*, accessed January 2020, https://joshuaproject.net/.
64. "Unreached of the Day: Podcast," produced by Mark Kordic, Joshua Project, accessed January 2020, https://joshuaproject.net/pray/unreachedoftheday /podcast.
65. "Mobile Apps," Joshua Project, accessed January 2020, https://joshuaproject .net/resources/apps; mobile app downloaded July 2017.
66. *Lift Up Your Eyes Prayer Guide* (Team Expansion), 4. Also on Joshua Project, accessed January 2020, https://joshuaproject.net/assets/media/prayer/guides /prayer-guide-thumbs.pdf. Not all missionary organizations include the *S* for Sikh. This one does.

67. "What Is the 10/40 Window?," Joshua Project, accessed January 2020, https://joshuaproject.net/resources/articles/10_40_window.

68. *Lift Up Your Eyes*, 4.

69. William D. Hart, "Secular Coloniality: The Afterlife of Religious and Racial Tropes," in *Race and Secularism in America*, ed. Vincent Lloyd and Jonathon Kahn (New York: Columbia University Press, 2016), 179, 185.

70. Mallory Shelbourne, "GOP Rep on Radicalized Islamic Suspects: 'Kill Them All,'" The Hill, June 5, 2017, https://thehill.com/homenews/house/336377-gop-rep-on-radicalized-islamic-suspects-kill-them-all.

71. Étienne Balibar, "Is There a 'Neo-Racism'?," in *Race, Nation, Class: Ambiguous Identities*, ed. Étienne Balibar and Immanuel Wallerstein (London: Verso, 1991), 21, 22, emphasis in original.

72. These observations are based on my attendance at the Tech Awards for Global Good in 2018. See also the Tech for Global Good website, accessed October 2018, https://www.thetech.org/tech-global-good. The idea that Western technology can be salvific is hardly new. David Noble calls it the "Religion of Technology" and traces it to the Western Christian quest to reclaim humans from the Fall and restore their "original God-likeness." Nowhere is this "religion of technology" clearer than in the Silicon Valley, where I live and teach. Here it has moved beyond a desire to make oneself more godlike through technology (though that quest is still omnipresent) toward technology to save the world. As a Tech Museum exec put it, "The world needs what The Tech has to offer." David Noble, *The Religion of Technology: The Divinity of Man and the Spirit of Invention* (New York: Penguin Books, 1999), 10, 3.

10. Continuing Counterscripts

1. Quoted in M. P. Joseph, *Theologies of the Non-person: The Formative Years of EATWOT* (New York: Palgrave Macmillan, 2015), ix.

2. Aram Bae, *Finding Aid for Ecumenical Association of Third World Theologians (EATWOT) Records, 1975–2006* (New York: Burke Library Archives, Columbia University Libraries, Union Theological Seminary, William Adams Brown Ecumenical Library Archives, 2007; reviewed and updated by Brigette C. Kamsler, 2014), 2, https://library.columbia.edu/content/dam/libraryweb/locations/burke/fa/wab/ldpd_6306796.pdf. On the history of liberation theology in the twentieth century, including a brief mention of EATWOT in the epilogue (256), see Lilian Calles Barger, *The World Come of Age: An Intellectual History of Liberation Theology* (New York: Oxford University Press, 2018). On evangelicals from the Global South "speaking back" to Americans on issues of "race, imperialism, theology, sexuality, and social justice," see also David R. Swartz, *Facing West: American Evangelicals in an Age of World Christianity* (New York: Oxford University Press, 2020).

3. On Césaire and religion see A. James Arnold, "Césaire at Seventy," *Callaloo*, no. 17 (February 1983): 111–119. On Fanon and religion, see Federico Settler, "Frantz Fanon's Ambivalence towards Religion," *Journal for the Study of Religion* 25, no. 2 (2012): 5–22.

4. Sun Ai Park, "The Poor Shall Rise," in "Worship Service: This Hour of History," by Elsa Tamez et al., in *Irruption of the Third World: Challenge to Theology: Papers from the Fifth International Conference of the Ecumenical Association of Third World Theologians, August 17–29, 1981, New Delhi, India,* ed. Virginia Fabella and Sergio Torres (Maryknoll, NY: Orbis Books, 1983), 181–183.

5. Elsa Tamez, "Reflections by Elsa Tamez (Costa Rica)," in Tamez et al., "Worship Service," 184. EATWOT had begun as a primarily male organization, and the women attendees demanded attention to their presence as "part of the irrupting millions seeking our rightful place in history" (Tamez et al., "Worship Service," 181).

6. Natalia Molina, *How Race Is Made in America: Immigration, Citizenship, and the Historical Power of Racial Scripts* (Berkeley: University of California Press, 2014), 6, 8.

7. Molina, 10.

8. Arnold, "Césaire at Seventy," 114.

9. Aimé Césaire, *Notebook of a Return to the Native Land,* trans. and ed. by Clayton Eshleman and Annette Smith (Middletown, CT: Wesleyan University Press, 2001), 19–20.

10. Césaire, 20.

11. Robin D. G. Kelley, "A Poetics of Anticolonialism," introduction to *Discourse on Colonialism,* by Aimé Césaire (1972; New York: Monthly Review Press, 2000), 8. Originally published in 1955 by Editions Présence Africaine.

12. Césaire, *Discourse on Colonialism,* 32–33.

13. Césaire, 33, emphasis in original.

14. Césaire, 41, 65, emphasis in original.

15. Césaire, 76–77.

16. Kelley, "Poetics of Anticolonialism," 7, 28.

17. John Drabinski, "Frantz Fanon," in *The Stanford Encyclopedia of Philosophy,* Spring 2019 ed., ed., Edward N. Zalta, https://plato.stanford.edu/archives/spr2019/entries/frantz-fanon/.

18. Leo Zellig, "Champion of the Wretched," *Socialist Review,* December 2011, http://socialistreview.org.uk/364/champion-wretched.

19. Frantz Fanon, *The Wretched of the Earth,* new translation from the French by Richard Philcox, with a foreword by Homi K. Bhabha and a preface by Jean-Paul Sartre (New York: Grove, 2004), 2, 7, 8. Originally published in French in 1961.

20. Fanon, 14, 60, 149, 235.

21. Fanon, 14, 19.

22. Fanon, 7.

23. Fanon, 20.

24. Fanon, 85–86, 147, 158.

25. Fanon, 236–238.

26. Fanon, 238–239.

27. Quoted in Gary Okihiro, *Third World Studies: Theorizing Liberation* (Durham, NC: Duke University Press, 2016), 17–18.

28. "A Non-white Struggle toward New Humanism, Consciousness," quoted in Okihiro, *Third World Studies*, 16. Okihiro explains that the students' demands for the creation of Third World studies as an academic field were never realized, and he calls for the field to be instituted now.

29. Virginia Fabella, preface to *Irruption of the Third World*, ed. Fabella and Torres, xii.

30. Aloysius Pieris, "The Place of Non-Christian Religions and Cultures in the Evolution of Third World Theology," in Fabella and Torres, *Irruption of the Third World*, 113–114; Fabella quotes Pieris in the preface, xiii.

31. "Declaration on the Relation of the Church to Non-Christian Religions: NOSTRA AETATE: Proclaimed by His Holiness Pope Paul VI on October 28, 1965," Vatican, accessed January 2020, https://www.vatican.va/archive/hist_councils/ii _vatican_council/documents/vat-ii_decl_19651028_nostra-aetate_en.html.

32. Ivone Gebara and Zwinglio Dias, "Everyday Life in India: Latin American Impressions," in Fabella and Torres, *Irruption of the Third World*, 178–180.

33. "The Irruption of the Third World: Challenge to Theology: Final Statement of the Fifth EATWOT Conference, New Delhi, August 17–29, 1981," in Fabella and Torres, *Irruption of the Third World*, 202–203.

34. "Irruption of the Third World," 194, 201.

35. "Irruption of the Third World," 194, 203, 201.

36. "Irruption of the Third World," 203.

37. See, for instance, Rebecca Kim, *The Spirit Moves West: Korean Missionaries in America* (New York: Oxford University Press, 2015); Scott Sunquist, *The Unexpected Christian Century: The Reversal and Transformation of Global Christianity, 1900–2000* (Grand Rapids: Baker Academic, 2015); Swartz, *Facing West*; and Melani McAlister, *The Kingdom of God Has No Borders: A Global History of American Evangelicals* (New York: Oxford University Press, 2018).

38. Joseph, *Theologies of the Non-person*, 44, 152, 172.

39. "Vine Deloria, Jr.," University of Colorado Boulder, Colorado Law, accessed July 2021, https://www.colorado.edu/law/vine-deloria-jr.

40. Vine Deloria Jr., *God Is Red: A Native View of Religion*, 30th anniversary ed. (Golden, CO: Fulcrum, 2003), 51, 68.

41. "Charles H. Long (1926–2020)," University of Chicago Divinity School, February 27, 2020, https://divinity.uchicago.edu/news/charles-h-long-1926-2020.

42. Charles Long, *Significations: Signs, Symbols, and Images in the Interpretation of Religion* (Fortress, 1986; repr., Aurora, CO: Davies Group, 1999), 137, 156, 163.

43. Long, 160, 75, 203.

44. Sylvia Wynter, "Unsettling the Coloniality of Being / Power / Truth / Freedom: Towards the Human, After Man, Its Overrepresentation—An Argument," *CR: The New Centennial Review* 3, no. 3 (Fall 2003): 257–337, esp. 262, citing Howard Winant, *Racial Conditions: Politics, Theory, Comparisons* (Minneapolis: University of Minnesota Press, 1994).

45. Wynter offers what might be called a "reoccupation narrative" instead of a straightforward replacement narrative. The ruptures she describes "remain

inscribed within the framework of a specific secularizing reformulation of that matrix Judeo-Christian Grand Narrative" and are "both discontinuous and continuous" (318). Wynter's reoccupation narrative straddles the line between the secularization thesis and secularism: the former emphasizes discontinuity (the Big Bang), telling us that religious difference becomes less important as the flesh becomes disenchanted or "degodded." The latter emphasizes continuity as it shows us how Christianity, in the words of Gil Anidjar, "*reincarnated* itself as secular . . . spreading its gentle and loving white wings*" over a world and making its norms seem universal and rational, while all other religions were made out to be particularistic and irrational. See Anidjar, "Secularism," *Critical Inquiry* 33 (Autumn 2006), quoted in Peter Coviello, *Make Yourselves Gods: Mormons and the Unfinished Business of American Secularism* (Chicago: University of Chicago Press, 2019), 43–44.

46. Wynter, "Unsettling," 287, 299.

47. Wynter, 329; Gayatri Spivak, "Can the Subaltern Speak?," in *Marxism and the Interpretation of Culture*, ed. Cary Nelson and Lawrence Grossberg (Urbana: University of Illinois Press, 1988), 271–313.

48. Sylvester Johnson, *The Myth of Ham in Nineteenth-Century American Christianity: Race, Heathens, and the People of God* (New York: Palgrave Macmillan, 2004), 19.

49. Johnson, 121.

50. Johnson, xi.

51. Johnson, xii.

52. Deloria, *God Is Red*, 288, 290.

53. Deloria, 296. See also Taiaiake Alfred's *Peace, Power, Righteousness: An Indigenous Manifesto* (New York: Oxford University Press, 2009), a more contemporary manifesto that sounds many of the same themes.

54. Long, *Significations*, 95, 90. Long uses the "phrase 'empirical others' to define a cultural phenomenon in which the extraordinariness and uniqueness of a person or culture is first recognized negatively" (90). He urges recognition of depth in the academy as well, given the "racist context" of the development of the study of theology and religion (203).

55. Long, 151, 157, 212–213.

56. Long, 152–153. Again, Long calls the academy to account, too. "On the practical level," he writes, "a method must be found whereby we deal with the religious history of all the American peoples. I suggest that we might begin by defining this culture as an Aboriginal-Euro-African culture. . . . This means that these meanings should always form the background for any discussion of American religion at any historical period" (168). To do American religion otherwise is to tacitly support the notion that America is different from and separate from what used to be called the "heathen world," or what Long calls the "primitives."

57. Johnson, *Myth of Ham*, 130–133.

58. Wynter, "Unsettling," 331. That Wynter concludes with "us" here is an indication of her primary audience: others in the category of the "damnés."

59. Eve Tuck, "Suspending Damage: A Letter to Communities," *Harvard Educational Review* 79, no. 3 (Fall 2009): 409–427, esp. 419–420.

60. Haunani-Kay Trask, "Nā ʻŌiwi," in *Night Is a Sharkskin Drum* (Honolulu: University of Hawaiʻi Press, 2002), 29; Trask, "Dispossessions of Empire," in *Night Is a Sharkskin Drum*, 33. Quoted by permission of University of Hawaiʻi Press.
61. Trask, "Nā ʻŌiwi," 30.
62. Trask, "Into Our Light I Will Go Forever," in *Night Is a Sharkskin Drum*, 60–62.

Epilogue

1. Marianne Chan, "Some Words of the Aforesaid Heathen Peoples," in *All Heathens* (Louisville, KY: Sarabande Books, 2020), 56. Quoted with permission of Sarabande Books, Inc.
2. Chan, 59.
3. Chan, 59.
4. Chan, 59.
5. Chan, 61.
6. Chimamanda Ngozi Adichie, "The Danger of a Single Story," TEDGlobal 2009, July 2009, https://www.ted.com/talks/chimamanda_ngozi_adichie_the _danger_of_a_single_story/transcript?language=en.
7. On the motivations of humanitarians, the difference between emergency and long-term interventions, and the ethical ambiguities of humanitarianism, see Michael Barnett, *Empire of Humanity: A History of Humanitarianism* (Ithaca, NY: Cornell University Press, 2011). On racism as structural and not just a matter of personal feelings and intentions, see Kimberlé Crenshaw et al., eds., *Critical Race Theory: The Key Writings That Formed the Movement* (New York: New Press, 1995), especially the Introduction: "The construction of 'racism' from what Alan Freeman terms the 'perpetrator perspective' restrictively conceived racism as an intentional, albeit irrational, deviation by a conscious wrongdoer. . . . The adoption of this perspective allowed a broad cultural mainstream both explicitly to acknowledge the fact of racism and, simultaneously, to insist on its irregular occurrence and limited significance" (xiv). By contrast, critical race theory seeks to "understand how a regime of white supremacy and its subordination of people of color have been created and maintained in America, and, in particular, to examine the relationship between that social structure and professed ideals" (xiii).
8. See Liisa Malkki, *The Need to Help: The Domestic Arts of International Humanitarianism* (Chapel Hill, NC: Duke University Press, 2015). Malkki explains that "the benefactor's own need to help those in need may generate actions that in fact help the benefactor him / herself in surprising and vital ways" (8).
9. Adichie, "Danger of a Single Story."
10. Gordon Wood, *The Purpose of the Past: Reflections on the Uses of History* (New York: Penguin, 2008), 83. See also Kathryn Gin Lum, "The Historyless Heathen and the Stagnating Pagan: History as Non-Native Category?," *Religion and American Culture* 28, no. 1 (Winter 2018): 52–91.

11. Dipesh Chakrabarty, "Postcoloniality and the Artifice of History: Who Speaks for 'Indian' Pasts?," *Representations,* no. 37 (Winter 1992): 23, 4.

12. Mark Charles and Soong-Chan Rah, *Unsettling Truths: The Ongoing, Dehumanizing Legacy of the Doctrine of Discovery* (Downers Grove, IL: InterVarsity, 2019), 163, 187.

13. Charles and Rah, 177, 188.

14. Phil Shackleton (arr.) and Eric Rainwater (words and music), "Humble Yourself," in *The Mission Connection* (Tarzana, CA: Fred Bock Music, 1992), 51–56.

15. Phil Shackleton (arr.) and Eric Rainwater (words and music), "Mission Connection [short]," in *The Mission Connection,* 6–9 (the end of "Humble Yourself" directs back to the "Short Version" of the song on pg. 6).

16. Toni Morrison, *The Origin of Others* (Cambridge, MA: Harvard University Press, 2017), 38–39.

Postscript

1. Therese Shaheen, "The Chinese Wild-Animal Industry and Wet Markets Must Go," *National Review,* March 19, 2020.

2. Linda Qiu, Bill Marsh, and Jon Huang, "The President vs. the Experts: How Trump Played Down the Coronavirus," *New York Times,* March 18, 2020.

3. Courtney Subramanian, Nicholas Wu, and David Jackson, "Trump Uses China as a Foil When Talking Coronavirus, Distancing Himself from Criticism," *USA Today,* March 20, 2020, updated March 21, 2020.

4. See Stop AAPI Hate, accessed June 2021, https://stopaapihate.org. On earlier waves of violence, see Beth Lew-Williams, *The Chinese Must Go: Violence, Exclusion, and the Making of the Alien in America* (Cambridge, MA: Harvard University Press, 2018).

5. Nicole Gaouette, "The US Is Asking Other Countries for Everything from Hand Sanitizer to Ventilators to Help Fight the Coronavirus," CNN, March 25, 2020, https://www.cnn.com/2020/03/25/politics/us-global-appeal-corona-supplies/.

6. Michael Nedelman, "'That's When All Hell Broke Loose': Coronavirus Patients Start to Overwhelm US Hospitals," CNN, March 25, 2020, https://www.cnn.com/2020/03/25/health/coronavirus-covid-hospitals/index.html.

7. Soumya Karlamangla et al., "How Bad Will the Next Few Weeks Be for California as Coronavirus Cases Surge?," *Los Angeles Times,* March 28, 2020; Dakin Andone and Paul P. Murphy, "What It's Like for Health Care Workers on the Front Lines of the Coronavirus Pandemic," CNN, March 29, 2020, https://www.cnn.com/2020/03/27/us/inside-hospitals-coronavirus-vignettes/index.html.

8. Jasmine Tyon (@jasminetyon), tweet and replies, 8:04 p.m., March 22, 2020, https://twitter.com/jasminetyon/status/1241923742378397698.

9. Jack Nicas, "He Has 17,700 Bottles of Hand Sanitizer and Nowhere to Sell Them," *New York Times,* March 14, 2020.

10. Andrew Hartman (@HartmanAndrew), tweet, 8:47 a.m., March 14, 2020, https://twitter.com/HartmanAndrew/status/1238854315516837888.

11. Tara Isabella Burton, "America's Civil Religion Is Capitalism. Trump's Coronavirus Response Proves It," *Washington Post,* March 26, 2020; Stephen Young, "'Restart the Economy' Is a Prayer to a Conservative God Who Demands Human Sacrifice," Religion Dispatches, March 25, 2020, https://religiondispatches.org/restart-the-economy-is-a-prayer-to-a-conservative-god-who-demands-human-sacrifice/.
12. Rosie Perper, "Trump Says He Wants to Lift Coronavirus Lockdown by Easter Because It's a 'Beautiful Time.' Dr. Fauci Says the Deadline Needs to be 'Flexible,'" Business Insider, March 24, 2020, https://www.businessinsider.com/trump-says-easter-beautiful-time-coronavirus-lockdown-timeline-2020-3.
13. Michelle Romeo, "I'm an ER Doctor. The Coronavirus Is Already Overwhelming Us," *Washington Post,* March 19, 2020.
14. Matt Stieb, "The Global Vaccination Effort Is Still Undercut by Deep Inequalities," *New York Magazine,* May 31, 2021.

ACKNOWLEDGMENTS

I could not have written this book without the wise counsel and community of students, colleagues, friends, and family who have surrounded me over the years. I am so grateful.

The interdisciplinary atmosphere at Stanford has enriched my scholarship immeasurably. I have had opportunities to workshop portions of the book at the Religious Studies Department Colloquium Series, the History Department's U.S. History Workshop, the Center for Comparative Studies in Race and Ethnicity's Emancipatory Performance and Racial Formation Faculty Research Network, the Stanford Humanities Center, and the Michelle R. Clayman Institute for Gender Research. My longtime mentor Richard White provided detailed and incisive comments on the full manuscript, which improved it greatly. I have also tried out the ideas that frame this book on the students who have taken my race and religion courses at Stanford and know that it has benefited immeasurably from their critical and honest engagement. Graduate students in the American Religions in a Global Context Initiative have built a supportive community at Stanford and I am thankful for their constructive feedback on an early draft of the manuscript. I am especially grateful to jem Jebbia for the thoughtful comments she prepared for an ARGC workshop of my manuscript, and to Joel Cabrita, Rachel Gross, and Adeana McNicholl, who also attended the workshop and provided important suggestions.

My student research assistants made this project possible from the start. I couldn't have asked for a better research and conversation partner than Thomas Graham when embarking on the project. Tristan Navarro wowed me with his ability to mine and organize data. I am grateful to the American Studies Summer Undergraduate Research Assistantship program at Stanford for supporting their work. My graduate research assistants, Chanhee Heo, Johanna Mueller, and Valeria Vergani, enabled me to finish the book during the chaos of the pandemic, providing constructive comments on multiple versions of the manuscript and helping me obtain permissions and images. Adeana McNicholl started as a graduate student soon after I began teaching at Stanford and watched this project develop from the beginning. Her detailed comments on two iterations of the full manuscript, and her moral support along the way, have been invaluable.

In addition to my students and colleagues at Stanford, this book owes much to the sage suggestions of so many generous colleagues at other institutions. Sylvester Johnson, Tisa Wenger, Shahzad Bashir, and Angela Tarango read the full manuscript and provided the most insightful advice that helped me tighten everything from the argument and framing to the title; the final version is what it is because of their generative feedback. My Young Scholars in American Religion family—mentors Laurie Maffly-Kipp and Doug Winiarski, and fellow Youngsters Kate Bowler, Heath('n) Carter, Joshua Guthman, Brett Hendrickson, Lerone Martin, Kate Moran, Angela Tarango, Steve Taysom, T. J. Tomlin, Dave Walker, and Grace Yukich—read a book proposal and early version of Chapter 6, helping me think through the scope of the book when I wasn't yet sure what it would become. Mark Valeri provided helpful feedback on Chapter 2 and Joshua Paddison offered detailed comments on Chapter 6. My graduate school writing group friends—Catherine McNeur, Robin Morris, Julia Guarneri, Francesca Ammon, and Sara Hudson—helped me reconceptualize the beginning and end of the book. Alison Greene, Jon Ebel, Jennifer Graber, and Heather Curtis offered productive feedback on my introduction and on Chapter 4. Alison re-read the prologue and introduction right before the manuscript was due and reassured me that I hadn't ruined it in the revising process. Paul Harvey (DGB) similarly provided incisive feedback on the book's bookends just before the manuscript was due. I am also grateful to Paul for inviting me to coedit *The Oxford Handbook of Religion and Race in American History* with him, which gave me the chance to learn from some of the best scholars in the field. And my academic support groups—DOPEsters Judith Weisenfeld, Nicole Kirk, and Jessica Delgado, and Team Kate (Kate Bowler, Kate Moran, and Grace Yukich)—helped me to survive the process of writing a second book while on the tenure track with small kids in tow.

I have also benefited from opportunities to share the manuscript and portions thereof with Tisa Wenger's and Zareena Grewal's course on religion and U.S. empire at Yale University; Jonathan Schofer's seminar on Sexuality, Body, Religion at the University of Texas at Austin; Jennifer Eyl's and Heather Curtis's classes at Tufts University; the Women in Intellectual History Workshop, organized by Caroline Winterer and Jennifer Ratner-Rosenhagen; the Rocky Mountain American Religion Seminar, led by Joseph Stuart and Colleen McDannell at the University of Utah; the Center for Religious Diversity and Public Life at the University of Colorado, Colorado Springs, run by Jeffrey Scholes; the symposium on Missionary Interests: Protestant and Mormon Missions in the 19th and 20th Centuries at the Church History Library, led by Christopher Jones and David Golding; the conference on Race and Religion in the Americas and the Atlantic World at Princeton University, helmed by Jessica Delgado; the Religion and the American Normal conference at Princeton, organized by Judith Weisenfeld; and the Unitarian Universalist Association General Assembly's Conrad Wright lectureship, arranged by Nicole C. Kirk. I thank also my fellow panelists and commentators at various American Academy of Religion, American Society of Church History, Society for the History of the Early Republic, and Society for the History of American Foreign Relations panels, especially Emily Conroy-Krutz, Kate Moran, Tisa Wenger, Terence Keel, Doug Winiarski, Joshua Guthman, and Jon Pahl. The invigorating feedback I received from all of these opportunities to share my work helped me to refine the book's arguments and analyses.

The Huntington Library, the Library Company of Philadelphia and Historical Society of Pennsylvania, the Stanford Humanities Center, and the Michelle R. Clayman Institute for Gender Research at Stanford University supported and made this project possible with research and writing fellowships that enabled me to devote sustained time to this work and to share its frame and claims with other fellows. Archivists, curators, and fellow researchers at these and other institutions—especially the Hawaiian Mission Children's Society Library, the Church History Library in Salt Lake City, the Rubenstein Library at Duke University, the David Allan Hubbard Library Archives at Fuller Theological Seminary, and Special Collections at Princeton Theological Seminary—generously shared sources with me and made this book possible. I am especially grateful to Peter Blodgett at the Huntington for his unwavering support of my work from hell to the heathen.

Many thanks to my editor at Harvard University Press, Kathleen McDermott, who shepherded the book with patience, and to Jon Butler, who led me to Kathleen (and, with Skip Stout, taught me how to write a book in the first place). I am also indebted to Debbie Masi at Westchester Publishing Services and copyeditor Ashley Moore, who guided the book through the final stages of production. My deepest thanks also to the readers for the Press, who provided important, encouraging, and detailed feedback, which made this a much better book. Thanks as well to Joseph Stuart, for the perfect index. I am also grateful to Philip Goff and the editors of and readers for *Religion and American Culture*, who provided insightful comments on my "Historyless Heathen" article, where I tried out some of the ideas that would inform this book.

These ideas have been floating in my head in some form or other since I was a child wondering about ancestors and relatives in China. My parents encouraged my wonder even as they, my brother—who sang in the church choir with me as a kid—and my other relatives, especially Paw Paw and Gung Gung, also showed me a wondrous faith. My endless gratitude goes to my family for their constant love and support, and especially to Mom for coming along on archival trips, cooking delicious meals, and playing with the girls so I could research and work. Anita and Wes also drove out to watch the girls and cook nutritious food during the pandemic, for which I am thankful.

And finally, to Nick, who accompanied me on months-long research trips (toddler in tow), took the baby on epic stroller walks so I could write, and provided 24-7 tech and grammar support, I can't thank you enough. To Phoebe and Clara, who remind me of what makes life worth living—baby giggles and big girl hugs, love-you songs and make-believe, baking challenges and movie nights—you make the world so bright.

INDEX